DESERT CHALLENGE

DESERT

CHALLENGE

An Interpretation of

NEVADA

BY

RICHARD G. LILLARD

UNIVERSITY OF NEBRASKA PRESS · LINCOLN

CONTENTS

I. ONE OF THE FORTY-EIGHT

II. BLUEPRINTS OF CREATION

III. HORIZON SEEKERS

IV. CHASING A DOLLAR TO HELL

[v]

V. WILD WEST IN NEON

LIST OF ILLUSTRATIONS

DESERT CHALLENGE

I

ONE OF THE FORTY–EIGHT

New West

NEVADA is ten thousand tales of ugliness and beauty, viciousness and virtue. " Old Virginia " Finney stumbles on a rock and smashes his bottle of whisky: " I baptize this ground Virginia City." Mark Twain hoaxes and outrages miners with a fake news story of a bloody massacre at Dutch Nick's. A trapper in Captain Walker's exploration party shoots a Piute Indian: " He looked like he intended to steal my beaver traps." Mary Pickford gets a divorce in three weeks because Owen Moore " happens " to come to the same county to take movies of a coal mine. Jim Butler grabs a piece of high-grade ore to throw at a lost burro and discovers Tonopah. Mrs. Sinclair Lewis #1 nervously approaches the hotel register and changes her residence from New York to Reno. Herbert Hoover pulls a twenty-five-pound trout from the green waters of Pyramid Lake. General Grant faints in the steam-hot depths of a silver mine: " This is as near hell as I want to get."

When gambling and six-week divorce are legalized the Washoe County sheriff says, " Thomas Jefferson would feel more at home in Reno right now than in any other place."

Nevada is full of contrasts and surprises. It is epics and anecdotes, geological records, newspaper headlines, Congressional documents, and divorce jokes. It is alkali flats, pine-stubbled ranges, and blue mountain lakes. It is an unspoiled virgin wilderness and an advanced civilization with stop and go lights. It is a home for " radical " legislation but not for radicals, a home for hard-rock miners, hard-riding cowboys, small-town folk, and silver senators. Seen by a Californian or a New Yorker Nevada is unorthodox, impious, backward, and undeveloped, and yet hospitable, individualistic, romantic. It is the home state for extremes — the smallest population, the biggest public domain, the greatest dryness, the largest proportion of men to women, the highest per capita income. It is everything or nothing, best or worst. The landscape belongs in Asia, or on the moon. State history reads like a novel. The people have come from everywhere in the world but, once acclimated, they can only be called Nevadans. They have acquired the Nevada spirit.

Nevada is the " Old West " streamlined. Even during depressions, Nevadans have held to the philosophy of the American frontier: a belief in individualism, an optimistic attitude, and a faith in men's future together, whatever their divergent pasts. The state is run by miners and cattlemen, lawyers and merchants who are veterans of the wide-open boom days in southern Nevada, early in the century. A growing minority of Babbitts has not replaced them. They contrast with the steady God-fearing farmers and the cautious, professionally circumspect finance-capitalists who dominate neighboring states. The best of the old-time freedom of the frontier remains in expansive, forward-looking individuals who have the idea that a man can make his own terms with destiny. They are Hamiltonian in that they believe in passing laws that make good profits for themselves; yet, too, they are Jeffersonian in that they say, in effect, " We are not perfect enough to say to others, ' You shall not be free.' " They consider their government best when it governs least. They say, " Live your life, but don't try to live mine."

Actual legislators are eager to build up their communities. Like county and state officials they are in close touch with voters. They are common men and any other common man can approach them with a " How come? " or a " I been thinking, maybe we ought to . . ." State senators talk to random Nevadans on the streets, and the governors are never too old to wave at a pretty girl or to make a U turn in the middle of the block and go back for another look.

As a result the legislature has given Nevada the least restrictive set of laws any American state has ever had. Human beings are free to get married overnight, gamble over a week end, get divorced over a summer's vacation. They can buy a meal or an automobile, collect a dividend, or die and leave an estate with blooded horses, and yet not pay one cent of tax to the state.

As it was in the days of the Old West, Nevada is a civilization of gay town-cities, lonely ranches, and mines. The talk is still on shafts and ore samples, range stock, hay, and horse-flesh. The townspeople are as tolerant of personal morals and as likely to ask a man to have a drink as were the Comstockers of John Mackay's time. Reno and Las Vegas are amazingly near in spirit to the Virginia City and the Tonopah of the past. Money comes easy, goes easy. Every night is a Saturday night, every Sunday an open house. Important men are informal. Friends are generous. All men are equal in opportunity to try to make money. Out in the long grassy valleys — the Monitor, Paradise, Pahranagat — cowboys still roll their own, brand calves, court the new schoolma'am, and bulldog steers at rodeos. And around the campfires in cow camps up in the ranges where the streams stop as soon as they start — the

Santa Rosas, Pancakes, the Tuscaroras — nasal voices wail on autumn evenings: " He was just a lonely cowboy, with a heart so brave and true."

Six deputies of the State Superintendent of Schools travel for thousands of miles each month as they visit schools scattered in counties as large as Balkan countries. Schoolteachers drill classes that could be seated in a coupé. In the remote districts, school is held in adobes, old log buildings, or the front rooms of ranch houses. Home missionaries carry their own bedrolls, food, and water when they bounce out on the two-rut side roads that lead to struggling one-family mines and homesteads sixty miles from the main highway. In new mining camps and isolated farming communities preachers hold prayer meetings in hotel lobbies, private homes, restaurants, and even in gambling halls.

A friendly, personal, unsophisticated society fills the great spaces. The huge areas, the meager population, the scarcity of water keep newcomers from settling up the state and crushing out the Western virtues. Nevadans are hospitable, neighborly, quick to offer help, and also downright curious about a stranger's business. As a tourist gets into his car parked at the curb, in Winnemucca or Ely, or somewhere else, a threadbare, lank, smiling old-timer may come up and ask for a lift, and even if he doesn't get it he will genially start an afternoon's conversation. " Where are you going? What are you going there for? " Lists of polling places are evidence of the human intimacy that fills the sun-swept gravel valleys. Henry Anderson, county clerk of Pershing County, officially announced the thirteen polls in the county for the primary election for United States senator, September 3, 1940, including

Mill City	John Herzog's Home
Imlay	School House
Lower Rochester	Kent Maher's Home

The enveloping space is as beautiful as it is simple. The whole vertical landscape is there, unchanged since Frémont's day except for the man-sized gopher holes called prospect tunnels, each with its dump of tinted dirt. At a colossal right angle to it, the horizontal landscape, farmed along the drainage bottoms, cut by a meandering road or two. The broad sweep of flood plains, the abrupt gorges that head them, the purple, crested ranges that curve out of sight. The cycloramas of cosmic blue above. The clean spicy air that a thunderstorm blows down from a sagebrush mesa. . . . On summer evenings the full moon is a luminous continent. Mark Twain would recognize it all as he would the ocher-colored buttes, the greasewood-covered mud flats, and the flocks of gawking sage hens along the side roads between ranches and prospectors' camps. The Ruby Range is as lonely, its glacial lakes as quiet, and the foxtail pines of the Toiyabe Mountains are as lovely and untouched as when John Muir tramped the timber-line zone and munched on raisins and chocolate bars.

This is not to imply foolishly that Nevada is a remaining fragment of the " Old West." It isn't. The original West was hunting and fishing grounds, where men baited hooks and pulled triggers for food, not sport. It was raw new towns thrown up without plan, haphazard in construction and irrelevant in appearance. The " Old West " was the hardships of camping. It was unbalanced diet, uncouth manners, midwives and quacks, casual homicide, too little water and too much whisky, and an unstable population that half built a town and then stampeded off somewhere to start another. It was a partial wilderness in which men had not yet settled into a permanent pattern of life. By and large, Nevada is none of

these now. The boosters may go ahead and call it " a last frontier " in the sense of economic opportunities, but they cannot
call it " Old West," which labels an expired phase of American history, dead and buried, the ghost town its sepulcher.

Nevada has held to the best of the institutions and attitudes
of the old days and meanwhile kept up with changing America. Along the sleek U.S. highways Nevada is a modern New
West. With state and federal money, enterprising engineers
have spanned the horizons with straight, wide roads. Service
stations and eating places, glowing in neons at night, have
sprung up to furnish autoists with gas and oil and rest-rooms
O.K.'d by *Good Housekeeping,* with coffee and flapjacks and
seventy-five cent special chicken dinners — all the brisk services travelers are used to where they come from. This is the
wayside population that led J. B. Priestley in his midnight mus-
ings on the desert to sense, mystically, that here the Time Spirit
was working hardest, harder even than in Russia; something
about these super roads in the Wastelands symbolized the
brave new world of mankind that America was leading the
way to. More likely, a Britisher was unnecessarily impressed
by superficial American service, which has followed human
traffic into Nevada along with alfalfa weevils and English
sparrows. Certainly, as far as Nevada is concerned, the asphalt
bands that stretch across more than 100,000 square miles lead
visitors across the state rather than into it.

Nevada adjusts to the manners of the automobile age, just
as it absorbs into its way of living such contemporary elements
as circulating libraries, airplanes, chocolate malts, freeze-pack
vegetables, union high schools, radios, and CIO organizations.
These and all that goes with them dominate the through-way
roads and the crowded town streets, but they do not dominate
life in Nevada as a whole.

The new Nevada of the past thirty years has its achievements to be recalled with pride and satisfaction. Quick to
catch liberal fire from the Progressives, it was among the very

first states to give its citizens the benefits of workmen's compensation, minimum-wage legislation, woman suffrage, the direct primary, the recall, the initiative, and a half dozen other such laws that enable men to regulate their social relations in the interests of personal freedom for all. Nevada voters had directly elected three United States senators and thus wiped up one kind of legislative corruption before the nation caught up with this democratic practice and ratified the Seventeenth Amendment.

In Reno is a people's university that affects the lives of students and public alike. The board of regents is elected by popular vote. A committee of professors accredits applicants' work in the high schools and junior colleges of other states. Students come from all over America to study on the shaded, friendly campus. A special attraction is the excellent School of Mines. One university agency especially aids consumers and six others assist ranchers and miners. The State Analytical Laboratory is of particular direct importance to the man in the street — or rather, the man in the desert ravine. It makes free assays for citizens of Nevada on minerals and ores taken from within the state boundaries. It identifies the samples and determines their richness per ton, their uses and market value. A strange rock may be the clue to a fortune in tungsten or manganese. A fragment of black ore from an outcropping may be a silver-lead ore worth $80 per ton — and $20 per ton is good ore any time. Copies of the reports are not made open to the public until the originals have had time to reach the hands of senders. Thus a keen-eyed Mormon boy in Moapa, a hopeful clerk's wife in Eureka, or a bilious old prospector on the Smoke Creek Desert can get expert advice he could not pay for.

Even the criminals in the State Prison in Carson City are treated like human beings. Inside the low-walled prison they have unrestricted sunshine and any occupations they choose to create for themselves. It's up to them, as individuals, to avoid boredom and spend their time profitably. Opportunities are there: a factory that makes the state automobile license plates, a library, tools and equipment for handicrafts, a lawn and flower garden to take care of, and recreational facilities that include a boxing room where Lou Nova trained during his attempted comeback. There is the baseball diamond in the old quarry, near by the exposed tracks of ground sloths and mammoths that the soles of visitors are slowly wearing away. A felon sentenced to death does not die by a public county hanging, as he once did, or by either of the alternatives formerly offered in the Prison Yard: the noose or two rifle bullets fired simultaneously from guns in mechanical holders. These brutalities of an older West are gone. In their place is the most humane killing method yet devised by man, the lethal gas chamber. Cyanide gas makes the victim unconscious in a few seconds. In a minute he is dead. Nevadans are justly proud of this invention of theirs, now copied in some of her sister " radical " states.

Nevada is not Utopia, however, and no complete unity lay behind progress in laws and institutions. A powerful faction opposed democratic innovations in government. The Republican party machine, led by a wealthy brewer, fought undisguised against the direct primary. Several times Puritanical pressure groups pushed through laws that reversed Nevada's traditionally tolerant handling of gambling and divorce. Nevada was caught in the propaganda wave of Prohibition and passed its own freedom-hampering " little Volstead " a few months before the Eighteenth Amendment was adopted; but the state was more itself when it was one of the last states to ratify the amendment. Too, it repealed its own enforcement act long before the New Deal put over the Twenty-first Amendment.

And, be it admitted, Nevadans do not always fully live up to their philosophy that government should free individuals and help them develop. For the lucky person thrives in Nevada, but the unlucky one, the down-and-outer, the fellow with the bad breaks and no friends — he may be left alone to starve. As a worker in the Welfare Department in White Pine County puts it, Nevada has the pioneer senses — horse sense, card sense, and money sense — but lacks social sense, an awareness of organized social responsibility to the unfortunate. In the copper center, Ely, regular and skilled employees of the mines and railroads have good standards of health, living, and housing. The life of casual and migratory workers, however, is below minimum standards for decency. These workers have no cash to build shacks, even, and property owners in mining towns do not build homes for renting. There is too little permanency of residence. These migrants have no contact with schools, lodges, churches, or civic clubs. Neither state nor county gives them any appreciable aid or encouragement. Also, indigent old people receive scant aid from the state. Counties give what little aid there is for mothers and dependent children. The only public care for orphans in the state is given in an ugly sandstone barracks on Prison Road in Carson City. There is no provision for feebleminded youngsters or for victims of tuberculosis and silicosis.

Many poor Nevada farmers need medical aid, for they are sufferers not only from isolation in space but also from economic evils: low prices for their products, intermittent drought, and unwise expansion of investments. They are trying to make a living on small, isolated homesteads. Proper diet is difficult to obtain. If illness strikes and a doctor is called out from town he will charge one dollar a mile in the daytime, a dollar and a half at night. The charge is defensible for a private professional man to make. A dollar a mile has long been the fee of the frontier doctor, but his price means that a poor man thirty or forty miles out grits his teeth or swallows patent medicine unless he is faced by death. In the same predicament are the numbers of men who are trying to mine on a small scale and live a barren life in remote canyons. One old miner said, "There's just one thing to do when a fellow gets sick. Either get married or go to a hospital." But women and hospitals are scarce in Nevada. There are only seven public nurses in the state. The hospital at Ely serves 15,000 square miles of territory.

Happily, misfortune seems really to be a minority problem in Nevada, and good fortune and optimism are the rule. The state is growing. Apparently Nevadans are right when they say there is plenty of work in the state and no one needs to go hungry. Ever since hit-and-miss prospectors stumbled on an outcropping of the Comstock Lode, Nevadans have felt there were fine futures ahead for up-and-coming individuals. When the state was three years old Myron Angel's *La Nevada Orientale* was distributed at the Paris Exposition. It told the world of "a country whose future is as bright as the glittering metal which is her staple and her pride." The idea was echoed in thirty years of private correspondence to California, the Eastern states, Europe, and China.

Officially and privately, men have had faith in the agricultural possibilities of the state, its opportunities for professional careers, homeownership, personal freedom, and wealth for poor man and capitalist alike. The revival of mining after 1900 and the first irrigation project, under Theodore Roosevelt, quickened Nevada to the publication of a batch of pamphlets filled with information and invitation for new residents. The Nevada Commercial League said in 1907, "Throughout Nevada opportunities await the man with brains and capital, and right in the City of Reno are the greatest opportunities of all." The State Bureau of Immigration recounted the resources of the sixth largest state. The Southern Pacific Railroad, scenting potential profits, published *The New Nevada: What It Is and What It Is to Be. The Era of Irrigation and the Opportunity of the Farmer, the Dairyman and Stockman.* This corporation, that had once used Nevada to subsidize

California, now acted on the prophecy of Roosevelt: "I feel that hereafter the most certain element of strength in the state will be the irrigated agriculture." Said the railroad:

Nothing necessary to the upbuilding of a great state was omitted when Nevada was created. The raw materials were abundantly bestowed and only the lack of human endeavor has prevented this rich and extensive region from taking a high place among her sisters.

Collis P. Huntington himself, hardiest of the railroad's Four, remarked to a prominent Nevadan, R. L. Fulton, "If I were a young man, I would devote my life to developing irrigation in Nevada."

Natural wealth and scanty population in a sovereign state are a combination that makes opportunity now as earlier, especially for young men who want a country to grow up in. In the spring of 1940 there was opportunity for a lawyer in Esmeralda County. The incumbent district attorney died, leaving an unexpired term of two and a half years, at $200 a month. The publisher of the Goldfield *News* pointed out that there was not a lawyer in the county. A young, upstanding attorney could settle there, get the unexpired term, and make a name for himself. In the same year Nye Togoni, twenty-two years old and a sophomore at the University of Nevada, ran for the legislature in Eureka County, canvassed personally from house to house, and won by a huge majority. Healthy, liberal, intelligent, he could anticipate a career. He served in an Assembly in which three-fourths of the members were under forty years of age. When Senator Key Pittman died in the late fall, just after winning re-election, the appointment for the one-year term before the next Nevada election came to a Las Vegan, Berkeley Bunker, who was thirty-four years old. Dapper and quiet, formerly the operator of a filling station, he was a bishop of the Latter-Day Saints. The Catholic governor, E. P. Carville, who selected him, said, "He typically represents the young manhood of Nevada. This nation today is calling upon its young men." Here was an encouragement to youth rare enough in years of depression and conscription. F. R. Payne, a retired operator of Penney stores, settled in northern Nevada a few years ago and expressed himself emphatically: " If I were a young fellow just starting out in business, by golly I would anchor down right here. This state has a future."

No state has a more promising future. What with new water projects, the growth of tourist travel in Western states, the migration of rich people to the state, the increasing recreational possibilities of Lake Mead, and the production of cheap Boulder Dam power, it is evident that Nevada affords opportunities for dreamers and doers. The electrometallurgical experiment station at Boulder City will develop practical industrial innovations for local manufacture of local mineral products. Already Las Vegas has a large manganese plant. Nevada is New West, not Old West. It is run by gasoline and electrical power, not by ox and horse power, but it remains, in new terms, a real, not a figurative, frontier.

Choked and Retarded

SENATOR FRANCIS NEWLANDS was overly optimistic when he said in 1901, " Spain, covering an acreage equal to Nevada and Utah, and, outside of its fringe along the sea shore, having climate, soil, topography and methods of irrigation and cultivation resembling theirs, has a population of over seventeen millions. The population of Nevada will someday be equally dense." Neither Nature nor Man has any such plan to make Nevada teem with people. The abstract forces of History point in the other direction. The dry land itself, the railroad that crossed it, the miners that dug into it, and the eco-

nomic and political peerage that seized control of it have kept
Nevada backward in development and poor in population.

With plenty of water Nevada would be one of the richest
areas in the world. It has the climate, the mountains, the valleys, the soil, but it doesn't have the water to produce the
woods and meadows of an Iowa or a Pennsylvania. As far as
sweet water goes, Nevada lives in an economics of scarcity.
She has always needed water control, irrigation, and federal
reclamation aid, and these have been slow to come. The Home-
stead Act with its promise of 160 acres free to any man who
took the trouble to patent it did no good in this dry land.
Most quarter sections lacked even morning dew, and what
naturally watered land did exist was pre-empted in no time.
Besides, even with water, 160 acres were not enough. Dry
land with springs and occasional streams could support a
ranch only if it extended for thousands of acres.

The Mormons could have made Nevada into an agricultural wonderland. They started the job but did not get to fin-
ish it. In 1854 President Brigham Young ordered many Mormon families into the Carson, Walker, Washoe, and Truckee
valleys, where they at once established stable farming communities by the conservation practices that had recently made
Deseret an immediate success at the foot of the Wasatch
Range. But a few years later, in 1857, Colonel Albert Johnston was advancing with an army on Salt Lake City, and other
trouble with federal authorities was brewing. As a matter of
theocratic defense, Young contracted the Mormon empire.
He called the Nevada settlers back to Salt Lake. Nevada lost
its best farmers and a chance to be developed by the expert
colonization that made Utah strong without railroads, capitalist millionaires, or federal subsidies. In the same year Young
recalled an infant missionary and farming colony at Las Vegas.
In the next decade Young established a settlement in the Virgin Valley, down off the Colorado River. The Mormon pioneers there paid taxes to Arizona Territory, in the form of

grain, cotton, and other produce, but when a government survey in 1869 put them inside Nevada, and Lincoln County officials demanded payment in gold for back taxes, Young ordered his people back into Utah. Nevada was the loser again until Young sent colonists back years later.

Lacking Mormons with their community water projects and United Orders, Nevada fell into the hands of the usual ego-minded land-grabbers of the frontier. The predominant population of transient miners didn't care, the few lucky farmers were happy to have no competition for the mining-camp market, and a clique of several dozen cattle barons enjoyed their undisturbed possession of the grass and water privileges on a public domain as big as all outdoors. Henry Fred Dangberg, a native of Westphalia, Germany, built up his 36,000-acre Land and Live Stock Company in Carson Valley. First to cultivate alfalfa in Nevada, he built dams and ditches to water dry benchland and increase the area in wild hay. Ohio-born Colonel T. B. Rickey acquired 42,000 acres in Antelope Valley, ranches adjoining in Bridgeport Valley, California, and water rights in Owens Valley that he later sold to the City of Los Angeles. He made a fortune selling beef to Silver City, Gold Hill, and Virginia City, and went on to own a chain of Nevada banks, build a five-story brick block in Tonopah, and become co-owner of the Nevada-California Power Company and the Goldfield Consolidated Water Company. An admirer said he had "the faculty of recognizing an opportunity and seizing it." Colonel John Tinnin and John Sparks built up a ranch in northeastern Nevada that was 150 miles long each way. It was as big as the four smallest Eastern states. Tinnin, son of a Mississippi planter, had fought Indians as a Texas Ranger and Yankees as a Confederate soldier. He started out in Nevada with $1,100 worth of cattle, three hundred pounds of bacon and six bushels of corn meal. Sparks, likewise born in Mississippi, grew up on his father's big cattle ranch in Texas. Baronial possessions and manners came natural to him. The two partners bought up the herds of little ranchers until they had 80,000 breeding cattle and 10,000 calves to brand each year. Their shorthorns and Herefords grazed along Thousand Springs Creek, forty-five miles long, and fattened in grass as high as a buggy along fifty miles of Salmon River. Scattered hay ranches raised thousands of tons of alfalfa, timothy, and bluegrass for winter feeding.

For years the indifference of public opinion and the political connivance of the monopolists counterchecked reclamation advocates. Finally, in 1902, Senator Francis Newlands obtained aid in Congress for the arid West and won Nevada its Truckee-Carson Project. The first federal project of its sort, it opened 87,000 acres for irrigation.

Agriculture has slowly progressed, but land and water monopoly is still holding it back, and with it the state as well. For seventy years the scarcity of land and the large-scale ownership that resulted raised a basic problem that was not met by government. During the last forty of these years livestock men were vitally concerned. They discussed plans for grazing regulation at their association meetings and got bills before Congress, but advice was divided and the bills remained unpassed. Several facts made Nevada more concerned than any other state. Though it has no more crop land than Delaware or New Hampshire, it contains more public domain and a greater percentage of public domain than any of the forty-seven other states. The whole agricultural organization of Nevada is virtually determined by the use that is made of this domain, but methods that work elsewhere to establish partial control over public grazing lands are futile here because of the dryness. The distances between watering places on the Nevada range are longer than in any other stock country in the United States. And the cold winters, which make winter feeding necessary, make control of stock water on the range less important than control of irrigation water, which raises the hay needed for winter feeding. And no state has less total irrigation water.

The huge ranches were a natural outcome. The Kenyon family, the Sadlers, Lamberluccis, Huffakers, Keoughs, and Chiatoviches, and others, were not conspirators. They were the protagonists in man's struggle against the desert. Some ranges lacked drinking water in summer and could be used in winter only. Others, snow covered in winter and grassy in midsummer, were adapted to spring and autumn use. Thus the sheepman (who did not practice winter feeding but did have his sheep eat snow in winter) and the stockman (who was slow to learn the advantages of winter feeding with cured hay) found it convenient to own ranches big enough or far enough apart to provide an open range for each season. Ranches as large as 100,000 acres grew up naturally in White Pine, Elko, and Humboldt counties. In western Nevada Henry Miller, already *the* cattle king in California's San Joaquin Valley, built up a domain that stretched from the Oregon line to Pisen Switch (now called Yerington). Miller's ranches commanded Walker River, Massacre Creek, Battle Creek, Virgin Creek, High Rock Creek, lower Quinn River, and hundreds of springs and natural wells. Careful with water and grass, tactful in his relations with his men and the public, this native of Württemberg, who had left Germany to avoid Bismarck's militarism, rode from ranch to ranch on horseback. He established a benevolent dictatorship that improved the range and developed a cow that could graze over the rough terrain and plumpen with a quality of beef that brought extra prices in California. The Seven S brand was almost a trademark for Nevada.

Over the state as a whole there was need for federal control and regulation of the parts of the public domain that were more valuable for pasturage than for cultivation. Cattlemen fought feuds, tied up rights of way in litigation, poisoned rivals' stock, murdered sheepherders, intimidated small farm-

Farm Security Administration; photo by Rothstein

SHEEP HERDER PACKING BURRO,
DANGBERG RANCH, NEAR MINDEN

U. S. Indian Service

PIUTES HELPING
IN A TRIBAL CATTLE ROUNDUP

Farm Security Administration; photo by Rothstein

COWHAND

ers, and constantly merged smaller ranches into bigger. Henry
Miller bought out pioneer settlers, Spragg, Bewley, Alcorn.
. . . He sued Colonel Rickey over water rights on the Walker
River and carried the case through to victory in the United
States Supreme Court. " Ang " McLeod of Mason Valley
sued Miller, charging that a dam on Miller's property had
flooded his place, washed away chickens, hogs, and calves,
gullied his pastures and deposited sand bars. Farmers who
were " experts " testified against Miller in an old saloon in
Dayton (the courthouse burned down during the trial) and
he lost; he appealed and won in the Nevada Supreme Court.
The Cattleman's Association in Elko County hired men like
Walter Scott (not yet the " Cowboy Millionaire ") to shoot
up sheep camps. Scotchmen, and Chinese, Mexicans, and
Basques, herding sheep out on the ranges, where seldom is
heard a discouraging word, felt the hot, sharp, thump of lead
bullets against their shins and temples. Flocks of sheep stampeded mysteriously in the night and ran until they fell panting. Off to the southwest of Tonopah, William Clifford and
Jack Longstreet disagreed on the boundaries of their cattle
ranges. Late one afternoon Clifford precipitated a pitched
battle with rifles. He and his son, James, and his son-in-law,
Joe Nay, came upon Longstreet and a Jim Smith as they were
riding down a wash. When 250 feet away they dropped to
the ground and started firing. Longstreet jumped into a small
ditch. The Cliffords put a hole through Smith's horse. Longstreet raised a blood blister under James Clifford's nose and
smashed Joe Nay in the knee. Darkness stopped the fight and
both sides slipped away.

Sheepmen trespassed, fought back, and built up their own
semiprivate domains. Dan Wheeler, pioneer, brought in
French Merinos and Shropshires and established a sheep ranch
in the Black Rock Desert country. He cursed and harangued
the " Boscos," Basque sheepmen from Bilbao and other parts
of Biscay province. They were thrifty, energetic, and peace-

ful, but they were tramp ranchers, they owned no land and paid no taxes, and they ruthlessly overgrazed the public lands. The Boscos stayed on, bought herds and acquired water rights, until they had a sheep country pretty much their own, a three-hundred-mile sweep from Winnemucca north to Crane, Oregon. At McDermitt, Joe Uguesia owned a large store, bands of sheep, and was worth $20,000.

Too many mouths nibbled off the grass blades and too many hoofs trampled out the roots. Many ranches were incorporated, stocks were sold on the open market, and ownership of some ranches came to rest with nonresident investors who were concerned with profits only and not the welfare of Nevada. Oscar J. Smith, native of Rhode Island, cowboy and miner from Colorado, moved into Nevada. He became a lawyer, got to be president of banks from Winnemucca to Rhyolite, and joined two other men in building up the Eureka Live Stock Company. William Dunphy built a 70,000-acre ranch in three counties, then sold to the Wilmec Corporation, and it in due time sold out to an Eastern capitalist.

The politicians helped the trend. They could have done nothing else. State laws made it possible for the state engineer, acting on the principle of priority by use, to allot to a rancher the exclusive rights to a well or spring or seepage on public land. In the 1880's Nevada congressmen persuaded Congress to trade barren, unsold school lands for sections to be specially selected by state officials for their salability. The state came into possession of large holdings that covered all the remaining hay land, irrigation water, and most of the stock water on the range. Then these state lands were sold to Nevadans. The law allowed a cattleman to buy public land in 40-acre lots at $1.25 an acre, with only twenty-five cents down and from ten to fifty years to pay off the dollar. With $5,000 cash a rancher could buy 25,000 acres in 40-acre tracts, and by selecting the tracts that controlled the water he would come into virtual ownership of a million acres. The unwritten laws of nature and of the six-shooter would keep off trespassers.

By 1916 less than one hundred farmers and corporations had come into control of three-fourths of the privately owned land in Nevada, and since they owned key supplies of water they dominated a still larger proportion of public range land. In 1929, a federal study revealed, 149 stockmen, who owned 6 per cent of the area of the state, claimed 63 per cent of the total area on right of custom and priority of utilization. No other state had so large a number of cattle and sheep per ranch, so large a proportion of migrant laborers per farm, so small a ratio of farmers.

The Nevada landscape has never nurtured in many breasts the illusion that land destined for cattle grazing alone could be made into dry farms. But homesteaders have challenged the Nevada desert. Possessing no cash and working toward a free patent, a homesteader would develop a spring or exploit a seepage from a mountain and set up a meager irrigation system, only to have a cattleman enjoin him from use of the water because of his own " prior rights." With dry farming impossible and no means for well drilling and water pumping, the settler could do nothing but pack up his wagon or his model T and roll on. Artesian well possibilities were limited, and he could get scant aid from old state and national statutes that granted free land or cash bonuses to persons who obtained flowing wells. He received no help from Senator Pittman's underground waters bill of 1922, for although it gave a citizen or a group of citizens a patent on 640 acres if they drilled for two years on a land area of 1,560 acres and got water, it required by implication an initial outlay of hundreds of dollars for the drilling work. All in all, a homesteader was very lucky if he established himself. The common man needed government credit, government wells and grazing regulation, but the decades came and went, the Wilsonian era of reform, even, and Nevada remained the " Beautiful Desert of Buried Hopes."

The Taylor Grazing Act of 1935, though favoring large stockmen over small ones, was a long step toward regulation of grazing on public lands. It licensed users and scientifically supervised the use of the land. It put an end to homesteading in broken, rocky, poorly watered country. It made cattle- and sheepmen get busy rounding up sworn statements from prospectors, cowboys, herders, and miscellaneous natives as to their long use of certain springs and streams, for priority of use is an important factor in the procurement of Taylor licenses, and there were conflicting or overlapping claims to one-third of the public domain. The Act gives to millions of grass-covered acres the same federal supervision that the tree- and brush-covered domain receives from the Forest Service. Sheepmen must own a home ranch. Stockmen must follow certain rules in their use of a subcontinent they refused to lease because of the rental or to buy because of the taxes. The American public and Nevadans in general gain only in that they stop losing. Overgrazing, soil erosion, range wars, starvation of stock from too little available winter feed — these need occur no more.

Although land and water monopoly and specialized single crops have brought profits, even wealth, to the owners, socially Nevada has lost. The absentee landlords have been indifferent toward political and cultural progress in the state. The resident landlords for years consciously delayed settlement and development by spreading a propaganda that Nevada did not either need or want more people and ranches. What was needed, they said, was fewer and bigger ranches, and certain parts of the state — which had at least been harboring the small population required for cattle ranches — could be more profitably and effectively used as winter ranges for sheep. An expert investigator for the United States Department of Agriculture in 1932 expressed the opinion that strategic control of water and therefore of public land " de-

lays the development of the State, as it has done for probably 25 years."

Cattle and sheep ranches offer steady employment, but
grain, sugar beets, potatoes, cantaloupes, and hay, especially,
do not, except in the Moapa and Virgin valleys in southern
Nevada, where the Mormon farmers do their own harvesting.
Consequently, Nevada is proportionately more of a migrant-
labor state than the California of *The Grapes of Wrath*. There
is a floating population of homeless boys and men and rootless
families. They are outside the regular institutionalized life of
churches, schools, and clubs. They cannot play a healthy
democratic part in the organized life of the state. The idle
men on the town streets — who once terrified the fastidious
Katharine Fullerton Gerould, author-wife of a Princeton professor — contribute to the " wide-open " industries but to no
fundamental public institutions. So many drifting men de-
teriorating in public are small asset to any community. Contrast Nevada, with her few huge farms and ranches and her
unfenced horizons and her " loafers " on the through-way
streets, and her neighbor, Utah, with her many small farms
and community water projects. In Utah local labor harvests
the crops. The population is relatively stable and steady, and
its life centers in the church, the school, and county events.

Another major reason for Nevada's laggard development
is the peculiar instability of mining, which has always been
her major industry and was for many years her only one.
Most of the states were more fortunate and began as agricultural areas, with mining and manufacturing later developments, yet, at that, states like Pennsylvania and Montana know
what it is to try to keep a state stable when the demand for
anthracite or copper goes down. Parts of all the Western states
have seen once-powerful counties become political relics when
the gold or silver petered out. But Nevada most of all has
known the vagaries of a mineral base for civilization. Witness

figures chosen at random to suggest ups and downs, the value
of the total production of precious metals for given years.

1867	$16,000,000
1877	46,000,000
1887	6,000,000
1894	900,000
1907	17,000,000
1917	54,000,000
1922	15,000,000
1929	33,000,000
1933	4,000,000
1937	34,000,000
1938	23,000,000

In the past, when Nevada's mines have boomed with the
fair weather of bonanzas, they have encouraged speculation
of all sorts, including agricultural products, and invited the
attention of the nation. When they have slumped because of
adverse federal legislation or the ill winds of borrasca — un-
productive ore — the state has tumbled into depressions and
been ignored or neglected. The population has ebbed dra-
matically twice, each time after the collapse of prolonged mining booms. In 1880, at the end of the great days of Virginia
City, the first height came in the census records, 62,000 citizens, though undoubtedly there were more residents in the
mid-seventies. Thereafter the population slumped to 47,000
in 1890 and 42,000 in 1900. The price of silver in 1873 was
$1.29 per ounce. In 1901 it was $0.60. In three decades the
price of silver had gone down one-half and the population had
declined one-third. Salaries of state officers were cut. Certain
offices were abolished. The Budget, always lean, was further
reduced. The United States Mint in Carson City closed its
doors forever. There was a Great Depression.

These facts imply the story that belongs to the chapters on
frontier mining, which was oddly migratory, unscientific, romantic, certainly exploitative. It had its Horatio Alger heroes

and its robber barons, but no empire builders. It directed Nevada's history for half a century and bossed a score of biennial legislatures. The background of Nevada politics for thirty years was a fight of mine operators against paying taxes. The fight ran through the territorial legislatures, two constitutional conventions, state legislatures, the district courts, the Nevada Supreme Courts, and the hierarchy of United States courts. Throughout Nevada's history the proceeds of mining have paid less than fifteen per cent of the state's ad valorem taxes, only two-thirds to three-fourths what agriculture has paid. Thus the major industry impoverished the state while the minor one built it up. The argument in defense of this was phrased years ago, by Charles E. De Long, during the Constitutional Convention of 1864.

But for the mines, all your stores would be removed, your farms would dry up and be abandoned, and your wagons would stop in the streets or be turned elsewhere. Every man you see . . . looks directly to the miner. . . . Every one charges, in the disposal of his wares and goods, sufficient to cover his taxes. . . . He makes the price large so that the miner shall pay it back to him.

Migratory miners established Nevada's government in the sixties, but in later periods, when state-building was no longer a task to call forth men's most serious efforts, the wandering, informal mining man was a far from ideal local statesman. A special session of the legislature met in 1908 to deal with a serious emergency. Governor John Sparks wanted a law to authorize the creation of a state police system. Certain mining magnates wanted the state police to use against the Western Federation of Miners. Labor, obviously, was against the bill. The issues were serious and called for immediate attention. Yet one day the legislators forced adjournment for twenty-four hours in order that all but a half dozen of the Senate and Assembly might board a special car and go to Reno for special events at the Wheelmen's Club. There were five four-round bouts, several of which ended in knockouts. Senators in the front row cheered on pugilists until gore flowed. Two days later the legislators were denying that they had adjourned to see the fight.

When the Governor first called this special session to assemble, the members had scattered so far in the intervening year that they had to be summoned not only from several other states but also from places as remote as Alaska, Canada, Mexico, and South America. At the close of a regular session fourteen members left the state, having no permanent interest in it. Here was a political evil accruing from dependence on a single product: ore. Since miners were migratory, the early territorial government had tried to hold the population somewhat stable by requiring only six months for residence and thus encouraging people to stay in the state by giving them a sense of being regular citizens. But the result was that miners got the vote or even an office easily without necessarily forming an attachment to the state.

This same mining, that furnished wealth for architectural splendor in New York and San Francisco, left the ghost town to enhance the landscape and the broken county seat to fight the efforts of newer towns to take away its political importance. Pioche replaced Hiko when it died a sudden death. Reno supplanted Washoe City; Winnemucca, Unionville; Tonopah, Belmont; Yerington, Dayton. At present Battle Mountain would like to get the seat of Lander County away from Austin.

Stampedes still take place, though on a minor scale, wildcat promoters are under controls they did not know in generations past, and mining has become a careful, regularized, predictable enterprise, with an effect that is healthful, if tardy, on the progress of the state.

Nevada was retarded for four decades by the Central Pacific (the Southern Pacific after 1884). The state prospered before a mile of track was laid, but when proposed the railroad seemed to promise more prosperity, more comfort, and more kinship with other states. It would mean no more jolting over dusty roads. Unfortunately, for Nevadans, as one local historian put it, the railroad turned out to be like the stork that a colony of frogs once invited to be their king because they were tired of their lowly log king, on which they hopped and sat. In contrast to their former meek king, the new ruler, with a long bill and ravenous appetite, proceeded to feed upon his subjects, devouring them without scruple.

The railroad controlled the transportation inlet and outlet of the entire state. From the first it made passenger and freight rates low enough to kill competition from stages and wagons and yet discriminate cruelly against Nevadans. Once competition was good and dead it raised its rates. It enforced the vicious long- and short-haul system to make huge profits at the state's expense. In 1877, for example, the railroad's charge was $300 to take a carload of coal oil from New York to San Francisco. From New York to Reno, a trip 306 miles shorter, the charge was $536. To Winnemucca, 475 miles shorter, it was $716, and to Elko, 619 miles shorter, $800. Goods destined for Nevada towns were shipped to San Francisco and reshipped back; a carload of coal oil for Reno cost $300 to San Francisco and then $236 for the reshipment eastward, and so on. This system of rates prevented any Nevada town from rising to occupy the place of Salt Lake City in Utah or Denver in Colorado. When Virginia City and Gold Hill foundries and machine shops could have supplied equipment to mines in eastern Nevada and Utah they were prevented by similar rates. Anything shipped east had to go to San Francisco first. It cost $200 more per carload to ship from Reno to Utah than from San Francisco to Utah.

All this was coldly deliberate. When the Big Four undertook to build the western end of the Pacific railroad their eyes glinted at thought of profits from the traffic to and from Nevada towns. The generous production of mines, from Virginia City to Treasure City across the state, made Nevadans reckless buyers, and all their necessities came from California and would be carried by the railroad. Here were chances for quick profits, for lavishly rewarding speculation in iron rails. Command of the Nevada territory, successful competition with horse-drawn vehicles, would annex a whole province to their personal possessions — their stores on K Street, Sacramento. Crocker and Stanford, Hopkins and Huntington were far from philanthropic, as Oscar Lewis makes clear in his recent book, when they bought their own stock on ten per cent deposit and awarded themselves construction contracts at high profit. Congressman Rollin Daggett of Nevada made it clear in Congress in 1880. "Their object seems to be to crush, not to develop, the industries of Nevada, and to this end the competition of special rates from California is employed when there is danger of an industry growing into importance."

California had supplied limestone needed in the Comstock ore-reduction works. When good limestone was found near by in Nevada and a quarrying industry started, Stanford and Huntington lowered the limestone freight rates so as to undersell the new quarry. When it had been bankrupted, they put the rates back to the former high level. Similarly the railroad stopped the mining of sulphur in Humboldt County, prevented the exploitation of soda and salt deposits, and reduced the acreage in wheat.

The Central Pacific bribed legislators and sometimes bought out a whole legislature, the session of 1879, for example. It kept Charles C. Wallace in Carson City to manipulate Republican politics, shut up opposing newspapers such as the Eureka *Daily Leader*, and even used pressure and threats to banish enemies from the state. F. E. Fisk, who openly fought extortionate freight charges and rate discriminations, had to leave Nevada and seek refuge in Oregon.

Crossing otherwise remote back country and being a permanent capital investment, the railroad did give some economic and financial stability to Nevada and create values in mines and land. It contributed directly to the public revenues more than any other single interest. It furnished over sixty per cent of the taxes in some counties. But even as a taxpayer the railroad showed its octopus tendencies. The assessed valuations were disputed by able attorneys, who valued lands high when for sale and low when being assessed for taxes, and when the railroad did pay its taxes it was likely to get them back in higher rates. When Washoe County raised the tax rate and made the Central Pacific pay an additional $45,000, it raised the charges for freighting wood from Verdi to Reno (about ten miles) from fifty cents to a dollar per cord. It raised other rates, to the extent that State Senator C. C. Powning estimated the blood money squeezed from the Reno area was $250,000.

From 1870 to 1910 the "railroad vampires" held on to most of the land for twenty miles on each side of its tracks, silently sucked Nevada like an orange, gave nothing much in return, and kept the state needlessly a desert in order to keep other railroads from coming west to gobble at the rich spoils of California. Nevada was a mere land bridge for the railroad from Ogden to Sacramento.

Decade after decade Nevadans protested against their King Stork that was swallowing whole all the good things in their state. Good citizens were outraged. Even the party of the railroads, the Republican, was "anti" as early as 1874. The newspaper editorials fumed, as did others in California and in the plains states. The Carson *Morning Appeal*, for example, said, "The Southern Pacific has never made the slightest attempt to build up Nevada and it declines to pay taxes on its lands in this State. If it were compelled to pay taxes on its unpatented lands at a valuation of $15 an acre, as it claims them to be worth, the tax would run the State Government." The Goldfield *News*: "The Southern Pacific will soon wake up to the fact that they have been playing the 'all hog' game a little beyond the limit and the people have reached the point where they are retaliating." The stage-line proprietor, Winder, in *The Ox-Bow Incident*, makes a speech that is no doubt representative of a hundred thousand unprinted opinions of Nevadans before the turn of the century.

They got the law with them; they're a legal business, they are. They killed off men, didn't they? . . . one for every tie their son-of-a-bitchin' rails is laid on. And they robbed men of honest to God men's jobs from Saint Looey to Frisco . . . and for what? For a lot of plush-bottomed, soft-handed bastards, who couldn't even drive their own wagons to ride across the country and steal everything they could lay their hands on in Californy. . . . By God, I hate the stink of an Injun, but an Injun smells sweet comparin' to a railroad man. . . .

If the railroad replied to the complaints at all, it pointed out that the line and equipment were the property of the stockholders and not of any state or even the nation, were theirs as fully as if actually built at their own expense. The railroad was built when it was a national necessity, during the Civil War, to protect the Pacific Coast from an English land grab. The government had secured able and responsible men only by inducing them with land grants and subsidies for each mile of track. As for the high rates, the railroad, like any commercial enterprise, had to discriminate between its several types of customers, and charge less for greater amounts of freight, more for smaller, charge less for points where there was competition, like San Francisco, reached also by steamboats and clipper ships, more for points like Reno and Elko, reached by no other freight carriers. Furthermore, Nevada would be a wilderness still without such progress as the railroad had made possible. Mr. Justice Davis himself had said, in *United States* v. *Union Pacific Railroad*, that the vast unpeopled area between the Missouri and Sacramento rivers was " practically worthless without the facilities afforded by a railroad for the transportation of persons and property."

Salvation for Nevada came only after the Granger movement, the Populist party, Bryan's fulminations, and the local Silver party came to a late climax. The State Railroad Commission, founded in 1907, locked horns with the Southern Pacific and Wells, Fargo. In 1910 the Interstate Commerce Commission decided against the railroad in a suit brought by the State of Nevada. RENO AS COMMERCIAL METROPOLIS headlined the *Nevada State Journal*. "Railroad Rate Decision Will Rejuvenate Entire State of Nevada." Discriminatory rates were at an end. Early in 1910 freight from Reno to all points east outside the state had been $4.29 per 100 pounds of first-class goods. Revised rates ordered were on a sliding scale with a lower top than before, $2.10 to Colorado, for example, and $3.50 to New York. Before, the rate from Colorado to Winnemucca had been $4.61. This became $2. The rate from New York was cut from $4.61 to $3.33. Editors had occasion to be jubilant. "This marks the relief of our people from heavy tribute which for more than forty years they have paid to the coast cities of California for the privilege of doing business in the state of Nevada." Troubles lay ahead to be ironed out in steamy sessions of the Interstate Commerce Commission. The new Panama Canal gave the railroad an excuse to cut rates to San Francisco — to meet competition — and leave rates to Nevada uncut. And for years the railroad nettled Nevada sheepmen by charging extra for wool shipped east. Little variant rates continued to work against Nevada's independence. But "heavy tribute" did disappear and Reno did begin to rise to its true stature as distributing center for the western portion of the Great Basin.

As Nevadans were dethroning their King Stork, who had proved so rapacious, a local frog, financially very plump, hopped into power. He was George Wingfield, "King George" to the wits, overlord of the political, economic, and therefore of the educational and moral life of the state. By the end of the World War this Oregon cowboy who had gone from a roulette table in Tonopah to the vice-presidency of the $50,000,000 Goldfield Consolidated Mining Company, was boss of Nevada. A man of his word, he grubstaked old prospector friends. To help the settlers on the Newlands Project he donated a $20,000 herd of purebred dairy cattle from California and built a creamery. The homesteaders could pay for this with half their milk profits. He manipulated the divorce law so that Reno's business kept prospering. The good deeds make a considerable list, but the bad ones loom larger.

Wingfield headed what was new in Nevada politics, a "bipartisan machine" that was powerful in elections and in the legislature for fifteen years. The traditional "interests" in the state, the railroad, utility, labor, livestock, and mining people, who had from time to time formed temporary alliances in political issues like the direct primary and the creation of the state police, sought favors from the Wingfield consolidated political organization, and thus made it all the stronger. It did not even interfere in the primary elections. Politicians who won played with Wingfield's machine or else they never tried to run again. Wingfield controlled mines, hotels, the Nevada Surety and Bonding Company, eleven state banks, and a dozen other financial enterprises. In one way or another he held the check on Republicans, Democrats, capitalists, and common men. The real capital of Nevada was Room 201 in the Reno National Bank Building, Wingfield's main office and headquarters for his henchmen, the lawyers George B. Thatcher and William Woodburn.

One good set of evidence of what this backroom government was like is a series of articles that appeared in the Sacramento *Bee* under the by-line of Arthur B. Waugh in early 1934. The series won high sanction when the Pulitzer Prize Committee awarded the *Bee* a gold medal worth $500 for the most disinterested and meritorious public service rendered by an American newspaper during the year. Waugh showed how Wingfield controlled the state government so completely that " a long series of machinations and deceptions, of fund-juggling and of political wire-pulling and trickery " went on for years until the stringencies of the Depression exposed matters to public scrutiny. Nevada taxpayers once lost $300,000 through connivance in the attorney general's office, the State Board of Finance and the state bank examiner failed to enforce the state banking code on the bookkeeping of the Wingfield banks, the banks did such things as loaning funds on chattel mortgages and loaning in excess of the legal limit, Wingfield undermined his country banks to support a tottering financial structure in his First National Bank of Reno. With no real security at all, Wingfield's Surety and Bonding Company wrote bonds for public officers and also for the public funds deposited in the Wingfield banks. United States District Judge Frank Norcross, apparently a cog in the Wingfield machine, was involved in very dubious proceedings in the Owl Drug bankruptcy and receivership case. A road-contracting firm which did not write its surety bonds through Nevada Surety and Bonding was driven to bankruptcy, and its equipment was given, by " legal " procedure, to a Wingfield-controlled contracting company.

What touched off the prize-winning exposure was the simple fact that Wingfield, even though his banks had been closed fourteen months and his enemies were advertising his misdemeanors, had control over the Nevada delegation to Congress when two proposed appointments were before the Senate: William Woodburn for the District Court in Nevada and Frank Norcross for the Circuit Court of Appeal. Nevadans did not object to the appointment of Norcross, for he was generally respected, but they did object, emphatically, to an obvious scheme to put Woodburn in a position materially to aid Wingfield. It looked as if bankruptcy was imminent for Wingfield, and Woodburn would be quite too kindly a judge to hear the case.

The *Bee* articles precipitated a delayed storm. The protests of Nevadans to Congress were so strong that the appointments were not voted. The First National Bank stayed open during the year and a half that the other ten banks were closed, but Wingfield went through bankruptcy — in an impartial court. All his banks were liquidated through various receiverships, the Reno one, too, and passed into other hands. The Nevada Surety and Bonding Company went out of existence. Wingfield walked the sidewalks of a hostile Reno. Since 1936 he has gained new wealth, including Reno real estate and a share in the rich Getchell Mine up in Humboldt County, but he is no longer king. Men run for office, win, serve only the public good, run again, and win re-election. Once again a politician is either a Democrat or a Republican. And to the average citizen the state government is good because it is visible. The capitol is a populous, clean goldfish bowl instead of a murky, muddy frogpond with one frog visible, half submerged on a rotten log.

Scorned and Exploited

For beauty and promise, Nevada is a name among names. Nevada! Pronounce the word aloud. Does it not evoke mountains and clear air, heights of untrodden snow and valleys aromatic with the pine and musical with falling waters? Nevada! But the name is all. Abomination of desolation presides over nine-tenths of the place. The sun beats down on a roof of zinc, fierce and dull. Not a drop of water to a mile of sand. The mean ash-dump landscape stretches on from nowhere to nowhere, a spot of mange. No portion of the earth is more lacquered with paltry, unimportant ugliness.

So wrote a novelist early in the century. His scorn was as orthodox as it was eloquent. Horace Greeley, it is reported, said on his trip west in 1859 that America would be improved if the Sierra Nevadas and the Rockies could be brought together and the intervening country eliminated from the surface of the earth. Arriving in Placerville, California, he said, "I believe God never made anything without a purpose. But the wilderness I have just crossed is certainly worthless for agriculture. Unless there shall prove to be great mineral wealth there, it has been created in vain." Another early visitor remarked, "If there is a State in North America where an active, experienced woodsman might perish, that State is Nevada." More than one arrival felt that Nevada looked like the breaking up of the world. Samuel Bowles of the Springfield *Republican* thought that Nature was incomplete here. Man had entered before she was ready for him and found her unprepared for his reception. "It is as though all hope had died out of mother earth," wrote J. H. Beadle, "leaving the dead embers of a burnt-out land as witnesses to the awful despair of nature."

Early in the sixties, Edward Hingston, manager for the humorist, Artemus Ward, wrote to a New York weekly that he was faced with the prospect of a trip across Nevada to Salt Lake City.

No nightingales will sing to me on the way, no locusts will chirrup in the grass, nor any bull-frogs grunt me salutations from the ponds, simply because the ponds are too alkaline for any reptile, not iron-plated to exist in; the grass don't grow, nor the grasshoppers either; and the nightingales don't sing, because they have no boughs to sit on to sing from, nothing to sing about, and finally, there are no nightingales.

Mark Twain, always an articulate commentator on Nevada matters, wrote letters home about his environment there. He wrote his sister Pamela that some people were malicious enough to think that if the devil were set at liberty and told to confine himself to Nevada he would go there and look sadly around awhile and then get homesick and go back to hell again. In a letter to his mother he added:

I overheard a gentleman say, the other day, that it was "the d—dest country under the sun," and that comprehensive conception I fully subscribe to. It never rains here, and the dew never falls. No flowers grow here, and no green thing gladdens the eye. The birds that fly over the land carry their provisions with them. Only the crow and the raven tarry with us. Our city lies in the midst of a desert of the purest, most unadulterated and uncompromising *sand*, in which nothing but that fag-end of vegetable creation, "sage brush," ventures to grow.

Nevada's scenery has been damned more than that of any other state. To patrons of busses and trains, as to the emigrants of the old trails (who had much better reason), Nevada is mileage only, a purgatory for tourists and a paradise for transportation and freight companies. Autoists feel that the only profit in the inevitable day's drive across the state accrues solely to the oil companies. Humorists condescend; romancers distort. Where Californians are professionally intolerant, Easterners and Southerners, who are used to abundant woodlands and streams, to summers of tall grass and verdant foliage, find Nevada occasion for indignation generally, though sometimes for curiosity and imagination, and rarely for appreciation.

Certainly, it must be admitted, Nevada is handicapped in having no sensational points of interest, for its artificial boundaries have clipped its natural wings. Death Valley lies just inside the California line and so do two-thirds of Lake Tahoe, which to the resort advertisers is a California lake. The Snake River gorge stays in southern Idaho. The spectacular salt beds of Lake Bonneville stop just east of the Utah line. The man-made wonder, Boulder Dam, lies half in Arizona. As desert, Nevada has the picturesque coloring but lacks the abundant cactus that have engendered a cult of the desert among selected natives and Easterners in Arizona and southern California. It lacks, even, the conspicuous erosion that can be canonized as national parks and monuments, like Arizona's Grand Canyon, Utah's Bryce, the Badlands of South Dakota, and the White Sands of New Mexico. Yet, as a later chapter will indicate, there is much in Nevada for the sightseer. Only now is a scattering of millionaires, divorce seekers, travelers, writers, and artists, James Swinnerton among them, seriously inaugurating a new understanding of the state.

The people living in Nevada have been impugned along with the scenery. Certain American cities, including New Orleans and Chicago, have long had the repute of being fester spots of immorality, but the state they are in has not been lumped with them in a sweeping charge of state-wide carnality. Nevada has fared less well. In the minds of a large portion of the American public the state as a whole is a symbol of brutality, vice, and antisocial conditions in general. The development of more conventional states on all sides has made its peculiarities stand out all the more. In particular, journalists and orthodox religionists have given it a reputation that is a part of American folklore and jokesmithing.

When the state was less than a decade old a Michigan paper referred to the citizens of Virginia City as " a semi-civilized race of savages." In reality they were the elite of the Pacific Coast. The San Francisco *Dramatic Chronicle* told about an Englishman who was disgusted with Virginia City, where he had been fleeced and bilked by crooked brokers. He entered a restaurant for dinner and was urged by the waiter to feast on sage hen. He refused: " D—n anything with wings that will stay in such a country." An article in the New York *Herald* libeled the mining town of Pioche. It said there were two hundred murdered persons in the town's graveyard, the merchants robbed the stagecoaches at night, the majority of the women were no better than they should be, and certain retired stage robbers never held up stages because they were in the pay of the express company. An English naturalist of sorts, Paul Fountain, who traveled through Nevada in the late sixties or early seventies and later published observations in two books, reacted violently to the free-and-easy life he encountered. Carson City, he said, was a hell on earth. No writer had ever described the shameless horror of Carson; no writer ever would. " It was past description, and an attempt to paint its abominable scenes would disgust all persons, without exception." Most of the population of Nevada was scoundrels, including killers, Yankee desperadoes, lost wretches in drunken orgies, saloonkeepers — bloated human spiders, and obscene women, who were the soul of every wicked act — " horrible sirens who kept dens." Carson outdid all other shameless places and was a moral ugliness that ill contrasted with surrounding natural beauty. Fountain's diatribe would be more convincing if in another passage he hadn't advanced the theory that a flock of birds he saw high above Salt Lake were flamingos.

Even the sympathetic historian of the Pacific slope, Hubert H. Bancroft, exploded abusively in one of his many volumes. He was speaking of Nevada in its early days, when it was nick-named Washoe. " It was then the paradise of evil-doers, as California had been in her day. From the frequency of assaults, assassinations, and robberies, together with the many minor misdemeanors and suicides, one would think that Washoe . . . had become the world's moral cesspool, the receptacle of prison offal from every quarter." And so on, in rhetoric about " bloated dissipation " that sunned itself upon the street corners, and grass widows " panting for new alliances." It is a decidedly unprofessional passage of history to come from the pen of either Bancroft or one of his assistants.

Of course, there was some fire for all the smoke fanned up by these writers and others. There have to be cards before a propagandist can stack them. Only, as the decades have passed, Nevada has received preponderantly negative treatment. She has remained a black sheep among the federal states. She has suffered from sneers, censure, obloquy. Things have been repeatedly said that question her whole ethical foundation. Her entrance to the Union was a corrupt political scheme. Her wealth has been used to corrupt legislatures and judges. Her leaders are corrupters of the press. Her chief industry, mining, is a grafting, gambling, swindling game. What steady population she has is of the baser sort — rowdies, gamblers, and breakers of sacred marriage vows. Her cities are crude mining camps in spirit, the rendezvous for *demimonde* elements. Her " rivers," even, are fraudulent pretenses, and her " forests " are sagebrush preserves. Many an outsider has asked, almost instinctively, " Can anything good come out of Nevada? "

At the turn of the century, when Nevada was one of two states that allowed prize fighting, the longhairs of America took punches at her morals, especially after the reporters sent to cover three championship fights sent home news features that grossly exaggerated the Sodom and Gomorrah qualities of Nevada towns. The state was a godless wallower in the mire before the temple of Mammon, attracting the " riffraff of humanity and the offscouring of the country," and " for the sake of the dollar . . . willing to sell all that is sacred and best." Slot machines were under fire; so were lottery proposals. Later, when Goldfield mineral properties were drawing the money of Atlantic Coast investors to Nevada, the Eastern press sneered at the mines — although it was impossible to sneer long at the Tonopah-Extension and the Mohawk. In 1924 the press of the country was in a furor over the execution of Gee Jon in the new lethal gas chamber in Carson. A little later editors whipped themselves up again over the second cyanide execution, that of Stanko Jukich. Painless? Humane? No! Brutal! Callous! Depraved! (This from states which allowed a criminal to twist and contort in the spasms of the electric chair or a killer to be hanged with such violence that his head is pulled clear off his torso.) The most consistent publicity and "exposure" has come to the legalized prostitution of Reno's Riverside District and Las Vegas's Block 16 and to the gambling and marriage laws. These have borne the brunt of a continent-wide assault.

These tolerant laws have long set "good people" by the ears. They have led more than one Christian to exaggerate Nevada's ways by calling the state names such as "the paradise of the corruptionist, the gambler, the pimp, the abandoned and the degraded, a menace to the progress of civilization, and despair of the church, the anguish of the angels and the anathema of God." Even before the World War it was accused of passing special laws to encourage "those whose vagrant and unholy passions led them to seek the easiest release from matrimonial bonds that they chose to regard as shackles and fetters." The Berkeley *Courier* once said that Reno was "a roadhouse for matrimonial joy riders" and that Nevada "has given an unmistakable endorsement to progressive polygamy." The expression was in vogue in other states: "If you can't do it at home, go to Nevada." The humorists were busy.

> Nevada, 'tis of thee,
> Sweet state of liberty,
>   Of thee I sing.
> State where our fathers flee:
> State that sets mothers free —
> Marriage, because of thee,
>   Hath lost its sting.
>
> My state that holds the key
> That sets the shackled free,
>   I love thy name.
> I love thy lawyers' ways,
> Thy dazzling divorcees,
> The briefness of their stays —
>   Their little game.

Reno, it is of thee,
Daughter of liberty,
    To thee we flee.
Long may thy streets resound
With freedom's joyful sound.
Scatter thy light around
    From sea to sea.

Especially did the torrent of nation-wide abuse break over Nevada's head in 1931 when gambling was re-legalized after a Puritanical interlude and the residential requirement for divorce was reduced to an all-time minimum of six weeks. Headline writers all over America had their way of slanting the news: " Nevada's Infamy," " Nevada Opens Up," " Nevada Goes the Limit," " Nevada Goes Whoopee," " Frank Nevada," " Pandora's Box," " Gambler's Heaven Opens," " ' Free ' Nevada." Editorial writers moralized on the same old theme of the state's immorality. The Montgomery *Advertiser* said, " Nevada is tired of cactus, alkali wastes, sparse population, hard times, and virtue." The Dallas *Morning News* talked of flushed and shaken men, women, and youths at the gambling tables. " These will Nevada gather in, to suck them dry and fling away the husks of humanity, quite careless whether they live or die." It recalled the old days when every town had its hell's half acre. " But Nevada seems ambitious that America shall have a sort of hell's hundred thousand square miles. She has made a propitious beginning already." The Los Angeles *Times* catechized:

Catering to the underworld is not the way to feed great enterprise.

Letting down moral barriers is not the way to draw population.

Making it easy to break up the home has not been lofty business for lawmakers.

Lifting the ban on gambling is an invitation to gangland.

Churchmen, notably those outside Nevada, had their say. Taking an absolute position on morals, overlooking modern psychology as well as Nevada sociology, the Presbyterians of Nevada and California in a synodical meeting adopted a resolution that was inspired by their " extreme embarrassment and hot indignation at the legalized vice and disgraceful divorce laws." They said that those responsible were both un-American and traitorous to the best moral interests of state and nation. They extended sympathy to their " fellow Christians who must live and labor to promote morality in Nevada under the unhappy handicap which the moral breakdown of the state presents."

Pious folk continue to find occasion to have their say about ungodly Nevada. A few years ago the Episcopalian bishop of Nevada, who was not a seasoned native, told a New York audience that in many towns " the people know the name of God only as it is used in cursing and swearing. In one town the little boys and girls bandy around the Holy Name with as much freedom as their basketballs. I confirmed a class of thirty not long ago composed of boys and girls who had never heard of God's name except as an expletive. There's a lot that is loose in Nevada, but there's no money loose for Christian work."

Nevada's low reputation made possible for years a crowning indignity, an articulate guerrilla attack on her statehood itself. Eastern interests tried for decades to oust her from the Union. They were irked by her equality in the Senate, by her aggressive role in silver history, by her activity in the powerful and dangerous Western farm bloc in Congress. Also, Easterners felt irritated when they reflected that what was virtually colonial territory should possess sovereign status. They did not see why an area so unlike theirs in appearance and tradition should be a state at all. As a Yale professor, William H. Brewer, confided to his journal in the early sixties:

I see no elements here to make a state. It has mines of some marvelous richness, but it has nothing else, nothing to call people here to live and found homes. Every man of culture hopes to make his fortune here, but to enjoy it in more favored lands. The climate is bad, water is bad, land a desert, and the population floating.

The attack reached its highest intensity during the nineties and early 1900's, when the Western states, under Bryan's leadership, were challenging the power of the Eastern states and their House of Lords on Wall Street. The wrath of those scared by free silver and Populism fell on the most vulnerable, in wealth and population, of the insurgent states. Eastern newspapers lambasted Nevada for its disproportionate place in the Electoral College and the Senate. From states bossed by Tammany Hall, the Yerkes interests, and the New Haven Railroad came the charge that Nevada was " a rotten borough." The standard moral charges against the state were rehearsed, whetted by the three big prize fights between 1897 and 1910. A state whose laws would allow Corbett *vs*. Fitzsimmons, Nelson *vs*. Gans, and Jeffries *vs*. Johnson was manifestly a den of moral turpitude. The press cried out: Strip Nevada of the state power it has so shamefully abused and that it neither appreciates nor knows how properly to use! Let it stand ashamed and humiliated in well-merited disgrace before the world! If it will not curb its own vile lawlessness let the nation do it and no longer bear the burden of such a corrupting and degenerating influence! Here is a vicious Babylon and the moment is ripe for another flood. Public opinion must see that this state is disqualified.

Alleged economic insufficiencies were brought forward. The Chicago *Tribune* in a widely quoted editorial, " How to Deal with Nevada," said, " The silver-mines which made her all she was have been exhausted. She has no other mineral wealth. She has no agricultural resources. She has nothing to attract people; and, as a consequence, she is flickering out." The *Tribune* urged that Nevada's statehood be canceled, or at least her Senators be excluded from Congress as were Southern Senators during the Civil War and the period of Reconstruction.

Defenders of Nevada from the attack, naturally, were Nevadans and other Westerners. They replied to both the political and the economic charges. They made it clear that " to degrade loyal States by depriving them of important attributes of their sovereignty would be radical, if not revolutionary." It would violate both the letter and the spirit of the Constitution, which provided in Article V for a restriction on amendments. " No State, without its Consent, shall be deprived of its equal Suffrage in the Senate." As for the argument that Nevada had two Senators for less than 100,000 population while states as large as Pennsylvania and New York, with many millions, had only two also, the reply was that senatorial equality was a qualitative, not a quantitative matter. Besides, Nevada had always had proportional representation in the House, only one Congressman to three or four dozen for New York; there was a just check and balance. Granting that Nevada's statehood arrived prematurely, even though with the approval, if not connivance, of Honest Abe, once arrived, it was perpetual, for a part of our governmental system, be it republican or democratic, was that states are sovereign, whatever their size in population or square miles, with senatorial equality the badge thereof. Only such parity in status and rights could hold together a federal government embracing Delaware and Montana, Wyoming and New York, or Rhode Island and Texas.

William E. Smythe, writing in *Forum* in 1897, adequately replied to the economic misinterpretation. The silver mines were not exhausted. They were not dead. They were only legally suppressed. Bonanza days were gone, to be sure, but not days of sober industrial development. There was much mediocre ore valued at from $8 to $20 per ton that new techniques could profitably reduce, if more railroads and cheaper

LOOKING NORTHWESTERLY across Truckee Storage Project lands. Reno is in the distant right

U. S. Department of the Interior

WINTER
FEEDING IN
MASON VALLEY

Nevada Photo Service—Reno

rates were available. The deep levels in the mines were untouched in most camps. Besides, there was other mineral wealth in the state: soda, salt, copper, gypsum, lead, zinc, mineral soap. As for lack of agricultural resources, the *Tribune* was woefully ignorant or willfully libelous. Land that had been farmed for years had demonstrated the excellence of sagebrush-covered land, provided it could be irrigated. Nevada hay and apples were exported to England for a duke's horses and a queen's table. The state contained at least six million irrigable acres (there were only two million in cultivation in Utah and Colorado). And Nevada was not flickering out. True, there were serious problems, the railroad rates, land monopoly, loot-prepossessed miners, but Nevada was " potentially one of the great States in the Union. Her natural resources were more varied, more valuable, and more extensive than those pertaining to most of the States east of the Mississippi, and even some of the States west of the river." Discounting some exaggeration, Smythe was sound, and the past half century has borne him out.

The big political assault on Nevada faded out with the discovery of bonanzas in Tonopah and Goldfield — which even Smythe did not foresee — and the beginning of agricultural development under the United States Bureau of Reclamation in the much-publicized Truckee-Carson Project, but the old issue turns up now and then. As late as 1931 a correspondent of a New York paper was writing that " sooner or later the rank inequality in representation in the Senate will bring a demand for reform which will have to be heeded " and proposing, in spite of Article V, that the Constitution be amended to provide for reasonable numbers of senators-at-large to be nominated at party conventions and elected at the same time as the president. Obviously, the East would elect these men.

Some foes of Nevada's political existence would solve her alleged insufficiencies by giving her back to Utah, except for a thin western slice for California. This would mean political annihilation for residents of the present Nevada, who would be backwoodsmen only to legislators in Sacramento and Salt Lake City. Logically, a more effective scheme would be to grant Nevada parts of the adjoining states. Honey Lake residents in northeastern California look to Reno for commerce and fun; so do cowboys and hay hands in Inyo and Mono counties. As a matter of fact, the California agricultural inspection on the state line, which has annoyed millions of visiting autoists with examinations of suitcases and bedrolls, quarantines certain eastern California areas right along with Nevada and other inland states, an admission of the natural unity of the whole area east of the Sierra peaks. Outlanders in parts of western Utah look to Pioche and Ely in eastern Nevada. But the argument the Sacramento politicos advanced two generations ago, when Nevada asked for all of California east of the Sierra divide, is now true. Our state boundaries are fixed by usage and tradition, and there is no changing them short of total reconstruction of the federal system.

The ironical side of the whole assault by Americans on the reputation of Nevada is that they themselves are responsible for whatever evils really existed. Statehood was thrust on the territory during a crucial year of the Civil War. It was men and women from all the states and territories who crowded into early Washoe to give it its turbulent, unregulated life. The badmen bragged of their origins in California, Utah, Texas. San Franciscans more than Nevadans promoted the slippery stock manipulations and the salting of mines on the Comstock. Miscellaneous non-Nevadans, especially Easterners, dominated among the wildcatters of Goldfield and Rawhide. The big prize fights were attended by men coming in special trains from both coasts, from states that prohibited fights. The gamblers of early days learned their trade elsewhere, and the profitable modern revival of gambling is made possible by tourists and temporary visitors. And as for divorce, Easterners first exploited it and they are the ones who have

made it a major state industry. Nevadans did not create most
of the conditions that have held back development of the
state. If the state is disreputable, it is not to blame. If it has
been unworthy of sovereignty, its fellow states and their citizens have been the unwitting cause, and they should have
proposed aid, not extinction.

VERBAL scorn, then, is one reason for Nevada's long and
gawky adolescence among sister states. But the social force
of low reputation has not been acting alone. Alongside, powerful economic forces have been at work to make Nevada an
imperial slave of the United States.

Nevada's original destiny, to furnish raw materials only,
explains why she has been a colony of the United States. She
has produced soda, borax, lead, copper, and wool, only to
find that Congress permitted these products to enter America
on the free list. Thus Nevada has had to sell these products to
Eastern manufacturers at a low price, kept low by world competition, and then buy back factory-made articles — copper
wire, borated soap, rifle bullets, and winter overcoats — at
high prices, kept high by a tariff on imported goods.

Also Nevada's bullion has been a subsidy to the nation. It,
however, has played a significant role in American history
and in world finance, not without glory to its place of origin.
For one thing, it was of crucial aid to the Northern cause
during the Civil War. " Nevada! coin thy golden crags, with
Freedom's image and name," wrote Emerson in his " Boston
Hymn." The production of Nevada and other states, including Colorado, helped strengthen Union credit, and the potential output helped demoralize the South, particularly after
several hopeless Confederate plots had failed to capture Nevada and California for Jeff Davis. Nevada was admitted as
a state, Charles Dana later wrote, to give Lincoln the three-
fourths majority he needed to pass the Thirteenth Amendment, a military measure that would change the national

slavery policy, break the continuity of ideas in the South, and be the equivalent of new armies in the field. Said Lincoln, " It is easier to admit Nevada than to raise another million of soldiers." He gave the New York and New Jersey delegations the political patronage necessary to win their support for Nevada's statehood. The state constitution was telegraphed to him at a cost of $3,416.77 and he signed it at once. Thus Nevada, with one-sixth the population then required for a congressman, became the " Battle-born State," rounding out the third dozen of sovereign states. It helped the North by contributing over $200,000 to the Red Cross of the day, namely, the Sanitary Commission, and aided the Union to resume specie payment after Appomattox.

The world watched Nevada, Virginia City in particular. New Yorkers talked familiarly of Comstock mines, and they were a prominent topic of the London Stock Exchange. This was partly because there was immediate profit to be made, partly because there was danger of serious long-range loss, for in both America and Europe Nevada's rich mines, along with others in the Western Hemisphere, exerted a seriously disturbing influence on the monetary system. The tremendous production of silver promised to aid the poor man by making money cheap and thus alarmed the rich. Nations like England and France, with gold for their standard, were heavy purchasers of Civil War bonds and feared that they would be paid in silver. A decade earlier the great increases in the world's supply of gold, because of the discoveries in California and Australia, had set European economists to theorizing. Some had seen great dangers threatening all the classes living on fixed incomes. Others had felt that a golden age of commercial progress would follow. The former prevailed as the production of gold quadrupled in a decade and that of silver remained stationary. National leaders argued that only silver would retain its value in terms of labor and commodity; therefore Belgium in 1850 demonetized gold and adopted silver as the standard metal, and in 1857 the German states and Austria established the silver standard. But now, as silver production swelled with the rise of Virginia City, Austin, and other camps in the West, Chile, and Mexico, European countries, whether on a gold or silver base, feared that they would collect the cheap money resulting from coinage of the abundant silver.

In 1864 Emperor Louis Napoleon sent C. Guillemin Tarayre to Mexico, California, and Nevada to report on the mines. He reported optimistically. Metallurgy, he said, was improving, the railroad was coming, production was large, and " loin de diminuer, croîtra d'année en année et augmentera." With increases each year, no one could say how much treasure would be extracted. In 1867 Napoleon called the first international monetary conference. Representatives met in Paris and discussed how to make money dearer. John Sherman of Ohio, the American delegate, as chairman of the Senate Finance Committee, was the author of a resolution that pledged the respective countries to work for the establishment of a gold standard. The German government, hearing amazing tales of Comstock silver, asked Philip Deidesheimer, superintendent of the Hale and Norcross and a graduate of the Freiberg Mining School, to report on values and extent of ore. After a careful examination he reported one and a half billions in sight! The German Empire went on a gold standard, made its silver coin into bullion, and sold it on the open market. Soon the Bank of France stopped coining silver. Therefore Belgium, Switzerland, Holland, Italy, and Greece did likewise. The Mint Bill was a center of dispute in Congress for three years, 1870 to 1873, and finally passed, after many tricky amendments and reconsiderations, without any provision for the coinage of the standard silver dollar. This so-called " Crime of '73 " legislated away the contemporary importance of Nevada, leaving only the " trade dollar " to be coined at the Carson Mint. This dollar, seven and a half grains larger than standard, was for use in Oriental trade. The Chinese garnered these dollars and sent many of them to India for opium, where they became rupees in the Calcutta mint.

The "silver question" was not settled by Congressional edict in 1873. In one form or another it has been before the country ever since, and among the ringleaders of silver movements have been Nevada senators — William Stewart, John P. Jones, Francis Newlands, Key Pittman. For a generation silver figured in every session of Congress and in every national political campaign. The prolonged debate as to what a sound and stable currency was got more Americans to thinking about economics than ever before or after, up to the beginning of the Great Depression.

Free silver was the symbol in a nation-wide struggle of poor man against rich man, of the agricultural West and South against the financial East. On one side were recruits from the Greenbackers, Knights of Labor, Farmers' Alliances, Populists, followers of Edward Bellamy and Henry George, members of Nevada's Silver party, and debtors everywhere. William Jennings Bryan was their apostolic leader. " You shall not crucify mankind upon a cross of gold! " On the other side were Cleveland, McKinley, the great bankers and industrialists, a mass of middle-class people who were well fixed, and a small army of creditors. The nation was in trouble. Money was scarce, credit inflexible, labor restless, and farming insecure. Progressive efforts to regulate railroads and trusts had failed. The state legislatures, bossed by " the interests," elected the United States senators. The Supreme Court's decisions supported property, not the people. Free coinage of silver, cried the champions of the underdogs, would solve all the major problems and give prosperity to the Common Man.

The Bland-Allison Act of 1878, pushed through over a presidential veto, provided that the Treasury must purchase each month not less than two nor more than four million dollars' worth of silver to be coined into regular dollars. The

Treasury thus bought little of the volume of silver the West could have produced, and the amount of money in circulation was not appreciably increased. The price of silver went down steadily, and Nevada mines began to close. Silver miners saw a relation between limited coinage of silver and the low price of silver, while farmers saw the relation between low commodity prices and high gold prices and between low circulation of money and high interest rates. Continued silverite agitation and the presence in Congress of twelve new senators from Western states admitted in 1889 led to the Sherman Silver Purchase Act of 1890, a maneuver by Republicans, which did not increase the amount of money in circulation, raise the price of silver, or stop the decline in prices for farm products. It was repealed at the special session called by Cleveland after the panic of 1893. Nevada's population dropped some more.

The Populists began the agitation that the Democrats took over for the hot campaigns of 1896 and 1900, for coinage of gold and silver at the ratio of 16 to 1, which was the ratio in 1860 before the Comstock began to increase the percentage of silver production in America. This scheme was intended to peg the price of silver. It precipitated the tumultuous battle of 1896.

Pamphlets and reprints flooded America. There was the speech of the senator from South Carolina, "Pitchfork" Ben Tillman: "Bimetallism or Industrial Slavery." Zach Montgomery of Los Angeles in "Bimetallism: Bondage or Blood," showed how the gold standard gave the bankers a picnic, made the poor poorer, lost Uncle Sam money, and made us subservient to Britain, while W. H. Harvey of Chicago wrote Coin's Financial Series. *Coin's Hand Book* and *Financial School* and *Up to Date* canvassed the economics of the entire struggle with vigorous though crude drawings to illustrate, and leveled darts at the British landlords who used the gold standard to buy up America. A map showed how huge areas in America, including a huge block overlapping the central Nevada-Utah boundary line, was owned by non-American plutocrats, men such as the Marquis of Tweedale, Lord Dunmore, and the Duke of Sutherland. Adolphus Fitzgerald, justice on the Supreme Court of Nevada, wrote *The Thirty Years' War on Silver*. He attacked the capitalists for wishing money to be expensive and men to be cheap. He held the government guilty of injustice toward its citizens who had stored years of sweaty labor in silver coin, silver bullion, silver mines and machinery, the buildings and homes of silver camps, who had given their lives to learning the craft of scientific mining.

Bryan's inspired campaign, his silvery oratory, the counterattack by Boss Hanna and his frightened Republicans, the testimonials of Wall Street's " goldbug " economists, the tension, the hysteria, and the final narrow victory for McKinley — all this is a chapter in the history of America rather than of Nevada, and is fully treated in the histories, though generally with Nevada's place in the background unmentioned or even the subsequent attack on her statehood because of her silver politics.

But even Bryan's defeat, his succession of defeats, did not end the controversy over silver. The bugaboo of " inflation " that haunts the economic system is in the American mind somehow related to federal purchase of silver, and every financial crisis brings the twin association to the fore again. In 1934, to give the most important example, Congress followed the leadership of Senator Key Pittman of Nevada and passed the Silver Purchase Act, which Eastern spokesmen have attacked vehemently as a crackpot machination connived at by vote trading, logrolling, threatening, and wheedling. The Treasury was required to buy silver from all sellers until the market price should reach $1.29 per ounce. Failing this goal, the Treasury was to buy silver until a fourth of all United States bullion (in monetary value) was in silver. By 1940 neither automatic shutoff was in sight and certain Eastern

senators were getting restless. To them the Act seemed to be
a subsidy to a small group of mine operators, half of them
living on the Atlantic, anyway. The Treasury had paid out,
in five years, $197,000,000 to Western silver producers, and
in the same time some $912,000,000 to foreign nations. No
one, they argued, could say that the American people in general were benefiting. (One of the plaintiffs was Senator John
Townsend of Delaware, whose masters, the du Ponts, were
receiving huge national defense orders from the government.)
They were motivated, perhaps, by the gold man's fear of silver, in the form of Republican fear of New Deal " inflation."
The ghost of Bryan was at large again: managed currency,
managed by the government instead of private persons on
Wall Street, a pegged dollar that will not change its purchas-
ing and debt-paying power. Senator Pittman and Senator El-
bert Thomas of Utah defended the Act and argued, furthermore, that the silver program of the New Deal had been of
great assistance to the United States in raising exports from a
low level, in so far as silver purchases from Mexico, China,
and Britain had enabled those countries to buy commodities
from us, Mexico in particular.

   Many people were interested in silver and wrote inquiries to
professional economists and to amateurs like newspaper editors. Both domestic and international issues were raised. For
by March, 1940, the government had made a profit on silver
of about $1,143,000,000, through seigniorage, the difference
between the circulating value of a coin and the cost of the
bullion and minting. As brought out during a discussion in
the Senate between Senator Pittman and Senator Alben W.
Barkley of Kentucky, if a miner takes 1,000 ounces of silver
to the Treasury he gets silver certificates — money — for 500
ounces. The Treasury keeps the other 500 ounces and can
issue certificates against them to pay government debts. Meanwhile a measure of mining prosperity was returning to Nevada and her neighbors as prospectors discovered new mines

and operators reopened old workings, inaugurating a new era in Virginia City, Silver City, Mina, Eureka, and a score more of the frontier camps. Most of the silver went east to be buried in the vaults at West Point, just as the gold went to its guarded sepulcher at Fort Knox, Kentucky. Philosophically it seemed absurdly comic that men should labor to dig precious metals from one hole in the ground only to bury them in another. Yet economically the result of this process, combined with paper work in Washington, brought livings to many human beings who might otherwise have been in grave plight during the depression, capitalists and proletarians alike.

Although Nevada's silver contributed less and less to the nation's income from 1873 to 1934, her other mineral products, gold and copper especially, gave wealth to many. Where her silver and gold of the sixties and seventies had redounded mostly to the glory of Californians, her succeeding production has gone in larger measure to capitalists in states to the east. The great days of Tonopah and Goldfield and Bullfrog in the era of Roosevelt and Taft found Californians asleep dreaming of the Comstock of General Grant's time, a generation before, and the big names of Nevada mining then and since have tended to be those of capitalists and operators in Pittsburgh, Denver, Philadelphia, New York. Fortunes were gathered in by W. A. Clark, Charles Schwab, the Guggenheims. In the last forty years Nevada minerals have built mansions on Long Island, Park Avenue, along the Schuylkill, have paid for European scholarships for young geniuses, have founded symphony orchestras and endowed libraries — all outside the state. They have added to the world's gaiety from Los Angeles to Newport, from San Francisco to Paris.

In 1918 a professor of economics at the University of Nevada estimated that 41 per cent of the assessed valuation of Nevada was public utilities, which were almost wholly owned by nonresidents. Mines, about 15 per cent of the assessed valuations, were mostly in the hands of absentees, and land and

range animals, 24 per cent were owned in considerable extent
by outsiders. He pointed out that safely two-thirds of the
taxable property in Nevada was owned by non-Nevadans.
Nevada was sovereign politically. Economically she was colonial. There was one consolation. So many direct taxpayers
were nonvoters that the native electorate could vote in liberal reforms!

California's Colony

LONG is the story of Nevada's subservience to California.
Nature began it long ago when she dried up inland seas and
lakes, ripped and crumpled the earth's surface into short
ranges and mountains all about the same in appearance, covered their bases with salty lakes, and then dried these up into
alkali sinks and mud playas, meanwhile raising up a high-
edged range on the California line to catch all the rain brought
eastward from the Pacific Ocean by humid air masses. Bluntly,
while Nevada is a fairly uniform desert that most strangers
dislike and misunderstand, California is a wonderland. Though
a sovereign state, Nevada has been automatically minimized
by being what it is right next to the empire that can brag
of Yosemite, the Big Trees, the redwoods, San Francisco Bay,
Mount Shasta, the orchards and vineyards of the San Joaquin
Valley, the bay at Carmel, the orange groves below snow-
covered Old Baldy, the wild flowers of Kern County, and
the fossil footprints at Grauman's Chinese Theater. Any state
next to California would play a minor role.

Boosters have beglamoured travelers into crossing a land
of desolation en route for a land of dreams come true. From
Lansford W. Hastings's *Emigrant's Guide to Oregon and
California* in 1845 to the last advertisement of Californians,
Inc., the Golden State has benefited from the pull of its scenic

attractions and famous places, climate, and notable personalities. Travelers plan to be interested in Salt Lake City — the Temple, the Tabernacle, the Lion House, memories of the Mormon sensations of long ago — and in California. Except for Reno, the intervening area is an anonymous land mass.

In fact, it is one of the nation's traditions to grab at the possibilities in California and ignore those in Nevada. Forty-niners hurried across Nevada to get to California and missed the outcroppings of Austin, Eureka, and Virginia City. The capitalists of the Central Pacific overlooked fertile agricultural land. Three generations of tourists were blind to Nevada's scenery, and recreationalists are just now awaking to its opportunities for out-of-door fun. Naturalists were slow to study its special plants and aniamals. Even the archaeologists, of all men those most tolerant of barren landscapes devoid of apparent human interest, almost missed the important pre-Columbian pueblo ruins of Lost City. They dug them up and explored the adjacent hills and washes just before blue waters backed up behind Boulder Dam and flooded the site. Forty years ago the Philadelphia *Evening Telegraph* admitted, " In speaking of the Great West today the name of California at once comes to our lips, but we seldom think of Nevada."

But Californians have always known of economically important features of Nevada, and there was a time when territorial conquest was proposed, the means to be legislative. In 1852 the California legislature created Pautah County on paper. In Utah Territory, where many Californians had settled, it took in the whole area radiating eastward from Lake Tahoe to Pyramid, Carson, and Walker Lakes. " Carsonville " was made the seat of justice. The Act was to take effect when Congress ceded the territory to California, but Congress did not, and California repealed the Act seven years later. In 1860 certain interests in the legislature at Sacramento made a similar proposal for a county to be called Washoe, but it failed to pass, and the newly discovered riches of the Comstock Lode were destined to be taken only by economic conquest from the Territory of Nevada, created in 1861, and the State of Nevada, proclaimed by President Lincoln in 1864.

The unsurveyed boundary between California and Nevada Territory, however, produced two misunderstandings, one of which has always been taken rather humorously, the other seriously. About a hundred miles southeast of Carson City was the early mining town of Aurora, near Mono Lake. In March, 1861, the California legislature organized the County of Mono and made Aurora the seat, for it assumed that the bounds of California reached eastward beyond this thriving place. In June a full set of county officials, except a judge, were elected. There was doubt aplenty that Aurora was inside California, and in the same year delegates from Aurora attended the territorial legislature in Carson City, where they helped Nevada create Esmeralda County. The two states took several years to agree on making an official survey. Meanwhile Mono County officials exercised jurisdiction over the Esmeralda Mining District, and California granted toll, water, and gas franchises in Aurora. In 1863, as the surveying party neared, it seemed likely to Territorial Governor Nye of Nevada that Aurora was in Nevada and he made it the county seat of Esmeralda County, appointed county officials, and sent Judge George E. Turner to hold court. Turner arrived and found a Judge Baldwin of Mono County there holding court. Neither interfered with the other. A litigant took his case to the court he preferred. The general elections were held on September 2, and since the survey had not yet reached Aurora, officials tactfully permitted two elections on the same day. Full tickets were nominated by Democrats and Republicans for both counties. The Esmeralda election was in Armory Hall, the Mono in the police station some distance down the same street. There was hilarity and good feeling. People voted at one place and then passed down to vote at another. If they missed voting for a winner at one place, they said, they might hit at the other! Almost the same constituents elected one delegate each to the lower houses of Nevada and California. In due time the survey conclusively established that Aurora was in Nevada, and California made Bridgeport the seat of Mono County.

More important than this believe-it-or-not was the border war over Honey Lake and Long Valley, a rich farming area just east of the present California town of Susanville. The cause of trouble here in 1863 was the artificial and unsurveyed boundary line. The eastern line granted by Congress to California in 1850 became the western boundary of Nevada Territory, with the proviso that California might relinquish land west of this line. This arbitrary demarcation ran north and south to the east of the Sierras, in desert and semidesert country. For the people of Plumas County living east of the mountains, which were snowbound in winter, there was more cultural kinship with Nevadans than with Californians. Nevada territorial officials early in 1862 visited Sacramento and tried to get the legislature to cede away all territory east of the High-Sierran summits. They got their hosts to admit this was a regionally sensible scheme, but despite a courteous hearing they returned to Carson City empty handed. They were defeated by state officials who wanted to be sure of taxes on the borderland mines, by the politicos of the mountain counties, and by the investors and miners and boosters who wanted to see California expand, certainly not shrink.

The result was that with the approval of many of the dissatisfied and independent folk who had settled in the Honey Lake area, Nevada included it, without benefit of legality, in Roop County, for which officers were elected in 1862. In the following January Judge Gordon Mott of Nevada appeared in Susanville to hold court for Roop County. He found no action to hear, but the officials of Plumas County in the seat, Quincy, west of the divide, resented this undoubt-edly illegal intrusion. The Plumas County judge enjoined a Roop County justice of the peace from holding court. Pro-bate Judge John Ward of Roop in return enjoined Judge William Young of Plumas from holding court in Roop. Judge Young ignored the order and was arrested, brought before Judge Ward, and fined $100. Then Judge Hogan of Plumas issued an injunction against Judge Ward and Sheriff William H. Naileigh of Roop County. Sheriff E. H. Pierce of Plumas County served it. Judge Ward replied with an injunction against Sheriff Pierce and his deputies. Sheriff Pierce and a deputy arrested Sheriff Naileigh and Judge Ward and started toward Quincy with them. A group of citizens, including Isaac Roop, a leader in the community, followed and rescued the prisoners. Sheriff Pierce returned to Quincy and organized a posse of between one hundred and two hundred men. A few days later he reappeared in Susanville with the posse and a piece of artillery. Again he arrested Judge Ward and Sheriff Naileigh, and a second time a band of citizens took them back, this time to put them in a closely guarded log cabin. A large body of men gathered with guns and ammunition. Next day Sheriff Pierce fortified his men in a near-by barn. After some exchange of words the two factions exchanged gunshots. The fight lasted several hours and a number of men on each side were wounded. At length the leaders agreed on an armistice. Their men withdrew and the matter was given to the two governors to investigate and settle. The affair made clear the need for a final boundary survey, which when made gave Honey Lake to California and settled the " war." Isaac Roop and his ardent fellow citizens had to become Californians.

Nevada engaged off and on for over half a century in her attempt to get a natural western boundary. Delegations visited Sacramento in 1874, 1877, and 1889. In 1915, when some Californians were circulating petitions to divide their state across the middle into a Northern California and a Southern

California, the Nevada legislature passed a resolution favoring the division of California lengthwise, east and west of the Sierra divide, the eastern strip containing the headwaters of Nevada rivers to go to the state nature meant to have it. Even the original line itself caused occasional trouble. A resurvey of a portion of it in 1873 gave 350 square miles of Nevada territory to California, and in 1899, after a long controversy, California took sixty-five square miles in the Tahoe area. The Tahoe boundary dispute threatened to flare up again in 1941.

The line still raises issues of states' rights. Nevada resents the California agricultural quarantine that keeps her potatoes and alfalfa from the profitable markets of the Sacramento Valley. During the Depression she disliked the caravans of new automobiles that California car dealers had groups of unemployed boys drive west from Michigan, for they used Nevada's roads and gave little in return, since the drivers were not tourists who spent. In 1933 Nevada began to require a small license fee on caravaning cars to defray the expense of maintaining highways. Nevada has a discriminatory beer statute aimed at California. In-state distributors of " foreign " beer are required to pay special license fees that are higher than those for distributors who sell the domestic product only. Nevada has passed and determinedly enforced laws that require Nevada licenses for all commercial delivery trucks at $20 a year, a statute that affects particularly California stores that would like to exploit the Nevada side of Lake Tahoe and the Reno-Carson area and pay nothing to the state. Also, Nevada weighs all trucks as they enter the state and charges them $1.50 per 100 pounds, unladen.

Obviously, since Nevada is not self-sufficient in many matters, it has not been in a position to attempt much barrier legislation of this sort, and what it has tried has not always been successful. In the early days, after popular pressure — including a soapbox session of a " Third House " — had forced the territorial legislature to pass a Corporation Bill, Congress, a year later, influenced by California, annulled it. Aimed at Californian economic dominance, the bill would have forced all mining companies to incorporate in Nevada and have their head offices there. In 1934 Reno passed a city ordinance that provided for the licensing and inspection by Reno officials of all bakeries selling their products in the city. When the law became effective early the next year, California bakers were prevented from making deliveries in Reno, for no move had been made to inspect their plants. California bakeries whose products sold in Reno, through Langendorf United Bakeries, Inc., secured a temporary injunction restraining the city from imposing its regulation, and a year later the United States District Court made the order permanent.

A few years ago officials in Las Vegas and Los Angeles tangled over an issue of taxes. The Los Angeles Bureau of Power and Light has transmission lines that start at Boulder Dam and extend forty-five miles in Clark County, Nevada, before reaching the California line. Clark County wanted $25,000 in taxes. The Bureau posted a bond for the taxes and obtained a temporary restraining order from a Nevada district court on the contention that the transmission lines that traversed Clark County were an instrumentality of the federal government and therefore not subject to taxation. Especially was this argued for the lines inside the Boulder City reservation. Only the appointment of new liberal judges to the United States Supreme Court and their several decisions tending to eliminate the doctrine of immunity from taxation made possible a settlement whereby the City of Los Angeles agreed to pay the taxes in full.

The most prolonged and complicated fight between Nevada and her powerful western neighbor was over the water of Lake Tahoe, cut through by the state line, which puts two-thirds of the lake and the outlet in California but allots Nevada almost the entire eastern shore and most of the course of the Truckee River. Fortunately for Nevada, the federal government was on her side most of the time.

Higher than any lake of its size except Lake Titicaca, as beautiful as the Alpine lakes of Italy, as colorful as the Caribbean Sea, Tahoe is a huge deep bowl of miraculously pure blue water. Under a cloudless sky it is a vast indigo dyeing vat. It drains hundreds of square miles of forests, streams, timberline meadows, glacial basins, and granite peaks, but for a lake twelve miles wide by twenty-six long the watershed is small. The Truckee River, which drains the surplus, is swift but narrow and seldom more than a foot deep. The simple truth is that, once the winter snow melts and runs off, the incoming water during the long, rainless summers little more than balances the evaporation into the dry air that blows back and forth the length of the lake each day. Tahoe is a magnificent catch basin to hold water but not to let it out for insistent powerhouses and thirsty irrigated farms out on the Nevada desert. This fundamental incongruity gave rise to controversies during a third of a century.

In early days the outlet of the lake lay in a land-grant section the government had given the Big Four. In 1870 the Donner Boom and Logging Company bought the land and secured from the California legislature a license to erect a log-crib dam to raise the level of the lake five feet and to clear the Truckee River for floating logs and collecting toll. It had the right to control the dam until 1895. For many years yellow pine and sugar pine and incense cedar logs swirled down the Truckee to mills below. This traffic stopped before 1895, but Donner Boom kept its control. Meanwhile many factories had appeared to make use of the water power along the Nevada banks, and in both California and Nevada were hydroelectric plants. Donner Boom asked these plants to pay rent. This robber-baron tactic led San Francisco capitalists, the Fleischhackers, who owned two of the plants, to acquire the fifty-four acres of land immediately surrounding the outlet

LAKE
TAHOE

U. S. Forest Service

AN AIR VIEW
OF A PORTION OF SOUTHEASTERN NEVADA

A WELL-MANAGED RANGE NEAR WELLINGTON;
SAGEBRUSH IN FOREGROUND

of Tahoe. They also bought up all the other plants on the river, made them all the Truckee General Electric Company, and operated the gates solely for their own benefit, which meant, of course, a steady flow the year round. Tahoe was high in late spring, awash the tops of piers and landings, very low in late summer so that piers were useless rickety trestles above the boats.

Tahoe water was now truly a baronial property. But perhaps modern engineering could go Truckee-canyon monopoly one better? In 1900 A. W. Von Schmidt, president of the Lake Tahoe and San Francisco Water Works, offered to sell to the City of San Francisco certain rights to the water of Tahoe, including a diverting dam in the Truckee, a patent to the forty acres of land on which this stood, and maps and surveys for a complete pipe and tunnel line that would deliver thirty million gallons daily. His price was $17,690,000. If the city was thirstier, he would put in a double line and supply one hundred million gallons daily. His price would go up accordingly. This grandiose scheme never got beyond print, but it gave Nevadans a scare. Schmidt took the San Francisco county supervisors to Tahoe to see how feasible his plan was. Whipped into action, R. L. Fulton of Reno, manager of the State Board of Trade, wrote to the supervisors. Nevada farmers and eastern Sierra industries, he said, had complete prior rights to the water. The Truckee water ran flour mills, smelting and reduction works, sawmills, a furniture factory, a box factory, a marble-working mill, a paper mill. It supplied half a dozen ice ponds and thus indirectly refrigerated food and drink during the hot summers. It turned the dynamos that gave light to a dozen towns. For half a century it had irrigated the fertile meadowlands just below Reno.

Three years later Nevadans were anxious again, when James A. Waymire, a San Francisco attorney, published a pamphlet to explain his plan for a tunnel. A better Jules Verne than von Schmidt, he proposed to tunnel from a point well below the rim of Tahoe to the Rubicon branch of the American River, in turn a tributary to the Sacramento River. This tremendous tunnel would provide power and ample water for San Francisco, which was tired of algae-tainted drinking water from rain-catch basins in the local hills. The attorney argued that the water could be legally appropriated, and said he had $500,000,000 behind the enterprise. This idea died, too, but more such fantasies might eventually lead to something deadly real. Nevadans got busy in Washington and encouraged the Department of the Interior to begin a practical program under the Reclamation Act of 1902.

And now, in 1903, the big fight began, for the United States Reclamation Service inaugurated its Truckee-Carson Project at Fallon. The Bureau appropriated all the surplus water of Tahoe and the Truckee for the use of its Nevada farmers. At the time the legality of this action was questioned. As the San Francisco *Call* put it:

It is not clear what rights the federal government has except as representative of reclamation and irrigation service. The waters of the lake are owned jointly by Nevada and California, and any powers asserted by the federal government can only be regarded as usurpation.

What was worse, the engineers in charge, under R. H. Newell, chief of the Reclamation Service, underestimated the amount of water necessary for the project and overestimated the amount of water available. This was an error over which a whole generation of Fallon farmers was to grow bitter.

The power company, which passed into the control of W. P. Hammon, continued to maintain virtual control of the gates at the head of the Truckee.

Soon enough it became plain that the Truckee-Carson Project was getting too little water. The government secured land near the outlet of Tahoe and attempted to construct a canal, but lake-shore owners got an injunction. Through Secretary of the Interior James R. Garfield, Theodore Roosevelt's lieutenant in conservation, the government tried to purchase the dam and gates, offering $25,000 and then $40,000. Refused, it threatened condemnation proceedings. The Hammon interests then began to negotiate with the government to give the land and gates away but in return to secure a right to 400 cubic feet per second. The discussions ignored any latent rights of California. An agreement was drawn in October, 1908, and submitted to the company about the time that William Taft was elected president. The company did nothing about the proposed contract. With Roosevelt going out and Taft coming in, it hoped for better terms from the new Secretary of the Interior, R. A. Ballinger, and in the reaction that followed Taft's inaugural it got a long way toward a more satisfactory agreement.

Ballinger drew up a new contract. It was made with no public notice of the negotiations and no public hearing. It left title to the dam with Hammon's Truckee Electric Company, and gave it perpetual rights in the public domain for reservoirs and pipe lines, wherever wished. What was more, it gave the company the right to locate a second point of diversion at any point and at any depth below the lake's surface, so that the company had the power to exhaust the waters of the lake almost indefinitely. Hammon had in mind a tunnel to drain Tahoe into Nevada. Ballinger promised to see the contract through, and the company prepared to float millions of bonds.

All that the government got in return was the excess water, badly needed on the Truckee-Carson irrigated lands, which were suffering from the original underestimate of available water and were threatened by failure. And the government would handle the outlet and thus be responsible for damage to property. Apparently, Newell and his engineers, desperate to make a success of the first desert project, which had been widely publicized, were willing to pay a huge price to avoid a debacle. From Nevada's viewpoint the prospect of ample irrigation water outweighed any possible disadvantage.

Since some of the lands involved in the contract were national forests, Secretary Ballinger asked Secretary James Wilson of the Department of Agriculture for his approval. Wilson and his chief forester, Gifford Pinchot, refused approval and vigorously protested against the contract on the grounds that it was against all the principles of conservation and was illegal to boot, because the only statute allowing the use of rights of way for electrical power purposes provided that such rights might at any time be terminated at the discretion of the secretary of the interior.

Some months later Ballinger referred the matter to President Taft, apparently without disclosing the protests. Pinchot, learning that the contract was on Taft's desk, awaiting approval, requested and obtained permission to submit a protest. After Taft had received it he asked advice of Senator Francis Newlands of Nevada, father of the Truckee-Carson Project. Newlands suggested a public investigation and hearing that would be " an object lesson as to what National Conservation means, and would tend to focus the discussion on lines of practical legislation." Congressman William Kent of California heard of the Hammon-Ballinger plan and protested publicly against the government's deeding away rights in perpetuity. He objected especially to the drilling of a tunnel fifty feet below the surface, on the Nevada side, which, obviously, would ignore the rights of lake-shore owners and make the " Gem of the Sierras " into a water tank. Not wishing to imply that someone was dishonest, Taft refused to call the public hearing, but did appoint a commission to investigate the Truckee Power Company. This, it appeared, was about to be merged into a corporation controlled by Harriman and Guggenheim to supply the Southern Pacific Railroad with power across the mountains and also sell power in San Francisco. The contract was held up.

The power company bided its time for two years, meanwhile merging into the Stone and Webster Engineering Corporation of Boston, one of the big utility corporations of the United States. In 1911 Congressman Kent learned that the Ballinger contract was again before Taft, in revised form. He asked for time to present the interests of the public as opposed to those of the corporation, and was given thirty-five days. He saw Newell, who desired only to save the irrigation project and explicitly denied any interest in Tahoe landowners, and he also saw the assistant attorney general assigned to the Interior Department, who said the contract was legal. California aroused itself to the very real danger that connivance between the government and a corporation would expropriate California waters for eventual use in Nevada. Sierra foothill towns sent official protests to Taft. The legislature passed a joint resolution that urged Taft to act against the Stone and Webster contract; it passed a law that prohibited the appropriation of water for use outside the state. The San Francisco papers editorialized. Governor Hiram Johnson, after a full hearing, telegraphed his objections. The protests killed the idea of a tunnel to drain Tahoe into Nevada but did not otherwise daunt the proponents of the contract.

At least, the issues were now squarely before the public. The conflict of public and private interests was clear, and perhaps it was the crucial issue, but the state line was there too, artificially splitting the lake. States' rights were equally involved. Nevadans argued fluently. Tahoe was in the Great Basin and was logically in Nevada's sphere of influence. All of California east of the Sierran divide should be in Nevada, anyhow. California had plenty of water whereas Nevada had precious little. The riverbank factories, the Truckee Meadows at Reno, and the Fallon farmsteads needed the water and had the older vested rights, and — quite beyond argument — the Truckee River supplied the water naturally.

Californians asserted that Nevada already used most of

the waters of the eastern slope of the Sierras and was unreasonable in supposing that it was entitled to all the waters of Lake Tahoe. They said these waters could be used to irrigate the upper Sacramento Valley (via a tunnel on the California side) and incalculably increase its agricultural and taxable wealth, and that certainly — to quote one of them directly — "the waters should be used in the fertile and semi-tropical lands of California, rather than on the comparatively bleak deserts of Nevada." Since the government, honest or dishonest, was partial to Nevada farmers, the California argument ran that, no question of navigation being involved, the government had no more rights or powers than any owner of private lands within the two states.

Both sides referred to the decision of the United States Supreme Court in *Kansas* v. *Colorado* (206 U.S. 43) that each state is entitled to its equitable share of interstate waters.

While more and more private citizens began to look to their interests, so were Newell and the Boston firm, Stone and Webster. The tunnel to drain fifty feet of Tahoe into Washoe Valley being too agitating an issue, they made plans to widen the river channel and straighten out some of the curves and kinks and to lower Tahoe 4.3 feet. This would give the company $1,500,000 worth of power a year and deliver abundant supplies of water to the farmers. It would also damage the appearance and the profits of the resorts and close the entrance to Emerald Bay; therefore, in 1912 Tahoe property owners were protesting to Taft and the Department of the Interior and using an injunction from the United States District Court to stop rim cutting by either canal or damgates.

The following year the Lake Tahoe Protective Association incorporated in order to consolidate action to keep the water level where nature put it. The California State Water Commission urged immediate action to protect California interests; namely, a suit against Nevada to have the waters duly apportioned between the two states in accordance with the *Kansas v. Colorado* case. It charged the power company with storing floodwaters, which damaged property in winter and spring.

A few months later President Woodrow Wilson's secretary of the interior, Franklin K. Lane, met at Truckee, California, with state officials, federal engineers, and property owners. The government and the company agreed to build a new dam and gates. The government promised to refrain for five years from cutting timber on the river to conserve water. It would clean out the upper part of the waterway to increase water flow and not take any more water from the lake than entered in normal inflow. Lane expressed his ideal: " We shall leave the lake as much a beauty spot as ever and provide regulation and control at government expense." In due time Lane had the government sue for condemnation of the dam at the outlet, in order to get water for lands in the irrigation district, now approximately 80,000 acres in extent. By the summer of 1915 the United States and the company attorneys had agreed on a price of $139,000 and on specified rates at which water would be furnished to the power plants.

Lane's 1913 agreement produced a surface calm for the five-year period, and then in 1919 the conflict reopened and passed through a final phase, California resort owners and lot owners *vs*. Nevada farmers and the Reclamation Service, a struggle not to be concluded until 1935. A pattern already established repeated itself over and over again: a move by Nevada interests, a checkmate by California.

The Reclamation Service asked many property owners to sign quitclaim deeds giving their property to the government. With a dam already holding the lake surface three feet higher than the normal 6,223 feet above sea level, the Service wished to raise the level to 6,229.5 feet. This would destroy thousands of dollars' worth of resort property and submerge the beaches on the California side. Congressman Kent protested. Property owners refused to sign. The San Francisco Chamber of Commerce fought the project. Secretary of Agriculture David F. Houston voiced his opposition to his colleague, Franklin K. Lane. The Sacramento Chamber of Commerce got worked up. The Grand Parlor of the Native Sons of the Golden West frowned at this plan to despoil its natural heritage. A California delegation visited Lane in Washington and he called off work at Tahoe until states' rights could be determined by law.

The next year, 1920, there was trouble again. By August the lake was down to a low-water mark set by the Reclamation Service. Instead of the 350 second feet estimated to be necessary there were only 240. The Truckee was a trickle beside the amount of water needed. The War Department sent an army engineer to report on the water problem and some observers wondered how the War Department came into the picture at all. Nevada farmers wanted to cut the rim. Again a compromise was reached by representatives of the two states, the Tahoe resort men, and the Service, now headed by A. P. Davis. The Truckee was cleaned of debris again, and the Service began to lay plans for reservoirs elsewhere on the upper Truckee that would leave Tahoe alone.

So much for an ideal future plan. In practice the old pragmatic quarrel went on. Three different years the lake went so low and the Fallon farmers needed water so much that the Tahoe property owners allowed pumping from the lake. Each time they said they would not allow it again. Each time Nevadans agreed to demand less in the future. Each time a new emergency arose. Resort and recreation men threatened suits when the lake rose too high behind the gates in spring and damaged piers and buildings. They threatened suits in the fall when low waters hurt business. Once, when Nevada farmers demanded water, the Tahoe people threatened an injunction and the farmers declared they would demand a $200,-000 surety bond against drought damage to Nevada crops.

There was a little " war " in 1930. The farmers and the

power men needed water again and were told that by previous agreements they could have only natural flow. On Saturday, July 26, at midnight, a steam shovel started a drainage ditch near the outlet on land belonging to the Truckee River Power Company. The shovel operator represented " certain farming and irrigation interests in Nevada." Resort owners had a warrant for disturbing the peace sworn out in Placerville, over eighty miles away, and by 3:00 A.M. the sheriff had stopped the shovel legally until 10:00 A.M. on Monday, when forty men began dynamiting the rim to make a long, deep ditch. A score of shore-land owners in fishing boats moved in near shore, mooring their boats over places picked for blasting and getting in the way of the dredger. Tuesday morning a routine blast of dynamite in the ditch some distance from the lake drew crowds from near-by Tahoe City, who thought the Nevadans had carried out their threats to destroy the dam and get water. About this time Sheriff Elmer Gum of Placer County, after a long dash from the county seat, served an injunction against forty John Does and their employers.

Lake residents organized a guard, the Tahoe Vigilantes, to patrol the dam in two-hour shifts. Feeling ran high in Tahoe City. Although people were aroused to the danger menacing Tahoe's beauty, they were callously unaware of the trouble and desperation on Truckee Meadows farms and on the project out near Carson Sink, where alfalfa and cantaloupes and sugar beets were withering and hardened settlers were again cursing both California and the Reclamation Service that had botched water estimates back in 1903 when calling the whole community into being. Californians were putting mere scenery and private pleasure against man's basic task of making a living. More legal threats. Again Nevada's demand for a $200,000 surety bond. In reply, California rationalization that " navigation " would be endangered when the surface fell above hidden rocks. Correspondence between Attorney General U. S. Webb of California and Secretary of the In-

terior Ray L. Wilbur. An injunction in the state courts and
then in the federal. Finally an agreement among all parties
that Nevada could pump two inches of water before October
1 but only natural flow thereafter. A three-year truce was
declared.

But 1931 was an even worse drought year. In March the
irrigation interests were already negotiating with the Tahoe
owners. In June a conference at the St. Francis Hotel in San
Francisco granted Nevada rights to pump five inches at once,
but no water below a minimum of 6,223.6 feet. This was
indeed a concession, the Californians thought, because Tahoe
was already three feet below average, but the Nevada delegation, headed by poker-faced George Wingfield, saw no
salvation in five inches, and walked out. Subsequent negotiations got nowhere. Truckee alfalfa was dying. Only three out
of twenty-eight ditches were getting water. A million-dollar
loss loomed. It looked as if the power plants would have to
shut down. "Lake owners must take responsibility," said
Nevadans. The governors met, two rollicking companions,
James Rolph and Fred Balzar, white camellias in their button-
holes, but this and other conferences gained Nevada only a
few inches late in the summer to save stock in Truckee
Meadows.

So things went for several years more. After a quarter of
a century the old dilemma was still unsolved. It was a fight to
the last. In 1934 owners of twenty miles of lake front organized the Save Lake Tahoe League to meet stanch save-the-
irrigation-project spirit. The possible construction by the
New Deal's PWA of Boca Dam on the Little Truckee, a
downstream tributary to the Truckee, would afford 41,000
acre feet of water, but would not go between the horns of the
dilemma, for much more water was needed by Reno, Sparks,
and the farms. Governors Frank Merriam of California and
Morley Griswold of Nevada urged Secretary of the Interior
Harold Ickes to make a complete investigation and settle

things once and for all. One by one the long-outstanding issues were agreed upon. The Truckee-Carson Irrigation District, the Washoe County Conservation District, and the Sierra Pacific Power Company (successor to Truckee Electric) compromised on the management of the diversion gates. The way was cleared for Boca Dam. But the toughest question remained until the last. What would the level of Tahoe be?

All agreed on a low of 6,223 feet, but where the farmers wanted a maximum of 6,229.1 feet, the Tahoe savers wanted no more than 6,228.1 feet. They argued that a fluctuation of six feet would damage the south shore, the beautiful shallow beach at Bijou. Reclamation engineers presented evidence, however, that in the old days nature had allowed the lake an eight-foot up and down. Ickes said he would not allow any valuable recreational area to be destroyed, but settlers in good faith in Nevada had rights, too, that could not be ignored. " This resolves itself to a point where there is only a foot of difference between you. A wise judge might divide the difference, but I don't know whether any would then be satisfied." During a month of study and deliberation, Ickes polled Tahoe property owners and found 417 in approval of 6,229.1 feet and 78 against. His formal decision of the maximum storage level was a victory for the Nevadans. They had won clear title to six feet of Tahoe water per year, less evaporation.

After thirty years of doubt and drought the Truckee-Carson people knew at last how much water to count on. California still had its lake shore, only slightly changed. America still had the " Gem of the Sierras," without a hole knocked in its bottom to drain its immaculate blue waters into either Nevada's Washoe Valley or California's Rubicon Canyon.

SENATOR CONNESS of California was partly right when he said in Congress during the Civil War, " Nevada is a mining community exclusively, and can never be anything else. It

must always be *fed from adjacent countries*." Nearly all of
the Nevada territory is served commercially by the Los
Angeles and Sacramento areas, which send it most of its fresh
fruits and vegetables, as one would expect, and also most of
its processed beef and mutton, which is more surprising, when
one remembers that Nevada is a sheep and cattle state. Carson
City drugstores send films to Sacramento to be developed.
Reno socialites buy their formal dresses in San Francisco. Las
Vegans have charge accounts at the May Company and Bul-
lock's in Los Angeles. Not the Salt Lake *Tribune* but the
San Francisco *Chronicle* and the Los Angeles *Times* appear
on the newsstands along with local papers. When a resident
of Lovelock or Austin needs special medical or dental attention he goes to San Francisco. Academically minded young
people whose parents can afford it go to the University of
California. Wealthy matrons bear their children in California
hospitals. Any Nevadan on his vacation heads, more than
likely, for the Golden Bear State. Life in Nevada is oriented
westward just as surely as southern Connecticut's is toward
New York City and southern New Jersey's toward Philadelphia.

It is true that in the early days Californians helped Nevada
get started. Nevada mining was initiated by California prospectors on the rebound east from the Mother Lode and was
carried on by California capital. The rush to Virginia City
was from California. Californians opened up the mines of
Aurora, and the Esmeralda Mining District was first incorporated under the laws of California. The state constitution and
the statutes imitated California's, and for good reason. Of the
thirty-four members of the Constitutional Convention of
1864, all except two came to Nevada from California, where
they had lived for an average period of nine years.

This was all constructive aid, but California also reached
over to control Nevada's commerce, transportation, banking,
and finance, and to sell her food, machinery, whisky, journal-

ism, and clothing. "Now when Californy has got more of a good thing than she wants herself," said an old-timer in the Sazerac Saloon in Austin, "she sells the surplus to Nevada, at a pretty considerable figure of profit." A double frame of mind was established. Californians looked on Nevada as the British mercantilists looked upon the American colonies. Nevadans looked on California with appropriate indignation but without revolutionary agitation.

The Washoe *Times* remarked that if Californians kept rushing into the territory "there will be no difficulty in settling the boundary line, for the whole of California will be on this side of the Sierra Nevada." The Virginia City *Territorial Enterprise* observed:

Nevada Territory being almost wholly settled by Californians, and being dependent, after the manner of a colony, on the mother country for her means of subsistence, might not inaptly be termed her first-born. Then the interests of no parent country and colony could possibly be more closely united than are those of Nevada and California. The colony has untold wealth of gold and silver, and the mother country manages, by feeding it and furnishing with utensils to set up housekeeping, to get it all as fast as it is dug out.

This was in 1862. Fourteen years later Franklin Buck, a Yankee trader in Pioche, a man who had lived in Nevada for a profitable ten years, wrote to his sister in Bucksport, Maine. His letter showed how a Californian in Nevada could make as few adjustments and attachments as the traditional Englishman at a tropical colonial post. He said, in part, "Nevada is a kind of an offshoot of California, a park settlement . . . it was all a mistake making a state of Nevada. . . . We all belong body and soul to California and could just as well have our laws made at Sacramento as at Carson. The state government of Nevada is a farce." For him California was the garden of America and his one true home. A sojourn in old

Nevada evoked the lyrical in Californians. Here is Albert
Evans of San Francisco on Treasure Hill, Nevada. A snow-
storm has cleared up. The sky is blue. The barren valleys are
soft outlines in the distance.

This strange, weird land never looked so attractive to our eyes
— but it is not Home. It is a land to toil and fight, grow rich
suddenly, or die in — but it is not a land to live and love in; not
a land in which to rear the household altar and set up the household gods; not a land one would wish to sleep in, when life's day
of toil is ended and the evening shadow falls. The home of our
heart lies behind the western horizon, by the waters of the sunset
sea, where the flowers bloom and the birds sing all the year round.
There is but one California on earth, and toward it we turn with
willing feet.

It was people like Buck and Evans that a prospector had in
mind when he referred to " them tenderfeet " who " come in
from the States on the railroads and make all the money, while
us pioneers . . . get the soup that the eggs was boiled in."
Although Californians have scoffed at Nevada and senti-
mentalized the vigor and glory of their own state, the fact
remains that in the sixties the Comstock, together with other
Nevada mining districts, was the making of California and
the salvation of its leading city. The Vigilance Committee of
1856 had damaged the reputation of San Francisco. The fruit-
less rush to Fraser River in British Columbia in '58 had partially depopulated the city and then sent back a horde of
penniless miners. Speculators were choked with real-estate
investments and deeply in debt. Values had fallen one-half.
As one writer put it, the city was overgrown and undernour-
ished. Confidence in the future was diminished. The placer
mines of the state had been exhausted, and agriculture, manufacturing, deep mining, oil, and tourists had not yet replaced
them as means of basic income. So the boom in Washoe (as
early Nevada was nicknamed) was a veritable godsend. The

" Sagebrush State allowed the rich current of her veins to be transfused into the bloodless arteries " of San Francisco.

The net result for San Francisco was many large buildings, Sutro Heights — famous for decades for its landscape gardens and Sutro Baths, nabob residences on Nob Hill — where the Flood mansion now houses the Union Club, tumultuous prosperity, powerful banks, the developments of large tracts of Bay Region property. Foundries and machine shops were brought into being by Nevada's need for mining equipment, as were steel and steel-wire cable works in the East. The oyster business flourished along the bay shore as did the fruit and vegetable business in the inland valleys. The cosmopolitan crowds of the Nevada and California gold and silver camps found inducements to root themselves on the hills of the old Spanish town, helping to make it the unique city it remains today. " The spirit of cordiality, conviviality, generosity, and democracy of the mining days was salvaged by the people of San Francisco."

Nevada enabled Californians to start mining-stock speculation in America with the organization in 1862 of the San Francisco Stock and Exchange Board, the first mining exchange on the Pacific Coast. Not California gold but Nevada silver produced the first barons in Western mining. It gave to George Hearst a fortune that helped elect him senator from California, that enabled him to buy the San Francisco *Examiner* for political purposes and later to give it to his son, William Randolph, who in turn used it to start a nation-wide chain of newspapers and periodicals. Stock gambling in Virginia City in the early sixties and control of Ophir Mine in the seventies projected J. E. (" Lucky ") Baldwin on a career of flashy money-making and spending that built the Baldwin Hotel and the Baldwin Theatre in San Francisco and established near Los Angeles several townsites and Santa Anita Ranch. Comstock bullion enabled W. C. Ralston to enhance the prestige of the Bank of California, erect office buildings, and raise the first Palace Hotel, which in its day was the most lavish hostelry in the world. After Ralston's bank crashed in 1875 the Bonanza Kings of the Comstock opened their powerful Bank of Nevada. Adolph Sutro, promoter and builder of the famous tunnel, bought up one-tenth of the city and county of San Francisco, the sandy western portion, introduced bent and Bermuda grass that held the dunes still, planted pine and eucalyptus forests, and got the area ready for its present concentrated population. Nevada started Marcus Daly on the mining career that culminated in Butte, and through Ralston's bank it gave national prominence to Darius Ogden Mills.

Other makers of notable fortunes and reputations were James Lick, who endowed the University of California with an observatory that enabled Professor Bernard to discover double stars and three-tailed comets, and Senator John P. Jones, who bought the Santa Monica Palisades as a front yard for his mansion and later gave them to the town for a park. The mansion itself, spacious carpenter's Gothic, became the Vista del Mar Hotel. Bonanza King John W. Mackay, an Irish immigrant who began as a mucker, built the Postal Telegraph system and laid a cable to Honolulu, Guam, and Manila without subsidy or guarantee. His widow and son endowed the School of Mines in Reno. The importance of Nevada gold and silver helped stimulate the building of the transcontinental railroad, and this same mineral wealth contributed to paying for it.

So Californians-in-Nevada took the eggs from Nevada's basket and shipped them home to incubate. They spent well in Nevada for personal comfort and entertainment, but when the ore production fell off and, as the saying went, miners began to pitch horseshoes, they were content to leave the dying camps, along with the gamblers and the prostitutes. Only the minority of immigrants to Nevada who stayed because of steady employment or a genuine liking for the state resented the whole looting process that produced a metropolis in California and a dozen ghost towns in Nevada, or wrote a history of California that made of Virginia City and other towns only a few paragraphs of incidental material in the story of the rise of northern California.

In general, Nevadans have accepted, because it was remote and hard to discern, the mercantilist exploitation of capitalists in faraway Philadelphia or New York, but they have regarded Californians — their immediate neighbors — as contemptible for giving nothing in return for bountiful bullion and plump profits. From the first days in Aurora and Gold Hill, when Nevadans sweated away for wages and Californians coolly speculated in stock and bought the legislature, Nevadans have taken satisfaction in their part in building up California but have felt also that they had something coming in return. It is still forthcoming.

Fighting Back

PATRIOTS of the Sagebrush State have frequently expressed sorrow and indignation at the way individuals have made millions of dollars in Nevada only to spend them elsewhere. Other states have fared so much better! Contrast Nevada with Colorado, where from the first mining fortunes built up the commonwealth. Hagerman planted the Midland Railroad on the continental divide and invested millions in the reclamation of arid Colorado lands. Tabor gave Denver its first important impulse by erecting splendid buildings. General William Palmer helped build railroads — the Union Pacific, the Kansas Pacific, the Denver and Rio Grande — aided in starting Colorado College, founded Colorado Springs, and built his home in the state. Why has Nevada been denied such good fortune? A representative complaint is that of the Episcopalian Thomas Jenkins, bishop of Nevada, in a speech in New York City a few years back. Addressing a meeting of church leaders and prominent citizens, he said:

Of all the men who have made fortunes in Nevada not one has sent back $1 for welfare work there. If I mentioned their names it would come near home. A will was published in the newspapers only a few days ago of a man who made his money in Nevada, but not one cent was left for Nevada.

What freebooters have hauled away to other states has been in part paid back, it must be added for the record, by Uncle Sam himself. Important federal co-operation and subsidy has helped Nevada build a fine system of highways, set up several reclamation projects, develop mining and agriculture, regulate grazing, and conserve forests, water, and wild game. Boulder Dam and Lake Mead are beginning to stimulate developments in the southern area. The Biological Survey has created a great game preserve in the northwestern corner. The Forest Service, with its improved campgrounds, fisheries, and fire lookouts, has created recreational assets. The Civilian Conservation Corps has bored wells, made range tanks (small dirt reservoirs to hold rain water for cattle), built campground furniture, cut public roads and trails into the hinterland, and fought rodents, insects, and fires.

According to anti-New Deal figures published in *Life* in May, 1938, the greatest per capita expenditures for Relief and Recovery (1933–37) were in Nevada, $1,114.12. New York was twenty-second with a per capita of $232.58 and North Carolina was last with $123.82. Yet the total in Nevada was only $111,412,000, as compared with the largest absolute sum, $3,008,440,000, in New York. In a letter to the editors Harry Hopkins explained the high per capitas in Nevada and Montana and other Western states by pointing out the naturally high costs of the great water-power and dust-control projects necessary in these states. He might have added that the mineral and agrarian Western states have so long been exploited by the industrial and financial East that there was moral justice in huge national outlays in the West.

Nevada is in the company of numerous other states in being the victim of the East. As Walter Prescott Webb has made clear in *Divided We Stand*, the West and the South are colonial properties of the East and always have been. But as a self-avenger, Nevada stands alone. None of the victimized states has re-expropriated with a zeal to equal Nevada's. A deliberate legislative campaign is doing what verbal regrets and recriminations could never accomplish.

For one thing, Nevada cashes in on the inhibitions of respectable people in self-consciously and officially " nice " districts in the United States. With open gambling, tolerated prostitution, and easy divorce Nevada does legally and constructively what vice must do elsewhere: cater to the " undercover " desires of virtue. In other states respectability promotes white-slave rings, adulterous marriages, gangs, rackets, and pay-offs. It gives Nevada a chance to be different — profitably. Nevadans argue that by legalizing the gratifications they remove social problems — a dubious principle. As Mayor Roberts of Reno put it ten years ago, " We believe the free are happy and the happy are not vicious." But Nevadans are not as aware of a frontier heritage of tolerance or of a modern morality like that in Walter Lippmann's *Preface to Morals* as they are aware of economic necessity. " Licensed indulgence " gives the state an all-important cash income.

Divorce brings $5,000,000 a year into Nevada. Half a million tourists a year leave behind $8,000,000, which includes about half the income of towns like Las Vegas. In 1931 Nevada startled the nation by re-legalizing gambling, frankly admitting that she was after out-of-staters who wanted a fling. " Dozens of places on the coast live entirely on the tourist trade. Why not Reno, too? " And now, after a successful decade, the bankers and politicians and even the good people (who claim that gambling and vice and divorce are a minor part in the lives of permanent residents) maintain that a change would be economic suicide. Mary Mullett of the *American Magazine* asked a prominent Reno attorney, " Wouldn't it be a good thing if there were uniform divorce laws throughout the United States? " and he replied, " Well — yes — I suppose so. But it would mean simply assassination for *this* town."

Nevada has best retaliated on California by offering individual Californians the old-style freedom not vouchsafed them by their own state. California's one-year interlocutory decree for divorce sends clients over the line for six-week service. Her premarital medical examination plus her three-day " gin marriage " law, which in reality allows matrimony only five days after application, make Reno and Las Vegas the equivalents of Gretna Green and Elkton, Maryland, much to the regret of California florists, jewelers, and preachers. Reno marriage licenses, normally 400–500 a month, jumped to 1,400 after the physical examination became mandatory. California's conventional antigambling and antibookie laws drive many a wallet into Nevada on week ends. For five years Californians who lived near the state line avoided the three per cent sales tax by crossing over into Nevada to buy automobiles, tractors, machinery, pianos, and other such expensive items. Reno merchants particularly profited, at the expense of California tax revenues and to the dismay of the California Board of Equalization. To plug the Nevada loophole, the Board's attorneys finally devised a " use tax " on property coming into the state. This also caught Eastern firms in interstate business making retail sales to Californians. After one of them carried a suit against California to the Supreme Court and lost, the Nevada merchants had to stop their guerrilla campaign. No longer could they refuse to report sales and encourage tax-shy Californians to be extra customers.

There was a time when Nevada's leaders fully agreed with

Barnum that notoriety is as good publicity as any. They echoed the slogan said to hang in the city council's chamber in Salem, Oregon: " Never mind what people say, as long as they talk about you." Easy divorce, open gambling, sex freedom brought in the crowds and rolled in the silver dollars, and indignant good people gave free publicity to the whole thing. But now the leaders soft-pedal divorce and muffle the sound of poker chips and play double forte on cash-and-carry government and financial freedom. The inhibited middle classes of other states are pay-ore, but politicians and businessmen have filed claim on an even richer gold mine, the millionaire stratum of American and European society. Now it is not only the churchmen who object to mention of wideopen conditions; it is also the native boosters and the early phalanx of millionaires, who want to make residence in Nevada more elegant and morally conventional. The wheels of fate have turned, and the Nevada that once saw its bonanzas flee over the state lines, east and west, the Nevada that was a poverty-stricken sister among the states, can now relish a great irony. The state lines that once were jail walls are now fortifications. Capitalists who once mocked Nevada from the distance are ready now to seek shelter there, bringing their treasure troves along. The lure is laws deliberately passed to prevent or reduce taxes. Nevada's lawyers and bankers and legislators have set out to make their state " The Cyclone Cellar for the Tax Weary."

The story goes back to 1925, when the legislature repealed the state inheritance tax, passed in 1913, so as to attract persons of wealth to take up legal residence. At first this did not seem to make any particular difference. Then in 1928 James Langford Stack, a former Chicago advertising man, died in his home in Los Angeles, leaving $4,318,000. Nevadans had never heard of him and no obituaries appeared in Nevada papers, but a few months later it came out that he was a resident of Nevada, his address being a summer home on Lake

Tahoe. His lawyer had tipped him off regarding the 1925 repeal. The United States collected $344,940 in estate taxes, but California got nothing. Land values on the Nevada shore inflated, and a colony of carpenters hammered away on handsome new cottages.

Meanwhile the Depression deepened and the state government's income dwindled. Bullion taxes except for gold were down almost to nothing. Because of drought and a slow market, little money came in from the stock-raising industry. The total assessed valuations, less than two hundred million dollars, fell off twenty millions, a large sum, indeed, in a state of 91,000 persons. The big railroads protested their taxes and impounded them. To top it all, in November, 1932, thanks to generous loans to cattlemen, coupled with financial juggling both unethical and illegal, one-half the banks in the state closed down and remained closed for several years. In them were one and a half millions in public funds and money of 27,000 depositors, totaling more than twenty-four millions. Until the banks were finally reorganized, with some loss to stockholders and depositors, ordinary people were in trouble.

Fortunately the state government had never been prodigal in spending money, and there were no overwhelming state debts. The constitution limits the state debt to one per cent of the assessed valuations, and any legislation creating a debt must provide a tax allocation sufficient to pay the interest and retire the debt in twenty years. Also, bond issues must be approved by a state commission and approved by the people at an election. Early in 1935, twelve per cent of the population were on relief, but the load gradually dropped as carpenters and copper miners and alfalfa workers found jobs opening up. Uncle Sam helped a great deal. Federal spending soon equaled the sums lost in the closed Wingfield banks. The FHA stimulated the building trades. Years of good spring rains improved the ranges, as did emergency wells and stock tanks put in by CCC boys. Boulder Dam drew tourists to Las

Vegas; so did the creation of Death Valley National Monument. The Silver Purchase Act and new techniques for the mining and milling of low-grade ore led to extensive reopening of neglected mines and discovery of virgin deposits. The state government kept within its budgets. It spent little on relief. Sufferers got federal aid or left their dusty farms and bankrupt small cattle ranches and joined the Okies in California. There were treasury surpluses of several hundred thousand dollars in 1935, '36, and '37, so that in June of the last year the treasury had a total cash surplus of $1,186,418, the largest per capita cash balance of all the states. Bonded debts outstanding amounted to only $851,000. This was nonscandalous but startling news about Nevada, and the metropolitan dailies gave it free publicity.

All this while the wide-open laws were bringing in riches to support local business with patronage and local governments with license fees. Other schemes were talked of, one of them a magnificent plan to transfuse to the state government millions of dollars from the financial circulation of America, a state lottery monopoly. This same idea had been toyed with in the 1860's and eighties and had passed the legislature, tentatively, in 1893. As introduced in 1937 by Senator William Marsh of Tonopah and Assemblyman Pat Cline of Las Vegas, it was in the form of a constitutional amendment which would create the monopoly and provide for bootlegging the tickets throughout the United States and bringing in a million dollars a month. The state and the lucky ticket holders would divide the spoils. Thus Nevada would make about six million dollars a year and abolish state taxes. Assemblyman J. E. Sweatt of Washoe County, a young man, argued earnestly against the bill. Opponents called him a graybeard. He returned to a session wearing a set of Santa Claus whiskers held on with a rubber band and took up the argument again. The Assembly passed a bill stipulating that any legislator with a beard over six inches long was to be taken out by the sergeant at arms and shaved. The joke stopped there, for the Marsh-Cline plan passed the legislature in the form of a joint resolution, and, complying with law, was held over to the next session. To become a part of the constitution it would have to pass the two houses again and win a referendum at a general election. The gamblers of Nevada opposed it (as they did movie bank night, now illegal in Reno). Reflective persons thought it would be too much resented by other states and would further damage Nevada's prestige. In 1938 it failed to get past the Assembly.

The task was to make Nevada respectable and attractive in the eyes of the rich, and the campaign begun with the repeal of the inheritance tax took a definite form. The legislature passed laws that restricted taxes. An amendment passed in 1936 limited taxes on personal property and real estate to an aggregate of 5 cents on each dollar of assessed valuation. The 1939 legislature reduced the state levy on real and personal property from 73 cents per $100 to 58 cents, but increased taxes on matters not likely to worry the rich: insurance premiums, Diesel oil, and cigarettes — a tax of one cent on each package bought.

These low taxes went hand in hand with the boosters' campaign begun in 1936. Sponsored by the First National Bank and the *Nevada State Journal*, both of Reno, a booklet entitled *One Sound State* was sent to 10,000 pedigreed prospects who were rich and might wish a residence where they could escape the nation-wide attack on entrenched wealth under the early New Deal. *One Sound State* pointed out how one could get residence in Nevada, indicated that there were no reds or labor agitators in the state, and gave data on the excellent fiscal conditions of state finances and the legal setup that made Nevada the least-taxed state in the Union. Solvent Nebraska could present no better story. The *Journal* followed up with special Scenic Sections called " One Sound State." Three years later the First National Banks and the Bar Associations in Reno and Las Vegas, respectively, published similar pamphlets and distributed them widely. The Virginia City *News* put out a *One Sound State Edition*, elaborate in format and obviously the work of Reno publicists. T. D. Vencill produced a pamphlet with colored illustrations: *Southern Nevada: " America's Investment Frontier."*

The campaign led the San Francisco *Chronicle*, in a state with rising taxes of all sorts, to ask in an ironic editorial:

What is Nevada doing? Getting ready to secede from the Union? . . . South Carolina achieved secession by firing on Fort Sumter. Nevada puts herself out alone by firing on Fort Taxation. . . . These people just do not belong in the United States.

These pamphlets in which the Babbitts of Nevada entice the Dodsworths of America have the Nevada flavor of the regular Chamber of Commerce literature, with its nonchalant mention of divorce and marriage facilities and frontierlike gambling. They contain matters never before issued by boosters, explaining with abundant citation of court decisions the lack of impropriety in tax avoidance, the ins and outs of legal residence, and the solution of the two homes problem. Ethically they are questionable, but legally they are watertight. Sociologically they are clear evidence that Nevada is using states' rights to pull the tail feathers of the American Eagle.

Nevada has no income tax, no inheritance tax, no death transfer tax, no sales tax, no gift tax, and no tax on intangibles. No such taxes will be levied. Nevada is the least-taxed state in the country. Where other states met the Depression with new taxes, Nevada met it with a lopping off of unnecessary " frills " in governmental expenses. The booklets might have explained, however, that this was possible because Uncle Sam was generous and Nevada had no large industrial centers and no permanent proletariat, instead, only a large body of transient farm workers who wintered in California and Arizona.

The boosters point out that even federal income taxes may

be pared down, since Nevada is a community property state. Married residents of the state may make separate federal income tax returns, thus avoiding taxes in the higher brackets, as would accrue if the husband made only one return for the total income of both spouses.

It is no crime for a taxpayer to change his residence, or in any other way legally to seek to avoid oppressive taxes. No millionaire seeking a cyclone cellar need be conscience stricken. The United States Supreme Court in *Gregory* v. *Helvering* (293 U.S. 465, 79 L. Ed. 596) said, " The legal right of a taxpayer to decrease the amount of what otherwise would be his taxes, or altogether avoid them, by means which the law permits, cannot be doubted." In *Superior Oil Company* v. *Mississippi* (280 U.S. 390, 74 L. Ed. 504) it said, " The fact that it [the company] desired to evade the law, as it is called, is immaterial, because the very meaning of a line in the law is that you intentionally may go as close to it as you can, if you do not pass it."

As to what constitutes residence, a layman is almost as well qualified to define it as a lawyer or court. A plutocrat who really came to Nevada and lived there would settle the matter, especially if he registered and voted. A person must reside in Nevada six months before voting but may register upon arrival if there is to be no election during the next half year. But " one does not have to live in Nevada exclusively, or continuously." A man has a right to select a new home and designate any place as the place of his residence. If the matter comes to trial a court will consider many matters, including

Making federal income tax returns and paying the tax in Nevada.

Declaring in a will that Nevada is the testator's residence.

Ownership of property and occupancy of home.

Transaction of various types of business at the new residence, in Nevada.

Mention of Nevada residence in legal documents.

Establishment of a bank account and keeping securities at place of residence.

Registration as a Nevada resident while stopping at hotels.

Membership in local clubs, societies, churches, and lodges. If one belongs to a national fraternity, it is a convincing move to transfer to the local chapter or lodge.

Declarations as to change of residence, both orally and in writing.

Payment of real property taxes in Nevada.

Generally taking part in the community life of Nevada.

For millionaires a new residence raises the problem of two or more homes. The rule is: " If a person has two dwellings in different places, and resides a part of his time in one place and a part of the time in the other, the question, which of the two places is his legal residence, is almost altogether a question of intent." Only his intention, the veriest of abstractions, determines the matter. This intent holds for the present and for an indefinite period in the future. If he dies, the laws of the state where he deemed his residence to be cover his estate. And he leaves more of an estate if he resided by intent in Nevada.

The legal setup is congenial, then, but what of those spooks of rich men's nightmares — " reds," " labor agitators," " irresponsible politicians "? Nevada's advertisers know how to assuage the nervous millionaire. Look at the tax laws themselves! " Nevada is not an overlegislated state." " Taxes are supporting politicians' sycophantic friends, but not in Nevada." " Nevada is a business-like state, administered by business men for business interests. Racketeers, crack-pot politicians, easy-money exponents find no welcome in Nevada." W. W. Hopper, president of the First National Bank of Nevada, is quoted in regard to the small legislature required by a small population: " These members are well known to their constituents and are intimately acquainted with the state and what the people want and need." Politics are safe.

Labor is, too. The strong unions of early Virginia City and Gold Hill are ancient history. So is the war of charcoal burners and law officers near Eureka back in 1879. The labor militancy that made the IWW of Tonopah and Goldfield first-page news is thirty years past. Labor is established in Nevada, but quietly. Nearly everything in Reno, for example, is organized, except ten-cent-store girls, who scab readily. The railroad brotherhoods have a strong lobby. But cattle and mining men are unconcerned about labor, and there is no need for anyone to worry about class-conscious workers as he putts on the Municipal Course or tells his chauffeur to turn home up California Avenue.

When labor trouble threatened once, a few years ago, the sound-state proponents forced the vigilantes responsible for it to stop. They were stirring up bad publicity. Boca Dam was being built in order to hold the waters of the Little Truckee River for irrigation on the Newlands Project. The California CIO organized the dam workers and then announced it was going to send men to organize the highway workers in Nevada. The Washoe County sheriff and special deputies met the organizers on U.S. 40 near Verdi, Nevada, and drove them back over the state line. News services began to send out details of this Boss Hague tactic, and suddenly the Chamber of Commerce woke up. Decorous CIO organization was better than noisy strong-arm suppression, pictures in *Life*, and newspaper photographs of university students pouring into trucks to rush to Verdi and repel the Red Tide. Rough stuff implied deep-seated industrial unrest. Fewer millionaires would immigrate. Nevada must live up to its early publicity: " The working class is closely associated, if not identified, with the employing class."

The Verdi incident was a minor botch. The " Cyclone-Cellar " Campaign has been a success. Nevada has convinced the rich of America that it is without parallel as a state where a person can have, hold, and bequeath a fortune without paying tribute at every turn to statehouse bureaucracy. It taxes best by taxing least. The first *One Sound State* drew about 1,500 letters of inquiry from all over the country, and the numerous pamphlets since have continued to stir interest. Favorable news stories and editorials appeared in *Collier's, Barron's, Business Week, Time,* the New York *Times,* and the *Wall Street Journal.* A map in *Look* showed forty-seven states black or crosshatched with taxes offensive to the wealthy. Nevada was the nation's one spot, a tax-free oasis. Rich folk are taking up residence in and about Las Vegas or buying ranches in the interior of the state, for pleasure places or for commercial investments.

And new arrivals are giving Reno a real boom. House contractors are busy, especially along the Truckee River above the business district and on the plateau southwest of town, where elaborate mansions compare with those in New York's Westchester County and Los Angeles County's City of San Marino. Bank accounts are swelling. Air lines, Pullmans, and telegraph services are busier than ever before — and they have always been busy. Retail sales are zooming. Values of downtown business property are up to $2,500 or $3,000 per foot of frontage. There is a rush to buy ranches in beautiful Washoe and Carson valleys. Handsome rustic private lodges and châteaux, emphatically fenced, are rising along the hitherto neglected Nevada shores of Lake Tahoe. Natural beauty and invigorating climate abet the tax laws that deal so liberally with conservatives.

From 1930 to 1940 Nevada's population grew 20.8 per cent. Only three other states did better, Florida, New Mexico, and California. But for no state did the federal government report a higher per capita income tax, and this, paradoxically, was something for Nevada to tell the world about!

Nevada's treasure hunt interested Californians from the start. Here was a chance legally to evade taxes and yet not rove too far from accustomed social life. When a New Deal-

ish legislature slapped on new taxes in 1933 and '34, Max C.
Fleischmann and other millionaires in Montecito, swank sub-
urb of Santa Barbara, hunted for a place to escape to and discovered Nevada. Polo player, director of Standard Brands,
and yeast king, Fleischmann was ready to buy up all of
Washoe Valley if his Montecito friends would join him; but
in a showdown they were firmly attached to southern California. Taxes or no taxes, they had been won by their semi-
tropical environment with its poinsettias, hibiscuses, and bou-
gainvillaeas, and their society routines in their foothill palaces
were too pleasantly fixed. He had to go it alone with an estate
on Tahoe. Santa Barbara felt his departure when, no longer
a resident, he stopped contributing generously to Santa Barbara charities and the Museum of Natural History, but Nevada knew of his arrival when he made the first donation in
history to the State Library.

George Whittell, a San Francisco real-estate operator,
bought eighteen miles of Tahoe frontage for a millionaire
colony, and built himself a $300,000 estate near Incline. H. B.
R. Bushard, another California millionaire, bought the entire
eastern slope of Mount Rose, which lies between Tahoe and
Reno, for a 50,000-acre stock ranch. J. C. McCausland, retired Oakland manufacturer, acquired two homes on Crystal
Bay, Lake Tahoe. E. B. Scott, a Beverly Hills capitalist, purchased a Reno home. Harry Duffill, Los Angeles capitalist,
established residence in Reno, as did Dr. Raphael Hermann
of Los Angeles, a " well-known scientist and philanthropist,"
and Frank R. Payne, a retired chain-store merchant of Salt
Lake City who was fleeing from new taxes in California.

When the Ham and Eggs old folks' pension scheme was
on the ballot in 1939 and seemed to stand a chance of winning,
many California firms, including the San Francisco Stock
Exchange, secured option leases on Reno property and made
plans for moving. Native sons do not love native taxes. Reno
real-estate men indulged in fantastic dreams, as did Floridians

some years earlier, when Upton Sinclair's gubernatorial campaign to End Poverty in California led Hollywood movie moguls to threaten to emigrate to the Palmetto State.

Recruits came to Nevada from Canada, Illinois, New York, Pennsylvania, and elsewhere. Prominent names among them are Arthur K. Bourne (Singer sewing machines); Lewis Luckenback (steamships); E. C. Ruckstell (axles), who has a home near Boulder City; Ralph Elsman (public utilities), who has a $300,000 country home in Washoe Valley; John J. Raskob and Errett Cord (automobiles), who have become Nevada mining magnates; Burton L. Bayes (insurance in Seattle and oil in Kansas); Pierre Mirc, retired (New York brokerage), who has a home at Crystal Bay; Philip C. Kauffmann (co-owner of the Washington *Star*); Richard Bonelli (opera); and Billie Burke (stage and motion pictures).

Socialites include Cornelius Vanderbilt, Jr., of New York and Beverly Hills; Mrs. Susie C. Snyder of New York and her daughter (the former Princess Karageorgevitch); Dr. W. B. and Mrs. Janet Newlands Johnston of Washington, D.C., and Paris; Mr. and Mrs. Allan Floyd, formerly of Pasadena and Chicago; Mr. and Mrs. Norman Biltz (Mrs. Biltz is the former Esther Auchincloss), who have a $100,000 home in Reno; Roma Ware, who has a ranch near Pyramid Lake; Mrs. Luella Rhodes Garvey of Los Angeles, who owns another of Reno's $100,000 homes; Jean Jacques Bertschmann, social registerite; Captain D. V. Shaw-Kennedy, social registerite and captain of the Coldstream Guards in the World War; Mrs. Beverly Blackmer (formerly Frances Frazier of New York), who owns the 250,000-acre Big Canyon Ranch on Pyramid Lake and has built on it a $200,000 home; and Dr. and Mrs. Vinton Muller (Mrs. Muller is the former Lady Astley, who recently possessed Checkers Court, the ancestral home of the Cromwells). No longer are cattlemen the only Nevadans interested in blue ribbons and pedigrees.

Permanently residing in his gleaming white country house

in Washoe Valley is Christian Arthur Wellesley, Fourth Earl Cowley, who has found Reno the " city of moderation," the taxes reasonable, the people " congenial, broad-minded and honest," the fun available in Washoe County equal to that in New York, Paris, or London, the golden silence surpassing that on Egdon Heath, and the climate " darned nearly perfect! "

The sudden influx of hundreds of such luminaries means prosperity for Nevada but at the same time raises the question What will they do to Nevada? Will it, like much of Florida and some of southern California, be New Yorkized? Will Reno and Las Vegas become imitations of Palm Beach and Palm Springs? Will ranches in Nevada valleys become mere adjuncts of Park Avenue, as have estates in bluegrass Kentucky and tidewater Carolina? Will the last unsettled shores of Tahoe, the Nevada bays, be private domains for new-stock rich men, with " No Trespassing " signs for the old-stock Nevada public? Will the westernness of Nevada, encouraged by the temporary indulgence seekers, be smothered out by the permanent tax refugees?

The questions are worth a thought, although they suggest no profound worry, because for many of these well-to-do persons the whole reason for residence in Nevada is a legal fiction. Obviously, the many who spend most of their time elsewhere do Nevada as little harm, or good, as the millionaire Stack did. Those that remain are a cultural minority, despite their wealth and prestige, and may be partially absorbed.

Frank J. Taylor asked a Reno banker about this matter and got, presumably, the answer of the bankers, journalists, native capitalists, and judges who help determine public opinion in Nevada:

We're going to keep Nevada a plain, freedom-loving frontier state where a man can go out on the highway and drive as fast as he wants to, or go into a gambling club and gamble all he wants to. He can go into the mountains and hunt all he wants to or out to the lakes and fish to his heart's content. We've got everything in this damn state!

Brave words, defying as they do several of the statutes of the state! But one wonders if the newcomers will ever more than condescend to native Nevadans, just as one wonders if capitalists who run away from the human society that let them get rich to begin with are a desirable type of immigrant. They are not colonizers but rulers in exile.

II
BLUEPRINTS OF CREATION

Older Than History

From any highway or trail in Nevada a person can look in any direction and feel " as if pretty near all creation were in sight " — a creation that is vast and colorful and romantic, with purple canyons, volcanic cliffs of all shades and tints, dark lava flows, creamy sands, and over all a canopy of blue with puffy white clouds. Spacious brown alluvial fans slope down from angular hills. Long valleys swim in pink and lilac haze, opaline mirages waver and wink on the distant flatlands, and mountains blur and change their outlines. Saw-toothed ranges drift on the horizons. It is a passive, imperturbable landscape, a sleeping grandeur laid in timeless space. It is a land that is older than history — the very blueprints of creation.

The story of Nevada's last 500,000,000 years is one of instability, extremity, and violence. Many an American state has a peaceful geological history. Illinois, for instance, grew an inch a century, as dust and mud settled in a shallow sea.

[96]

But Nevada was for millions of years in one of the most extensive zones of disturbance and confusion on the surface of the earth.

At the dawn of recorded geology, the Archean era, mountain ranges of lofty granite peaks with broad, smooth surfaces covered Nevada. Millions of years at a time, a magnificent routine rolled its course. Nevada sank beneath the surface of the ocean and then rose to be part of the ancestral land mass of the Rocky Mountains. It sank again and was covered by a continental sea.

In the Paleozoic, the first great era of life, western Nevada was part of a continent. From Austin eastward the state was a deep sea-trough. Newborn brachiopods swam in the salty waters and then grew two shells, that looked like miniature Roman lamps, attached themselves to the bottom by a fleshy peduncle, and used ciliated arms to pull in food. Trilobites, primitive segmented creatures, ancestors of crabs and spiders, crawled about. Algae in spherical colonies and radiolaria floated in masses of mucilage. Crinoid columns, spiny-scaled feather stars, grew in the warm bays. Protozoans grew in masses on the bottom. They were tiny, part-naked, shelled globules of streaming protoplasm, spindle shaped. As they died they piled up like heaps of wheat grains. Meanwhile, sediments of the western continent were washing in and accumulating as fine shales, conglomerates, mudstone, and oil shales, but mostly as limestones. Several times the land and sea changed places and the former ocean bottom became high mesas that either became wind-blown sand under the silent sun or ocean sediment on top of the former continent. This up-and-down continued until the deposits were six and seven miles thick.

The Mesozoic era arrived and reddish sandstones accumulated on top of the original Archaean range. The earth warped and twisted. Bays and estuaries rolled over Nevada. There were mollusks, coral reefs, and shell banks of fluted oysters.

Flat spiral ammonites grew and multiplied. Fishlike reptiles swam about with paddle-shaped limbs and snatched at food with conical teeth.

The earth began to shrink, buckle, and snap. Nevada rose from the sea. It was squeezed, folded, and crumpled. Horizontal compression moved the sites of Sacramento and Ogden halfway to Nevada. Blocks of rock ten miles wide and fifty miles long lifted up from the sedimentary strata and formed the monumental basin ranges. They were upright mountains four to six thousand feet above the valleys — faulted crust blocks from which the streams spilled straight off. Then, as now, they were without outlying foothills, spurs, lakes, or baylike indentations. Mount Davidson rose, with faults on all four sides. The Sierras and the Humboldt Range rose part way. Earthquakes shuffled the ranges like a pack of cards. Peaks tipped and tumbled, as do a row of books when some are pulled from a shelf, creating wedges that pried out mountain blocks and thrust them over their neighbors, on which they fell in slow motion like colossal sledge hammers, fracturing and grinding. Great fissures opened deep into the interior of the earth. Diorite and diabase intruded into the earth's crust, as around the Comstock Lode. Red-hot lavas poured out, wrenching the cracks, layering the older ranges, and forming new hills. Volcanoes flamed and blasted near the site of Lake Tahoe. All over Nevada hot springs and geysers boiled, building up mounds of opal, amethyst, and quartzlike sinter. Superheated streams and rivers gushed up through cracks and fissures, bearing solutions of silica, gold, silver, and copper in a multitude of chemical combinations. In the Humboldt Range the solution cooled to become sulphide-bearing quartz. Monzonite porphyry pushed into the split and sundered limestone of Ely. The volcanic waters ascended through the limestones of Eureka and the parallel cracks in the old granite of Austin and deposited bonanza veins and seams, which were later shaken and displaced by earthquakes. The silver of Treasure Hill formed in fissures between limestone and shale and in chambers in the limestone. During long successions of years, half millions at a time, rain water ran down the mountains above Virginia City, Austin, and Ely, leaching the ores, oxidizing and carbonating them, concentrating them. *114414*

The earth bent up and lifted Nevada taut like an arch. The Sierras lifted abruptly at the western edge, forming bastion-like scarps from Honey Lake south to Owens Valley. A placid vale, Little Valley, near Marlette Lake, was lifted to the summits of Genoa Peak and Slide Mountain. Dozens of quakes shook the region, and on both sides great blocks of earth sank to form the Tahoe basin and Washoe Valley. A lava flow burst from volcanoes to the west and flowed so as to cut the Tahoe trough in two. Tahoe filled with water, spilled over to form the Truckee River, and started to cut a gorge through into Nevada. The Truckee slowly lowered the lake level and left old bay bottoms exposed as land at Incline and Glenbrook.

The fires of lava burned into Cenozoic time, the third great era since life began. Molten, flaming matter repeatedly broke through the deeply riven rocks of earlier eras. Cooling slowly below the surface, the matter became granite and other intrusive rocks, to be revealed by later erosion. Bursting to the surface and cooling more quickly, it became lavas — andesite and rhyolite and basalt. When full of gases that brewed and simmered, it hardened into bubbly scoria. Whole new volcanic ranges appeared in western Nevada. Again rain dissolved surface mineral, trickled down the cracks, came in contact with superheated matter, and evaporated, leaving behind new ore deposits in veins and stringers. Earthquakes hammered and shook the lava mountains and cracked them open. Fresh flows squeezed up, joined by smoldering water that deposited free gold in Goldfield, and also gold combined with tellurium. Lava filled the deep valleys between the limestone ridges in the Pahroc Range; elsewhere it formed level valley floors. Parts of Nevada were scorched and sterilized from the stratosphere to the center of the earth.

Lakes were formed, dried up, lifted and spilled into adjoining basins, smothered out by cataracts of scoria. A fresh-water lake formed in northeastern Nevada. It was deep enough to catch two thousand feet of clay, shale, and limestone. An earth bulge lifted it out, its waters evaporated or ran away, and a fold tipped its bottom to an angle of forty-five degrees. The Virginia and Pine Nut ranges rose and the Carson River began cutting a gorge that is now three hundred feet below the old river gravel, perched on dry slopes above. Lakes in western Nevada caught the debris of volcanic activity. Colemanite, a former source of borax, was deposited in the Muddy Mountains in the southeast. Other nonmetallic deposits collected in basins. Southern Nevada wobbled and trembled, and the Charleston Mountains emerged as a massive block.

The climate was humid. In central Nevada it was two to five times what it is now. Torrential rains fell. Soil was deep, moist, and fertile with the magnesias and potassiums of decomposed lava. The forests of California extended out into Nevada, into the present Black Rock Desert, Newlands Project, the Esmeralda District. There were stands of pines, firs, and a species of giant Sequoia as big as the redwoods of California. There was a luxuriance of ferns, water lilies, peaches, barberries, maples, willows, oaks, black walnuts, cedars, figs, myrtles, and sycamores. The forests bordered large lakes, which covered much of Nevada. Birds circled above and cranes patrolled the shores. Fresh-water diatoms thrived in waters filtered by volcanic ash. In their microscopic pillbox shells of silica they formed white beds hundreds of feet thick, fifty million individuals to a cubic inch. The lake-shore grasslands and the woodlands supported an abundant fauna, which varied in long periods. Toward the first there were several species of small three-toed horse, peccaries, deer, snakes, moles, four-horned antelope, camels, bearlike and hoglike creatures. There was a small rhinoceros the size of a wolf. The teleoceras, a big, heavy, short-legged beast, one horn on his nose, one on his forehead, sloshed through the grassy lake margins. Later came the dire wolf, mastodons, lions, and tigers.

Fed by the rains, streams cut actively into the ranges, wore gorges through the lava headlands, and bisected the table mountains. Some mountains were eroded back a mile, leaving an even rock floor veneered with thin patches of gravel slanting down to the plains. Fans of gravel, boulders, silt, and sand covered the lower hills. Mud flows carried rocks as big as houses several miles from the canyon spillways. Peaks buried themselves in their own debris — disappeared to become mere rubbish heaps. Volcanic pebbles accumulated on top of dust and sand, lengthwise to the wind, to form the deceptive " desert pavement " that yields beneath one's step.

Volcanoes burst out again and covered the forests and the bones of animals with yellowish ash mud that formed opalbearing petrifactions. Much of the new lava, as in the Thousand Creek area, ran in the new creek channels, that were far below the older lava flows on the ridges above. Railroad Ridge, seven miles long, is two hundred feet above much younger lava in Virgin Creek Valley. Cinder cones vomited slag and scoria. On the high mesas north of Granite Creek Desert the lava cooled so quickly that it formed obsidian and basalt glass, a boon to later arrowhead and spearpoint makers, who squatted on the intervalley rises and chipped.

The epoch of the glaciers arrived and the climate turned cold. Ice masses formed on the Sierras and the high central mountains to the east, on Arc Dome, summit of the Toiyabe Range, on Mount Jefferson in the Toquimas, along the crest of the Ruby-East Humboldts. Glaciers converted V-shaped stream valleys into U-shaped glacial valleys, scalloped out cirques, and slowly carted millions of tons of rock to be dumped in terminal and lateral moraines. A glacier carried boulders six feet through from Donner Pass, dumped them from its snout into the Truckee River, and it in turn rolled them most of the way to Reno. They lie on the old river terraces near Verdi.

As water ran off the glaciers, and as they melted away successively during the series of ice periods, new lakes formed. One rose south of Hamilton, where a beach bar reposes sixty feet above the present sagebrush valley floor. Carson Valley was a lake. Washoe Valley contained a lake instead of the swamp of nowadays. Finally the glaciers melted away. Huge deposits washed down to join those of previous ages. Alluvial material filled up valleys with 2,000–5,000 feet of loose gravel and graded them level. No desert streamlet could ever start to flow across them without filtering down and out of sight. Erosion covered the lower ranges and left exposed only the " lost mountains."

Meanwhile, with low temperatures, little evaporation, and the runoff from the ice masses, Lake Lahontan rose and sprawled over northwestern Nevada. At its height, 2,500 to 25,000 years ago, it had 8,422 square miles of surface and at its deepest point, the present Pyramid Lake, was almost 900 feet deep. Streaked with basin-range islands, it stretched from Walker Lake into Oregon, from Winnemucca to Susanville, California. Trout, suckers, shiners, minnows, and whitefish swam in its clear, fresh waters and in the tributary streams, which spanned the whole width of Nevada. As the lake surface varied, up and down, a series of shore lines formed — terraces, as west of Lovelock, sand bars, as just east of Hazen. Giant ground sloths nibbled at the leaves of bushes and left their footprints in the shore mud. Prehistoric men camped around the edges, scratched rock inscriptions, threw darts at humpless camels, and lured ducks with feathered decoys.

When the glaciers were finally gone except for the tag ends in the highest hanging valleys, Nevada began to change into the desert of American history. The epoch of sagebrush was at hand. The climate warmed and for thousands of years evaporation from Lahontan exceeded inflow. The water contained increasingly concentrated amounts of salt and carbonates. In rock-shaded water, algae and associated bacteria removed the calcium carbonate and deposited it as a stony tufa on the shore rocks so that they grew like mushrooms. As the tufa grew outward and upward toward the light, it became porous, bulging concentrically, one layer outside another. A time came when the carbonate collected too rapidly for the algae to keep up, the lake waters became relatively concentrated, and the chemical precipitated itself out as crystalline tufa — aragonite — which was later covered by algae-laid deposits. As Lahontan's surface became smaller and the level fell more and more slowly, the algae caught up with the carbonate and removed it faster than it washed in, forming stacks of tufa that were exposed as the lake shrank further. Finally, the old limestone formations were hundreds of feet above the water line. The Humboldt River, lengthening as the lake rim pulled westward, cut the gorge through old bottom sediments that is now filled by Rye Patch Dam. A gulf bottom north of Winnemucca became a wasteland of sand dunes, seventy-five feet thick, forty miles long, and ten wide, that slowly drifted eastward, burying bushes and — later — telegraph poles. Lahontan sank below the valley rims and shattered into a dozen lakes and catch basins.

Fish that had evolved into unique species during the epochs of isolated inland lakes were further segregated. The gamy mountain whitefish survived in the Walker, Carson, and Truckee rivers. In Pyramid and Winnemucca lakes was a large, clumsy, sweet-flavored sort of sucker, called quee-wee by the Indians and eagerly harvested by the ton during the annual spawning migration up the Truckee. From the upper Truckee to upper Reese River the royal silver trout found streams to swim in. He was steel blue on the back and silvery with easily lost scales on the sides. More common was the cutthroat later famous as the Tahoe trout, with a dark-olive body and large black spots. He reached two pounds in the high brooks, ten pounds in the mountain lakes. He grew to recorded extremes of thirty-five pounds in Lake Tahoe and sixty-four pounds in Pyramid Lake. He was the largest trout in America.

The ancient sources of Lake Lahontan remain in the hanging creeks that never leave the ranges and the " rivers " that rarely reach their lower ends, and in the Walker and Truckee rivers, that still support large perennial lakes several hundred feet deep. The Truckee is the living link between lovely Lake Tahoe, high and pure in a green bowl of pines and manzanita, and the magnificent sump, Pyramid Lake, which gleams between barren, desolate, russet-brown ranges. Its surface is a map colored in sea green, cyan blue, brownish yellow, and glassy pink. White deposits scar the shore line, along which are the amazing tufa formations, black and grayish blue. They are domes and monoliths, mammoth mammillary glands, colossal sponges, gigantic bunches of grapes. Some of the shores are soggy with partly formed tufa. The crescent, sloping beaches are covered with small, faintly polished pebbles like navy beans (lime concretions around sand grains). On curving sand spits, Caprilike crags, and Anaho and Pyramid islands are hundreds and hundreds of California gulls, Farallon cormorants, American mergansers, and great blue herons. Far outnumbering them are ten thousand or so white pelicans, which stay during the warmer half of the year and eat tons of chub minnows, suckers, and quee-wee. They dive for fish or form paddling semicircles that drive schools toward shore and then scoop them up in the shallows. The nesting places on the islands, isolated breeding grounds amid the Nevada desert, resemble the bare rookeries of the Pacific Ocean.

Other than Pyramid and Walker lakes, all that remains of Lake Lahontan is numerous dry and intermittent lakes. Among the ephemeral lakes are Black Rock Desert and Hum-

PYRAMID LAKE,
SHOWING TUFA FORMATIONS

PELICANS ON ANAHO ISLAND,
PYRAMID LAKE

DESERT, AUSTIN AREA

A LOCALIZED RAIN OF HIGH INTENSITY

boldt, Carson, and Winnemucca lakes, which have dried up since Nevada became a state. There are similar lakes outside the Lahontan water system, in central and southern Nevada. All these lakes that come and go, sometimes persisting for a couple of years at a time, are always a dry spell or two ahead of mapmakers. Their life story is a simple round. Rain falls from gloomy cloud masses on the uplands. Torrents flood the channels, dissolve compounds of sulphur, boron, sodium, and potassium, flush down rocks, sand, and clay, and dump them on the widening flood plains. Yellow water, roily with suspended mud, slips over the flats, spreading out for miles. When full, North Carson Lake is twenty miles by fourteen and only a few feet deep. Franklin Lake, fifteen miles by four, may dry up in summer. Largest of all the mud lakes is Black Rock. On the rare occasions when Quinn River runs to its end and really floods, a lake forms sixty miles long by twenty wide. The next summer the sun dries up the water, bakes the mud, cracks it, and draws the alkalines and salts to the surface. The lake becomes "a tessellated pavement of cream-colored marble" so hard that it rings beneath the hoofbeats of galloping horses and scarcely shows the prints.

Years ago a scientist remarked of Nevada, "What a study for the geologist! No trees to hide the hills, no grass to cover the rocks. You can read the story like an open book." Everywhere are illustrations of prehistory: the lava spillways near Massacre Lake, the fossil forests and ancient shore lines in Virgin Creek Valley, the diatom deposits along U.S. 40 southwest of Lovelock, the sand-carved, red Jurassic mountains and petrified logs in Valley of Fire, the vapor plumes of Steamboat Springs and the dying geysers at Beowawe, and Castellated Gorge, its 2,000-feet perpendicular walls cut by glaciers atop Mount Wheeler.

Frémont's name for Nevada and western Utah was "the Great Basin," a brilliant but misleading metaphor. The area is a basin in the sense that it is a self-contained drainage system with no streams that reach the sea, but there is, obviously, not just one broad plain of evaporation. There are scores of lake basins totally unconnected, caught between the dozens of basin ranges, which are but the broken relief of a continental swell that rises in the middle of the " Great Basin." If Frémont had known central Nevada when he coined his phrase, his figure of speech would have been different. Except for West Virginia, perhaps, Nevada is the most consistently mountainous of all the states. It is currycombed throughout its whole area by short ranges running north and south. The valleys average 4,000 feet above sea level. The ranges rise from 1,000 to 5,000 feet above them. Many peaks are over 12,000 feet in altitude, the highest one, Boundary Peak, reaching 13,145 feet. The California Sierras and the Utah Wasatches are the rims of Frémont's " Basin," yet the Ruby and Snake ranges, halfway between, in eastern Nevada, are as high.

" The whole idea of such a desert . . ." wrote Frémont in his report of his first visit to Nevada, " is a novelty in our country, and excites Asiatic, not American ideas. Interior basins, with their own system of lakes and rivers, and often sterile, are common enough in Asia . . . but in America such things are new and strange, unknown and unsuspected, and discredited when related."

The famous pathfinder was only the first to find the scenery of Nevada suggestive of the Near East and the heartlands of Asia. Richard Burton was reminded of the Suez country, of the Arabian seaboard behind Aden, and of Takhashshua near Zayla. As General Lew Wallace rode along the Humboldt Valley in a Pullman car, he exclaimed, " How much this is like the River Jordan; the same winding stream, the same green fringe along the banks, the same brown and tree-less hills." In a multitude of ways the American desert resembles the Old World desert that stretches from the western Sahara through Mesopotamia to the Gobi. There are parallels in Nevada to the salt flats near Jericho, the dry terraces

of Granada and Castile, the dry stream bed of Wadi Biskra in
Algeria, the gravel desert of Rajputana, India, and the Arabian
river, Wadi Rummah, that is a thousand miles long and rarely
damp at the lower end. The undrained intermountain basins
have counterparts in Central China, Eastern Turkestan, and
the Sahara. The chemical water bodies, Pyramid Lake, the
soda lakes near Hazen, and Columbus Marsh, are hydro-
graphic kin to the Caspian, the Dead Sea, the Shotts of Tu-
nisia, and also the Lake Eyre basin of Australia.

The strange and glorious wasteland of the early explorers
and emigrants remains essentially unchanged down to the
present. It is the " sagebrush country " that Mary Austin
found as distinctive a type of landscape as the moors of England and the Campagna of Italy. It is the desert of John C.
Van Dyke, Mary Austin, J. B. Priestley, and many another
who has experienced the golden fire of a Nevada sunrise, the
varying shadows and colors and outlines of each hour of the
day, the sunsets with their pink summits and knife-edged
ridges of amethyst, their iridescent clouds, and the afterglow
that reminded William Morris of Italian skies. And at night
the stars shimmer and dazzle the crests of the desert ranges
so that they seem half sisters to the towering Rockies, half
sisters to the icy, lifeless mountains of the moon. This is a
subworld in which any human being is a trifling interloper, a
land that is " geology by day and astronomy at night."

Surviving in Drought

LONG dry spells, torrential rains, unremitting glare and heat,
unexpected frosts, sudden changes in temperature — these
make Nevada a perennial challenge to nature and man. The
Nevada environment has always been dominating and vigorous in its effects on the lives of plants, animals, Indians, farm-

ers, and cattlemen. All living things that have entered the state and remained to reproduce have had to make special adaptations that are of scientific interest, if not aesthetic.

The Nevada air is so arid it can evaporate from seven to nineteen times the amount of water that falls as rain; and some Nevada valleys see no rain for a year and a half or more. Areas larger than Eastern states contain only a few scores of water sources, some of them warm and unpalatable. Rain and snowfall are unpredictable from one year to the next and vary greatly. In 1906, for example, the average rainfall was 15.8 inches; in 1928 it was 4.2 inches. Winter blizzards whiten the mountaintops while no rain falls in the valleys. When the snow melts in the spring there are trickles on the mountainsides, but once they reach the valleys, they evaporate or sink into the soil. These seepages make life possible, however, since they supply pools, springs, and artesian wells. In summer, moisture-laden air comes in from the Gulf of California. Black clouds collect and roll over a square mile or two. A wind blows and then stops for a period of silence. Scattered drops the size of a bird egg pelt the dusty earth. Suddenly the saturated clouds completely condense, as if great bags of water were rupturing. Water boils knee-deep in what was an oven-dry ravine. It gouges at the roots of plants, sweeps away the paper-thin topsoil, and gurgles into burrows and dens.

In parts of Nevada the annual range of temperature is around 124 degrees. Killing frosts come late in May and begin again in September. On most days there is uninterrupted, brilliant sunlight (but, because of the low humidity, no sunstroke). All the upper end of the spectrum, including ultraviolet, is present to a remarkable degree. Swift masses of air pour up and down the state, unobstructed clear to the surface of the ground. They throw trillions of sand grains against leaves and stems, wrench trees, and wreck buildings that have not been double braced.

The lack of moisture and therefore of humus restricts the

accumulation of topsoil and produces a pale-gray landscape. Not restrained by turf, sand accumulates in drifts. There being no streams to cut channels and flush the valleys into the ocean, soluble mineral salts accumulate in the basins — sodium chloride, carbonate, and sulphate — and further restrict organic life.

Yet over 2,600 species of plants have migrated in from Mexico, the Sierras, the Columbia River country, and the Rockies and made manifold adjustments to the Nevada environment. Moisture-loving plants compress their lives into a short season of a few weeks. The ground is full of seeds awaiting the spring rains. Plants leaf out and flower more explosively than they do in the East after the long winter. All of a sudden there are patches of such colorful annuals as pink verbena, purple phacelia, and orange gilias. More representative of the desert, however, are the perennials that resort to year-round adaptations by means of resiny coats, leathery leaves, sunken breathing pores, huge underground root systems for storing water, and hooks and barbs to keep off rodents.

For example, the cactuses, those strange relatives of violets and begonias, bud slowly. The fruit ripens over a long period of time. The terminal buds of their stems are stunted and transformed into spines. The roots, which may spread for thirty or forty feet in the top four inches of soil, grasp at any rain that falls and carry it to be stored in the thick, green stems. The creosote bush, the only plant that grows on many gravelly plains near Las Vegas, formally spaces itself, as if planted by an engineer, so that each root system will have enough moisture for itself after a rain. The delicate sparse foliage on the springy slender boughs is varnished outside and stink-flavored inside. Even when the yearly rain is only two inches, the creosote bush will flower out in yellow in the spring and grow on through the summer. It can endure three straight rainless years, though not without dropping most of the leaves.

Nevada plants automatically zone themselves by elevations, in the fairly permanent belts of temperature and humidity. This is nowhere better illustrated than in the Charleston Mountains. In the alkaline bottom of Las Vegas Wash are green greasewood, desert saltbush in gray thickets, and, in the dunes, the thorny mesquite, which will send its roots down fifty feet or more to find ample moisture. On the well-drained slope adjoining is a stand of creosote bush and Mojave yucca. At 3,500 feet above sea level Joshua trees appear, the giant yuccas that stand in twisted attitudes and thrust their huge fists of spiny leaves into the sky. Between 6,000 and 8,000 feet are sagebrush, brush oak, pinyon pine, desert juniper, and mountain mahogany. The thickset little nut pine, rarely over fifteen feet high, sends its knotty branches in every direction in stiff zigzags and then turns them up gracefully at the end. The tough mahogany, which resembles a gnarled apple tree, grows very slowly for as long as nine hundred years. As fuel it surpasses hickory, being much heavier and leaving even less ash behind; bearings made of mountain mahogany wood wear as well as metal ones. In the next thousand feet above this group are faster-growing, less drought-resistant trees and shrubs, white fir, yellow pine, wild currants, stiff-leaved Oregon grapes, and tall red roses. From 9,000 feet to timber line at 11,500 there are white pines, dwarf juniper, dense groves of small, ladylike aspens, and the foxtail pines, with long, dense leaf tassels, eccentrics that John Muir found "irrepressibly and extravagantly picturesque, offering a richer and more varied series of forms to the artist than any other species I have yet seen."

Animals are even more varied than plants in their adaptations to Nevada. Small mammals and snakes hide from the hot sun by lying in the shade of bushes, burrowing into sand, and getting under rocks or into caves. The round-tailed squirrel runs rapidly from the protection of one bush to another. Bats cling in deep crevices. Grasshoppers, beetles, and lizards, being cold blooded, simply heat up and go their way, not minding soil or rocks that are 124 degrees in the sun. Deer flies and mammoth horseflies warm to aggressive activity under the white-hot sun as they pester twitching flanks. At night the big food hunt begins for day resters. Trade rats, their bat-like ears alert, their prominent black eyes staring, crawl from their nests of sticks, rocks, and bones, get through the protecting wall of cholla cactus joints, and search for seeds. Spiny pocket mice, half as long as a thumb, and harvest mice gather their crops. The coyote makes his nightly round of up to twenty miles, running along his beat with an aimless, soft-footed gait, scenting out rabbits, rats, drought-sick cattle, newborn foals, wild berries, and the best watermelons and muskmelons in farmers' patches. Millipedes crawl out from under rocks and eat decaying vegetation, the relatively harmless scorpions capture insects and spiders, and the desert lynx, shy and secretive, brings his huge padded paws down on sleeping birds and roosting chickens.

The desert denizens get water in many ways. Termites get it when intestinal protozoans break down their woody food for them. Other insects get it from green stems and leaves, seeds, and dead plants, which, like hay, never fully dry. Dragonflies roam thirty miles to and from water holes. The tortoise stores water in sacs between his flesh and shell. Lizards and rabbits get water from the insects and plants they eat and are, in turn, an indirect water supply when they are prey for hawks, owls, kit foxes, snakes, and coyotes. Bighorn sheep dig juicy bulbs and tubers. Squat badgers, speedy at excavation, get their water from the several dozen mice, ground squirrels, and gophers they eat each day. Mourning doves, desert quail, cactus wrens, sage thrashers, flycatchers, and other birds obtain their water from insects, morning dew, and rain pools under boulders. Frogs and toads, deer, antelope, and aquatic birds restrict their movements to the areas that contain springs, streams, or lakes — the water islands in a sea of dry earth.

As protection from enemies, including the sun, the desert creatures use camouflage. By avoiding a black color they keep from fully absorbing the sun's rays. Their skin and hair assume the general pallid tint of the humus-lacking desert surface. On the dark lava flows, however, ground squirrels, grasshoppers, rats, and mice are darker, as they are in the wreaths of forest around the mountaintops and in the wooded canyons that finger down the northern exposures. Many animals have color patterns that conceal them against a background of twigs, leaves, or bare rocks. In the rock-strewn mountains are bighorns, with variegated coloring, and brush-inhabiting chipmunks, striped from the ends of their tails to the ends of their noses. In the brushy canyons and washes are the spotted skunk and the pale, dotted lynx. On the plains are the antelope squirrel, striped to its shoulders, and the silver-spotted grasshopper, that lives only in creosote bushes.

More spectacular protection on the open plains and mesas is the speed of some of the animals. The antelope gets off to instantaneous starts and flashes out of sight, his rump gleaming white, a heliographic warning to his fellows. The little thimble-sized pocket mouse leaps three feet at a time. The sidewinder, looping along rapidly, strikes in stride without rattling or coiling. Many of the thirty-five or more other Nevada species of snakes and lizards move with hummingbird velocity. The gay, prankish ground cuckoo or roadrunner, who is poor at flight, streaks after flying insects. The black-tailed jack rabbit springs away, jerks this way and that, makes a long leap now and then, slows down to a lope, and crouches behind a bush, holding its long jackass ears flat while it hides or erect while it listens for danger. What wild horses remain of the huge herds of thirty years ago escape wolves and coyotes, bronco busters, and dog-food manufacturers partly by

JOSHUA TREES

PRICKLY DESERT POPPY

AIR VIEW OF
THE TOWN OF
ALAMO AND
PAHRANAGAT
VALLEY

sagacious suspicion of fenced-in water holes and funnel-shaped canvas traps in canyon bottlenecks, partly by phenomenal endurance and agility in running unshod over rocks. Heads erect, slender legs pounding, manes and tails flowing, a band of these Americanized Arabians can run twenty miles, take a fresh spurt, and run on another twenty, meanwhile shunting off to the side one by one, so that finally an inexperienced pursuer finds that what was once a band of two dozen horses is now only three or four individuals, still strongly racing on.

Prehistoric man, already trained in desert living by his long sojourn in Mongolia, met the challenges of the Nevada environment by evolving a simple but stabilized civilization. He lived in limestone caverns such as Lovelock Cave, Hidden Cave, near Fallon, and Gypsum Cave, north of Las Vegas. Along the Muddy River he built an intermittent village thirty miles long, climaxed in Pueblo Grande de Nevada, or "Lost City," now under Lake Mead at Overton. Here was a flourishing town with buildings as large as twenty-one rooms, advanced arts, and careful agriculture. This culture was fully developed fifteen or twenty centuries ago, before the age of cliff dwellings and mesa-top pueblo apartments in Colorado and Arizona. In the same climate that Nevada has today, Indians made brush dams and irrigation ditches and raised maize, beans, squash, and cotton. They harvested natural products, including mesquite pods and cactus tunas. They made cheesecloth and feather fabrics and wove fine textiles and dyed them red, blue, and purple. They used strips of rabbit fur to make blankets and overcoats. Advancing beyond the manufacture of baskets only, they produced bowls and jars, cooking pots and canteens. They colored them gray or red or white and decorated them with black designs. They rounded and drilled turquoise beads and skillfully chipped arrow points, awls, and knives of many-colored flint. Near Lost City was a twisting cave with vaulted chambers of solid salt. Men worked in the flickering light of bound-brush torches as they loosened oval slabs of salt with stone picks and hammers, dusting away the chips with yucca-fiber brushes. When hungry they sat by their lunch pots and ate ground mesquite pods and roasted corn on the cob.

Nevada was not a favorable country for the nomadic pre-Frémontian Indians. They were kept so busy merely getting food that they did not develop extensively the leisure-time activities of the corn-fed Eastern tribes — interminable ceremonies and continual warfare. Shoshones, Piutes, and Washoes were unceasing in their search for edibles, but regularly they saw the weakest die of starvation. Indians dug basketfuls of carrot root from the marshes, roasted it, and ate its sweet-potato flavored flesh. They dammed up streamlets in the hills and flooded the holes of badgers, gophers, and trade rats, in order to get meat and skins. There were other food supplies for ingenious aborigines. If the cane that grew in the marsh-lands was split open and laid in the sun, the sap crystallized. Squaws scraped it and rubbed it into tasty sugary balls. Bunch grass produced milletlike seeds. Squaws bound up sheaves and then stripped off the heads between sticks tied together like scissors. They ground the seeds on a flat stone, together with wild-sunflower seeds, and ate the meal or baked it in cakes. In drought winters they boiled white sage — later consumed by some Comstockers as a " cure " for balding heads. The waves of Humboldt, Carson, and Mono lakes cast ashore the larvae of a fly. Heaps of them were gathered up, dried, winnowed to get rid of the enclosing cases, and stored in willow baskets for winter meals. The squaws gathered grasshoppers and large crickets, pounded them up, and mixed them with animal grease to make a palatable chocolate-colored compound. In September and October the tribal divisions migrated in a mass to their natural orchards, the pine-nut plantations, knocked down the cones with long poles, collected them in heaps, lightly scorched them, shook out the slightly roasted nuts, and stored them for precious nutriment during the next year. Exploiting to the full their natural resources and keeping on the move, the historic Indians managed to live, even though they never knew the economics of abundance.

Present-day Indians want to live self-sufficiently out of the soil. They are buying land, fighting brush fires and cricket invasions, digging wells, developing springs, diverting water for irrigation, reseeding overgrazed grass land and fencing out cattle and sheep. They are competently raising beef and dairy cattle, turkeys, and chickens, practicing trades and art-crafts, mastering the science of nutrition, and — thanks to the Indians' New Deal under Commissioner John Collier — governing themselves through tribal councils. The spirit of the Indian school at Stewart, just south of Carson City, is

The land is ours, and we belong to it. . . . But we're learning the white man's ways. . . . In return for our labor, we will keep part of the proceeds from the school's crops. . . . Then we will use the money and newly acquired skills to cultivate our own land on the reservation back home.

Indians are eager to farm because they can see how the white man has learned to exploit the desert soil. The pioneer in the Atlantic states thought that " land that won't grow trees won't grow anything," but the settler on treeless and even grassless lands in Nevada, Mormon or Gentile, showed that proper irrigation could raise extraordinary crops. In early days Nevada wheat commanded a one-cent premium in the Chicago pit, sugar beets contained up to twenty per cent sugar, mixed timothy and clover hay was in demand at Saratoga and was shipped by James B. Haggin to his stables south of San Francisco. Barley, potatoes, and apples won prizes at world's fairs, and butter and beef brought advanced prices in California. Turnips, honey, corn, and cantaloupes brought good prices in the local towns.

A warm, fructifying sun shone down, and though " zephyrs " blew there were no tornadoes. Decomposed lava made soil that equaled in richness the volcanic valleys of Sicily, productive for over twenty consecutive centuries. Thanks to aeons of dryness, Nevada's soils had not been leached of limes, potashes, and magnesias. The low humidity meant that little dew fell to dampen the hays and then leach away the precious vitamin A as it evaporated. Only water was a problem. The valleys in the obtuse angle on Nevada's western boundary were amply watered by rivers, where Mason and Smith and Carson were early the show places that they are now. Along the desert ranges every rill was taken up, every artesian-well basin, in many a site that lay inconspicuously here and there in out-of-the-way places, marked nowadays by Lombardy poplars, an old apple orchard, corrals, a barn, haystacks shaped like old-style beehives, and a tall faded farmhouse. Near the river sinks, tule land, cleared and drained, became bumper-crop alfalfa land. The Mormons built long community ditches like the six-mile one down the Virgin River Valley to Bunkerville. After a cloudburst or flood had broken across the life-bringing aqueduct and men had repaired it, the most exhilarating cry in the world was " The water's in! "

Out in the terrible deserts, where frantic forty-niners once threw away grindstones and walnut dressers, are fertile farmsteads. These are evidence of what to a pious reclamationist of forty years ago was " man joining hands with God." Rye Patch Dam on the Humboldt, Lahontan Dam on the Carson, Boca Dam on the Little Truckee, and the six feet of peaceful Tahoe waters that run through the gates bring waters to reclaimed lands that formerly were sandy loam and compact adobe impregnated with substantial quantities of salts, or " slick spots " that supported no natural vegetation, or flats that dried hard and tough. Often the root zone of good topsoil was so full of salt and boron as to retard or stop the growth of plants. Aided and advised by the government and the state university, farmers have used chemical and cultural methods.

They have changed the chemical nature of the soil by adding gypsum and alum. They have disked in tons of manure, aerated the soil, and initiated cultivation with a crop of sweet clover, or they have spread sand over adobe as a seedbed and later mixed it in along with the cover crop. The result is productive fields around Fallon and Lovelock — husky cabbages, Hearts of Gold melons, tall corn with turkeys and chickens chasing grasshoppers between the rows. Snow surveying, a methodical measurement of depth and water content of the seasonal pack in the mountains, enables the Nevada Agricultural Station, which developed the technique under Professor J. E. Church, to forecast the summer's water supply with an accuracy as high as ninety-five per cent.

From the first Carson Valley farmer of the 1850's to the last 1942 settler to take up newly irrigated public land, agriculturists have had things to learn about their organic environment. The taller the sagebrush is, the better the soil. Wherever creosote bushes grow, the soil is excellent. Weeds wait ready to thrive in cleared land: scrawny pigweeds and the rotund tumbleweed, sour-smelling dock, velvet-leafed mullein, and ticklegrass. Nut pines make good fuel, timber, charcoal, and fencing. Yucca roots make an excellent, costless soap. Honey mesquite will supply fuel, fence posts, and tool handles; the skinny, string-bean pods are nourishing feed for horses and cattle; when dissolved in cold water, the gum exuded from the bark makes a good mucilage or throat gargle. Ground squirrels and pocket gophers have to be poisoned or fumigated. Grasshoppers infest alfalfa and must be poisoned. Jack rabbits nibble everything planted and must be fenced out, shot, trapped, or clubbed to death in community rabbit drives. Coyotes ravage among the fruit crops and the farmyard animals. They must be trapped at their urinal " scent posts " or near carcasses; litters must be dug from the dens and killed.

The most famous scourge in Nevada, the Mormon cricket

of the north central counties, hatches by the billions from eggs laid halfway up the mountains. In summer, when fully grown into fat, black, shiny, clumsy, wingless grasshoppers, the crickets start downhill. Sometimes they are so thick in the brush and timber that a horse can barely make his way through them. The catastrophic hordes crawl down the slopes like waves of molasses. Birds land among them and gorge until glutted, but make no impression on the flow of migrants. Crickets fall into ditches and fill them. They tumble into creeks in writhing heaps until they have made a living bridge to the other bank. They cross paved highways and squash under tires until they form a slimy surface that endangers cars, especially after a rain has lathered the whole stinking mess into a skiddy mucilage. Highway maintenance divisions are kept busy cleaning them up. But, most serious of all, they march over fences, over house porches, and, crossing cultivated fields and meadows, they consume every kernel, every tender stem, every leaf, and creep on, the only sound being the clicking of their jaws and the soft rustle of multitudinous body cases.

This droughtland plague is hard to fight. Practical measures are troublesome: a fence of flattened tin cans, a six-inch wooden fence with a curved tin top and all knotholes plugged, or a fence that is thirty inches of common burlap with seven inches of oilcloth sewed to the top. At present the United States Department of Agriculture is trying to stop the annual invasions by dropping poisoned bran from open-cockpit planes.

Cattlemen and sheepmen, like farmers, have faced problems of survival, the solution of which demanded time and energy. Grass raised the greatest problems. In overgrazed meadows the soil washed off, gullies formed, and worthless rabbit bush moved in. Alkali came up from the subsoil to ruin hay land that had been too slowly irrigated and drained off. The herds and flocks had to be kept in good grass or hay or

BOULDER DAM

AERIAL VIEW
OF BOULDER DAM
AND SURROUNDING
COUNTRY

U. S. Bureau of Reclamation

they were tempted by poisonous range plants. Cowboys and sheepherders had to search out the high, nutritious mountain grasses, the bunch grass on the stream benches, the rye or wheat grass, and the glossy-fruited desert grass. They had to know where sheep could find the short, tasty winter fat and the sweet white sage. Cows and sheep were killed or had convulsions when they ate greasewood, locoweed, the low-growing larkspur, lupine when in full pod, or chokecherry leaves before early September. The narrow-leaved milkweed and the arrow grass poisoned calves and sheep; the awns of squirrel-tail grass embedded in their jaws and faces and caused pus-filled abscesses or jabbed into their eyes and blinded them. In the spring, rabbit bush, despite its pretty crown of golden flowers, was poisonous to sheep. In certain Sierra canyons was the fitweed with its fragrant white flowers. After cows and sheep ate it they had convulsions. Their muscles twitched, their lips chewed on near-by objects, and their breath came a couple of hundred times a minute. The creatures ran in any direction in short spasms, and then they fell rigid. Early stockmen learned all these things the costly way and developed ways of avoiding losses that present-day stockmen profit by.

Droughts like those of 1889 and 1934 dried up the springs and water holes, killed thousands of stock animals, and raised urgent problems of range management. Coyotes pulled down calves and weak cattle. Wolves singled a ranch horse from the remuda and ran it down in relays. Elk and wild horses ate the none-too-abundant range grass. Black-billed magpies, hungry in winter, pecked the eyes of cattle and picked wounds in the sheep's backs or drilled holes in their sides to get at the luscious fatty layer over the kidneys.

Nevadans have been harder pressed than the citizens of most other states to adjust permanent civilization to the blueprints of nature. The social problems of water and freight monopoly, or scorn and exploitation by other states, have been just another set of difficulties. But just as Nevadans have found ways to equalize their state with the other forty-seven, so have they continued an increasingly victorious struggle against an environment " not yet ready for man to enter in." They have been experimental, patient, and determined. Practical men and women on the farms and ranches and Indian reservations, and laboratory scientists at the university have figured out ways to overcome the odds of climate and pestilence. The air-conditioned buildings in the busy towns, the plump white-faced cattle along the unfenced roads, the fat sheep like cotton tufts among the sagebrush, the reclaimed marshes covered with lush alfalfa are evidence of man's triumph. The greatest single victory over the desert is Boulder Dam. Rainless, useless creosote-bush country has become a far-reaching blue lake and a national recreational area. Energy has been seized from a muddy torrent. A dark gorge has been wedged tight with a tremendous block of cement. At the bottom are the dynamo- and control-rooms where congregations of tourists worship the Electrical Energy that runs their civilization. Boulder Dam is to Americans what Chartres Cathedral was to medieval Europeans, what the Temple at Karnak was to ancient Egyptians. The clean functional lines, the colossal beauty, and impersonal mass and strength of the dam itself are as symbolic as real. The dam is a symbol of how physical science, guided by enlightened social principles, can turn desolation into green valleys and thriving cities.

III
HORIZON SEEKERS

Hazard, Misery, Endless Toil

NEVADA has long been a means to an end. Part of its destiny is to be a thoroughfare for Americans eager to get across. The faster the better. Nevada has been a huge wedge separating California and the East, an obstruction to challenge the path-finder, the hardy "mountainman," the emigrant, the team-ster, the stage driver, the railroad builder, and the autoist. It has tested their bravery, endurance, and resourcefulness. The long procession of Western history has made its way along the Spanish Trail, the Humboldt Valley route, and the central route, called Simpson's by the Gentiles and Egan's by the Mormons. From the Armijo party, that opened the trail between southern Utah and Los Angeles, to the latest migrant divorcee entraining after a six weeks' stay, Nevada history has been made, to an extraordinary extent, by groups of tempo-rary residents eager to depart.

The Spanish did not explore Nevada. They skirted it to

the east and south. For them, as for the mapmakers of the seventeenth and eighteenth centuries, it was the "Northern Mystery," either a blank or else a vast area drained by three mythical rivers that ran from Utah into the Pacific. Rio Buenaventura rose in the Rockies, flowed through Lake Salado, and terminated in San Francisco Bay. Rio Timpanagos flowed from Utah to the ocean, as did Rio Los Mongos. Weird tales were told of groveling savages in stone houses, scorching deserts, icy mountains, disappearing rivers, and stupendous canyons. Even in the century of Meriwether Lewis and Zebulon Pike, Nevada remained the last part of the United States area to be explored, the final wilderness to be penetrated by the white man. The first men to cross it, solve its unknowns, and survive its rigors were automatically heroes.

On July 17, 1827, Jedediah Smith, at the Little Lake of Bear River, in what is now Utah, wrote to General William Clark, superintendent of Indian Affairs.

Sir, my situation in this country has enabled me to collect information respecting a section of the country which has hitherto been measurably veiled in obscurity to the citizens of the United States. I allude to the country S. W. of the *Great Salt Lake* west of the Rocky mountains.[1]

In his modest letter he briefly sketched a daring trip across Nevada. In August, 1826, he departed from Salt Lake with seventeen men, went south up the Sevier River and then westward along the rivers now called Virgin, Colorado, and Mojave. His party was attacked by Indians on the Spanish Trail in the Las Vegas area and suffered from thirst, which they allayed by chewing "Cabbage Pear," a hedgehog cactus. They reached San Gabriel Mission, had trouble with the Spanish authorities, and wintered in California. In June, 1827, accompanied by two men, Smith clambered up the canyon

[1] Reprinted by permission of the publishers, The Arthur H. Clark Company from Dale, *Ashley-Smith Explorations and Discovery of Central Route to the Pacific, 1822–1829.*

of the Stanislaus River and, on his second attempt, crossed the Sierras at Sonora Pass. He arrived at the edge of the desert with five horses and a mule carrying hay and provisions. He crossed Nevada by the central route, Utah by Salt Lake Desert,

travelling over a country completely barren and destitute of game. We frequently travelled without water sometimes for two days over sandy deserts, where there was no sign of vegetation and when we found water in some of the rocky hills, we most generally found some Indians who appeared the most miserable of the human race having nothing to subsist on (nor any clothing) except grass seed, grasshoppers, etc. When we arrived at the Salt Lake, we had but one horse and one mule remaining, which were so feeble and poor that they could scarce carry the little camp equipage which I had along; the balance of my horses I was compelled to eat as they gave out.[1]

Smith, a pious New Englander who had caught the exciting challenge of the West while clerking on a Lake Erie freighter, had found nothing in Nevada of value to the trapping firm of Smith, Jackson, and Sublette. But he had made the first trip across the full width of the Great Basin and had given Nevada its first, though inadequate, description.

In the late 1820's Peter Skene Ogden, chief trader for the Hudson's Bay Company in the Snake River country, led a brigade of trappers into the Owyhee and Humboldt valleys. He called the Humboldt the Unknown River and discovered that it did not reach the Pacific. Others called it appropriately after him, Ogden's River. Somehow, too, the name Mary's River got attached to it.

In 1832 a trapping party under Milton Sublette and Nathaniel Wyeth reached Humboldt Wells in northeastern Nevada. Joe Meek, one of the party, shot a Digger Indian who was prowling along the stream. Wyeth asked, " Why did you

[1] *Ibid.*

shoot him? " " To keep him from stealing traps." Wyeth
asked, " Had he stolen any? " " No," replied the hardened
mountaineer, " but he looked as if he was going to! " Wyeth
and Sublette separated, the first going north to the Snake,
the second heading off into terra incognita toward the Owyhee River, where the men, though tough and seasoned frontiersmen, had their troubles with Nevada. Their stock of food
ran low. Hunters found little game (though they were in an
area now a favorite with sportsmen). Beaver were available,
but were judged inedible because they had been eating poisonous wild carrot. The horses lost weight. Water was hard to
find. Men bled mules and made a soup of the blood. They
arbitrarily chose a fellow's mule, quarreled with him when
he protested, and butchered it for meat. They were as much
reduced to extremes as were the later, inexperienced emigrants. According to Meek's untrustworthy but lively account:

I have held my hands in an ant-hill until they were covered with
ants, and then greedily licked them off. I have taken the soles off
my moccasins, crisped them in the fire, and eaten them. In our
extremity, the large black crickets . . . were considered game.
We used to take a kettle of hot water, catch the crickets and
throw them in, and when they stopped kicking, eat them. That
was not what we called *cant tickup ko hanch,* (good meat, my
friend), but it kept us alive.

The next year a detachment of Captain Benjamin Bonneville's exploring expedition made the first round-trip journey
across Nevada by the Humboldt route. This famous party
contained Meek, George Nidever, Zenas Leonard, and about
thirty-five others, and was led by Joseph Walker. Once again
expert frontiersmen found Nevada a challenge to their craft,
to their very existence. " Poor and dejected " Indians, " entirely naked and filthy," stole enough of their traps so that
they had to stop trapping. Traps were worth $15 to $20

apiece and were, of course, irreplaceable. The trappers killed
several Indians without Captain Walker's knowledge. The
party traveled down the Humboldt, which they called the
Barren River. For days they found no sticks large enough for
walking-canes and had to go without fires except when they
found driftwood on the sand bars. They were impressed by
the dryness, sandiness, the salt springs, and the scarcity of
grass. Leonard wrote in his journal, " Everything here seems
to declare that, here man shall not dwell." Lower down on
the Humboldt they came to a place where there was ample
grass. Here eight or nine hundred Piutes approached menac-
ingly to within a hundred and fifty yards. Walker had the
men pile up their baggage as a barricade. Seeing through murderous intentions, he refused to let chiefs come behind to
smoke. The trappers shook their guns threateningly. They
shot at some ducks on a marsh near by. At the noise of gunshots the Indians fell on the ground, and when they arose they
were astonished to see the ducks dead. The Indians put up a
beaverskin as a target and the trappers shot holes in it. The
Indians left for the night, but next day they trailed along and
repeated their requests that the party halt and smoke. A saucy
group of from eighty to a hundred approached. Walker was
worried and excited. His party outnumbered, he determined
to teach the obstreperous savages a good lesson. He felt he
had done his best to avoid a clash. " We must kill a lot of
them, boys. It will never do to let that crowd get into camp."
Thirty-two trappers tied their extra horses to shrubs, mounted
their choice steeds, surrounded the Indian party, and closed
in. They fired a volley and about thirty-five redskins fell,
while the rest ran howling into the grass and tules. The trappers took the bows of the dead and put the wounded out of
their misery. It was a decisive blow, wrote Leonard, " even to
a greater extent than we had intended." Unmolested further,
Walker and his men trapped on down the river, but in the
Carson Sink country they ran out of food. They had reached

the last of their dried buffalo. Their hunters brought in only rabbits. South of Walker River they were reduced to eating dried lake flies. The horses were tired and scrawny. The party skirted the Sierras to south of Owens Valley and crossed them on Walker's Pass, where snow gave them difficulty.

While returning eastward the following spring, in 1834, they had a torturing experience. They tried to cut eastward from Owens Valley instead of going north to the Humboldt River, and as a result they fared worse than Jedediah Smith had seven years before. They got into the arid area between Death Valley and Tonopah. Inside of a few weeks in April they lost sixty-four horses, ten cows, and fifteen dogs. Game was scarce. The only water was stagnant seeps. Some camp-sites lacked any sort of water, fuel, or grass. Dogs gazed pite-ously into their masters' faces, howled, and dropped dead. Men took the hides of dead beasts and made moccasins for footsore animals. There was an altercation between those who would go ahead and those who would turn back to the Sierras. The latter won but could not find tracks to retrace their route. Horses finally led them to a stream. They fol-lowed the eastern escarpment of the Sierras until they found landmarks from the year before. And once again on the Hum-boldt they had to massacre annoying Indians. They killed fourteen and wounded more. Three trappers were wounded. The party followed up the Humboldt until their provisions grew scarce and then crossed to the Lewis River (now called the Snake) and followed it until near Captain Bonneville's camp on Bear River.

In the 1840's the mystery of Nevada rapidly evaporated, even though its ardors did not. Inspired by the California boosters, Marsh and Roubideaux, the John Bartleson party crossed in 1841. The first emigrant party to make the cross-ing, these thirty-two persons hazarded a short cut around the north side of Salt Lake, over Silver Zone Pass, and through the Pequop Mountains. They were following advice given them by men at Fort Hall on the Snake River, which, as John Bidwell remembered it later, was that

we strike out west of Salt Lake . . . being careful not to go too far south, lest we should get into a waterless country without grass. They also said we must be careful not to go too far north, lest we should get into a broken country and steep canyons, and wander about, as trapping parties had been known to do, and become bewildered and perish.

They carried flintlock rifles and dragoon pistols with flint locks. Bidwell had asked old hunters in Missouri what guns to bring and they had replied, " Don't have anything to do with those new-fangled things called caps; if you do you will lose by it. If they once get wet you are gone; but if you lose your flint you can easily pick up a stone that will take its place." But they found no use for their guns. There was little enough game to shoot, and Indians offered no trouble.

At one stop, when the Bartleson party were reducing their loads and even burning a few wagons for fuel, an unusual incident occurred. A Shoshone sage appeared and said the Great Spirit had sent him thither from the mountains to find a strange people who would give him many things. They gave him a pair of pantaloons. Immediately he turned toward the sun and commenced an eloquent harangue fully a half hour long. As he was perfectly naked, they showed him how to wear pants. They gave him article after article, and following each presentation he turned toward the sun and gave thanks in a lengthy speech. As more things were given him his talks grew shorter, but he gave some sort of a prayer for each gift. The emigrants called him the Persian.

The party made from eighteen to twenty miles a day down the Humboldt. " The principal growth, on plain and hill alike," John Bidwell recalled, " was the interminable sage-brush, and often it was difficult, for miles at a time, to break a road through it, and sometimes a lightly laden wagon would be overturned." Bartleson, who had turned out to be an inadequate leader, ran away ahead of the party, taking with him seven men and some oxen. By the time they reached Carson Lake they were happy to eat fish and pine nuts given them by friendly Piutes. A portly man before he left Missouri, Bartleson was already a lank skeleton in bulging clothes. He now fell sick, as from cholera morbus. " Boys," he swore, " if ever I get back to Missouri I will never leave that country. I would gladly eat out of the troughs with my dogs."

In 1844 and 1845 John C. Frémont made the first official explorations of Nevada while spying on California for such expansionists as his father-in-law, Senator Thomas Benton. His party of twenty-five men included such noted veterans of the Rocky Mountain fur brigades as Thomas (" Broken Hand ") Fitzpatrick and Christopher (" Kit ") Carson. On New Year's Day, 1844, a few days after leaving Klamath Lake, Oregon, he was on the edge of Black Rock Desert. In the distance were the vapor plumes of hot springs. His party made its way down a creek, impedimented by ice, snow, and salty soil, amid formidable burnt scenery that looked like monumental heaps of coal and cinders. Mules floundered as they pulled a twelve-pound howitzer of a kind invented by the French for mountain wars in Algeria. Two days later the expedition found itself in a fog so dense that one could not see beyond a hundred yards. Men who went after horses got lost. A man named Taplin climbed a mountain and was surprised to find himself in brilliant sunshine. Frémont admitted in his report, " We were evidently on the verge of the desert which had been reported to us; and the appearance of the country was so forbidding that I was afraid to enter it." He reconnoitered southward, walking into the Granite Creek Desert, looking in vain for Mary's Lake or, better, Rio Buenaventura, alongside which he expected to have an easy trip to San Francisco. Together with Carson he did unexpectedly discover a deep green-blue lake, where he saw herds of mountain sheep, flocks of ducks, and trout as large as the salmon of the Columbia River. After the entire exploring party came up, Piutes gave them fish and there was a paunch-filling feast. From one point on the shore, an island in the lake " presented a pretty exact outline of the great Pyramid of Cheops," which suggested to Frémont a name for the lake. The party went up the Truckee River and crossed to the Carson River, arriving there on January 18. Kit Carson kept hunting for " beaver sign." He held that if it could be found it would be proof of a major stream running into the Pacific. Always in the distance were the smoke signals of Indian watchers. Frémont, Kit Carson, and Fitzpatrick explored the lower Carson River, where they ran into a phenomenon that baffled them. They could not tell for sure which way the water was running. (The reason was that in preirrigation days Carson and Humboldt sinks often filled and joined. The first to overflow changed the direction of the water on the lower reaches of the other.)

Even this splendidly equipped government expedition had troubles. The men ran out of horseshoe nails and then out of the iron substitutes in their possession. The feet of their mounts were torn. The Buenaventura eluded discovery. Ever energetic and resourceful, Frémont determined on a daring exploit. He would take his party across the Sierras in midwinter. He had no maps, no precedent to follow, no reliable information of any sort. Washoe Indians who gave him pine nuts attempted to discourage him by sign language: the snow was too deep. But even when he saw the icy Sierras from Antelope Valley, Nevada, he refused to give up his foolhardy plan. And by sheer pluck and endurance he did get his entire expedition over Carson Pass to the warm California valleys. Only the howitzer — no luggage to carry over ten-foot snow — remained on the Nevada slope.

In April Frémont had recrossed the Sierras from the lower
San Joaquin Valley and was traversing the Mojave Desert
and southern Nevada. His route, he found, was the roughest
and rockiest of all those he had followed on his Western
trips. The "foot evil" destroyed many mules and horses.
Grass was scanty, even at the watering places along the Spanish Trail. Luckily, the annual trading caravan had not yet
come westward from Santa Fe. Indian visitors carried extra
long bows and water in gourds strengthened in meshes of
cord. April 29 at Agua de Hernandez the explorers saw omi-
nous evidence of Indian hostility. Outside willow shelters
near a spring lay the bodies of two Mexicans who had come
ahead of the caravan and camped. Hernandez was pierced
with arrows. His hands and legs had been cut off. Santiago
Giacome, who had been large and strong, was likewise full
of arrows. Because of the oppressive heat and glare, the expedition traveled during the "warm, moonshiny" nights.
Horses with sore feet were continually falling back. Fuentes,
a Mexican who had escaped the massacre at the spring, cut the
tails and manes from dead horses in order later to make them
into saddle girths. Springs contained bitter water, and an
April gale flung sand in their faces, but Frémont continued
equably to exercise his natural gift as an observer of topography, geology, and botany.

The country had now assumed the character of an elevated and
mountainous desert; its general features being black, rocky ridges,
bald, and destitute of timber, with sandy basins between. Where
the sides of these ridges are washed by gullies, the plains below
are strewed with beds of large pebbles or rolled stones, destructive
to our soft-footed animals, accustomed to the grassy plains of the
Sacramento valley. . . . But, throughout this nakedness of sand
and gravel, were many beautiful plants and flowering shrubs,
which occurred in many new species, and with greater variety
than we had been accustomed to see in the most luxuriant prairie
countries; this was a peculiarity of this desert. Even where no

grass would take root, the naked sand would bloom with some rich and rare flower, which found its appropriate home in the arid and barren spot.

As the expedition approached Las Vegas it had to make long dry *journadas*, days' journeys on which a stop would be disastrous. On May 3 the grass and vigorous springs at Las Vegas (the meadows) were a welcome relief. Next day the men and beasts endured the fifty-five mile journada to the Muddy River. Frémont recorded their "intolerable thirst while journeying over the hot yellow sands of this elevated country, where the heated air seems to be entirely deprived of moisture." The men chewed sour dock to moisten their mouths and ate the bisnaga, a cactus with juicy pulp, slightly acid. They camped all day May 5 on the Muddy. Indians crowded around the camp, lurked in the river bottom below, and harangued in Ute from a bluff near by. The explorers kept their guns in their hands all day and enclosed the horses. The natives held two or three arrows in each hand, ready for use; they had partially drawn out the thirty or forty arrows in their quivers. The arrows were barbed with clear, hard opal and when shot from the powerful long bows were "almost as effective as a gunshot." To the apprehensive Frémont the Indians had "an expression of countenance resembling that in a beast of prey; and all their actions are those of wild animals. Joined to the restless motion of the eye, there is a want of mind — an absence of thought — and an action wholly by impulse, strongly expressed . . ."

A man who appeared to be a chief, with two or three others, forced himself into camp, bringing with him his arms, in spite of my orders to the contrary. When shown our weapons, he bored his ear with his fingers, and said he could not hear. "Why," said he, "there are none of you." Counting the people around the camp, and including in the number a mule which was being shod, he made out 22. "So many," said he, showing the number, "and we — we are a great many;" and he pointed to the hills and mountains round about. " If you have your arms," said he, twanging his bow, " we have these." I had some difficulty in re- straining the people, especially Carson, who felt an insult of this kind as much as if it had been given by a more responsible being. "Don't say that, old man," said he; " don't say that — your life's in danger," — speaking in good English; and probably the old man was nearer his end than he will be before he meets it.

The expedition moved on east, up the " desolate and revolt- ing " valley of the Virgin River, a region in which Indians were waiting to pilfer from Santa Fe wagons. Frémont placed scouts on the flanks ahead, armed men in front and rear di- visions, and the animals, baggage, and horned cattle in the middle. The procession was a quarter of a mile long. Every- one took turns guarding at night, frequently one-third of the party at once. One rest day an able man named Tabeau, with- out informing his superiors, rode back to the last camp in search of a lame mule. Late in the afternoon Frémont saw smoke rise suddenly from a cottonwood grove below camp — an Indian sign warning distant tribesmen to be alert because a blow had been struck. Carson and several other well- mounted men set out and searched the old camp and the banks of the Virgin. They found the mule, shot dead and ready for butchering, and the blood of Tabeau, spattered on the ground, but " no vestige of what had belonged to him could be found, except a fragment of his horse equipment. Horse, gun, clothes — all became the prey of these Arabs of the New World."

Returned safe from this trip, Frémont wrote his *Exploring Expedition to the Rocky Mountains, Oregon, and California.* Published in 1845, it was one of the few Congressional docu- ments to be reprinted many times in many editions and to become a popular classic. In its descriptive, dramatic pages Frémont discussed the first official proof that Rio Buenaven- tura was a legend. He had flanked the Sierras from Oregon to southern California and found only small rivers that ran east. Giving Nevada its first analytical description, he commented on the physical nature of the Great Basin, its lack of appreciable drainage into the Snake and the Colorado, the need for further investigation, and the agricultural possibilities.

In that branch of agriculture which implies the cultivation of grains and staple crops, it would be inferior to the Atlantic States, though many parts are superior for wheat; while in the rearing of flocks and herds it would claim a high place. Its grazing capabilities are great; and even in the indigenous grass now there, an element of individual and national wealth may be found.

In the fall of 1845 Frémont was at the south end of Salt Lake on another Far Western expedition. He made the first trip westward across Great Salt Lake Desert, a feat that Utes had claimed was impossible. His scouts, including Carson, Walker, and several Delaware Indians "making the grand tour," easily found streams, natural hay, and passes that led to the upper Humboldt River. He might well have spent the winter in exploring central Nevada, but his real purpose was to make a military reconnaissance in California and help the American settlers if hostilities broke out with the Mexican authorities. But the better to explore in stride, he split his party. He put the larger part under the command of Edward Kern and sent it exploring down the Humboldt, with orders to cross to the Carson and head on south to a rendezvous at Walker Lake. With ten picked men he himself dropped south past Franklin Lake, and then explored southwest past the alkali deserts of northern Nye County, arriving at Walker Lake a few days ahead of the Kern party, during invigorating, subfreezing November weather. The trip was unexciting, but Frémont had been surprised to find, as he wrote his wife, "Instead of a barren country, the mountains were covered with grasses of the best quality, wooded with several varieties of trees, and containing more deer and mountain sheep than we had seen in any previous part of our voyage."

In 1846 James Clyman, veteran Rocky Mountain trapper who had gone to Oregon by way of Idaho, led a party back to the States via the Humboldt River route. In the group of eighteen men, three women, and three children were James Hudspeth, later sponsor of a cutoff, and Lansford Hastings, who dreamed of setting up an empire in California. Once east of the Rockies, Hastings sought to encourage emigration westward by loudly advertising a cutoff south of Salt Lake (Frémont's salt desert route of 1845). But his only dream of Nevada was a nightmare. Clyman's journal recorded what there was to see: naked savages making rope of rabbit hides and fishing tackle of weed lint; colored basalt mountains, rough slag, chalk beds, clouds of dust that made the mules sneeze and cough, "volcanic mud salt and soda," and springs that ran only twenty feet before sinking. On Carson Desert Clyman's water spaniel, Lucky, leaped impetuously into a spring to cool off and drink. The water was boiling hot and killed him. May 16 was a representative day. The party was following the Humboldt east of the present town of Winnemucca. "The whole of to day has [been] verry crooked but the earth has been so dry that we can not ventur cut off." Nevada was the "most Steril, Barren countrys I ever traversed." It had the "most thirsty appearance of any place I ever witnessed."

This was the year of the successful William H. Russell party, joined by Edwin Bryant, that went through Silver Zone Pass and the Humboldt Valley, and of the ill-starred Donner party of ninety persons, misdirected and delayed by the bumptious Hastings both in the Wasatch Mountains and on the Salt Lake Desert. No worse advertisement for Nevada ever passed from one man to another than the classic tale of the Donners' misfortunes in Nevada, which led to their equally classic calamity in the California Sierras. They were doomed from the first, and their troubles had a terrible, dramatic concentration. Ignorant of the route and of the challenges of the desert, they wasted vital energy and irreplaceable time as they wound blindly among Nevada ranges. Homicide and death plagued them. At Gravelly Ford on the Humboldt two good friends quarreled. One was James F. Reed, highly regarded, well-to-do head of a family. The other was John Snyder, a handsome young athlete who put the hindgate of his wagon on the ground at night and danced clogs, jogs, and the pigeon wing. The two men exchanged sharp words while getting their teams up a steep, sandy hill. Snyder struck Reed on the head with the butt end of his heavy whipstock and repeated the blow until blood ran over Reed's face and eyes. Mrs. Reed ran in to stop the scuffle. Reed's hunting knife jabbed into Snyder's left breast. Snyder staggered and died in fifteen minutes. Angry migrants propped up a wagon tongue with an ox yoke and proposed to hang Reed. Others proposed banishment and won. Reed started out walking, empty handed, except for a gun and ammunition that his daughter Virginia rode out and gave to him. Along the lower Humboldt, as oxen died or were stolen and killed by Piutes, many persons had to walk. Old Hardcoop, a Belgian cutler, walked until he gave out, and was left behind to die. On the desert near the Truckee River, a rich German named Wolfinger, who was driving at the rear of the train, failed to catch up when camp was made for the night. A member of the party murdered him and took his money. At an encampment where Reno now stands, William Pike and a friend were cleaning or loading a pepperbox pistol. As one was handing it to the other, it went off accidentally and killed Pike, who died in twenty minutes. The wooded Sierras, generally the delight of migrants, brought the Donners only dismay and terror — inundating snow, starvation, mental aberration, even cannibalism. Only forty-eight of the original ninety survived to reach the balmy, oak-shaded Sacramento Valley.

By the time the spring sun of 1847 had melted snow from the bones of Donner party members, the seekers of Nevada horizons had learned much that the previous American frontiers had not prepared them for. Water lore was crucially important in a land where in summer a man needed seven quarts of water a day and a pack animal needed twenty gallons. In Nevada mountains a man went uphill from water sign, not downhill, as in Missouri or Wisconsin. A dry flat looked like a cool lake when heat waves created a mirage. In winter the best water was boiled snow. Springs, especially in the southern part of Nevada, were so few that a water hole became "the polar star of the desert traveler towards which he turns his face with inflexible determination." At that, it might be hot and require cooling, or be so impregnated with soda, lime, and borax that it gave fearful cramps and dosed like epsom salts. If a well were to be dug, palatable water would more likely be found under a completely dry lake (or stream bed) than under a damp, muddy one. Where a spring, like Desert Wells at the southern end of Smoky Valley, was a pool of bluish muddy slime overlain with a slight film of stagnant water, a new pit dug near by would partially alleviate the sufferings of men and animals. Prolonged thirst raised urgent medical problems. Dying of thirst, observers claimed, involved three stages, normal thirst, functional derangement, and structural degeneration. The victim became clamorous and could be relieved by water and fruit acids; then he got cotton mouth, and his only salvation was quarts of water in very small sips over a long period of time; next was the shriveled-tongue phase, complicated by high fever and irregular heartbeat, requiring the same water treatment and medicine; finally came the "blood sweat" or "living death," with unclear mental state, no pain, and certain death. As for animals, mules and donkeys had more endurance than horses. An utterly exhausted horse, in the condition known as *resté*, took a long time to recover and had to be left on the trail. A fatigued mule, given water and grass, recovered overnight. Driven by thirst, a mule would chew mud.

Indians could give all-important directions and information, and one needed all the sign talk and aboriginal vocabu-
lary he could acquire. Much sometimes depended upon being
able to speak or understand Piute:

> pah-punip   spring of water
> hy-ko   white man
> ossowam   blanket
> za-me-ti-moeb   bread
> tah-ho   today

or Washoe:

> go-ding-ah?   Who is that?
> ac-tag-go   no
> ah-leah   today
> bah-hah-ging   small

or Ute:

> neur-ne-marang!   Give it to me!
> ah-ra-wa-co-do-jin?   Where is it?
> peki pah-gur-nap pee-pee-che.   By and by rain comes.
> huk-ah-bah ko-mush pah-kare-re?   Where is the next water?

UNFORTUNATELY, the golden news from California started
an impetuous mass migration before the desert lore of the
pathfinders had become general knowledge. Needless suffering and death resulted, but Nevada could no more stop the
stampede than it could stop the wheels of destiny.

The rush of '49 was a crucial episode in American history,
one of the great mid-century events that changed the map
and the civilization of the country. To participants it was an
experience to record, to recall. Hundreds of men and women
kept diaries and journals or later penned reminiscences. As
a result the crossing to California is the most documented
mass movement in history. The migrations of ancient Jews,
of stout Vikings and bellicose jarls, of Napoleonic armies, and

of Irish peasants after the potato famine may have affected world history more, but none is so intimately and multitudinously set forth for all mankind to read. And in the eyes of some people, none is more important. Bayard Taylor put the positive case long ago for the single year 1849:

The story of thirty thousand souls accomplishing a journey of more than two thousand miles through a savage and but partially explored wilderness, crossing on their way two mountain chains equal to the Alps in height and asperity, besides broad tracts of burning desert, and plains of nearly equal desolation, where a few patches of stunted shrubs and springs of brackish water were their only stay, has in it so much of heroism, of daring and sublime endurance, that we may vainly question the records of any age for its equal.

The gold seekers were a cross section of prosperous and hard up, town reared and farm reared, educated and illiterate, competent and shiftless alike. Preachers, lawyers, and schoolmasters were among them, and future governors, senators, state supreme court judges, authors, and college professors; and also among them, in great numbers, was the poor-white type, the " Pike." He was from Missouri or anywhere in the Mississippi Valley from northern Texas to southern Illinois. He was an abstract of Wolverine, Sucker, Hoosier, Buckeye, and Jayhawker. Gaunt, sallow, lanky, scant bearded, he wore soiled homespun clothes that had once been butternut dyed. His slouched hat generally had a hole in the top. He wore large shoes and no socks. He was the backwoods version of the Yankee — ingenious, droll, whittling, spitting, and both loquacious and laconic. One observer said he was the " Anglo-Saxon relapsed into barbarism." He was potentially either a poet or a ruffian.

All these Americans found Nevada the greatest obstacle in their way. From the City of Rocks on the Idaho line to Ragtown on Carson River, Nevada was a crescendo of misfortune. The summer of '49 was unusually hot and dry, but the crossing was just as hard for California-bound travelers throughout the fifties.

At City of Rocks, amid colored buttes and white lime and quartz hills, men and beasts were already breaking under the strain of the overland journey. Men who had been model citizens in Illinois and Ohio lost their tempers, cheated friends, broke contracts, and ended arguments with bloody knives. In order to hasten on, some individuals unloaded and abandoned their wagons and piled necessities on animals. A few persons, half crazed by misfortune, started walking back to the States. Cattle were nervous and wild, many cows were unmilkable, horses and oxen were hollow-bodied and bony. A day farther on, at Thousand Springs Creek, Nevada began auspiciously with broad meadows and " bottomless " wells of sweet water. This was a fine resting spot for man and beast. Here also were enjoyable curiosities, hot springs that sent up tall clouds of steam with the odor of a tan vat, and started a wide, foaming stream. Once under way again, the wagon trains ascended Thousand Springs Creek to the summit that led to Bishop's Creek. From a narrow trail on the edge of a precipice, the gold seekers looked west to see two strips of willows that lined the Humboldt River as it meandered through a vast desolation.

At Wells the argonauts started their long trek alongside the Humboldt, which was welcome for its water, unwelcome for its everlasting zigzags. The route went in straight lines from point to point, crossing to crossing, so that the trip was a jointed series of fifteen- to twenty-mile deserts. One hour the wagons sank hub-deep in loose sand; next hour they mired up to the wagon beds in swampy muck. The Humboldt Valley was hundreds of miles of torture, and there was no mood for enjoying its scenery. As Alonzo Delano wrote of the Applegate cutoff through Black Rock Desert: " Descending a couple of miles through a defile, we passed the most beautiful hills of colored earth I ever saw, with the shades of pink, white, yellow and green brightly blended. Volcanic mountains were around us, and under ordinary circumstances we could have enjoyed the strange and peculiar scenery." The majority opinion was as hot as the shimmery air above the toiling caravans. Nevada was the Creator's dumping ground. The devil had scraped a little together. A Pike said:

Rocks an' mountains an' sand; an' sand, an' rocks an' mountains — miles on miles of it. Sometimes the water was white as soapsuds with alkali, an' sometimes as red as brick-dust, not one time in five sweet an' clean. . . . I've drove all day 'thout seein' a spear o' green, or a speck of any thing but sand. . . . I reckon God knows what he made that country for — he hain't told any body, though.

Water was an ever-present problem. From Humboldt Wells on, drinkable pools were semistagnant and tarnished by foundered oxen that lay dead in them. The river shrank as it ran and became more heavily laden with carbonates. People put citric acid or vinegar in vessels of water, hoping to counteract the alkalies, but they still suffered from diarrhea and diuresis, nausea and vomiting. Cream of tartar made water palatable. A cure for alkalied cattle was a plug of tobacco between two slices of bacon. This cured cattle or killed them. Another remedy was to feed them acid and bleed them. It was unsafe to water animals in motionless water. Cattle had to be whipped at the crossings to keep them from drinking too much. Horses fell to the ground and died, but exhausted oxen frequently cooled off at night and wandered away to become food for Indians. So many beasts lay dead of poor water and overwork that agile foot travelers could almost have walked across Nevada on corpses without touching the ground. One emigrant counted fifteen hundred dead animals in sixty miles.

Fodder was scarce. Oxen and horses nibbled at what willows and tules were left after a few thousand emigrants had cut off branches for fuel. Grass and edible sedges grew in swamps and marshes along the river, but cattle mired and floundered in the bluish mud. Men stood in nauseating water up to their waists and cut hay with knives, while a comrade ferried bundles ashore in a calked wagon box.

Human food was at a premium. Inadequate stocks of goods from Council Bluffs and St. Joseph gave out. At first, men caught a few black-spotted trout in the Humboldt, shot some ducks and Canadian geese, and bagged a few antelope, rabbits, and sage hens, but by the time twenty thousand persons had passed by, no game was left. Families dug up the wild-parsnip roots, not knowing they were poisonous when raw. As antidotes individuals tried bacon grease, whisky, and gunpowder. Hungry folk killed sick or weak oxen and jerked the meat. The carcasses contained no fat. The marrow was liquid and bloody. Some oxen were so poor that two men could pack all the flesh in two knapsacks. Children searched among the dreary charred sagebrush of campsites for such scraps as delicious morsels of fatty bacon rinds. When ravenous enough, a man would devour a steak raw as he tramped along. If desperate, men cut the hams from dead and decomposing oxen along the road and culled meat from decaying horses. Self-preservation was stronger than reason or fastidiousness.

Men and women begged passers-by to sell them surpluses of anything, but few could spare a hatful of potatoes and onions for $2, twenty-five pounds of flour for $12.50, or a little hard bread for 50 cents. One man was herding two dozen sturdy oxen west from Salt Lake City. Men in one party offered him $200 for an ox and he refused. Next day a score of determined men with guns marched into his herd, selected the fattest ox, butchered it, and divided it up. The owner demanded $100, but they told him he had lost his chance for any recompense.

The one abundant commodity was hardship. The dust irritated eyes and noses and blistered lips. It gave the horses glanders unless their nostrils were treated with alum. Children cried for water and their helpless mothers walked ahead of them to keep out of earshot. Sick women and children jogged on the wagon beds, their throats parched and their heads throbbing. They dreamed of the mossy wells and fragrant pantries they had left behind. Tense, they listened for the steps of the exhausted oxen, dreading to hear them falter and stop. Walkers found that hiking through soft sand was like treading water. Their legs wore out and their feet impeded movement like leaden weights. People who picked up epidemic erysipelas suffered from fever and inflamed skin. Others caught the dreaded Asiatic cholera. They had diarrhea and cramps, they vomited and turned blue, and their faces looked pinched. As soon as thirteen hours after taking sick, they collapsed and were thrust into hastily dug graves. Their markers were wagon chains or pieces sawed from the tailboards.

For hours at a time the only sound was the gritty turning of wheels, the clink of traces and neckyoke, the clump of shod feet, and the squeak of brakes. " Deadhead " animals dropped back and let their mates pull. This let the doubletrees scrape the wheel and made the other animal and the driver nervous. These were tiresome sounds on the braided ribbons of road through the sagebrush in endless bowls of dull earth. They combined with other circumstances to wear down nerves. Frantic adults threatened suicide. There were quarrels between emigrant parties, fellow travelers, and partners. Men cut each other with " California toothpicks " (bowie knives). Mosquitoes swarmed in the hot evenings. At the rocky passes and grades on the benchland straightaways and at the murky fords, there were traffic jams, cursing, and fighting. Wagons upset. Wagon bows broke. During an argument, one emigrant hit another over the head with a wagon wrench and killed him. A quick trial followed. A wagon tongue was elevated to make a gallows pole and the killer was forthwith hanged. Lorenzo Sawyer came on a dead man who had been abandoned under a tarpaulin between two stakes. Beside him were a cup of water and a piece of lard bread. A card announced: " Please give this man a cup of water and bread if he needs it. He was not able to travel, and wanted to be left."

Indians shot arrows into oxen and drove off stock. In the daytime they traded good mounts for ailing ones; then they sneaked in at night and drove off the good ones. An emigrant followed a stolen horse and came on it drying as strips of jerky, hung on a willow tree. A few Humboldt travelers were shot through the body and scalped. One died slowly. His heels dug holes a foot deep and his fingers scratched up dirt as far as his arms could reach all around. There were massacres on the Applegate Trail from Winnemucca west. Circling spots in the sky, dark birds sweeping with majestic curves, dipping and tilting without the quiver of a wing, signified a burned wagon, warped irons, charred ends of boards and spokes, and a dog howling over what was once a man.

For all the disasters that encouraged violence and selfishness, there were people who did good deeds. Wives stuck by husbands who had bungled preparations for the trip. Ministers held services that comforted, and doctors worked themselves haggard as they rode back and forth along the line and aided the sick. Families delayed their journey to stop and help a screaming mother through childbirth brought on prematurely by the stench of rotting animals and bouncing of the wagon on rocks and sagebrush stumps. Young men scouted for food for bereaved widows or drove the teams west for them. Friends asked forgiveness after violent disagreements and proposed a congenial session with a " California prayer book " (deck of cards). Jokers and minstrels strove to raise the spirits of the depressed. " Oh I wish I was single again! " " Frog went a-courtin' he did ride." The many-versed " Sweet Betsy " helped pilgrims to the Golden State take hard-

ship more easily. The stanzas counteracted furnace heat, pow-
dery dust, and stinking sloughs.

> Oh don't you remember sweet Betsy from Pike,
> Who crossed the wide mountains with her lover Ike?
> With two head of cattle, a large yaller dog,
> A grand Shanghai rooster and one spotted hog.
>
> *   *   *   *
>
> They passed through Salt Lake to inquire the way;
> Old Brigham declared that sweet Betsy should stay.
> But Betsy got scared and ran off like a deer,
> Leaving old Brigham pawing the ground like a steer.
>
> *   *   *   *
>
> The wagon tipped over with a terrible crash
> And out on the ground there spilled all sorts of trash.
> Two little didies all done up with care
> Looked highly suspicious — but all on the square.
>
> *   *   *   *
>
> The cattle ran off and the grand Shanghai died,
> The last piece of bacon that morning was fried,
> Ike looked discons'late, sweet Betsy looked mad,
> The dog drooped his tail and looked wondrously sad.

At the lower end of the Humboldt, near the present town
of Lovelock, were the Big Meadows, acres and acres of wild
rye and blue-joint grass. The tired migrants camped for several days. They cooked their careful doles of food over sagebrush fires, gathered rye grass, cured it quickly under the
withering sun, and loaded it on the wagons. They stuffed it
in the mattress ticks and filled the wagon bed until the vehicle
was piled high with bundles of grass. They twisted the hay
into strands to be tied over the backs of the beasts. The men
tested all the harness, soaked the wheels, and checked all the
wagon parts, especially the tongues, axles, brakes, and hounds.
The women cared for the sick and helped with the haying.

A few adults relaxed by reading. Many caught up with lost sleep. All prayed for divine aid, for the last and worst ordeal remained, the Forty-Mile Desert, over portions of the sinks of the Humboldt and Carson. Everything that could be abandoned to lighten the load was dumped — walnut tables, turning lathes, oak chests, carpenter's tools, a six-volume set of Rollin's *Ancient History*.

Many parties left the Big Meadows at noon in order to cross the Carson Desert at night. The bed of Humboldt Lake was smooth and dry, but then came miles of soft sand in which the oxen stumbled. At first there were a few bodies of cattle lying on both sides of the trail, then a few wagons. Every mile the evidence of panic increased. Dead animals lay in front of wagons. Personal belongings were scattered all over the ground, but no life remained. Wagons were stuck and newcomers had to turn out around them. Some wagons were overturned, some burned, blocking the road. A man counted over a thousand abandoned wagons in forty-two miles. Littered about were possessions carried two thousand miles only to be dropped. Mill saws, life preservers, gunlocks, wagon covers, tents, feather beds, chisels, crowbars, log chains, cast-iron stoves. The sands were covered by ransacked trunks, empty casks, cardboard boxes, and wagon parts. Books strewed the wastelands — *Memoirs of Aaron Burr*, Wayland's *Moral Science*, Chitty's *On Contracts*, Cooper's *Prairie*, Milton's *Paradise Lost*, Byron's *Sardanapalus*, Shakespeare's *Tragedies*, *The Laws of Iowa*. Books more likely to be carried on to California included Horn's *Guide Book to Emigrants*, Frémont's *Narrative*, schoolbooks, *Book of Common Prayer*, and *Baptist Hymn Book*. The Carson Desert was like the rear of a routed army. It was a dry-land Sargasso Sea, a graveyard of overland schooners. Part of a nation was in flight, leaving a junkyard of maladjusted civilization. Forty-Mile was Nevada's first ghost town.

There was small respite at Desert Wells, where men dipped

bad water from shallow holes. Some emigrants unhitched their teams and urged them on toward the Carson River, planning to return later for their wagons. Desperately thirsty men and women begged for drinking water. They paid $15 for a glassful, $100 for a pint. People went insane and were tied down in the wagons. The oxen moaned and staggered, and anxious watchers saw their heads droop lower and lower. On and on the wagons rolled, until finally the great moment came when the oxen picked up their heads, sniffed, and quickened their movements. Unhitched teams strained forward, walking so fast a man could hardly keep up with them. Trees came in sight and the animals stampeded. Drivers tugged on reins and lead ropes. Dangerously speedy traffic rushed from the top of the hillbank down to the edge of water.

The Carson River was tea colored from alkali but drinkable and cool, and above it were " trees — real trees, green trees, shade-giving trees. We instantly became . . . initiated into the tree-worshipping sect." It was wonderful . . . " cold sparkling waters meandering between banks of rich verdure and beneath the wide spreading arms of the Umbragious Cotton Wood of the Desert — an oasis of Eminent Coolness." Animals plunged in and their masters had to jump in with them and beat them out on the banks before they swallowed too much while heated and frenzied. Emigrants spread up and down the river. They blissfully enjoyed the luxury of lying down under something larger than a sagebrush. They took baths and threw their sweaty, fouled, tattered old clothes on the bank. Fabrics of every hue and color gave the place the name of Ragtown.

After a rest the emigrant parties, now almost in sight of California, took one of the several passes over the Sierras. Many crossed over to the Truckee River, followed it up to the abundant grass of Truckee Meadows, where Reno now stands, and went over Donner Pass toward Auburn. Other multitudes followed up the Carson River to Mormon Station

(Genoa), where they could purchase the greatest luxury of all, a pint of fresh milk. From there they crossed to Placerville or struck southwest over passes that took them toward Sonora, Queen of the Southern Mines. As they went along the Nevada base of the Sierras, the travelers never tired of drinking the ice-cold water of the tumbling creeks. This was a different Nevada. Truckee Valley, Washoe Valley, Eagle Valley, Carson Valley, Diamond Valley were inexpressibly beautiful. There were meadows of thick deep clover and blue-joint grass, novel hot springs, and forests of " pitch " pines eight feet in diameter. There were cool, snowy, monumental peaks that held up a clear blue sky. It was all a paradise finale to the desert and an introduction to California, the Land of Promise.

Evolution of a Thoroughfare

THE RAPID rise of California in population, wealth, and prestige after 1849 made it important to the Pacific Coast and the nation that regular communication be established. In the fifties the government gave out mail contracts to various staging firms, which tried several routes and finally settled on the central. For several winters a Norwegian named Thompson carried mail between Placerville and Carson Valley. He fashioned rude skis. Using a stick for braking uphill and supporting downhill, coasting at a mile a minute, leaping ten-foot precipices, he successfully crossed through the blizzards of the snow-blocked Sierras with a heavy pack on his shoulders.

In 1860 the famous but unprofitable Pony Express was organized. This spectacular demonstration of speed and hardihood lasted only eighteen months and lost its backers one and a half million dollars, but it did an unprecedented thing: it took a letter from St. Joseph, Missouri, to San Francisco,

1,950 miles, in ten days. The operating firm, Russell, Majors, and Waddell, had five hundred tough, fleet horses, which were distributed at relay stations from sixty-five to a hundred miles apart. The horses were expected to go twenty miles an hour and were, accordingly, well fed and cared for. Riders wore thin, close-fitting clothes, light shoes, and sat on a pancake saddle with a tiny blanket. They carried ten pounds of mail, which cost senders five dollars in gold per each half ounce — five dollars for a letter written on feather-light thin paper. They changed horses and the flat mail-pockets in two minutes, aided by two hostlers. Every third station, riders changed. For exciting but dangerous work, riders received $120 a month.

No airplane record nowadays is more impressive than the Pony Express was then. Riders carried the news of Lincoln's election from St. Joseph to Denver (665 miles) in two days twenty-one hours. In a famous Nevada relay of this same news packet, " Pony " Bob Haslam, his revolver ready, rode the 120 miles from Smith's Creek to Fort Churchill in eight hours and ten minutes. The Piute War was beginning, and the route ran through a country hostile with Indians.

People who were so lucky as to see the Express in action recalled the memory with a thrill. A stagecoach party, including Adolph Sutro, was about to descend Myer's Grade toward Lake Tahoe during an April storm. Flakes of snow and pellets of hail blew into their faces, stinging and blinding. Trees swung to and fro. Wind howled and broke off branches. " On the very summit," wrote Sutro later, " we met a lonely rider dashing along at a tremendous rate. We wondered what could possibly induce him to go on through that gale . . . It was the Pony Express! " When Twain was heading west on the overland stage, a rider was sighted. " Here he comes! " A black speck rushed eastward toward the stage, became a horse and rider, burst past with a hail, and swung away like a scudding cloud.

The overland telegraph contributed to the quick demise of the Pony Express. In four months during 1861 the California State Telegraph Company ran a line from Fort Churchill to Salt Lake City, a distance of 570 miles. It placed twenty-five to thirty poles every mile, fully a third of them hauled from the Sierras. Immediately the Texas woodpecker got to work riddling this miraculous feast of dead timber. The construction gangs battled against alkali, soft shifting sand, solid rock, and lack of drinking water and animal feed. In October a message went clear through from Frisco to St. Joe. Congratulations followed from every state in the Union and every civilized nation in the world. Many a Westerner said, " It is the great achievement of the nineteenth century."

Every thirty to fifty miles there was an office or repair station. Rains and floods loosened the poles. Brush fires burned them down. Lightning knocked them down and " burned " the instruments. In marshes and sinks of mushy alkali, fallen wires shorted. In the Sierras the menaces to unbroken communication were multiplied by falling timbers, avalanches, sleet, washouts in spring, forest fires in summer. In a severe storm there might be as many as thirty breaks in a hundred miles. When wires could not be connected, men on horseback carried dispatches from the two last stations on either side of the gap. A San Franciscan wired a friend in Virginia City and had his response in six hours. " How is this? Allowing full time each way for transmission, delivery, and probable delay, I should have had this answer at least four hours ago! " He did not know that the message passed through a dozen breaks, was carried over several gaps by mounted men, through floods and blinding snowstorms.

In the long-lived freighting business the key figures were the brawny, bearded teamsters. Their faces smeared with dust and dirt, their mouths full of original verbal inflections and climaxes, their hands wielding the galling lash of the bullwhip, they were empire builders in a thousand districts that were not

reached even by the narrow-gauge mining railroads. They
drove tough teams of from six to twenty mules. Commonly
the team was sixteen mules, which pulled three lumbering
wagons hitched together. The wagons, which were six or
seven feet deep, were covered with canvas to keep dust and
rain off the merchandise. Teamsters had two methods of guid-
ing their mules. One was the blacksnake whip. The whip
handle was three feet long; attached to it were twenty feet
of braided rawhide lash. The slightest move of the handle or
crack of the whip started, turned, or stopped the team. The
other method was the jerkline. Drivers rode the near (left)
animal of the last team and guided the animals ahead with a
line that passed through the rings in their hames and ended
in the bit-ring of the leader.

There was a solid stream of wagons crossing the Sierras.
Strings of small bells hung on metal arches over the fur collar
of the harness. The jingle warned travelers around the bend
that big wagons were coming. From Sacramento to Austin,
from Austin to Salt Lake City, from Las Vegas to Tonopah,
mule teams pulled and jerked, groaned, fell back, lunged forward, tumbled down, slipped on rock and ice, sweated and
steamed, kicked, bit, buckled to it again, and tugged on, carrying manufactured articles in, lugging raw material out.

At night the station yards were full of wagons, mules,
horses, and men. Wagons were grouped at the tying rail or
around trees in old-fashioned camp style. Animals were tied
to the tongues or sides of wagons and fed barley and hay
in long boxes. Tired and dusty, the drivers sat around fires in
the barrooms or squatted on the verandas and told of marvel-
ously intelligent mules, incredibly bad roads, wagon races,
sexual exploits in bonanza camps, and fights with churls who
would not turn out far enough at narrow places. One team-
ster told how he had pulled a record tonnage with a small
team. Another teamster had siphoned many gallons of whisky
from a heavy load of liquor without being detected. A third

told how he once won a fifty-dollar bet in Tonopah. He stood in a bar, glass in hand, and, calling out commands, turned his team around in the narrow street in front of the Mizpah Hotel. The immemorial orders were sufficient. " Gee " — to the right, " haw " — to the left, and so on. The team did the rest. The wheel horse stood his ground and several times helped turn the wagon by pulling one side back four or five feet. The pointers ahead stepped over the wagon chain. Such reminiscences helped fill an evening until about nine o'clock, when the teamsters crawled under their wagons with a roll of blankets and slept till dawn.

No means ever used to cross Nevada has been more glamourized than the stagecoach, but no horizon seeker traveled more uncomfortably than he in the stage. It was rarely the cradle on wheels that Twain tells of in *Roughing It*, swaying and swinging as it whirled along at a spanking gait. There were many discomforts. The stage was crowded. As likely as not, a passenger was crammed between heavy men. The man on one side persisted in talking about a patent amalgamator; the other man smoked bad cigars and blew the nauseating smoke out the side of his mouth. A family ate a bag lunch. The odors of sausage, mince pie, bread, and peanut butter mixed with alkali dust, tobacco smoke, and sweat. Elbows jabbed ribs, heads butted shoulders, booted feet kicked shins, and trousered legs stretched past faces to rest on the window ledge. Sleep was a dozing head on a wobbly stalk of a neck. Company might be stimulating conversers who told good stories and smoked fragrant pipes or passed a friendly flask of brandy. It might be downright alarming. E. P. Hingston was traveling from Glenbrook to Carson. A fellow passenger drew a revolver and pointed it toward Hingston, clutching it convulsively. " By God! there will be a man for breakfast tonight! " He rolled his head and muttered. His lady companion, who had mischief in her eyes and diamond rings on her fingers, urged him to put the gun away. But he yelled, " Boys, look out! By God! I'm on it. There'll be a man for breakfast over in Carson. I tell you so — sure." At a halt Hingston asked the driver about the couple. " Not a bad fellow; but he has an ugly kink in his brain. He's not to be played with. . . . She. Wh-e-e-e-ew! . . . She's a blazing ruin."

Coaches were tough. They were built for what they had to do. They pulled through mire, bumped over ridges of rock, crunched over blocks of stone and slabs of ice, and glided like a sleigh over snow. They fell in chuckholes and lurched, while the passengers hit the roof, bit their tongues, and fell in a scrambled heap. The stages leaned and rolled from side to side like ships becalmed on a rough sea, or they tossed like cockleshells, but they held together and rolled on. Passengers were a ballast that shifted about inside. On steep grades in the early days, especially in the Sierras, the rear wheels were tied fast and the coach slid down with them as a brake.

In winter the leather curtains flew open at the corners and let in cold blasts. Experienced travelers who crossed Nevada in the snowy months provided themselves with thick blankets, black-felt vicuña shirts half an inch through, and moccasins lined with wool and provided with buffalo hide straps to pull on over their boots. They took roast fowls to munch on, a demijohn of bourbon to pass the time, and a bag of unground coffee to use at station houses. At night hungry coyotes yelped near the road. Wolves trailed a stage over a summit until the driver turned in his seat and shot at them.

In summer the stage moved in a pillar of dust. Powdered alkali and pulverized soil floated in clouds like smoke from burning hay, and the coach plowed on through it hour after hour, as if wading in ash drift. The horses sneezed and wheezed dust from the mildewy hairs in their nostrils. Passengers were coated like millers. They looked prematurely aged. Their scalp hairs were porcupine quills. Dust clung to their eyebrows and mustaches and made little white beads on the ends of their eyelashes so that their eyes blinked under a feathery fringe work. Powder went up their noses and into their ears. Every square inch of their bodies was gritty. Their faces were smeared with muddy perspiration. Dust mixed with sweat to form a slimy jam between their toes. Feet swelled and blistered. Misery was compounded if the stage passed a marshy area in the early morning or evening. Gnats and speedy desert mosquitoes swarmed in and explored trousers, sleeves, and collars. The scenery outside was hateful, " a vast waveless ocean stricken dead and turned to ashes," "a series of horrible deserts, each worse than the other." Only at night, when humidity kept down the dust considerably, could the passenger enjoy the "mournfully grand desolation."

On the overland route from Salt Lake City westward, the stone or juniper station houses were ten to fifteen miles apart. Those that provided food were ready, when the stage pulled in, to serve diluted coffee, greasy beans, and bacon for a dollar a plate. Conductors, who were in full charge of mails, express, and passengers, had beats of 150 miles. Drivers changed every fifty miles. At every station the horses were changed fresh. They were graceful and hardy. Samuel Bowles thought they " would shine in Central Park and Fifth Avenue equippages." Twice each day the overland coach going west met the one coming east. For a moment the panting horses stopped and the two great curling dust storms met and blended into one. "What news from the States? " "Give us some San Francisco papers." "Did you have any trouble? " Then the conductor: "All set. Go on, driver."

The most celebrated stage trip in the West was the one over the Sierras between Carson City and the railhead at Folsom, twenty miles east of Sacramento. During boom days in the Nevada mining camps this stretch became one of the main streets of America. Since it carried an immense traffic of stages as well as wagons, it was smoothly graded, and water wagons sprinkled it daily to settle the dust and keep the surface hard. A coach swept up hills at a round trot, rolled down grades at a sharp gallop, turned abrupt corners without a pull-up, twisted among and past the freight wagons, ran casually along the edges of high cliffs, and swerved gracefully between giant red firs, sugar pines, and incense cedars. The schedule for the 165 miles between Virginia City and Sacramento was eighteen hours, twelve and a half hours for special coaches with many relays. The average speed was ten miles an hour. One seven-mile stretch along a ridge top toward Placerville was made in twenty-six minutes, a truly exhilarating experience. Travelers were greatly impressed by the rapid pace and by the wonderful scenery of the upper Carson, Johnson Pass — 7,200 feet in elevation, and the American River Canyon. One New Englander said the trip was " the finest bit of stage travel in all our continental journey." There was no equal in the world to this feat of mastering distance and exploiting horseflesh.

The central figure in stagecoach days was the driver, who was looked up to as much as the pilot on the Mississippi steamboat. He made heroic dashes across long distances. He was " a great and shining dignitary, the world's favorite son, the envy of the people, the observed of the nations." People hung on his words and were happy for days at a facetious insult from him. He dressed better than the passengers, wore gloves, which he drew on and off with deliberation, and took pride in his team and his silver-inlaid whipstock. Seemingly reckless, the driver was proud of keeping on schedule. " Horace " said Hank Monk to Greeley of the New York *Tribune*, during the fast trip to Placerville that became a classic anecdote — " Horace, keep your seat. I told you I would get you there by five o'clock, and by God I'll do it, if the axles hold! " A driver was conscious of his record for holding the reins for years on end without an upset or a hurt passenger. He would bring the stage in even if he was shot through the lungs by Indians or road agents or injured by the kick of a horse so that a leg hung limp and twirling like a shoe held by the laces.

from Richardson: Beyond the Mississippi

DOWN THE SIERRA NEVADAS IN 1865

from Williams: THE PACIFIC TOURIST

PALACE-CAR LIFE
ON THE CENTRAL PACIFIC RAILROAD

There is exaggeration of detail, not spirit, in Bret Harte's "Stage-Driver's Story." As a stage came down Geiger Grade, north of Virginia City, three wheels, one by one, flew off the stage, but the driver raced the stage to the next station without a spill.

Two stories further illustrate the character of the stage driver. Among a group in a saloon in Austin was "Uncle John" Gibbons, who drove stage between Austin and Belmont. Someone told of a well-known ghost that appeared nightly in one of the levels of the North Star Mine. Uncle John expressed his doubts that there was such a thing as a ghost. The speaker said all the men on the mine level had seen it. " The ghost is there, and if you'll go down I'll show him to you any night."   Uncle John, who knew his horses, harness, and Concord wagons, had never been in a mine. He shuddered.

I'm afeared of mines, and don't want to drop down none o' them thar straight holes; but I tell you what I'll do: You trot your ghost out into the big road, and I'll harness him up, and drive him tandem all day with Brown Bill and Dick. I ain't afeard of anything with a bit in his mouth.

Twain tells about Jack, a New York youngster who had been to California and back on one of the stages operated by Ben Holladay. Later, when a learned elderly tourist was impressing Jack with the great work of Moses, who guided the children of Israel the three hundred miles of desert from Egypt to Jericho — guided them with unfailing sagacity for forty years over sand and rocks and sheer desolation, and landed them safe in the Promised Land — a marvelous achievement — Jack only replied, " Forty years? Only three hundred miles? Humph! Ben Holladay would have fetched them through in thirty-six hours! "

Some drivers rarely spoke. Others talked a little to be sociable, or for the same reason listened attentively to a stale

joke that was dinned in their ears by a smart aleck. Drivers
cussed at a male who spoke to them tactlessly and were fa-
therly and polite to ladies in their charge, ready any minute
on a freezing night to surrender wraps they needed to a
woman who complained of cold. Widely known were occupational heroes such as Baldy Green, who was frequently
robbed in Six-Mile Canyon on his way down from Virginia
City, Bill Blackmore, who "managed ribbons" over every
grade in western Nevada, Richard Gelatt, who once took a
loaded stage downgrade from Tahoe to Carson with a broken
brake staff — no brake at all, and Frank Jordan, who drove the
old overland route from Austin eastward. In one respect Jordan's Maine upbringing set him apart from other drivers. " I
don't drink; I won't drink; and I don't like to see anybody
else drink. I'm of the opinion of these mountains — keep your
top cool. They've got snow, and I've got brains; that's all the
difference."

Many of the drivers were creative masters of the Western
art of poker-faced tall-story telling. The Sierran drivers had
a certain kind of macabre tall story all their own, inspired
particularly by the steep and precipitous Kingsbury Grade
that twists down a mountainside from Tahoe to Genoa. The
stories told of terrible accidents, of how drivers used the king-
bolt to kill mutilated passengers so they wouldn't sue the
company, of corpses left in deep ravines for buzzards and two-
legged bastards who didn't mind picking dead folks' bodies.
A driver named Charlie told J. Ross Browne that he drove
through the mountain dust by the sound of the wheels.
" When they rattle I'm on hard ground; when they don't
rattle I gen'r'lly look over the side to see where she's agoing."
When Browne asked him if people got killed on the route, he
replied, " Some of the drivers mashes 'em once in a while, but
that's whisky or bad driving. Last summer a few stages went
over the grade, but nobody was hurt bad — only a few legs'n
arms broken. Them was opposition stages. Pioneer Stages, as

a gen'r'l thing, travels on the road. Git aeoup! " Charlie
told of the behavior of a San Francisco gentleman along the
American Canyon grade near Strawberry, where the rocks
of a glacial moraine projected above the road:

He was so 'fraid them rocks 'ud be shook loose and fall on his
head, he kept a dodgin' 'em all the time. His hair stood right up
like a hog's brussels. Every now and then he was peerin' around
for a soft spot of road to jump out on; an' when he seed he
couldn't find it, he held on to the railin' with both hands till his
fingers wos all blistered. " D-d-driver," sez he, " d'ye think there's
any danger? " "Danger! " sez I — "ov course there's danger!
Supposing that 'ere rock was shook loose by the rattlin' ov this
'ere stage — , what d'ye think 'ud be the consequences? " " I
r-r-really can't say," sez he; " p-p-possibly it would crush the
stage! " " No," sez I, "it wouldn't crush it; but it 'ud make sich a
damned squash of it that bones couldn't count. Your bones an'
my bones an' the bones ov three passengers above an' four behind
an' nine down below, 'ud be all squashed, an' the verdic' of Corner's Inquest 'ud be — 'Eighteen men, six horses, an' a Pioneer
Stage squashed by the above stone! '" "D-d-driver," sez he —
his teeth a-chatterin' like a box o' dice — " is that so? " " You bet,'
sez I, " the last time I see it done, three ladies and ten gents from
Frisco was squashed." " Good gracious! " sez he, turnin' as white
as a sheet, " let me down at the next station! " And sure 'nuff he
got down at the next station and made tracks for Frisco. He
changed his base, *he* did. Git aeoup! "

" Is that true, driver? . . . Is it on the square, I mean? "
Browne asked. "Stranger," said Charlie solemnly, " I don't
make a habit o' lyin'; when I lie I kin lie as good as any body;
but gen'r'ally speakin' I'm on the square."
    " There is more true poetry in the rush of a single railroad
train across the continent than in all that gory story of burning Troy." So wrote Joaquin Miller after the railroad was
a fact. For many years the iron horse was only the hope and
prayer of people in Nevada, of sunburned emigrants walking

beside their wives, sea travelers with mal de mer and sour memories of Cape Horn, merchants who needed to replenish their stocks, miners in need of equipment or rich and ready to return east in comfort, and ranchers with fat cattle but no way to ship them to city markets. In the 1850's, when public clamor was loud for a railroad to reach west to California and tap the commerce of Asia, the War Department, headed by Jefferson Davis, explored five routes to the Pacific, three of them crossing Nevada. The secession of the South, which had deadlocked plans for a railroad by insisting on a Texas-Arizona route, and the war emergency in the North made possible the building of the road. In 1862 Congress passed a bill " to aid in the construction of a railroad and telegraph line from the Missouri river to the Pacific ocean, and to secure to the government the use of the same for postal, military, and other purposes."

Steel rails were laid across Nevada in one of the great construction feats of the century. Five thousand Chinese laborers in blue-denim overalls and shirts and coolie hats drilled, placed blasts, made grades, built stone culverts, leveled the bed, laid ties, and spiked down rails. They built pine-timber bridges over the Humboldt River. They unwound coil after coil of wire, fixed it to insulators, lifted tall crosses upright, and planted them. Wagons of timber and iron rolled eastward. Orderlies and gang foremen galloped, cussed, and yelled. Charles Crocker, the Sacramento dry-goods merchant who had become one of the Big Four, stormed up and down the unfinished line, noisy, cocky, energetic, urging on the work. His large face was caked with sweat and dust, and his sorrel mare was lathered. The Chinese ate dried cuttlefish and rice, worked tractably and industriously in gangs of forty or fifty, and were satisfied to get $35 a month. In 1868 they built 362 miles of track and reached the Utah line. The final race began with General Grenville Dodge's Irish crews that were building the Union Pacific westward, competing for federal subsidies. The famous meeting of the rails occurred at Promontory Point, Utah, on May 10, 1869, where spikes of Nevada silver and California gold were driven into a tie of California laurel by a hammer connected to the telegraph so as to carry across the country tap sounds of the great event. California had been linked to the nation and Nevada could be crossed in luxury.

For several years Americans sought Nevada horizons by means of the world's leading travel novelty. There was much rattling, and in summer there was heat and dust. The roadbed was uneven, and the open vestibules between cars were dangerous. The ice in water containers melted between filling places and the tepid water tasted of wet wooden floors and damp burlap. The wood-burning, funnel-stacked locomotives occasionally jumped the tracks or collided with cattle and held up the train for many hours. The first observation cars resembled modern coal cars with seats around the sides. But the Silver Palace Cars of the Central Pacific, later supplanted by Pullman Palace Cars, had scrollwork, gilt, velvet upholstery, carpets with floral designs, potted ferns and rubber plants, wood stoves, fairly rattleproof windows, and organs with hymnbooks. At night there were oil lamps and porter-made beds. Protected from sun and wind and biting cold, on a roadbed that was, at its worst, far superior to a rutted wagon road, the elite of America rushed down the Humboldt and up the Truckee at twenty-two miles an hour. Three times a day the train stopped at private, supervised restaurants for twenty minutes while the passengers ate good table-d'hôte meals at long tables laden with thick crockery and steaming platters of food at seventy-five cents per plate.

Passengers shot at rabbits and antelopes through the windows and from the vestibules, conversed, read books, ate out of baskets of food and sweets they had providently brought along, sang songs around the organ, and either pitied or sneered at emigrants in wagons on the old trail alongside. Observed at leisure from a comfortable seat, Nevada began to be interesting. At the stations were Indians with papooses, miners in outlandish costumes, cowboys with ten-gallon hats; and the background was strange pinkish vistas in which the anatomy of the earth lay exposed. Guidebooks appeared, Henry Williams's *Pacific Tourist* among them, to explain the features of the landscape and relate some of their most interesting history. Someone in a railroad party showed the new, mellower attitude toward Nevada: "With water to settle the dust and congenial companions, Nevada would be all right." But ex-Senator Ben Wade of Ohio, no whit lenient, replied, "With plenty of water and good society, Hell would not be a bad place to live in."

Emigrant trains had coaches that were cushioned better than day coaches on the Eastern roads. They even had sleeping arrangements, though not upholstered as on the Silver Palace Cars. Emigrants purchased bed boards to suspend between their seats and mattress ticks stuffed with straw. Those with foresight brought along pillows and curtains to hang around their boudoirs. The agent assigned families and single ladies to berths in one car, single men to another, Chinese to a third. These trains, too, stopped at the regular eating places, although many a family carried their own food the whole way, cooking it on the wood stove. A newsboy peddled soap, towels, tin washing dishes, coffee, tea, and cans of hash and beans. The average rate of speed was but twelve miles an hour, but the ticket from Chicago to San Francisco was only $55.50 for third class (in 1880), and certainly the train outspeeded the covered wagons alongside. At that, chivalric young men jumped from the front cars, picked yellow primroses and purple penstemons, boarded the last cars as they came by, and presented fresh bouquets to admiring girls. There were long halts when engines were changed, and twice a day the train was backed onto a siding while the regular trains rushed by and roiled up a huge cumulus of gritty dust.

More than likely a car contained a persevering mother who used up all the lavatory water in washing her children's dirty pinafores and then turned to the ice water and used it all up. If she was a frau directly from Mannheim or Wermelskirchen, so much the worse for fellow travelers who tried to remonstrate in English. In Robert Louis Stevenson's emigrant train was a cornetist who lengthened the faces of the other passengers by cruelly repeating "Home, Sweet Home" until a hard-looking man with a goatee said, "Stop that damned thing. I've heard enough of that. Give us something about the good country we're going to."

For half a century, while the Central Pacific linked northern Nevada to the nation, southern Nevada remained the last huge area in America without a railroad. All who sought to cross this wilderness of scorched earth and creosote bush were either masters of desert craft or else tenderfeet who risked the horrors of death by thirst. In 1905 gangs of sweating Greeks completed William A. Clark's San Pedro, Los Angeles, and Salt Lake Railroad (now the Union Pacific). The last spike was driven near Goodsprings. But until the tracks were ballasted, depots built, and dependable water supplies secured, the southern Nevada desert was no safer than the Mojave for greenhorns. During the construction of the railroad, several dozen workers died while trying to cross one way or the other between the camps and San Bernardino, California. Twelve employees of the Clark company died inside of a single six-month period. A foreman died of frenzied thirst on his way to camp. Prospectors found a laborer, naked and sun blistered, groping blindly for water that he claimed he could hear trickling. A stage driver picked up two workers near Dead Man's Well, a source of brackish, unfit water. Both insane, they resisted rescue and died before the stage reached Moapa. Surveyors found many bodies torn and partially eaten by buzzards and coyotes.

Up northwest another desert area was crossed by Nevada's

third transcontinental road, the Western Pacific, built by "bohunks" with hand labor and teams. It crossed the Sierras via the Feather River Canyon and over the pass discovered in 1850 by James P. Beckwourth, threaded between Smoke Creek Desert and Granite Creek Desert, and joined the Humboldt River route eastward from Winnemucca. With its completion in 1910, all the most inhospitable landscapes in Nevada could be seen through double plate-glass windows as one ate a $1.50 diner meal complete with silver service and finger bowls.

Safely traversed by railroad trains, Nevada became a setting for novelty seekers and stunt men who disdained locomotive power and used antiquated means to make crossing the state still tedious or spectacular. Through wagon roads had begun to relapse into wilderness with the completion of the Central Pacific. At the end of the century Captain Willard Glazier crossed via the Humboldt Valley as he rode from ocean to ocean on horseback. Some years later William D. Rishel, president of the Cheyenne Bicycle Club, was assigned by the Hearst press to find a practicable bicycle route from Salt Lake City to San Francisco. He experimented with many trails and finally determined on a route that approximated the Humboldt Trail of '49. A Hearst publicity stunt resulted. Six hundred bicycle riders relayed a message from Manhattan to the Golden Gate in thirteen days. About the same time Edward Payson Weston walked across the continent; later Jack Eldredge was walking westward, trying to surpass Weston's time. At a brief stop in Winnemucca he ate a pound of steak, twenty eggs, six potatoes, one pie, and one gallon of coffee.

THE COMPLETION of the Western Pacific left one great conquest to be made, that of the automobile maker and highway engineer. In the days of prosperous mining camps, toll roads and bridges and county roads were kept in good order for wagon and stage traffic, but when a new era came in American transportation, and Haynes-Appersons, Overlands, Dorts, Maxwells, Packards, and tin lizzies roamed the lanes at twenty miles an hour, Nevada had only an emaciated embryo of a highway system. As the camps declined, the roads were neglected and fell into disuse. Cloudbursts washed out whole stretches. Patches of road that remained contented local farmers and miners but gave despair to travelers, who were as helpless as the emigrants of '49. Two deep ruts wound among tumbleweeds, rabbit bush, and overgrown sagebrush, and crankcases leveled off the dusty crown between them. A smooth stretch abruptly changed into a slithery sandy curve or a treacherous jaw-smacking chuckhole. Where the ruts were too deep, ridged with dried mud, the motorist straddled them, fearing all the while he'd slip in and get jammed. There were sudden steep pitches over railroad grades and down into creeks and washes. If one met another car on a narrow mountain pass, he had to back perilously, buck, and maneuver until there was room. On the flat desert a meeting meant that one had to chance turning out into sand even softer than the roadbed. In the open valleys there was often a bewildering tangle of ruts and trails that pushed out in all directions. A short cut? An alternate route? A smoother lane farther on? There were no signs, no persons to ask. The traveler put his measuring stick into the gas tank, studied the wetted end, estimated the mileage left in his tank, cogitated on the directions he had picked up at the last town, and worriedly tried what seemed the most-used road. There were periods of fairly hard surface where the braided sandy tracks looked little used, less used than the turnoffs that led to ranch houses or small mines. The driver, who hadn't seen another car for two hours, turned a strained face to his companion. " Where are we? "

   In winter or spring the wheels spun in the putty clay of the playas and the motorist piled brush under the wheels, wrapped the tires in burlap or rope, and worried himself into an attack of biliousness. In summer he shoveled sand and choked in the dust that boiled up through the floor boards and hid the ruts and holes. The car shivered and trembled over corduroy roads and jiggled sideways toward the loose sand and the roadside litter or sharp basalt and scoria. If it rained, one stopped wherever he was unless he was in a dip or wash. The one task was to look for the shelter of a ranch house, miner's cabin, or deserted branding corral. If a man's business was urgent, he struggled on, squinting through the blurred windshield, spinning his wheels and slapping mud against the underside of the fenders, racing in low gear through the wettish-looking spots and twisting the car through the rocky gullies — all to get on twenty-five or thirty miles in an eighteen-hour day.

Even at the time of the war of 1914–18 Nevada's main roads lacked double-track widths, durable surfaces of concrete or rolled gravel, locations free from snowdrifts and annual washouts, and the removal of dangerous curves and railroad crossings. Routes were roundabout. Heavy grades and steep pitches were unnecessary. Bridges were ready to collapse of their own weight. The first and second reports of the State Highway Commission had much to say of the problems Nevada presented to travelers.

The first vehicle through the country has generally made the location for the future roads, with a result that in some cases the roads are very poorly located. The heretofore secondary importance of the roads has resulted in their being promiscuously relocated to make room for railroads, flumes, ditches, fences, and other improvements in the country.

Except in the immediate vicinity of our larger towns and cities, the existing roads are single-track desert trails, and for the most part made by the wheel-tracks of the vehicles traversing the territory, and taking the line of least resistance. Rank growths of sagebrush, greasewood, and mesquite mark the limits of this

single-track roadway, so that, if one were to view our State from
the air, he would distinguish our highways from the rest of the
landscape by great strips of barrenness six or seven feet wide.

In 1914 about fifty motorists crossed Nevada on transcontinental journeys. The next year the number was nearer
five thousand, as the European war diverted Eastern travelers
westward. Also, the Lincoln Highway Association, the pioneer organization to focus national attention on the problem
of automobile roads, urged people to " See America First "
and arranged for caravans to see it. Motorists had their troubles with bridges out in West Virginia, detours in Indiana,
and gumbo in Iowa, but the climactic disasters came in the
unmarked alkali wastes of Utah and Nevada, where cars sank
in lonely bogs and sand pits. " See South Africa First! "
sneered the motorists. " See the Moon First! " People in good
out-of-state cars said to people with Nevada plates on their
cars, " Why don't you fellers build some roads that decent
people can ride on? " Henry Joy, president of the Lincoln
Highway Association, admitted that the worst spot on the
whole trip across America was a twenty-mile stretch of sand
and marsh near Fallon. " We want the tourist," said Mayor
Frank Byington of Reno. " We want good roads, and Nevada has 425 miles of proposed Lincoln Highway between
its borders . . . but a population of less than eighty thousand. What can we do? "

The Federal Road Act of 1916 began a reform in Nevada
roads that slowly gathered momentum. Road surface, drainage, and grades were the major technical problems. The
United States Bureau of Roads, unaware of the meager traffic
in Nevada, insisted on twenty-four-foot roads, and Nevada
officials countered with arguments for nine- to eighteen-foot
roads. There were problems of right of way over private land,
county land, and the extraordinarily wide 400-foot right of
way alongside the Central Pacific. For an isolated, under-

populated, huge state there were tremendous costs involved
in obtaining equipment, building roads, and maintaining them.
Federal aid helped. The government donated a large amount
of leftover war equipment — harness, compasses, Manila rope,
wagons, wheelbarrows, pumps, tires, tanks, autos, parts, and
trucks with the camouflage still painted on their sides. The
Lincoln Highway Association passed on donations from General Motors and Willys-Overland. Convicts from Carson
Prison furnished man power. California automobile clubs put
up road signs in western Nevada from Pyramid Lake to
Searchlight and pioneered in the preparation of adequate maps
and information service.

Segments of graded gravel road began to appear here and
there, and also concrete bridges, ample culverts, narrow but
two-lane highways, fills to level off incessant ups and downs,
hard shoulders, strategic road signs that hunters and other
small boys riddled with bullets.

But it was not the roads alone that were irregular. Cars,
even in the early 1920's, were far from perfect for the rigor-
ous tests of Nevada roads. Only the unwritten code of stopping to help made travel possible. Motors heated up. Water
evaporated from the radiator almost as fast as put in. Passengers pushed cars up grades while the driver wrenched the
engine along in low gear. Carburetors jiggled out of adjustment, and tires blew out. Brakes gave way on hills. The front
bearing burned out. Lights shorted out at night on signless
roads. Many a gasoline buggy was hitched behind a pair of
horses and pulled to the nearest town.

Cars stalled in the midst of nowhere. While the father,
peevish and profane, tinkered in the glare of his fenders and
tried to make repairs, the family fought discomfort and killed
time as best they could. They sat in the niggardly shade of
Joshua trees or pinyons. They watched whirlwinds lift giant
tumbleweeds as if they were balloons. They nettled their fingers picking the prickly white poppy that grows along the

roadside. They exchanged stares with lizards. One Midwestern family sat stalled for four hours until a car came along. Its driver found the gas pipe broken and the vacuum tank not working. There was no repair tape. He bound the pipe with his handkerchief. A few rocky miles farther on the pipe broke right where it joined the gas tank. A car sank up to the hubs in a mudhole. The driver dug, packed in sage and rocks, raced the engine, strained the chassis, and popped out the universal shaft. The nearest building was a deserted ranch, seven miles away. The nearest town, Pioche, was sixty miles away. It took a day to wait for a car to pass, get a ride, buy the part, and return to the stranded car. Another car clumped to a stop in a mudhole. Trying to back out, the driver killed the engine. Something stuck inside the engine. The driver sat helpless. Several passers-by stopped and made futile efforts to push the car and get it started. Finally a country doctor passed by. Nevada roads had taught him automobile mechanics. He took a cold chisel and unmeshed the gear of the starter.

Michigan met the challenge to build foolproof cars. Nevada met the necessity of constructing good roads. The Highway Department grew until it was the largest and busiest department of the state government, a distributor of potent political patronage. Nowadays Nevada is amply provided with wide, safe transcontinental highways, from which the old roads angle off like airfield runways. The Arrowhead Trail crosses via Las Vegas from Zion Park to Los Angeles; Roosevelt Highway crosses from Ely to Mojave by way of Tonopah; U.S. 50, the Lincoln Highway, cuts Nevada in two through the center. It is the most varied and charming of all the long crossings. It is the old Pony Express route, the early overland stage route, and the wagon road laid out by Howard Egan, the Mormon, and also Captain J. H. Simpson, the army explorer. To the north, U.S. 40, the old Humboldt route, now called the Victory Highway, passes through busy towns, Elko, Winnemucca, and Lovelock.

The excellent highways, a surprise still to travelers conditioned by stories of the California rush of 1849, have all the features of well-engineered roads anywhere: flattened curves, railroad overpasses, guardrails on mountain grades, caution signals, wide shoulders, white strip lining, sodium lights at underpasses, retaining walls where the sides of cuts are loose, first-aid equipment at gas stations. Where emigrants once suffered and died, now there are auto camps, eating houses, fancy motels, elegant service stations that wipe off one's car before asking, " How many? "

But the signs, like the scenery, make the roads unmistakably Western and Nevadan. " Caution: Cattle Grazing." " Drinking Water 100 Yards ⟶ " " Dip — 300 Feet." " Danger. Slippery When Wet: Crickets." " Advise 40 Miles Per Hour." A scrawled sign points to two wavering ruts through the sagebrush or shad scale: " Golden Pheasant Mine, 5 Mi." It is only on the shores of Tahoe that notices put up by the newly arrived millionaires strike an alien, jarring note. " Keep Out." " No Help Wanted." At the imposing entrance of a Zephyr Cove estate is this: " Electric Gate. Hands Off."

All America in an endless procession zings toward the horizons on the east-west roads. There are limousines driven by colored chauffeurs, Chevrolets and Fords filled with middle-class families, " oil-burning crates " bearing kids to national parks, jalopies loaded with mattresses and washtubs and migrant crop harvesters working the routes between Imperial Valley peas and Idaho potatoes. Divorcees and elopers, G-men and B-girls, soldiers and traveling salesmen, capitalists who speak to people through their secretaries, and New York Communists who travel to hear the people talk — all the cross-currents of the nation's life are canalized on the Nevada highways. Replacing the wagons of the old days are the mammoth Diesel freighters and trailers of the interstate truck lines, each with an appendage of half a dozen states' license plates. The dark smoke from their vertical exhaust pipes drifts along the road. At night, lit up with dozens of red, yellow, and blue safety lights, the trucks resemble monster caterpillars. In place of the stagecoaches reined so surely by Frank Jordan and Richard Gelatt are the sleek, luxurious, air-conditioned, and carefully driven buses of Burlington Trailways and Greyhound Lines. And remote in the sky, droning faintly, are the transcontinental planes of United Air and TWA.

IV
CHASING A DOLLAR TO HELL

Prospector

"WHITHER BOUND? " asked the editor of the *Reese River Reveille* of a roughly dressed man who stopped to water his burro at a trough on the main street of Austin, Nevada.

"Don't know."

"Where are you from? "

"Over yonder." The man pointed vaguely west.

"Prospecting? "

"'Spect so."

He was giving no information to a news-hungry mining-town editor. The editor could only wonder. Did this miner have a rich mine staked out? Did he have a hunch that led to treasure in the Sulphur Springs Range more fabulous than any in the Virginia Range to the west? For the miner was professionally silent. He watered his animal, parried the questions like a down-East Yankee, and plodded on.

When Thomas Jefferson Bell, veteran prospector of Nye

County, who found the outcroppings at Southern Klondyke, was filling out papers for a Masonic aid society he gave mining as his occupation. A reply came back: " Can't you give some less dangerous occupation than mining, and who is your family physician? Where did he graduate? " Bell wrote, " The only risk in being a miner is that of starving to death. As for the family physician — the nearest doctor is a hundred miles away, and we have never seen him." Thomas Jefferson Bell was a free spirit, working on top of the ground, in the sunlight, moving freely over a pastel landscape.

He was master of his environment. Indians were harmless, and poisonous " varmint " were easily avoided. Food was a matter of calculation. The one real problem was drinking water, but he knew the desert craft of water signs: clumps of aspens or cottonwoods, mesquite patches, converging tracks of rabbits or wild sheep, pointing cairns left by Indians, the flight of doves and bees to hidden springs or water holes in twisting canyons.

The prospector lives in popular stories and novels, a frontier type as enduring as the cowboy, and he lives in history as well. He has played one of the great roles in Nevada's history. He opened the door to settlement. The flag and commerce followed his pick. The discovery of the Comstock by Peter O'Riley and others was the first magnet that attracted any considerable number of persons into the territory and started the American frontier rebounding eastward from the Pacific Coast. Prospector's discoveries in the Reese River and White Pine country first opened up central and eastern Nevada. Southern Nevada remained a wilderness until investors and railroad builders heard of the discoveries of Jim Butler, who founded Tonopah in 1900, Harry Stimler and William Marsh, whose Sandstorm was the first claim in Goldfield, and " Shorty " Harris, who staked out the first location in Bullfrog.

And once camps and mines produced ore, Nevada's trade

and manufacturing developed. Farms were laid out to feed new residents, cattlemen drove in herds to graze in the river bottoms, railroad companies laid tracks, and carpetbagging politicians set up local governments. The enterprise begun by the prospector in Nevada was the touchstone in determining her governmental policies. The tale is similar in Alaska, Australia, Siberia, in many a tropical colony and Western state.

The frontier prospector was a man of imagination. With hardly a jingle in his pocket, he owned a million. He scorned the tedious work of digging and developing a mine, but endured tremendous hardship while looking for it. Hope and persistence kept him going. He walked afoot and alone with a pack mule or burro, or with a pony pulling a cart. His equipment included a pick, shovel, gold pan, canteen, great horn spoon, an ax, blankets, a few pans and cooking utensils, a blackened coffee pot, and a battered tin pail.

The prospector's food supply was bacon or sowbelly, flour, baking soda, beans, coffee, whisky, and maybe some canned milk. He made " sourdough " biscuits by fermenting batter and cooking it in a well-greased pan. He brewed " prospector's soup " with bacon fat, browned flour, canned milk, and a cubed onion for seasoning.

He was wise in mineral experience if not in mining-school knowledge. He knew a great deal of geology, mineralogy, metallurgy. Mining regulations varied from district to district, decade to decade. He understood their ins and outs. He searched for gold along dry ravines and canyons where he hoped to find float rock — quartz fragments washed down from ore-bearing ledges above. If he found float, he licked it to make gold particles shine and looked at it through a magnifying glass. He crushed it on a flat stone and carefully shook about half a pound of powdered rock into a spoon. This was the hollow half section, carved lengthwise, of a cow's horn. As he poured water from his canteen into his gold pan, he stirred the spoon under the water with a dexterous motion of his wrist, and washed away powdered quartz so as to recover particles of gold, if any. He could detect a particle of gold as small as the end of a hair.

In early days almost every prospector was prepared to locate silver. He carried a vial of nitric acid and one of salt dissolved in water. When he found a quartz vein he broke off a piece and pounded it up. He boiled it in acid and filtered the solution. Then he dropped in some salt solution. If white clouds or a white sublimate formed, he had an " indication " of silver.

When float bore gold or silver, the prospector began a search for its origin in veins and lodes up the ravine. He made many testing holes and trenches. Days or weeks passed until he found the original lode, for it might be miles away. He examined all the outcrop he could find and determined its approximate limits. Then he paced off one or more claims to include his find. Usually these were rectangular areas, no longer than 1,500 feet along the vein, no wider than 600 feet. He piled up rocks to make a location monument four feet wide and two feet high, filled out a location notice, put it inside a tobacco can, and laid it in the monument.

NOTICE IS HEREBY GIVEN that the undersigned hereby locates and claims the following-described piece of mineral bearing ground as a lode claim. From this discovery monument 400 feet in a northerly direction and 1100 feet in a southerly direction and three hundred feet on each side of the middle of the vein.

The general course of the vein is northerly and southerly.

This claim shall be known as the Merry Christmas, situated in the Silver City Mining District, Lyon County, Nevada.

Located this 10th day of May, 1875.

Daniel Pettis
Locator

In this process of location there was much the prospector had to know. Was he on private land, public land, land withdrawn from entry? If there was already a monument on the lode, or an old shaft, had the first claim become invalid? Naming the claim, as required by law, called only for imagination or a sense of humor and gave the prospector his one chance to be literary. Ledges had such names as Home Ticket, Red Bird, Wide West, Wild Cat, Wake-up-Jake, Queen Victoria, Dan Webster, Bubble Creek, May Queen, Daisy, Royal Hawaiian, Paymaster, Thanksgiving, Gouge Eye, Let-her-Rip, Dry Up, Grannie, Leviticus, and Deuteronomy.

The prospector put ore samples in a sack and took them to the nearest assayer, who was very likely a methodical German from the Harz Mountains. The assayer fired up his little furnace. He " bucked down " the samples with a mortar and pestle and bucking board until the fragments would pass through a screen with one hundred meshes to the inch. He carefully mixed each sample on a piece of oilcloth, quartered it with a knife, and took a small quantity. He mixed all these small quantities together and weighed them. He stirred in borax, flour, and litharge, weighed the total mixture, and distributed it in six crucibles. These he lifted with tongs and put into the fire, banking fresh charcoal around them.

There they remained until the contents melted. The assayer took them out with the tongs and poured the liquid from each into a conical iron mold, where it soon hardened into slag and slowly cooled off. When the six pieces were cool, he set each in turn on a small anvil and struck it with a hammer. This separated a glasslike top mass from a small button of gold, lead, or silver that was at the bottom tip of the cone.

More figures to jot down: the weight of the button, the weight of the waste.

Now the assayer put each button in a numbered cupel and heated it white hot in his muffle furnace. This drove off the lead and left a two-layered button of gold and silver at the bottom. By a series of weighings, he determined the proportion of the metals to each other, and by some simple equations he computed the weight of metal in relation to the weight of the ore samples, the proportion of metal per ton of ore (assuming the samples to be representative), and the value of the ore per ton (on the basis of metal prices on the current market). All this done, the assayer drew up his certificate and gave it to the prospector in return for a fee.

If the ore was of sufficient value per ton — $20 a ton was satisfactory — the prospector performed the location work. He sank a discovery shaft four feet by six feet wide and at least ten feet deep, or deeper if necessary, to show an exposed deposit of mineral in place. Or maybe he made an open cut or tunnel. At any rate, he removed at least 240 cubic feet of earth or rock. To hold title he had to do this within ninety days. If the mine looked promising, within these same ninety days, he filed a detailed certificate of location with the mining district recorder and the county recorder. Thereafter, to hold possession, the prospector had to expend on the mine at least $100 each year in labor or improvements. The cost of a day's labor (eight hours) was fixed at the prevailing wages of the district. Any expense counted that improved the claim; for example, building a road to an inaccessible claim.

By now, if not before, he was ready to try to induce a grubstaker to finance him in sinking a shaft a hundred feet or more. He hoisted the ore to the surface by a hand windlass or a mule whim and piled it for future removal. High-grade ore went in one pile, low-grade in another. If the ore was very rich and the prospect equally favorable, it was soon time to ask for more capital, perhaps to incorporate and issue stock, in order to sink deeper and also to explore sidewise in drifts (along the vein) and crosscuts (at right angles to it). Perhaps such explorations on several levels indicated a large lode encased within the worthless country rock. A promoter was sure to be interested by now, and the hole became a mine. A small mill went up to smash the ore into powder and extract the metal. If other promising ledges lay in the vicinity, a boom town sprang up around the original prospect hole. If the strike was isolated, prospectors and promoters went away, leaving the mine almost as solitary as the original dry ravine had been.

The account presupposes that the prospector's original float led to a paying mine which he could develop or sell to a promoter. Generally it didn't. He kept repeating the whole routine in other draws and gulches, on other buttes and ranges, over and over again, staying out until his bag of red beans was gone. Then a spree in town, fresh supplies, and noncommittal answer to local reporters. The important thing was that he kept at his search. A favorite old joke kept circulating. A geologist, a prospector, and a promoter went out hunting game. Eventually they found tracks. The prospector followed the tracks forward, the geologist backtracked to find where the animal had come from, and the promoter went back to town for a wagon to carry out the animal after it was shot.

When the strike was made the prospector and some partners or hired miners went to work in the prospect hole and set up a wisp of civilization quite different from that in the metropolitanized mining towns. They lived in a cabin made of the materials nearest at hand: stone and mud, brushwood covered with sod, rawhide with big stones in the corners, adobe bricks, a stockade of logs placed close together and upright in the ground. Smoke rose through a hole in the roof against a bank or through an actual chimney made of wooden slabs, scraps of sheet iron, nail kegs, or whisky barrels with the end knocked out. At a distance, the outside of one of these out-of-the-way habitations was as hard to see as a Washoe Indian wigwam. It would seem too primitive to house men who knew gneiss from schist and selenite from limonite. But inside, civilization triumphed. There were walls papered with *Harper's Weekly;* bunks covered with blue blankets; pegs for old boots, shirts, flitches of bacon, bunches of onions,

Farm Security Administration; photo by Rothstein

PROSPECTOR TESTING ORE SAMPLES

from Browne: APACHE COUNTRY

THE HURDY-GURDY GIRLS

from Browne: APACHE COUNTRY

HOME FOR THE BOYS

frying pans, and tin cups; a coffee pot hanging over the fire; rough shelves heaped with yellow-backed books and manuals, hardware, crockery, groceries; guns leaning in the corner; a jug under a pine or juniper bedstead; a litter on a table. In this surrounding, jolly bachelors in the '49 tradition did their own washing, mending, and bedmaking, cut each other's hair on Sunday, greased their own boots, and wrote many love letters.

The first generations of Nevada prospectors used the burro in preference to any other animal, so that in mining areas it was as much a feature as the horse was in cattle country. The burro was an accepted personality. While his master tightened the cinch, he swelled up and doubled the size of his paunch. He watched his master make camp. At night he sang his " Hynaaw-hee! Hynaaw-hee! " and was affectionately known as the " Washoe canary " or " mountain canary." He was slow but hardy and dependable and could go anywhere a man could. But his plaintive note is growing fainter and rarer in the desert ranges, to be replaced by the roaring of automobile engines in second gear. Miners have taken to old high-centered automobiles and to jeeps that can easily follow a sheep trail to the high-altitude herdsmen's camps, and the burros have been turned loose to run wild. Herds of these obsolescent aides to Nevada history graze on the upland benches. Social fraternities of burros in southern Nevada have been rounded up by California chicken ranchers and slaughtered for hen food. Like the " desert rat," the burro is no longer an important figure, but he is warmly remembered. Five-cent photographs of him cling to the postcard racks in Nevada drugstores and sell in amazing numbers.

The automobile prospector first appeared in Tonopah and the camps it fathered. " Chug wagons " frequently broke down, and when they did run well they bounced riders through a holocaust of fine dust, and if impending brush was cut away they outsped burros and wagons. On October 29,

1906, when the government threw the Walker Lake Indian Reservation open to mineral entry, and a blast on Mount Grant above Hawthorne gave the signal, several powerful automobiles were among the impatient throng of men that rushed eastward. A few foot and animal prospectors, sensing an unfair advantage, pinked tires with gunshots. The "benzine bus" was a luxury, its gasoline costing seventy-five cents a gallon, and it was of most service to rich investment millionaires like William Andrews Clark and Charles Schwab, who maintained stripped cars in Tonopah and Goldfield waiting to rush off to any newly reported strike, carrying agents to stake out claims. As costs went down with the appearance of the Ford car, ordinary prospectors piloted their "gasoline camels" over the harder spots in the sand, across the sun-baked dry lakes, and along the traditional prospect trails between springs and water holes. Rough hummocks and rock-strewn gulches required low gear. On the alkaline flats the car could purr in high gear as fast as a mile a minute.

Nowadays the excellent state highway system and graded county roads greatly facilitate the movement of prospectors. At the same time the Mackay School of Mines, the State Bureau of Mines, and the State Analytical Laboratory with its free analyses of minerals and ore have educated the prospector so that he is no mere badger-hole inspector — though every hole is worth a look. He is no lucky, unsystematic interloper. He is an informed geologist who carefully examines clues and makes practical use of the latest technological knowledge. Such a man is S. Frank Hunt, who pursued a lead for years and finally made an important copper strike in 1931 at Rio Tinto, near Mountain City.

With gold and silver and copper valuable now, and with industrial demands for a dozen strategic minerals such as manganese and tungsten, Nevada prospectors have every incentive to work public and private domain alike (the right to own discovered ore holds on most private land, too) with every hope of rising from a grubstake to a bank account. Important discoveries are frequent. One especially publicized strike came in 1935. "Red" Staggs and Clyde Taylor located the Jumbo claim off west of Winnemucca and sold it for $10,000 to a local storekeeper named George Austin. A year later when Jumbo ore assayed at $1,495 a ton, John J. Raskob, Herbert Hoover, and other experts came in to investigate. Raskob offered a million dollars for a half interest, but Austin held on. Another headliner was a strike made by E. M. Booth and his wife in 1938 in the Cimarron District, north of Tonopah. Their ore assayed up to $2,000 a ton. They sold twelve of their sixteen claims to a mining company for $185,000 and other considerations.

The biographies of most prospectors cover many states and usually several countries or continents. In the sixties and seventies, prospectors knew parts of California, Idaho, Oregon, Arizona, Montana, British Columbia, and Mexico, as well as Nevada. In the time of Theodore Roosevelt, the range of background also included South Africa, Canada's Northwest Territories, Arabia, Peru, Alaska, Brazil, Colombia, Siberia, Colorado, and New Mexico.

Pertinacious at sweaty searching and exploratory pick swinging, the prospector is often singularly unfaithful to his discovery. After years of sourdough bread and biliousness, he sells his mine for a song. He wants cash quick so that he can feel a dollar in his trousers. He doesn't want the delays of mine development. He lacks the capital necessary. Or, he wants to keep on the move and hunt some more.

Alvah Gould sold his half of the prodigal Gould & Curry claim on the Comstock lode for $450. Later, when the mine was the talk of brokers on three continents, he was the proprietor of a Reno peanut stand. Charlie Swiggart was an experienced ore hunter who spent years prospecting in the Mojave Desert and elsewhere in the arid Southwest. He was "bitten by the bug." With high hopes but a low grubsack, he felt that someday he would locate a good mine. Eventually he staked a group of claims in Searchlight, a brand-new district in extreme southern Nevada. He called his group the Quartette. Then he sold the Quartette to a man named McCready for $500 and a team of mules. A friend of Charlie's told of the negotiation later: " There was nothing then of the Quartette but a dry hole twenty feet down with no ore in sight. Swiggart unquestionably had the best of the bargain on the showing, for if it had not been for luck and the generosity of nature in endowing the spot with gold, McCready would certainly have been out of mules and money." As destiny worked things out, McCready also let slip a fortune. He lacked money to develop the mine and sold to Charlie Dunn of San Bernardino for $60,000. Within six years the Quartette had produced over a million dollars' worth of bullion. It was netting $10,000 a month for shareholders. In sight was $900,000 in unmined gold.

In a state rich in minerals, freaks of fortune are inevitable. Many mines have been discovered by pure chance. Good-luck stories, some authentic, some legendary, are part of the atmosphere of Nevada. A prospector shot at a snake and split a rock of high-grade ore. Three drunken men rolled a boulder down a hill; it chipped off rock and exposed a vein of rich ore. It is said that Henry Comstock found the famous Virginia City lode when he saw queer-looking stuff in a gopher hole. In Searchlight a shaft sunk 225 feet for water struck valuable deposits of silver, gold, and copper. Men digging an outdoor toilet in Tonopah uncovered a " pockety pay shoot " of rich ore. Two young miners' sons panned a badger mound at Weepah; two feet down they discovered gold ore worth $78,000 a ton. Guy Pritchard, after failing for years as a prospector, gave up and got a job repairing the old road between Hawthorne and Bodie. After lunch one day he sat down to rest, reached lazily for a rock to throw, and discovered silver and galena worth $90 a ton.

Above all, lost pack animals get the honor of bringing about discoveries, a theme that popular fiction like Dane Coolidge's *Trail of Gold* and Mark Requa's *Grubstake* have exploited until it is growing stale. From the Spanish conquest of South America to the arrival of the first Stanley Steamer in Goldfield, the lost burro, mule, or horse had his chance, at least in legend, to lead the course of empire.

The classic example in Nevada lore is Jim Butler's discovery of Tonopah. According to Butler's early version of the discovery, in May, 1900, he and his wife set out from Belmont to go to the Southern Klondyke Mining District. On the night of the eighteenth they camped at a spring in a desolate spot at the foot of a hill. Next morning they found that their pack burros had strayed. Butler set out uphill to find them, cornered them, and headed them toward camp. To speed their return trip, he picked up a rock and was about to hurl it at their rumps when he noticed it was mineralized quartz. Near by was the outcropping. The Butlers gathered specimens and went on the remaining ten miles to Southern Klondyke. They showed their samples to the camp assayer, who expressed the opinion that the rock was worthless and demanded an assaying fee that they could not pay. On their return trip to Belmont they picked up more specimens.

Butler gave them to young Tasker Oddie, district attorney of Nye County, offering him a half interest if he would get an assay made. Oddie was equally poor in cash, and in turn he gave the specimens to Walter Gayheart for one-half of his interest. Gayheart, an Austin engineer, made the assay and found values of $80 to $600 a ton in gold and silver. After Butler had leisurely harvested the hay on his ranch in Monitor Valley, he led his partners to the spot, and there on August 25 they located the Desert Queen, the Burro, the Mizpah, the Buckboard, and many other claims. They staked off every foot of ground anywhere near the richest outcrop, that on Mizpah Hill. Their very location monuments were made of high-grade ore. From one fifteen-foot shaft they filled two wagons with ore. They hauled the loads to Austin. The net proceeds were $600. The Tonopah rush began; and during the next twenty years Tonopah produced metal valued at $125,000,000, almost half of it from the original mine.

"The palpable sense of mystery in the desert air," which, as Mary Austin once wrote, "breeds fables, chiefly of lost treasures," bred a batch of tales in early Nevada. Where Butler and Humphrey discovered mines that founded towns, Hardin and "Alkali" Jones glimpsed mines, only to lose them, and the world has yet to know just where they are. Like the Southwest, Nevada is specked with lost mines and treasures, and some of Coronado's children are ever on the hunt. J. Frank Dobie points out that there are no legends about the gold at Fort Knox or the silver at West Point. It is the gold not yet found that draws and lifts the human spirit. Stories of unfound gold and silver are based on facts or on "mere hope, imagination, hallucination, aye, plain fertility in lying — who can say? " Professional mining men smile. Rule-of-thumb prospectors admit their skepticism. But if enough realistic details are piled in, even the cynic will have a moment's thrill: "If only the story is true and I can find that mine! "

The stories follow a fairly regular pattern, be they about the Three Little Lakes of Gold, the Whiteman Lost Cement Mine, the Lost Golden Eagle, or the Lost Chicken Craw. The outcropping or rich float is found under some emergency (thus the discoverer has no time accurately to find his bearings). Some rich samples are exhibited (which prove there is ore at the place described). For one of several reasons, return for rediscovery and location is delayed, or else the mine simply cannot be found again. Indian hostilities keep whites out of the region. Indians cover up the outcropping to keep whites from stampeding in and scaring away wild game. Years elapse and the finder's memory fails him. The area is topographically too regular, and the specific spot eludes identification. Cloudbursts cover the lost ledge with debris. Or, necessity and circumstance keep the finder distracted elsewhere for years, and when he finally does organize a party he is blind or feeble or about to die. He draws a map, which is so vague that followers cannot make sense of it. If he is still healthy he may be killed accidentally before the party sets out. Sometimes the sole evidence of a fabulously rich mine is in ore fragments that an Indian brings to a trading post. But however the story may manipulate man's destiny to leave Nature her secret, it always provides charts and circumstantial descriptions, and witnesses who saw either the discoverer or the ore he brought in.

Most of the stories go back to very early days in Nevada. One such concerns the " Hardin Mine." In 1849 a party of fourteen emigrant wagons was crossing northwestern Nevada on the Lassen cutoff, which cut west from the Humboldt River route near Winnemucca. They camped at Double Hot Springs to rest and to give their cattle time to graze in the tall grass. When they started westward again, three hunters went out, including a man named Hardin. The three planned to cross a near-lying mountain and rejoin the wagons on the other side. They found no game and, what was worse, they got lost. They saw a team on a road in the distance. As they wandered toward it they got into a burned, black, igneous country, part of the Black Rock Range. In one place they floundered through soft, gray, sifted ashes. The ashy place was near the margin of a shallow gulch. Along the gulch and in the ashes were chunks of whitish metal, some the size of beans, some forty or fifty pounds in bulk. Everywhere there protruded pieces the size of bricks. Metal lay around by the wagonload, as if Aladdin's cave had been blown open. One of the hunters had been in the Mexican War and had later worked on pack trains in the Sierra Madre before returning to the United States. He identified the slabs as silver. They gathered up all they could and clambered down to the valley floor, where they found an emigrant with all but one yoke of oxen dead. He was at work with hammer and saw cutting down his wagon from a four wheeler to a cart, so that his famished cattle could pull it and wife and child to California alive. The hunters tried to get him to pull the silver to California. He said he wouldn't pack it, even if it were pure gold. Hardin threw down the largest piece by the road, the three divided the smaller pieces, and went on to Mud Meadows. They found their party and showed samples of their find. Steve Bass saw the silver and watched Hardin melt it into buttons in a gouge in his ax handle covered with hot coals. The emigrants left some fragments at the meadows and took others on to California.

The men told their story in the mining towns around Mount Shasta, but no one was particularly excited, because gold was more valuable and more accessible. One of Hardin's companions wandered to Oregon, where a Rogue River man, A. B. Jennison, heard of the silver. Later he heard the same account from Hardin himself, who became a blacksmith in a wagon shop in Petaluma, California. In 1852 a doctor crossed the same desert area and found the big piece of silver Hardin had thrown down by the road. He did not take it but realized later it was pure silver. He planned to return, but just before his trip was to start he fell mortally sick. Before he died he gave all particulars to Tom Harvey and George Lathrop. A party of emigrants camped near Mud Meadows in the same year and found small pieces of the silver left by the Hardin party. These they took to Shasta City and sold to a jeweler named Lewis. He displayed the silver in his window, where it was seen by L. D. Vary and Isaac Roop.

Indian hostilities in the Black Rock area kept searchers away till 1858. In that year Jennison was there with a party and Hardin himself returned. He searched for three years. There were dozens of men hunting for the marvelous silver deposit, but they found nothing. The face of the mountains had been changed. Perhaps the original silver chunks had been uncovered by a cloudburst, and after Hardin saw them water spouts cut new deep gullies and sent down avalanches of broken rock and totally buried the silver again. Hardin left during the Indian War of 1860. Later he helped the settlers during the Honey Lake border war, but his search was over. In 1865 an Albert E. Jamison discovered rich prospects in the area and in 1866 the camp of Hardinville was established, but no mines there ever uncovered the bricks of virgin silver.

The most famous of all Nevada's lost mines is the Breyfogle. Its history, told in almost a dozen distinct versions, is the most elaborate native fiction in Nevada. Most accounts put the mine in the Funeral Mountains. The sure fact is that there was once a man named Jacob Breyfogle who thought he could relocate a rich ledge. A Pioche merchant wrote in 1873: "This man Breyfogle has been luring parties out in the vicinity of Death Valley and hunting for a mine for years past, and he gets a party every year."

Donald F. MacCarthy, a retired prospector, told a version to J. Frank Dobie. Briefly, Breyfogle and two other men were in Los Angeles when the Reese River mining excitement broke out around Austin in 1862–63. Afoot, they crossed the Mojave Desert and the Panamint Range, at the eastern base of which they camped one night around a water hole in the rocks. Indians killed Breyfogle's sleeping comrades. He seized his shoes and ran barefoot to the floor of Death Valley. Day came, and in hot glaring sunlight Breyfogle fled across the valley to the Funerals. While searching for water he found rich float, pinkish feldspar speckled with gold. He tied specimens up in his bandanna. Surviving somehow on roots, mesquite pods, and alkali water, he walked northward across the Funeral Range and the Amargosa Desert. Two hundred and fifty miles away, at Baxter Springs, he found fresh water. He crossed into Smoky Valley, where a rancher named Wilson found him. He was still carrying the bandanna full of ore. His head was so sunburned it looked scalped. Wilson took care of him for a few days and then took him to Austin. In the fall, when the weather was cooler, Breyfogle, a Jake Gooding, and others, well outfitted, returned to the Funerals, but a war party of Panamint Indians drove them off. In the winter Breyfogle led back a second expedition. He found all the landmarks of his trip except the pinkish float which would be a clue to the ledge.

" Old Man " Finley, who died near Bullfrog in 1905, had spent years searching Death Valley for the Breyfogle. Johnny Mills, living a few years ago, looked in the Funerals for forty years. It is said that back in the early days George Hearst kept prospectors in the field for two winters looking for the lost vein. For a time all prospecting was locally called Breyfogling.

Some folks think Death Valley Scotty's " secret mine " is none other than the Breyfogle. When the Jumbo Mine in Goldfield produced ore at $2,000 a ton, the ore was compared with alleged Breyfogle ore samples in Austin: the two were identical. Was the Breyfogle any of a number of known mines? The mine at Johnnie? " Bob" Montgomery's Shoshone in Rhyolite? One of the mines at Bullfrog? A mine at Lida, Hornsilver, Silver Peak, or Southern Klondyke? Is it still to be discovered?

Mining Camp

THE MINING camp never grew slowly and gradually. It began with a rush. It started suddenly and often went suddenly out of existence, spending its vitality with the speed of the desert annuals that go from germination to seeding in less than a month. The prospector had made his strike, located a ledge, recorded his claims. The news had leaked out, rich specimens had been exhibited, and from the whole Pacific slope men had speedily set out. Romantic, Byronic they were — individuals spurred on by hope of gain and power. Granted legal title to any minerals they discovered and moral title to any profits they made, they rushed through obstacles to be first, richest, strongest. They abandoned established businesses or farms to lose their heads and probably their money over rocky seams. But maybe not! That was the thing! To try *and* seize the Main Chance!

Virginia City, Aurora, Austin, Ione, Schellbourne, Treasure City — whichever it was, the new camp became a fever, a state of mind involving dreams of grandeur. Each virgin province in Silver Land was a glittering El Dorado. Sane men were the exception. Everybody, his uncle, cousin, brother, and son-in-law was going there. The editor of a California mining-camp paper wrote in his last issue, " The discovery of the rich mines on the other side of the mountains has carried off a large proportion of our most enterprising business men, who have now become permanent residents . . . and we have determined to pull up stakes and follow them."

Men crammed into stages for a speedy dash at high ticket rates. A heterogeneous caravan plodded from sunrise to sunset, camping out at night or sleeping in the crowded shacks that served as inns — Chinese, engineers, brokers, tobacconists, clothiers, day laborers, Jezebels from every mining camp between Sonora and British Columbia, lawyers who scented lucrative litigation, Pikes who turned their quids in leathery jaws, a few Saxon mining experts from Freiberg, strangely slow and systematic in a turbulent stampede far from twelfth-century watchtowers and reverberating cathedral bells. Footpackers carried blankets and luggage, picks and shovels slung on their shoulders. Irishmen pushed wheelbarrows containing food, tools, bedrolls. Dapper San Francisco capitalists rode mares. Mexican vaqueros lounged on lean mustangs as they drove cattle to be butchered at the camp. Urged on by furiously swearing teamsters, mule and ox teams tugged at heavy wagons loaded with mill machinery, provisions, hardware, whisky, mule feed, lumber, clothing, more whisky.

A makeshift town sprang up around the mines. Men dug caves in hillsides, built stone huts, and set up shanties of mud, rawhides, willow branches, cotton cloth, juniper posts, pine logs, woolen blankets, green lumber, or flour sacks, castoff shirts, coats, and pants sewed together like a quilt. Mining paraphernalia lay scattered about. Streets appeared, but they dodged about at acute angles, as if following the dips and spurs of the mineral veins beneath. Newly arrived stampeders slept on the floors of stores, saloons, restaurants, or on the open ground, which was often just as good. The " Restaurant and Lodgings " was probably without a roof. The " Law Office " was just a shanty with a canvas door and no window. A Californian who stayed at Edwards & Evans Exchange in Unionville found himself in a room that was lathed but not plastered. The International Hotel in early Austin was a canvas-and-wood affair. The front room was a barroom, stage office, parlor, drawing-room, and general rendezvous. The next room was a dining-room furnished with a rough plank table and a hard-mud floor. Beside and behind the table were bunks, wine-rack fashion. People did not mind these makeshifts as long as they could hope. " If we strike it, what a town you will soon see here! " Even before the place had a name there would be a platted townsite, lots selling at from $500 to $2,000, and a thousand inhabitants.

Prices were high. In Treasure City in 1869 lumber that had been hauled across Nevada from Carson City cost $450 a thousand board feet plus a freight charge of $260. Fuel was $30 a cord, water 10 cents a gallon. All restaurant meals were $1. Fifty cents bought a night's use of dirty blankets in a tiny bunk-room containing eleven other sleepers. In Aurora in 1863 it cost $1.25 a day for hay alone to keep a horse in a stable. Hen eggs were $1.50 a dozen. One old mountaineer gathered duck and gull eggs on the cinder-cone islands in Mono Lake and sold them for a tidy profit.

Only metallic money was in evidence. People were hostile to paper, for they remembered devaluated greenbacks in the past, and in Nevada they were isolated from centers of business. Gold and silver were being produced in abundance, men said, and most emphatically these metals were the proper sort of money. The nickel was a nasty little coin, half dime and half brother to arsenic. Small change was despised as it still is in small old towns like Carson City. Paper bills were jeered at as they are now in Las Vegas, where they are called " cabbage " or " Jewish lettuce."

Everywhere were bars and gaming tables in impromptu buildings. It is no accident that the early Westerner fell into the habit of bragging how big his town was by giving the number of saloons on the main street. Amid the hum of voices, the clink of money, the gleam of lights, miners found relief from their cheerless huts. The bar often held bottles of Old Crow and Golden Wedding and other famous brands, all filled from the same keg of green whisky. But whether the liquor that contained it was good or bad, ethyl alcohol was the principal fuel in camp.

However new a camp was, graveyards began to fill at once, from disease, exposure, and homicide. Graves were merely the mounds of rock necessary in coyote country and an occasional pine slab with a carved inscription. Their occupants were, for the most part, young men.

Newspapers, at that time the surest evidence of freedom of speech and of literate democracy, arrived early and were eagerly welcomed. In Unionville, when the first issue of the *Humboldt Register* came off the press, on Sunday night, May 3, 1863, a large crowd was waiting outside, and soon copies were all over town. By midnight thirty-four anvil rounds had saluted the paper and an impromptu brigade commanded by a Captain Pfersdorff had marched to the music of a cornet up to the office front and given a salvo of nine cheers. Pete Hopkins of the Magnolia Saloon in Carson City, well over a hundred miles away, had sent Proprietor W. J. Forbes a package of liquor to celebrate the first number, and this was duly consumed. In March, 1864, when T. W. Abraham arrived in Como, south of Carson City, with the press material for the *Sentinel,* he was met outside of town by a brass band in full force. It was in a wagon pulled by decorated horses. There were drinks for the teamsters. Miners joked and punned. Abraham was told to press on. As the procession entered Como there were cheers from working miners in shafts and tunnels. Men banged anvils and shot off guns. The equipment arrived at the *Sentinel* office amid more cheering while the band played " Yankee Doodle " and " Hail, Columbia."

Unsettled mining camps were animated by the nervous, crude, but dynamic life of an improvised civilization. Streets were crowded with mules, wagons, and men. On the sidewalks and in the saloons and stores were men who showed ore samples, sold mines, discussed ores and ore processes, played with small silver bars in their pockets; miners whose clothes, torn by rocks, had been patched so as to give their nether garment a medley of clashing colors; prospectors who jammed their pockets with rolls of duplicate location notices and assay certificates; idlers and bummers who claimed they were pioneers of '49, drank at the expense of strangers, swore, and swapped outrageous lies. Bartenders were incessantly in motion in their frantic efforts to keep orders filled. In the crowded clubrooms the dealers astutely furnished drinks every few minutes, and players gambled with calm recklessness: " Chicken today, feathers tomorrow." Serious men jammed the Wells, Fargo office as they wrote letters or sent home packages.

Carpenters hammered and sawed on the frames of livery stables, theaters, sporting houses, hotels, stores. Bricklayers slapped down mortar. Near town, in the mines already established and down one level, there was blasting, drilling, and pounding. On less-developed ground, prospectors ran around like ants, developing shafts. "Shots" exploded every few minutes. Miners were in a hurry, and they lacked lumber to lay over shafts before setting off blasts. They lit a fuse and called "Shot!" and ran for the nearest cover. Some careless miners did not call. Passers-by scurried in all directions. Bang!! and a volley of rocks rubbled down on anything below.

A brand-new mining camp improvised its recreations with zest if not with brilliance. In Summit City a debating society lasted for a while and was followed by the Nasty Club, which tried its members for various offenses. One night a miner was arraigned for malpractice. He had unskillfully felled a tree. In a fantastic parody of a coroner's inquest, witnesses gave their testimony. The death of the tree was attributed to beavers, volcanic eruption, and lightning, but all experts agreed that the tree had been dead for twenty years. The verdict was: "We, the jurors, find that the tree was not felled by human hands, but was thrown down by some cause to the jury unknown. We furthermore find the Coroner guilty of the drinks for the Club, for holding an inquest on a tree that has been dead for twenty years — the same being barred out by the statutes of limitation."

During the first winter in Treasure City, 1868–69, a crowd gathered in Main Street each day about noon. With lively interest they placed bets on the horseback messengers who daily grabbed the mail sacks of rival express companies from the stage in Hamilton, three miles downhill, and galloped up.

"Two to one on Wells Fargo and Company!"
"That's me! Come out with the scads."

"One hundred even that the Pacific Union wins by a minute and a half."
"That's me!"

There was much confusion and pouring of twenty-dollar gold pieces from buckskin purses into hands. At last two dark spots appeared moving against the snowdrifts on the brow of the hill toward Hamilton.

"Hi! hi! hurrah. Here they come! Wells, Fargo and Company are ahead!"
"No, they ain't; the gray is the Pacific Union!"
"Bet you a hundred on that."
"Take you for the drinks; I'm short today; the game beat me last night."
"I don't make four-bit bets. What'n thunder d'ye take me for!"

The horsemen were lost to view behind the snowdrifts. Now they turned into Main Street. The crowd roared. The riders plied whip and spur. The horses strained their muscles and bulged their eyes. They splashed through slush and snow, neck and neck. One horse stumbled to his knees. The other gained half a dozen yards. The rider threw his bag into the door of the Union Express Company's office. A yell went up. Citizens paid their bets and talked over the race, while hostlers threw blankets over the horses and led them up and down.

As unstable as their camp, men entertained themselves sadistically by firing revolvers in all directions on a street, by throwing bad eggs at a violinist, by hurling snowballs at a sleigh party, by fighting drunkenly in a saloon over the singing of "Flag of Our Union." For the prominent and physically powerful Tom Peasley, chief engineer of the first fire department in Virginia City, and doorkeeper at one session of the Territorial Legislature, "to knock an acquaintance over with a slap upon the back was a playful style of salutation. To break a door down instead of unlatching it only denoted a particular intimacy with the proprietor." There were badger fights, burro fights, dog fights, wildcats *vs.* bulldogs. One cinnamon bear had to fight four bulldogs in succession. A rooster-pulling contest was held. Any man who wished deposited a dollar, placed a rooster between his legs, with the head downward, and pulled on the rooster's legs. If he pulled the legs off, he won a dollar. An English visitor asked why the cocks made no noise. "They can't," replied a native; "they are too much absorbed." A Gold Hill blacksmith took great delight in attracting tame ducks to his shop by throwing them pieces of raw liver. Then he beat a small bar of iron red hot and chopped off small bits, which he chucked to the unsuspecting birds. He almost went into convulsions of laughter when he saw the hot bits of iron burn through their crops and drop to the ground.

Often theater buildings were as impromptu as the audiences were uncritical. Early in 1863 the nation's leading humorist, Artemus Ward, lectured in the new camp of Big Creek. He spoke in a saloon which was just a sagebrush roof over a bare dirt floor, with no sides at all. At one end there was a wood fire. Ward spoke from behind the drinking bar, amid decanters, pictures of race horses and prize fighters, with the barkeeper beside him. His lecture was his funny assemblage of gags and wit called "Babes in the Woods." At the close of one hilarious point, the barkeep pounded the bar with his fist. "Good boy from the New England States! Listen to William W. Shakespeare!"

New camps celebrated traditional public holiday with boundless energy, well illustrated by the first Fourth of July in White Pine, in 1868. Cave City (soon to be called Hamilton) and Treasure City both wanted to have celebrations of their own because of the intense rivalry between them. Then they realized that they didn't have enough people for two. On the third of July they compromised on duties and honors and combined their efforts.

The Parade Committee had no troubles. Its plan and personnel were easily arranged. But the Flag, Music, and Ball Committee ran into grief. There was no flag in the two towns. At the store they bought a piece of the white drilling used to line houses and tents. They ripped the red from the quilt cover of an " aristocrat's " bed. The blue was hardest to find. Hearing that a Mormon family had pulled in and camped below town, one of the committeemen strolled down to see what blue fabric might be picked up, and there he finally obtained a blue veil that the wife dug out of her trunk. How the music and dance problems settled themselves will appear later.

On the Fourth the males of Cave City lined up in twos and marched up the three miles of trail to Treasure City. There being no band in town, the two best local whistlers strode at the head, producing " Yankee Doodle " until the altitude above 9,000 feet took their breath away. The procession was met by the citizens of Treasure City, and all trooped into saloons for certain obvious formalities. Then they all marched back to Cave City.

Literary exercises followed. The chairman was from Treasure City. He introduced the orator of the day (a Cave City man) and for a while the eagle screamed. Then he introduced the poet of the day (a Treasure City man), and after hearing the poem the crowd sang patriotic songs, enthusiastically organized the White Pine Pioneer Society, and, in honor of the makeshift Old Glory that floated o'erhead, made it the first sacred relic in the archives of the Society.

In the evening a hilarious Grand Ball took place in a " hall " that was an incomplete store. It was a cheap board structure about forty feet by twenty. Only the sides were up. There was no front, no rear, no roof. It was on the downhill side

of the street. The front floor was one foot off the ground
and the rear six feet — presenting a hazard to festive cele-
brants. Cloth for the ceiling had been sewed in one big piece.
It made a canopy between the sides.

The music was furnished by a fiddler who sat on a three-
legged stool and called the figures. Several hundred men attended in gray shirts, overalls, and stogie boots. The two
women resident in Cave City were there, as were Heberine
and Brighamette and two other daughters of the Mormon
family, who wore homespun dresses, and leather brogans
thoughtfully provided by the committee for their customarily
bare feet. They danced square dances but not round dances
(which were danced only by Gentiles and apostates).

Behind all the surface turbulence of mining camps, sober
citizens were setting up a stable society. American institutions, the defenses of free men, that had slowly evolved on
the Eastern frontier, were boldly imported and established,
even before the permanence of the camp was known. A self-
appointed committee kept order, county sheriffs arrived to
watch things and appoint deputies, a United States marshal
appeared, daily mail service was arranged, a post office was pe-
titioned for, and soon municipal machinery was set up. With
the camp still chaotic in appearance and manner, there were
courts, a mayor, a common council, primary meetings, elections, official recorders and surveyors, torchlight processions,
and hat waving. There were plans for a public school and
ward organization. Before Hamilton was half a year old, its
citizens set up a school district, elected a board of trustees,
dedicated a lot for the house and fixed the salary of the schoolma'am. They also reserved a tract for religious purposes and
formed a lyceum with a debating club and reading-room. To
get the immediate revenue needed to begin and maintain local
government, mining towns passed a license tax. A general
property tax would not do because permanency could not be
assumed and, besides, mineowners would object to it. Thus

stage companies, hotels, stores, saloons, and banks paid taxes from the start, and even if the mines should peter out and the population dwindle away, all governmental debts would be paid.

Most important of all, in a mining community, an established principle of landownership had the sanction of custom. A special kind of law, a common law of miners, sprang up in California and Nevada and spread throughout the West. Acting on their own initiative in each newly discovered district, miners called a meeting and formed their own rules and formally adopted their own customs. They exercised popular sovereignty in a very fundamental sense. Equivalent to the New England town meeting, this procedure was an original contribution to the art of self-government. By 1866 there were over two hundred mining districts in Nevada. Whether phrased by lawyers or educated men unversed in the law, or frontiersmen, the regulations were well worded and clear in meaning.

They established that use was proof of ownership, that equality in size of lots was of prime importance, and that land not in actual possession was common land. They laid down rules for the legal size of a claim, the requirements for ownership, conditions whose constant fulfillment was necessary, circumstances that would forfeit all right to title, methods of procedure to settle disputes.

When territories and states were set up, mining laws always made full provision for the miners' districts. The laws of Nevada Territory provided:

In all actions respecting mining claims, proof shall be admitted of the customs, usages, or regulations established and in force in the mining district embracing such claim; and such customs, usages, or regulations when not in conflict with the laws of this Territory, shall govern the decision of the action in regard to all questions of location, possession, and abandonment.

In 1866, when Congress began to legislate on mining claims, Senator William Stewart of Nevada and other Western senators saw that it sanctioned local laws that did not conflict with the laws of the United States. Later amendments to the law extended the application of the original squatters' covenants; for example, Congress asserted that mineral lands of the United States are " open to exploration, occupation, and purchase " under regulation " prescribed by law and according to the local customs of miners in the several mining districts."

Reality, of course, fell short of the ideal. The existence of a mining district with perfectly plain rules did not prevent crime and violence. Claim jumping was a phenomenon in any new camp. " A personal occupation and a good revolver " might very well constitute clear title. The so-called " Battle for the Washington and Creole " at Pioche in 1870 is an example. Two big operators, Raymond and Ely, had acquired many claims in town, including the Washington and Creole, which promised only mediocre returns. Tom and Frank Newland, who owned adjacent claims, asked for and received permission to tunnel below the Washington. To their surprise, they tunneled into a thick, rich vein, assaying $300–$500 per ton. Quietly they asked Raymond and Ely for permission to mill the ore they tunneled. They got thirty days. When Raymond heard about the ore, he was pleased, not angry, for he was eager both to build up the fame of Pioche and to get plenty of ore to work at the near-by mill he owned at Bullionville. At the end of the thirty days the Newland brothers wanted to keep the mine they had found; so they gathered up some roughs and jumped the mine. They built a fort at the tunnel entrance, stationed men and guns there all hours of the day and night, and mined full blast. The sheriff tried to drive them off, but guards ordered him away at the point of guns and warned that they would shoot Raymond and Ely, should they approach.

Soon after, four young miners approached the owners and said they would drive off the intruders in return for a right to use the claim for a month. Raymond and Ely told them to try if they thought they could win. The four, Michael Casey, Barney Flood, Morgan Courtney, and William Bethers, all under thirty, watched their time, waiting for the guard to relax. One day one of them passed the entrance and offered his flask to the guards, who drank heavily. About three in the afternoon the quartet rushed downhill, firing their pistols. They drove the guards away from their guns and hid behind rocks so as to cover the persons in the mine. While a crowd of spectators watched from the hill above, the fight continued off and on for several hours. The attackers killed one guard, wounded several others, and finally drove out the Newland gang. During their month of mining privilege they netted $60,000.

The hectic early period of a mining camp was the heyday of the " badman," as distinguished from the normal law-breaker and from the " gunman," who might be a good citizen. Badmen killed because of drunkenness, inferiority complexes, grudges against society or individuals, sheer bravado, sometimes because of mental illness brought on by syphilis or bad liquor. They killed during quarrels over women, land titles, card games, and " insults." Half the time the cause was trivial. They seemed to enjoy taking human life. They solved social and psychological problems, not with intelligence, but with animal cunning and brute force. Red-whiskered Sam Brown of early Washoe ran a knife into a man named McKenzie, turned it carefully round and cut the man's heart out, wiped the blood off his knife, and lay down to sleep on a billiard table.

Hasty use of the revolver as a weapon of assassination, not defense, was a peculiarly Western American tradition. It was not found at all in the busy frontier camps along the Fraser and Cariboo rivers in British Columbia or in the Yukon and

Klondike country in northwestern Canada, where mounted police moved in alongside migrating prospectors. Gunwork had no part in the amazingly orderly search for gold in Siberia by the Soviet Union, as described by John D. Littlepage, but Sam Kemp is authority that Westerners did carry wild gunplay to Johannesburg during the gold rush there from Pretoria, and they carried it to Alaska over Chilkoot Pass.

In Nevada towns, as elsewhere in the West, law enforcement lagged at first behind violation of law. A man had to assume the responsibility for his own protection, and therefore he carried a gun. The omnipresent gun and the sensitive code of honor combined to produce the inevitable killing. Normal feminine and domestic associations were lacking. There was no conservative agricultural counterweight in the population. There was always a chance of being wiped out by a " difference " with someone. Men lived in a society where a man was admired if he was " heavy on the shoulder " and could " hit out straight from the hip." Gunplay was easily provoked in an atmosphere of rum, corn whisky, stale tobacco, cards, and oaths. A Virginia City barkeep named John Wilson, employed by J. L. Moore of the Pavillion lodging- and boardinghouse, asked for his pay to send to his family. Moore pulled out his six-shooter and said, " I'll pay you off. Where shall I shoot you? " Wilson, surprised, replied, " Anywhere," and grinned. Moore scowled and fired. The ball struck Wilson just above the navel and passed out near the backbone. As soon as Moore saw what he had done, he stuck out his hand to the wounded man and said, " John, shake hands, I was only joking! " Wilson died a few days later.

The low percentage of convictions encouraged killings. According to tradition there were seventy-two graves in the burying ground below Pioche before there was one death from natural causes in camp. Myron Angel's *History of Nevada* compiled a list of 402 homicides between 1846 and 1881 — an admittedly incomplete list — and showed that nothing was done about most of them. Three of the killers committed suicide, thirteen were hanged by vigilantes, and only sixty were so much as taken to court. Of these, twenty-one were acquitted, twenty-three were sent to the state prison, and eight were hanged by county sheriffs. Judges and prosecuting attorneys were zealous enough, but juries were easily influenced by friends or intimidated by foes. Since desperadoes tended to kill their own sort, peaceable citizens were likely to leave them to themselves. As an old-timer recalls, " These ' bad men ' and their ' companionate marriage wives ' lived in a section of the town that was isolated, and no attention was given to how many were killed." If one of them wanted " trouble," he could find it. If a stranger ran a bluff on gun-play, one of them would call him on it.

One winter day a sleigh was making the three-dollar, 1,500-foot climb from Hamilton to Treasure City. On board was a female in moire antique, furs, and gaudy jewelry, her face gaily painted. When the sleigh stopped in front of the Wells, Fargo office, two six-foot gallants jumped out. Both were bearded and costumed like Eskimos. Each offered his hand to assist the lady out. Neither would yield. She made no move to make her own selection. They shoved, pushed, and one of them struck a stinging blow. They pulled their revolvers, but their heavy clothing interfered with their aim. The crowd scattered. Some of the bystanders pulled their guns and shot, too. Finally a bullet blasted an artery of one of the horses and blood spurted over a combatant. Thinking himself shot, he threw down his revolver and ran down the street, groaning and crying murder. Meanwhile the woman sat an impartial spectator, waiting to see which would survive to help her descend from the sleigh.

Another type of gunwork that caused trouble in Nevada was the duel. The many Southerners who went to California in the fifties and then to Nevada in the sixties took with them their elaborate ritual for blood atonement in matters of honor.

In the sagebrush, however, this notion of genteel fighting never acquired the decorum and finesse it had in the parklike estates of South Carolina and Louisiana.

The Constitutional Convention debated on means of stopping this threat to life and peace and tentatively required all voters to take a nondueling oath but finally included in the Constitution an oath administered only to state and county officials, directors of corporations, and schoolteachers. " And I do solemnly swear (or affirm) that I have not fought a duel, nor sent or accepted a challenge to fight a duel, nor been a second to either party." This proviso, which was in the official oath until 1914, no doubt helped to discourage dueling, but even when coupled with a criminal statute did not stop it among Nevadans, especially newspapermen. In early years in Virginia City duels were either fought or scheduled between Joseph Goodman of the *Enterprise* and H. C. Bennett of the *Herald*, Goodman and Tom Fitch of the *Union*, Sam Clemens of the *Enterprise* and James Laird of the *Union*. All were based on trivial points of honor. " The code seems to becoming quite fashionable," remarked the *Union* in 1863.

Unrestrained, sarcastic frontier editorials were the most common affronts to honor, as witness the incident that led H. F. Swayze on January 23, 1863, to give a death wound to Editor George W. Derickson of the Washoe City *Times*. About eight days earlier Swayze, a resident of near-by Ophir City, had attempted " to palm off " a plagiarism on the *Times* and Derickson had replied with a severe personal article of a sort then common in the press.

" ICHABOD." — A tall, gawky greenhorn, dressed in a buckskin suit, stepped into the *Times* offices yesterday, and handed us an article, which he was very anxious to have published. He said he had spent a great deal of time in getting it up, and wanted a dozen or so copies of the paper, containing his article, when published, to send to his friends. The article was headed, ' How I got my Wife,' and was signed, ' Ichabod.' The said greenhorn, whose real name, he informed us, is H. F. Swayze, is hereby informed that he can have a dozen copies of the *Times*, containing his article, by calling at this office and paying for the same. His article, which he says cost him so much trouble and study to get up, was published in the second number of the *Times*, word for word, and we have the same for sale. The same greenhorn, who seems to think printers are as green as himself, brought in a long article several weeks since, ridiculing the town of Ophir and its inhabitants, and was very much surprised because his literary efforts were not appreciated and published. The manuscript copy of the last article of the said H. F. Swayze is at his disposal by calling at the *Times* office; and he can also purchase, for cash, several copies of the *Times*, containing this notice, to send to his friends.

Editor Derickson was at a dance at Steamboat Springs on Thursday, the twenty-second. He heard that Swayze was looking for him and armed himself. Next day they met in a Washoe City saloon, and from there they went to the office. Swayze said Derickson was to retract his charges, and pulled his gun. Derickson said the language in the paper was true and that he would retract nothing. Swayze replied, "You are a damned liar," and as Derickson retreated through the open door both men fired simultaneously. They fired several times more. A ball lodged in Swayze's mouth, cracking the jawbone and carrying two teeth with it. He spat out the ball and teeth. Derickson was mortally wounded. The sheriff took Swayze prisoner, while citizens, who had liked the editor, were incensed almost to lynching fever.

Killers were less numerous, fortunately, than robbers and road agents. Holdups were common on the dark camp streets. Nowadays a fellow down on his luck merely panhandles. In the age of Colt's pistol he said, "Hands up!" The editor of a Pioche paper wrote, "The practice of robbing strangers is disgraceful and should be stopped." Stage robberies were a natural event because concentrated wealth, bars of gold and silver, was carried in the stages, and they had to pass along narrow roads such as Virginia Gulch, below Aurora. These bottlenecks were an invitation to bandits. The Wells, Fargo Express Company was rather generally disliked because it was a corporate monopoly, as highhanded and extortionate in rates as the Central Pacific was later, and as fully protected by law. Since the high tariffs of the company took the gold away from the miner, average citizens thought it a pleasant irony to have the company in turn despoiled by a brave common man with a gun. Wells, Fargo put a shotgun messenger on each stage to protect the bullion bars, then two messengers, but still there were holdups. These called for an organization. There were spies in express offices, in the ore mills, and in the stables. When a stage with treasure aboard was leaving town, the spies signaled to confederates.

Vigilante organizations formed sporadically whenever crime became too frequent. There was a protective association in Hamilton and Treasure City for a couple of years, and so many robberies took place on the Egan and White Pine road that inhabitants formed the Egan Canyon Property Protection Society with a preamble and rules and regulations. The most celebrated incident of vigilante work in Nevada took place in Aurora in 1864. The Daly gang had been guilty of several crimes, and when it killed W. R. Johnson citizens organized extralegally to stop further violence. The gang had a grudge against Johnson. He had refused to tell them the whereabouts of a man named Rodgers, who had legitimately killed a horse thief, one Sears, a friend of Daly. Early in February, 1864, Johnson, who kept a station out of town on the road toward Carson, came to town to dispose of some potatoes, and his enemies set their wits to work to contrive a killing that would not point to them. One of them affected friendship for Johnson, induced him to take a walk and to visit several saloons, and at a late hour decoyed him to a somewhat obscure locality, where other gang members were secreted behind a woodpile. They killed him, rifled his pockets, and separated, leaving him where he lay. Daly went to a saloon, where, shortly afterward, he referred nonchalantly to a dead man in the street a little way off.

Daly was at once suspected. Next day a man named "Italian Jim," who was somehow aware of the plot, was pursued to West Walker River and arrested. He confessed the details. Three of the leaders, Daly, Masterson, and Jack McDowell, alias Three-fingered Jack, were arrested. A posse finally captured Buckley in the sagebrush near the edge of Mono Lake.

A Citizens' Protective Union organized, encouraged by the evident conscientiousness of the newly elected United States marshal, Bob Howland. It was time for reform. In the preceding three years about thirty citizens of Aurora had died by violence — one every six weeks. The members of the safety committee felt no disregard for due process of law, but law officers had been indifferent. There had been delays, high costs in the trials for poor people, unnecessary postponement of trials of underworld characters, and difficulties in obtaining witnesses.

The vigilantes began rounding up miscellaneous badmen and unconvicted criminals and banishing them from town on threat of lynching. Some villains fled town on horseback. For the murderers of Johnson, outraged citizens began setting up a gibbet. Up in Carson City, Governor Nye received telegraphic dispatches describing disorder. He wired back to learn the condition of affairs. Bob Howland replied, " Everything quiet in Aurora; four men to be hung in fifteen minutes."

At noon on February 9 the members of the Protective Union formed in line, marched to jail, took the four prisoners, and mounted them upon the scaffold erected in front of Armory Hall. Every miner had long since left his tools in the shafts and tunnels around Aurora, and there was a great crowd, but the local militia and the Union kept strict order. The doomed men were allowed to speak. Buckley, who was cool and brave, assured the hearers that only he and Daly were guilty. Daly, who was drunk, confirmed this. Johnson had killed his partner, and he regretted only that there was but one Johnson to kill in return. Masterson said he was innocent. Three-fingered Jack raved drunkenly and called heaven to witness his innocence, and just before being pinioned he drew a derringer and pointed it at his breast. It snapped, and he dashed it to the ground with a curse. The four were placed in position, their hands were tied, their eyes bandaged, and the nooses slipped over their heads. The signal gun went off and the men dangled.

OFTEN enough, after an excitement had produced a stampede and a mushroom town, men found that there was no excuse for a town. There were a mayor and a fire department, a politician aspiring to the United States Senate, a gun-sporting badman and a fire-eating editor, but the all-essential ore failed to extend downward or sideways. It declined in richness until it was low-grade that would not pay for its own mining and milling. Or it pinched out before it got any distance at all. What a competent geologist could have predicted in a brief, sane exploration of the area had been discovered only after several hundred or thousand people had gone through the process of setting up a community. Worse, sometimes the mines were all right, but " richer " mines were heard of somewhere else near.

Whichever way, the camp died without getting within gunshot of permanency. The citizenry moved to prosperous camps or joined the rush to the new strike. Everyone left, taking the portable possessions he had brought not so long before. The editor took his Washington hand press, the merchant his canvas walls and iron cashbox, the constable his notched gun, the miner his pick and shovel and dynamite caps. The huts of mud and sagebrush remained behind, as did the stone houses and the skeletons of frame buildings, but many one-room frame shanties were put on runners and dragged away to the new camp. The camp of Gold Creek, in the Owyhee region near Idaho, was established on the mere rumor of gold. A town was set up and immediately abandoned. One fire plug still remains. In some camps there were elaborate mills to leave behind — built before the limited ore supply was known — and roasting furnaces with tall chimneys of solid masonry, put up at great expense to extract precious metals that were never found. Generally not enough remained in a few years for the camp to be called a ghost town. It was merely a former site, a dimly remembered name — Yandleville, Yankee Blade, Pizarro, Geneva, Coral City.

If a strike made good, however, the camp took on the appearance of a real town. Excess population drifted away. The wild manners of the days of roughing it toned down. Law, comforts, conveniences were fully established. Tents became houses; booths, stores. Real-estate values leveled off and general property taxes became possible. Mining stocks were less a matter of wild speculation, more a matter of sober investment. Families arrived and good schools went up, staffed by well-paid teachers. Several newspapers competed for subscribers and influence over state politics. Churches were built, with special features in redwood. Marble shafts and family plots with ornamental iron fences appeared in the graveyards; the epitaphs named men, wives, and children. Sure of their town's future, citizens put up sandstone courthouses strong enough to last a century. Stage and freight lines settled down to regular schedules. The Fourth of July became a carefully planned, impressive occasion with rock-drilling contests held after a great pageant — military companies marched in immaculate order, the fire departments pulled their costly and ornate engines and hose carriages, decorated horses pulled the car of state containing gay girls labeled to represent the states of the Union, and brass bands played brave tunes that rebounded from the mountain slopes. Fraternal orders flourished. Saloons, at their best, became community centers where men settled business matters and strengthened friendships. The thick red carpets, the mahogany bars, the glimmering graded glasses helped give éclat. The paintings in their gold frames were art, the out-of-town newspaper rack was literature, the mechanical piano was great music, the cabinet of curiosities was science, and the gamblers were high society. A " permanent " mining camp was set up that might last from four years to twenty, and, with rare good fortune, to eighty and beyond.

The Nevada mining camp that actually lived on and grew up was a new sort of community in the America of the day. Houses clung to the steep hillsides above the commercial streets. On all sides was evidence of the basic industry that kept the whole community on the go. Ore ran out of tunnels in little cars. Waste dirt sprawled on the dumps. Steam engines puffed white vapor. Thick smoke writhed from stacks. Quartz batteries stomped on ore. Ball mills roared and rattled. Underground blasts shook the earth. In front of the mill offices visitors stood around and saw an amazing sight. Bullion bars of gold and silver were carelessly thrown into wagons and coaches as if they were but useless window-sash weights.

The business streets echoed with noise, and people were everywhere in motion. Fruit vendors peddled the latest berries and peaches from California. Wagons rolled into town loaded with hay, merchandise, and mining equipment. Auctioneers shouted off the stocks of delinquent mine stockholders, and gaping crowds of speculators bought them. Organ grinders ground away. Billstickers posted advertisements, sometimes gorgeous ones, for auctions, theaters, lectures, new saloons. " LOOK HERE! *For fifty cents* You Can Get a Good Square Meal at the HOWLING WILDERNESS SALOON! " Newsboys cried papers just off the press, con-

taining the latest telegraphic news and filled with every species of notice and advertisement. A small crowd watched a
blacksmith knock out a man's aching tooth with a punch and
hammer. Clothiers sold off prodigious assortments of gar-
ments. " Now or Never! Cheapest costs in the world!! Pants
Given Away!!! WALK IN, GENTS." " You wants to puy
sometings sheap — eh? Vat? Se cote ers too larsh? Oh mine!
Feets be-auti-fool! and den he feets zo nice een ze dail — in ze
dail, monsuer. Shoost look at eet." Stages dashed in from San
Francisco, or Carson City, Elko, or Battle Mountain. Wells,
Fargo agents distributed letters, packages, and papers to a
multitude who stood around amid piles of silver bricks, scales,
letter boxes, clerks, account books, and twenty-dollar pieces.

Among the crowd were boosters, ecstatic " natives " of a
year or two, who insisted on a number of opinions that a
stranger had to hold. He had to find the climate healthful, even
if only one day in ten was good; to admire the fertility of the
soil, the luxuriance of vegetation, in spite of the evident bleak-
ness of an area robbed of its sagebrush for fuel; to agree it was
a fine place to live, despite sore throats, diarrhea, loss of appetite, heart disease, and erysipelas — a frequent scourge of early
days; to discover Elysian repose at night, even if the ore crushers and the whisky drinkers made bedlam at all hours.

Most of the male population were of a type that followed
the mines and loved mining-camp life. They were merchants,
lawyers, doctors, saloonkeepers, politicians, journalists, mineworkers, engineers. Even when they had families, they felt
no strong ties to any particular community. They were a virile, enthusiastic group of men, brimful of push and energy,
conscious in a way that they were making history, even more
conscious that they were alive on a new frontier where personal conquest was possible. They believed actively in liberty
and freedom of opportunity, in social equality for all (except
Indians and Chinese), in civil liberties (except for Confederate sympathizers). They judged a man on his record for char-

acter and achievement. When they turned vigilante or pulled
a gun on another man, the basis of their action — they thought
— was democratic idealism; they did not sense in it what their
grandsons would label "fascism." They worked, played, and
dreamed with gusto and zest, for they had the get-rich-quick
temperament of a society of dream millionaires. No man
could go amiss, even if he worked his imagination or his jaws
more than his pick. Quite absent was the steady spirit of commerce and agriculture. The most common sentence in town
was "Let's take a drink." The second most common was
"How are stocks today?"

The men who walked from the mines, their day's work
over, were not dispirited Siberian saltworkers or dulled Alle-
gheny coal miners. Their working environment was inor-
ganic, the most lifeless surroundings men have ever willingly
submitted to — the dead crust of the earth, where the only
life, if any, is that which seeps and trickles in water. But out
of the mines they were "the boys," ready for the recreations
of downtown or the pleasures of well-rounded domestic life.
Convivially they worked in gangs, ate in gangs at the board-
inghouses, slept in gangs in the rooming houses. In contrast to
the prospectors and solitary miners in the ravines and high
valleys, they were metropolitanized.

Ethnic minorities added variety to the scene. Indians were
in the towns from the start; they came in from their squatters'
shacks or campoodies to do housework, buck wood, or scav-
enge. Many nations and tongues arrived in due course. Each
had its spot of congregation, a saloon, café, or beer cellar. This
was especially true of the Germans, French, Mexicans, Chinese, Cornish, and Irish. The Cornishmen, or "Cousin Jacks,"
long famous as tin miners in southern England, were socially
cohesive enough to be called, punningly, "Clannishmen."
The French had their Café de Paris. In their beer cellars the
rotund Teutons sat and dreamed of the Vaterland amid banks
of smoke from meerschaum pipes. Modest little signs, advis-

ing the public that L. Sam or Yee Lung did washing and iron-
ing, pointed the way to hot, ill-ventilated rooms where " Ce-
lestials " chattered in high voices.

Austin, Pioche, Eureka, Tuscarora, Silver City, and Gold
Hill lasted longer than most of their contemporary Nevada
towns. Gold Hill, sitting astraddle one end of the Comstock
lode, would probably have been the glory of the age had not
a more brilliant mining metropolis flourished one mile north
of it. For in Virginia City the Nevada silver frontier reached
apotheosis.

Climax in Virginia City

OF all the mining towns that have been sensations in the West,
the most famous is Virginia City. Its mines were the richest
yet discovered in the United States, and a whole set of circumstances gave it a crucial importance no other mining camp
has ever had. Successive ore finds and delirious stock gambling
kept it at a higher pitch for a longer time than any other
Western camp. It made precedents galore. Good fortune gave
it a half dozen unusual journalists who won it regional fame
at the start and later began a tradition of literary glorification
of the town on a national scale. The history of Virginia City
is to a very considerable degree the history of Nevada. It is
part of the economic and political history of the United States.
It is both a representative and a unique part of the history of
the frontier.

The depth of the veins gave Virginia City a permanence
that the California placer camps and most Nevada hard-rock
camps never knew. By 1864, five years after the original rush,
a complete city pattern of life had been established. Streets
were straight and business was centered on C Street. Land had
been subdivided into lots, with preferred frontages of forty to

fifty feet selling for $10,000 to $20,000. Above C Street were residences of merchants and mining officials. Below were a Chinese section and the rickety huts of Washoes and Piutes, who throve peacefully on the wastes of town. Near by was a section of whitewashed cabins, gaudily furnished, with inmates sitting in uncurtained windows. Throughout the town, in hotels, rooming houses, and shacks, the mineworkers lived. Livery stables were common. Saloons were everywhere. There were established schools, churches, and courts. The mine shafts were just downhill from town, but tunnels ran in all directions beneath the streets. According to the Bureau of the Census, the number of permanent residents in 1860 was only 2,500; 7,000 in 1870; and at the peak, in 1880, about 11,000. Estimates of reliable visitors during the booms between census years give a top total of 25,000 persons in town.

In make-up the population that hurried to Virginia City was a hodgepodge. In 1860 there were already men from all the states of the Union and thirty-nine foreign countries. Young men were abundant. At the first state constitutional convention, in 1863, the average age was about thirty-nine, the youngest delegate being twenty-four. As late as 1883 the average age of miners was thirty-six. Young or old, interesting and original characters were numerous and many of them became famous in the West. One was James W. Nye, former police commissioner of New York, whom President Lincoln appointed territorial governor. Even the Piutes liked him, since he was fair to them. He was popular in Virginia City for his stories and for his interlarding of profanity and the Scriptures. His repartee later helped him get into the United States Senate. As C. C. Goodwin remembered him, he was once speaking out of doors when a donkey brayed vociferously and interrupted him. The crowd bellowed with amusement. Nye stretched out his hand. " Ladies and gentlemen, that does not disturb me in the least. I have never tried to make a Republican speech in Nevada that the opposition has not trotted out their best speakers to try and down me."

"Sandy" Bowers emerged among the first legendary figures of Washoe. He was married to a Scotch boardinghouse keeper, Eilley Orrum Cowan. Miners gave her a ten-foot claim on the Comstock, in Gold Hill, that turned out to be immensely rich, for running through it was a streak of decomposed rock, two feet wide and half gold. Although the muckers secreted high-grade ore in their clothes and carried it off, for three years the illiterate owners netted $10,000 per month, until the ore pinched out 190 feet down. Meanwhile, they decided to go to Europe, and gave a great free banquet at the International Hotel, at which Sandy said:

I've got money to throw to the birds. Thar ain't no chance for a gentleman to spend his money in this country, and thar ain't nothin' much to see, so me and Mrs. Bowers is agoin' to Yoorup to take in the sights. Outside of Horace Greeley, the only great men I've seen in this country is Governor Nye and Old Winnemucca. Now me and Mrs. Bowers is going to see the Queen of England and other great men of them countries, and I hope you'll all join in and drink Mrs. Bowers' health. There's plenty of champagne and money ain't no object.

They went. They spent lavishly, with bad taste, and failed to get an audience with the queen. They returned to a mansion in Washoe Valley which cost at least a quarter of a million dollars, including $3,000 mirrors and window curtains at $1,200 each. It was the Scotty's Castle of its day. Entertaining prodigally they squandered their fortune in a few years. Sandy, the "sagebrush Croesus," died, and Eilley made a living as the "Washoe Seeress."

One of the best-known Comstockers was William Wright, who called himself Dan De Quille. He was a popular reporter on the *Territorial Enterprise* from 1862 until the paper suspended in 1893. He wrote local news and features and ranked as the leading mining reporter in the area. He made the newspaper a notebook for his richly detailed observations of life, and also wrote for San Francisco publications, especially the weekly *Golden Era,* which called him " our cherished contributor. . . . Far and wide are Dan De Quille's stories, sketches, his notes of travel, quaint conceptions and sober suggestions, copied, commended, and spread abroad through the land."

A humorous, patient, thoughtful Quaker who had been raised on an Iowa farm, he never became soured when companions like Mark Twain left him behind and went on to wide fame. He had no enemies and many admirers. His rivals on the Gold Hill *News* wrote, " Dan is a favorite, deservedly so, with all who know him . . . the old wheel horse of the reportorial corps." Which was to say, he was the dean of newspapermen in two hillside towns where eighteen papers were started during the sixties, where on July 4, 1864, six competing dailies appeared. Keenly observant, witty, sympathetic to suffering humanity, De Quille was a submerged novelist, an incipient literary man fated to be a mining-camp reporter.

The most famous of Comstockers is, of course, Samuel Clemens, who walked 120 miles from Aurora to work on the *Enterprise* and remained about two years. He soaked up life and lager, leaned against doorways watching people and listening to them, and unconsciously stored up data for future books. He was " abnormally lazy " and made Dan do more than half the local-news reporting. (He later quit the San Francisco *Call* because " They wanted me to w-o-r-k a-t n-i-g-h-t-s, and d-a-m-n m-e if I'll work n-i-g-h-t-s for any man a l-i-v-i-n-g! ") According to William Stewart, he was " the most lovable scamp and nuisance who ever blighted Nevada." He printed stories about people, whether true or not. He wrote burlesques on fellow reporters, on society parties, on the territorial legislature and the constitutional conventions, and he published his celebrated hoaxes, " The Massacre at Empire City " and " The Petrified Man."

Clemens was not overly worried at any "enemies" he made. "Over in Washoe," he wrote in the *Golden Era*, "I generally say what I please about anybody and everybody, because my obliging fellow citizens have learned to put up with it. . . ." He was "sloth-like in movement," his speech drawled, he "sneered at those who offended him" but he was genuine and he was funny, and the Comstockers found him interesting. With his curly red hair, angular nose, and drooping mustache, he was a well-known citizen. He first called himself Mark Twain in the *Enterprise* on February 2, 1863. In the next few years San Francisco writers variously labeled him "the Moralist of the Main," "the humorist of the Sage Brush and Silver Land," and "the Wild Humorist of the Pacific Slope." By 1866, two years after his departure for California, the *Enterprise* was already maintaining what some recent critics have claimed, that while in Virginia City Twain "developed that rich and inexhaustible vein of humor which has made" him famous; "the solid foundation . . . was laid originally in our native alkali and sagebrush."

Dan De Quille, and hundreds of his fellow citizens, obscure or prominent, lived through extraordinarily unstable years. For two decades there were excitements that came and went, wrecking some individuals but never dismaying the general public. The rush of 1859, encouraged by the original Ophir and Gold Hill ore bodies, flattened out during the next year. New discoveries came along, and in 1863 the second boom arrived. Many mines flourished. Freaks of fortune were both exciting and commonplace. A miner named Plato paid an Irish prostitute with the title to ten feet near the Bowers claim. Miners uncovered rich ore, the ten feet rose to $150,000 or $200,000 in value, and Plato had to marry the woman to get back the fortune. Once six tons from the Belcher mine yielded $770 per ton. Mine officials in Virginia City received the highest salaries in the United States. Superintendent Palmer of the Gould & Curry got $40,000 a year. Virginia City was rich and great, and the population reached 15,000. But the ore bodies terminated at five hundred feet, the boom deflated later in the year, and continued flabby for two years, ending in an acute panic in late 1865, when the population was down to 4,000. Early in 1866 new ore bodies revived the town and gave a year of prosperity. In 1870 this third boom subsided. No new ore was being found below a thousand feet. Pumping was stopped in most mines. Perhaps the Comstock was through.

Then toward the end of the year an unprecedented bonanza came to light 1,100 feet down in the Crown Point Mine in Gold Hill. Once again the Comstock became enormously busy. "Exciting times," went a song sung in San Francisco.

> Exciting times all round the town,
>   Glory, Glory to Washoe,
> Stocks are up and stocks are down,
>   Glory, Glory to Washoe.
>   Washoe! Washoe!
>   Bound for the land of Washoe,
> And I owned three feet
> In the "Old Dead Beat,"
>   And I'm bound for the land of Washoe.

Closed mines reopened and new operations commenced. The fourth boom reached its height in 1872 and began to quiet down. Low-grade ore turned up in the Consolidated Virginia at the 1,200-foot level. And then, early in 1873, came the biggest cache of all, the Big Bonanza, which by 1880 produced $135,000,000 in gold and silver and paid $78,000,000 in dividends. Stock of the "Con Virginia" went up as did the values for all Virginia City mines. But at last the Comstock reached its superclimax. By January 7, 1875, according to Grant Smith, the market value of all Comstock mines reached about $300,000,000, an absurd value. On January 8 a panic set in that ruined thousands of people. The Crown

Point ceased to pay dividends, the rich Belcher stopped in 1876, and thereafter only the Con Virginia and the California, which also tapped the Big Bonanza, paid dividends; and they stopped in 1880. In 1881 the market value of all the mines on the lode was only $7,000,000. Great hopes were in the past. Ghosthood loomed in the future.

During the gilded twenty years prospectors and stockholders and merchants often made large amounts and lived well, and the daily laborers had a standard of living possibly unparalleled in its day. For two decades the strong Miners' Union kept the wage at $4. It forced the Nevada legislature to pass America's first eight-hour law for mine work. Workers as well as capitalists could afford the luxuries of life. The stores sold quantities of raw oysters on ice from San Francisco, fresh beef, California fruits, wines and liquors, fresh milk, potatoes, and green vegetables. Boarding tables set bounteous repasts. Drinking was universal and respectable. The saloonkeeper was an important member of society, powerful, often for the good, in politics. The world's finest liquors were served in all the mixtures and concoctions for which Americans are noted, and behind handsome mahogany bars were glasses and bottles of all shapes and sizes. Sawdust Corner, the Roadside Club, Hennessey & Breen, the Crystal Bar — and richly appointed gambling-rooms such as Gentry and Crittenden's lured miners from lonely cabins and rooming houses. They played faro, monte, vingt-et-un, rouge et noir, and roulette.

Work and recreation were both unceasing, even on Sundays. A visitor wrote, " There floats up to the ear the sound of innumerable stampers, punchers and crushers, stamping, pounding, punching, cracking, crushing, ganging, smiting, and smashing the silver quartz unceasingly day and night." Among the equally prolific evidences of fun were excursions to Steamboat Springs and Lake Tahoe, brass bands, jolly stag parties at the firehouses, elaborate parades on political occa-

from Tarayre: DESCRIPTION, *1871*

PANORAMIC MAP

of the metallurgic region of Washoe. In center, a map of Washoe is seen from vertically above. Rim shows the view from Mt. Davidson. Virginia City shown in rim to east; Gold Hill in rim to south

SCENE IN VIRGINIA CITY

CLIMATE OF VIRGINIA CITY:
THE "WASHOE ZEPHYR"

sions, carousals on election nights, games in the richly furnished billiard rooms. The Storey County Miners' Union held dances and picnics and, on occasion, funerals that sometimes ended up in total intoxication. Fire stations were select clubs. A local variant among social parties was the mill warming. Richly dressed ladies and gentlemen drove to the new mill. After workers had started the stamps pounding ore, the guests gave toasts with bountiful wine and champagne, danced between the amalgamating pans, and consumed a buffet feast.

"This ain't no place for libraries and such things," a hotelkeeper told a stranger. "Men come here to make money, and they haven't time to spare loafing around reading." But there were reading-rooms in several clubs, and books and magazines were available at the newsstands for the small minority who wanted them. In the year 1867, for example, 325 Comstockers bought subscriptions for *Harper's Monthly*, 112 for the *Atlantic Monthly*. In the summer of the year they bought almost 1,200 copies of English monthlies, 194 separate copies of Dickens, 23 sets of Froude's *History of England*, 44 copies of Shakespeare, and 50 copies of *Snow-Bound* during the first week it was offered.

Of variety entertainment and straight dramatic fare, Virginia City had the best the road could furnish, which meant, in a decentralized age, the best in America. There were several large theaters. At one time four were running at once. Programs ranged all the way from farce to Shakespearean tragedy. McKean Buchanan appeared in *Othello* and *Colleen Bawn*, Frank Mayo in *David Crockett*, Marie Duret in *Miami, the Huntress of the Mississippi*, Adah Mencken in *Mazeppa*, Modjeska in *Camille*. Lotta Crabtree, Dion Boucicault, James O'Neill, E. A. Sothern, Edwin Booth, baby Maude Adams, and young David Belasco played in Virginia City. Belasco claimed later that the killings and hangings he saw in Nevada made him "all the more particular in regard to the psychology of dying on the stage. I think I was one of the first to bring naturalness to bear in death scenes and my varied Virginia City experience did much to help me toward this." Virginia City heard Adelina Patti and the Howson Opera Company, and Louis Gottschalk, and Ole Bull with his violin. Several music halls offered a miscellany of entertainment such as bar acts, the shoofly and cancan, jokes, pantomime ballet, Negro dances, monologues in dialect — especially Negro, Irish, Yankee, and German, and living tableaux that " would hardly do for a Sunday school festival." Barnum brought Tom Thumb, Commodore Nutt, Miss Minnie Warren, and the India Rubber Woman. Said another traveling showman, " The sides of Mount Davidson must ache with laughter, for Virginia City is continuously gay and festive."

In Virginia City business pennies and nickels were inconsequential. Most drinks were priced at one bit — twelve and a half cents. If a man put down a dime he got the drink and the bar lost the two and a half cents. If he put down a quarter he got only a dime in change and the bar got the difference. Men were equally nonchalant about larger sums. Pretty singers or dancers, like Little Lotta Crabtree, often collected small fortunes after a successful number, for if miners liked it they showered a hundred dollars on the stage and tossed on a silver brick or two.

Extravagant, even in Virginia City, was Johnnie Skae's fishing party as remembered by such old-time mining men as Harry Gorham and Frank Leland. Skae made his first stake when he was a telegraph operator because he had the ability to decipher code messages for his own use. He later became president of the Sierra Nevada Mine. When a small bonanza came to light late in the seventies, Sierra Nevada stock rose from sixty-five cents a share to several hundred dollars. The stock of all the local mines went up for a time, too. As part of a stock deal he was contriving, Johnnie invited several hundred guests to a fish fry. The guests included stockholders, newspapermen, brokers, politicians, lawyers, and mine superintendents. The place was the Virginia and Gold Hill Water Works Reservoir, down a steep grade from town. The reservoir had been specially stocked with trout from Lake Tahoe. Guests caught their own trout, handed them to chefs from the International Hotel, who stood near by in white caps and aprons, and they were cooked at once. There were cigars by the hundreds, buckets of coffee, huge stacks of food, and so much whisky, gin, and champagne that hilarity was dominant over caution, and numerous vehicles were wrecked on the grade back up to town.

Not only were eager miners and speculators careless in their magnificent dreams of private treasure and their expenditure of actual cash on hand. Also they were wasteful in their stewardship of claims and ore. By the spring of 1860 none of the original holders of the first locations on the Comstock lode retained his shares except a John D. Winters. Five-sixths of this fabulously rich strip of 1,166 feet had been sold for $70,601. Until the riches of the lode were fully understood, men preferred to get what they could rather than take chances. In the recording of mine claims on the lode and in surrounding regions, miners loosely observed the self-imposed regulations of the local mining district regarding accurate description of claim boundaries. They did not wish too specifically to describe claims until they knew about the ore underneath, for they might wish to shift the boundaries. Records were kept haphazardly. The first recorder at Gold Hill was a blacksmith who kept the books on a shelf behind a saloon bar. Miners would take it whenever they wished to consult it and would change statements of location boundaries to take advantage of their newest knowledge. A formal recording might be as vague as " We the undersigned claim this spring and stream, for mining purposes." In Virginia City the records were no better kept, though even by 1860 there were approximately four thousand claims within a radius of thirty miles, and thousands more were taken up in the years following, most of them of a speculative nature. Prospectors claimed to have found huge ledges of iridium and platinum. One Washoe speculator claimed he had stumbled on an ambergris mine. Not one of a hundred claims was worth prospecting, and not one of twenty " promising " claims made good in any way.

Heedlessness in recording was matched by wastrel mining and milling. Bad use was made of great wealth. Tons of low-grade ore were totally disregarded. Ignorance in the face of new technological problems, absence of raw supplies, and the haste of unrestrained exploitation led in early years to a waste of one-third of the ore mined. Half a dozen big fortunes in an amalgam of pulverized ore and quicksilver ran off from mills into Carson River and down it to Carson Sink. For a while after the railroad came to Virginia City, ore was loaded from bins into hopper cars, and the wind blew away tons of fine dust. An assay could be obtained from anywhere on near-by hillsides. A commissioner of mining statistics for the United States said, " All the explorations in the barren mines of the Comstock could have been executed with the money flung away by the mines that have had, for a time, rich ore." A few Germans with experience at Freiberg offered their services, but although they knew silver metallurgy their processes were too slow. Americans experimented for themselves and made unequaled progress — though with unequaled lack of benefit to capitalists or the general public.

When techniques were developed they progressed so rapidly that huge mills were outdated as soon as built. The Gould & Curry Mine built an elaborate $900,000 mill after levying assessment after assessment on stockholders, and then discarded it almost as soon as it was built. With overhead costs like this in mind a metallurgist remarked that gold went into the mines faster than silver would come out. True to the Mexican proverb, it took a mine to work a mine. Salt, mercury, machinery, and other mill supplies were bought at ruinously high prices.

Stockholders put pressure on superintendents, who spurted up profits, not by running plants more economically and recovering more bullion from ore, but by mining more ore. The expense sheet did not matter. The profit sheet did. Speculators, not being investors, did not worry over waste. " Oh, snake it out," was an ordinary exhortation to President Alpheus Bull of the Gould & Curry, in San Francisco. No mystery, then, that mining was unsystematic! And small wonder that dividends were meager. Several hundred millions of production in the sixties paid less than $25,000,000 in dividends.

Dishonest trickery was as common as honest carelessness. A prospector noted, " I think near all the scoundrels and smart fellows I have ever known in California are assembled here." In the early days, before systematic geology made mining a relatively predictable industry, mining enterprise was mostly gamble, and like gambling it easily became crooked. Virginia City miners collected mining-claim assessments for working mines that they had hardly touched. Innocent newcomers were shown worthless rock ledges and urged to buy stock. Persons outside the territory were sold, sight unseen, stock in granite and dirt ledges. Comstock mines were salted with bullion fragments. Ore from rich mines was dumped in barren shafts, for which stock was then sold. The richest ore in mines was assayed and its value given as the value of all the ore. The press printed warnings against these practices, apparently with no success. No mere newspaper notice could affect the American dream of easy wealth. Samuel Bowles of the Springfield *Republican* punned, " Some purchasers invested with so little care that they will never be able to find even the ground where their pretended property lies — *lies*, indeed it does! " There was an early Nevada joke about salting. A claim buyer, after seeing the assay report, remarked that the ore was just as good as that of the Comstock lode. The seller replied, " It ought to be. I got it from there."

Pseudo assayers and mining engineers worked out technological frauds. At the start, when silver milling processes were unknown, quacks furnished all sorts of chemical and botanical decoctions, most of them useless. One " mining expert " was on trial for deceit. When asked what a mining expert is he answered, " A man who wears glasses, looks wise, and talks Dutch." There were assayers who would be able only to guess at ore contents or who would underreport values and keep the difference. The lawyer, William Stewart, was losing a mine case that hinged on the exact location of certain ore bodies in dispute. He could not break down the positive testimony given by the so-called surveying expert on the other side. Just as the witness was about to leave the stand, he had an inspiration. " How many degrees are there in a circle? " he asked. The expert cast a triumphant glance at the jury. " Why, a schoolboy would know that depends upon the size of the circle."

Many capitalists and mine superintendents engaged in undercover practices. There was a premium on shrewdness and a crooked financial juggler got a long way. There was wealth enough for everyone; ironically, this abundance created the imperative that a few get all of it. Such was the dominant spirit of the times. A superintendent on a nominal salary of about $15,000 grew very rich in four years. He owned the lumber mill that furnished the mine its timbers, and he remilled privately the tailings from the company mill. Several times conniving superintendents, using a scheme invented by the controllers of the Gould & Curry, suppressed the news of rich strikes in order to make a financial killing. They imprisoned the miners underground in Virginia City with fine foods and champagne as rewards, or they blasted over the find with worthless rock. Simultaneously they had friends or agents in San Francisco start false rumors that the ore was pinching out, thus lower the price of stock, and buy it up cheap. Once they owned the stock, they announced the bonanza and voted themselves huge dividends or resold at a spanking profit. A broker once foiled this scheme by getting a job as a miner. He carried a bottle of emetic. When a strike was made, he drank his bottle and got sick, and as an emergency case he was taken up to the top and home. His wife made out she was running for a doctor, but went to the telegraph office and bought stock. Capitalists assessed stockholders until they balked and then bought them out below par. Brokers willingly let stock bought on margin go down, collecting money to keep themselves safe. As soon as the decision was known in a crucial court case involving the Savage and the Potosi, a sharp broker rushed to the telegraph office and contrived for about $300 to monopolize it for nearly two hours, until his friends in San Francisco had bought up all the stock procurable. Persons who rushed to Gold Hill to break the communication were unable to do so. John Kelly, a " bear " operator, made a good bit of money shorting worthless securities; during Johnnie Skae's Sierra Nevada boom in 1878, he whispered among his friends that he had a five-foot vein in his Lady Bryan down in Six-Mile Canyon. Purchasers lost everything.

The Comstock courtrooms, naturally enough, reflected these business ideals. Tampered juries, fixed judges, manufactured evidence, false witnesses to be had for hire for either side, trumped-up suits to cloud titles to ledges — these were common during the first five years in Virginia City. A crucial suit between the Ophir and the Burning Moscow lasted several years and cost $1,170,000. The case of *Chollar* v. *Potosi*, lasting from 1861 to 1865, cost $1,300,000. The Ophir and the Yellow Jacket were each involved in over thirty suits at one time. The three-man territorial supreme court was so generally suspected of bribetaking in these suits (their salaries were small and living costs were high) that the *Enterprise* was able to publish three and a half double columns of names in small type, demanding their resignations. A table in H. H. Bancroft's history of Nevada shows twelve mining companies involved in 245 suits, 168 as plaintiffs and 77 as defendants. S. H. Marlette, surveyor general of Nevada, estimated that the cost of litigation for the first half of the sixties was $9,000,-000. Stewart, who made $100,000 a year in fees, estimated the entire cost of litigation up to January, 1866, at $10,000,-000, or one-fifth the total production of the lode.

Virginia City was an everlasting refutation to the theories and arguments of " classical " laissez-faire economists. A visitor wrote home to San Francisco:

Here, corruption is at a premium, and men's virtue is to be estimated in an inverse ratio to their professions. California in '49 was a kind of vestibule of hell, but Nevada may be considered the very throne-room of Pluto himself. I have seen more rascality, small and great, in my brief forty days' sojourn in this wilderness of sagebrush, sharpers and prostitutes, than in a thirteen years' experience of our not squeamishly moral State of California. The principal occupation of the denizens of this God-forsaken angle of creation seems to be the administering to one another of allopathic doses of humbug, which are received with an air of gravity and relish which betokens an abiding and universal faith in their virtue. God help me! I never saw such a land before. The description by Leo Africanus of the City of Murderers in Biledulgerid, of the old Taurica Chersonesus are the only instances which history affords of such an anthropophagus, soul-devouring state of society. Mammon is the god of their idolatry, and slavishly submissive to the behests of their demon-lord are all his wretched worshippers. . . . *Nota bene.* — If I resided here six months I should turn out a consummate rascal.

Yet the individualism of the miscellaneous citizenry of the Comstock in the sixties and seventies did attract and develop leaders with constructive ability. The number of talented men was unprecedented. Grant Smith thinks that " No other community of equal size in this country ever contained so many men of great ability in various directions." There was Philip Deidesheimer, a German from the Harz mining region, with California experience, who invented a method of timbering mines which is now used the world over. Joseph Goodman made the *Enterprise* a leading paper in the West. As notable as any was William Stewart, a " red-headed, light-bearded, foaming-hot politician," six feet two inches high, with the bearing of a lion and the knack of giving people what they wanted. A hostile editor said he towered above his fellow citizens like the Colossus of Rhodes and contained as much brass in his composition as that famous statue had. Born in New York, he grew up in Ohio and got his education at Yale. He went to California in 1849, prospected near Nevada City, led antilynch mobs, fought hunger, cold, and Indians, became district attorney and then state attorney general. In 1859 he came to Virginia City, where as the leading lawyer and politician he fought the erroneous theory that the Comstock lode was made up of many ledges and won much litigation through his defense of the single-ledge theory. He helped Nevada through a brief war against the Piutes, aided it to become a territory, forced the resignation of the whole bench of the corrupt territorial supreme court, coined the phrase " the honest miner," supported the miners in their insistence on the $4 wage, helped Nevada to become a state in 1864, became the first senator elected, shaped the United States mining statutes, wrote the Fifteenth Amendment, helped defeat the Force Bill and proposed a Universal Amnesty and Universal Suffrage Bill — thus winning Southern support for Western silver, got a mint established in Carson City, fought for bimetallism for years, and opposed the rise of colossal fortunes.

Stewart well represents the democratic leadership that tried to control the Comstock until about 1865, when competitive enterprise began to give way to monopoly. This change, common enough on other sectors of the frontier, came about through the very nature of the mines. Where diggings in Gold Canyon and the early placers of Virginia City had been surface mines which demanded few tools and gave easy profit, if any, the deep quartz mines of the lode called for heavy machinery and capital investment such as few men could afford. Many California miners of the mobile, transitory, individualistic forty-niner sort came to Virginia during the early booms, only to leave with curses because the work was underground labor on a wage basis. Immigrant labor came to do much of the mine work, and control passed from miners to independent capitalists. Then these mineowners were in turn supplanted.

For by the middle sixties laissez-faire competition had snarled Comstock business. More than a hundred stamp and amalgamation mills had been built on insufficient capital. The cream of the lode croppings had been skimmed. Property rights were tangled in litigation. Little local banks were loaning more money, at three to five per cent a month, than they could collect. Speculators still dealt in " feet," linear measurements along ledges. Miners were going unpaid. The important banking house of Stateler and Arrington failed when some ore bodies petered out and market values fell from $6,000 to $700 per foot. It owed $40,000 to W. C. Ralston's Bank of California. At this time William Sharon, small, quiet, dandyish, and calculating, appeared in Virginia City, established a branch of Ralston's bank. He subtly replaced Bill Stewart as boss of the Comstock and began calmly to acquire a mining monopoly for the bank. The capitalism of the expert businessman had reached the Washoe frontier and taken the place of the democracy of the inspired leader. Sharon established regular paydays for miners and a standard interest rate of two per cent per month. He introduced speculation in shares. He made loans to mines, encouraged additional borrowing, foreclosed, and got mines cheaply. He organized a monopoly milling company for the syndicate's mines, fought the building of Sutro's tunnel because he would have to pay it royalties for ore carried out through it, and in 1869 brought a railroad up a tortuous grade from Carson City, thus ending a picturesque business of wagoning and stagecoaching. Mining became a comparatively sober business, although the Sharon ring had opponents and big operators competed for huge spoils. In 1871 John P. Jones and Alvinza Hayward took advantage of a fall in stocks to buy under the Bank of California faction and get control of important mines, notably the Crown Point. About the same time John W. Mackay and James G. Fair, ex-superintendents and genuine mining experts, and James Flood and William O'Brien, saloon-keepers, began buying into mines and purchasing the hardly developed strip, between formerly rich mines, that held the dazzling ore casket, the Big Bonanza.

Here, on a desolate and barren range of mountains, by the mid-seventies, had grown up a city in which extraordinary things happened. Underground were the most extensive tunnelings yet made in America, and in them a quarter of the city's population was always at work. The streets of the town were the roof of a subterranean building that grew downward and was seventeen levels down by 1877, or the equivalent of about two Empire State Buildings. There was said to be as much lumber underground in Virginia City as there was in the whole city of Chicago. The size of the machinery and the ore dumps showed what great things were done. On top were the buildings that symbolized the wealth and energy of the place. Piper's Opera House cost $50,000. The Storey County Courthouse, sturdy to this day, was a $117,-000 building on ground that cost $30,000. The Catholic Church, St. Mary's in the Mountains, with its rose window, its redwood columns and arches, its Italian marble and Spanish bells, was commodious and beautiful. The International Hotel, six stories high, contained 160 large, high-ceilinged rooms, and the first elevator west of Chicago. Its elegant appointments symbolized the metropolitan pattern of life in the camp. In it was the bed occupied — on separate occasions — by General Grant, Dom Pedro of Brazil, Adelina Patti, and President Rutherford B. Hayes. In this hotel, according to the story, the Bonanza Kings entertained the Duke of Sutherland with five hundred bottles of champagne.

Social distinctions became more pronounced than in other camps. The elaborate Victorian homes of mineowners, superintendents, brokers, and merchants were furnished with the best that money could buy in an age of ornate interior decoration. Ladies and gentlemen dressed exceedingly well. Prince Albert coats, stovepipe hats, and Paris gowns were as abundant, proportionately, as in San Francisco and New York. Private card and dinner parties were gay and stylish. Millmen's wives and daughters exhibited diamonds and laces to their rivals as did social leaders in Eastern cities. Common were the phrases "high-toned," "genteel," and "the haut ton." Elegant ladies in silks and corals liked Virginia City for its cloudless skies, that were a contrast after their visits to "the bay," and for the bustle and activity of the town, which electrified and invigorated them. While the lords of creation gave their lives to money-making, their wives read novels, played Boston-made pianos, sang at the Choral Society on Thursday nights, went on picnic excursions where they ate chicken and ices and drank champagne, and peddled gossip. Occasional grand balls sponsored by fraternal organizations, and governor's levees and balls in Carson, had all the elegance and display and courtliness of a reception at Mrs. Vanderbilt's. There were the Ivy Social Club, the Washoe Club for the leaders of the Comstock, and the exclusive Entre Nous Club, noted for its waltzes, quadrilles, and mazurkas.

The generous production of the mines enabled Nevada to play its significant role of building San Francisco, helping to win the Civil War, giving America its first mineral kings, and upsetting the silver standard in the Western world. In the struggle to obtain the bullion, the mines and mills of the Comstock added to the technological knowledge of the time. There were tough problems to solve. There were no big trees on the Virginia Range to timber the mine workings. There was no pure water in or under the town. What water was there was unhealthfully if not poisonously filled with chemicals. Tunnels caved in. Clay earth swelled and snapped off uprights or sank and compressed twelve-inch yellow-pine planks into three-inch slabs as hard and dark as teak-wood. Whitish sulphate masses — epsomite and pickeringite — grew like cauliflower heads and shredded, displaced, and broke the lagging, the side boards in the drifts and tunnels. Hidden lakes poured into the shafts, and Cornish pumps had to labor to lift out the water. Fires burst out and trapped clambering men in smoke and crashing timbers. The Crown Point-Yellow Jacket fire in 1869 was the most terrible metal-mine disaster in America up to the time. Between thirty-five and forty-nine miners were burned, smothered, and crushed to death. Dynamite caps blew too soon or too late. Workers and animals fell into shafts and winzes. Cables parted and tumbled miners down shafts in cages. Most continually per-plexing was the ventilation problem caused by steaming min-eralized waters from hot springs at the bottoms of the deep mines. Hot water was struck at about 1,200 feet. The far-ther down the hotter, generally one degree for every twenty-eight feet. At 2,100 feet the temperature miners worked in was about 120 degrees. Below 3,000 feet it was 138 degrees. Miners worked in seven-minute shifts, dousing themselves with ice water and sucking the ice liberally provided, while sweat ran down and filled their loose shoes.

"By the contest waged in this district," wrote a federal expert, "against the forces of nature, contributions of the first importance to mining science have been furnished; the foremost practical miners of America have been trained." Among the inventions developed or experimented with were

compressed-air drills in tunneling, electric signals, giant powder cartridges, pressure ventilation, steam hoists, safety ele-
vator cages, and the largest and most efficient water pumps
known at that time; the Deidesheimer square-set system of
timbering, honeycomb-wise, tunnels in loose ore, which took
millions of board feet of timber into the mines and made them
"the tomb of the Sierra forests" east and west of Tahoe; the
V-shaped flume, for floating logs fifteen miles from the Sierras to Washoe Valley; processes of ore crushing and reducing that far surpassed those used for centuries in Mexico
and Peru, including variations of the trip-hammer quartz mill.
A great feat in its day, completed in 1873, was the piping of
water 38,000 feet from Lake Marlette in the Tahoe Alps,
down through Washoe Valley, and up around Mount Davidson to Virginia City, which is about 1,500 feet above the
valley. Adolph Sutro ran his celebrated tunnel from the Carson River to the 1,640-foot level of the Virginia City mines.
The railroad from Carson City was an engineering triumph.
It rose nearly 1,600 feet in thirteen and a half miles of track
so curving that its aggregate curves would make seventeen
full coils. Across Crown Point Ravine in Gold Hill was a
sensational trestle 390 feet long, 90 feet high, containing about
20,000 tons of steel, bolts, pins, and cables. This fifty-two
mile narrow-gauge railroad from Reno, owned by William
Sharon and Darius Ogden Mills, was for a time the most
prosperous railroad in the United States. Forty or fifty trains
a day carried loads at monopoly rates.

One important reservation must be made. Although the
miners of the Comstock met and overcame greater obstacles
than any miners before in history and showed great skill in
erecting machines and adapting European timbering, they
made little advance in the application of geology to mining, as did later miners in Colorado, Michigan, and Montana.
They accentuated the gambling phase of mining at the expense of the industrial.

WITH the passage of decades Virginia City changed. Just as shrewd William Sharon and hard-working John Mackay supplanted convivial Governor Nye and persuasive Bill Stewart, just as the locomotive engineers of the Virginia and Truckee Railroad replaced colorful stage drivers and teamsters, so did comparatively sober and domesticated miners succeed carefree bachelor miners. By 1885 saloonmen and gamblers were leaving for new strikes; the C Street rooming houses were emptying, and the "boys" who remained were married and thrifty. Miners had started to pitch horseshoes; it was time to get out. Easy money disappeared. As one bartender put it, the railroad brought in "only dead brokes and stiffs."

Abandoned shaft houses became dilapidated and were dismantled or fell in. Mills were torn down. Homes were moved to Reno, where they remain neatly groomed relics of the Victorian age. General Charles Forman, superintendent of the Overman and Caledonia mines, who had built a new home in 1875, moved it to Los Angeles in the late eighties, at a total cost of over $6,000, and located it on ten acres near Pico and Figueroa streets. In 1893 the veteran paper, the *Enterprise*, suspended publication. Empty stores were torn down for wood. Old shacks blew down. Outlying structures vanished in the slow fragmentary way that no one can ever fully account for, and the soil of the city was so littered with split-iron nails that finally the state highway department had to bring in a huge six-ton magnetic machine for picking up the old nails from the streets. Sagebrush and rabbit bush moved into the vacated lots and abandoned lanes. The International Hotel, with its mansard roof and baroque windows, stood well into the twentieth century, despite a startling bulge, and then burned down, to be replaced by a wrecked-car lot. The Wells, Fargo building was sagging in 1914; by 1930 it was a ruin with both roof and floors fallen in, and finally it was demolished.

The ground sank as abandoned mines decayed below and as an earthquake slip slowly spilled a mountain on Gold Hill. In the seventies an immense crevice formed east of the town, and mine timbers a foot through were crushed to the thickness of a few inches. About 1870 the Savage chimney, 150 feet tall, began to lean. It was three feet off center in 1874, and was straightened by sawing out a notch on one side. There were frequent cavings farther south over the Chollar Mine, where some ground had been mined within two hundred feet of the surface. When a couple named Woods returned, after a short trip downtown, to their house where they had left a fire in the stove and a dog to guard the premises, they found that the house had dropped from sight and was covered with broken earth. In 1903 the Chollar hoisting works also tumbled into the depths below. Buildings leaned in various directions, especially over the Savage and the Gould & Curry. Several brick rooming houses leaned like squashed crates. Often, settling ground bent four-inch pipes into kinks as if they were rubber hoses. In 1912 the Fredericks Building had a " series of twists and displacements " and the Tonkin Building was leaning four feet.

There were souvenirs for decades: old stamps, checks signed by the Bonanza Kings, portraits of the leading men of the great days, copies of the *Enterprise*, lamps, chairs, mineralized timbers from the mines which were as heavy as rock and took a high black polish. As property values crashed, bourgeois heirs of the aristocratic past made shrewd bargains. The Virginia Hotel sold, fully furnished, for $550. The house of the superintendent of the Ophir Mine, with its Brussels carpets and walnut and mahogany furniture, sold for $250 cash and $170 in back taxes. The building that houses the Crystal Bar, with its three-way chandelier (electricity, gas, and kerosene), and the upstairs rooms of the once-exclusive Washoe Club was built in the seventies for $80,000. In the 1920's it sold for $335 in delinquent taxes. Gleaners found a few bonanzas of pin money. Harry Gilmore cleaned up $1,325 in gold and silver in the ball mill of the Mexican Mine and $650 in the bullion room of the old Con Virginia.

In the late 1930's and early 1940's "historic landmarks" were fast disappearing. The armory building collapsed, settling and slipping earth pulled a wall off the Biroth Building, the Virginia Hotel — once the headquarters for Confederate sympathizers — burned down, and fire also wiped out the surface workings of the Con Virginia and California, not used for nearly twenty years. Gone were the vestiges of the greatest mines of the Comstock lode: hoist, compressor, cable house, main hoist house, offices, and outbuildings. The Crown Point trestle was torn down. The Virginia and Truckee Railroad went into receivership, and most of the twenty-seven locomotives it had once used became Americana, committed to veneration and oxidation.

For fifty years after the last boom subsided, mining operations continued off and on, large scale and small scale, without glamour. Companies experimented with new processes, introduced electrical power, hunted for hidden lobes of the lode, and milled both low-grade and the mill tailings of the old days. According to one authority, between 1881 and 1931 over forty millions were expended on the Comstock, producing millions in bullion but less than five millions in dividends. In 1930 the Census Bureau found only 667 inhabitants in all of Storey County, which includes both Gold Hill and Virginia City.

Yet Virginia City neither disappeared nor died. It was not forgotten. The visitor there today, especially if from the East, says, " This is a sight I'll never forget! " No new industry has come along to rebuild it and alter its appearance. Except for the macadam, the automobiles, a couple of service stations, and a few white bungalows built to rent, the main street has about it the air of old times. There are brick and wooden buildings like those in movie sets for Western towns and also elaborate stores with overhanging cornices, Roman-esque second-story windows, pilasters, Italian Renaissance façades, and elaborate capitals on porch columns that reflect all the architectural extroversion of the Gilded Age. The style is irrelevant to the purpose of the buildings, their site, their destiny as monuments to the " Old West," but it does have all the fascinating ugliness of the General Grant period, which architects now label " The Reign of Terror." The climate has been at work to counteract its effrontery. Fronts are weather-beaten, and paint has faded or peeled off. Porches and balusters sag. Shingles are loose and ruffled. But the board walks remain fairly busy thoroughfares. The thresholds of granite or cast-iron plate await the further use of millions of feet. Hinged iron shutters bearing aged green paint give their medieval protection to windows. The wooden porches with their balustrades keep off the bright Nevada sunlight, and the rise of the street south over the horizon toward the Gold Hill divide suggests what once was there, a metropolis continuing on out of sight. The Presbyterian Church, built in 1867, is still in service. The obsolete, baroque public school bulks on South C. Isolated and paintless is the firehouse of Company No. 2. In the middle of town the Enterprise Building remains. The Tahoe House serves meals. Numerous dark, cramped shops offer goods. Decorating their windows are potted geraniums and succulents and sunflowers. A half dozen bars, including the Wonderlode and the Old 62, sell liquor superior to the lightning-rod rotgut of 1860 and inferior to the imported delicacies of 1875. The Masonic Hall on North C is intact, although propped up on the north side, where a neighboring structure has vanished. The one really jarring note is struck by a self-conscious novelty and "antique" shop, advertising itself as " The Museum of Memories " and an occupant of the building once the Bloody Bucket Saloon. Here the spirit of the Comstock has sunk to the level of cheap commercialism and still cheaper souvenirs.

C STREET
VIRGINIA CITY

Frasher's Photos—Pomona, Calif.

LOOKING
NORTHERLY
along Comstock Lode mining
area between Dayton and Virginia City; Silver City in the
middle ground

U. S. Department of the Interior

Up the mountain on B Street are the Miners' Union Hall, a flagpole atop its gable, the county courthouse, and the Knights of Pythias Temple, with a cast-iron railing framing the top of the disintegrating porch. The skeleton of Piper's Opera House stands like a great barn, its shingles a loose thatch. When no longer a Mecca for the talent of the American theater, it became a silent-movie theater and a floor for high-school basketball games. Now it is a monument of scrap lumber waiting for fate to set it on fire. Its floor is warped like an accordion bellows. The stage slants dangerously. The galleries are propped up. The ceiling and roof are slatted. Positive weather and negative repairs have made them a mere latticework to strain snow and rain before they drip on the floor and swell it into further contortions.

Below C are the Episcopal Church, weathered brown and nailed shut, and, the width of a street away, St. Mary's in the Mountains, built in 1868, burned in the great fire of 1875, and rebuilt in 1876 with a water pipe installed in the cross on the steeple. The railway station is boarded up. No more receptions for Ulysses Grant, Rutherford Hayes, and Herbert Hoover! Dirt filters into the unused roadbed and covers the rails.

Scattered about the town are many pleasant homes set off by picket fences and shaded in summer by locusts, Lombardy poplars, and cottonwoods. In the gardens are apple and pear trees, sunflowers, golden glows, and bachelor's-buttons. Hop vines clamber along the fences and over the verandas. The WPA has built several public buildings and new high-gear roads to replace the steep Gold Canyon road up from Carson City and the dangerous Geiger Grade up from Reno.

Few of the original Comstockers are left to warm themselves in rocking-chairs on sunny porches. The memories are down to the fourth generation. It was not so in the forty years between 1880 and 1920. At every new stampede and mining camp that opened in the world there were veterans of the Chollar and Yellow Jacket and Con Virginia, of the Metropole Saloon and the Sawdust Corner, prospectors and miners still, ready to believe the new strike might be good but unwilling ever to concede that it might eclipse the Comstock. That was impossible. Full of anecdotes, replete with the innate dignity of " I saw it happen, my boy," they made the later generations of Tonopah and Goldfield, Searchlight and Rhyolite, the promoters in khaki, and prospectors in gasoline buggies, hope all the harder that their new camps would surpass the unsurpassable, leave the illustrious Virginia City far behind in the fine dust of its dump heaps. The Comstockers who drifted away into big cities recalled a golden age it had been their great luck to live in.

> In youth when I did love, did love
>   (To quote the sexton's homely ditty),
> I lived six thousand feet above
>   Sea level, in Virginia City;
> The site was bleak, the houses small,
>   The narrow streets unpaved and slanting,
> But now it seems to me of all
>   The spots on earth the most enchanting.

The sons and daughters of the Comstock are scattered, but they have a sentiment for it. They are aware that they are of the one noble lineage of Nevada. They were born there or they grew up there. They are connected with something big in American history. Some of them are Joe Farnsworth, Nevada state printer; Miriam Michelson, writer; the late physicist, Charles Michelson; George Lyman, San Francisco pediatrician; Grant Smith, San Francisco lawyer; Ed Lyman, Los Angeles lawyer; Newton Drury, head of the National Park Service; the late John Fulton, head of the Mackay School of Mines. Ogden Mills was so sentimentally attached to the Virginia and Truckee as to maintain its rising deficit during his last years out of his own pocket.

Present-day inhabitants of Virginia City, seasoned mining men among them, retain a faith in the lode. There are huge fortunes yet undiscovered, they feel, especially in the unexplored lower levels. The creed of the sixties is still alive: Once a silver mine, always a silver mine. There is always more to be found. "There's many a good mine in the sneer zone of an old one."

A visitor can approach Virginia City by the new Geiger Grade from the north, rounding one sagebrush ridge after another and wondering when the town will appear. He can come on it up narrow Gold Canyon from the south, eager to stop climbing and get out of low gear. Either way, he is riding into what is as much a historical legend as a physical relic. If Salem, Massachusetts, and Charleston, South Carolina, have a wider renown in the folklore and popular history of America, it is because they are older and because those who made them famous continued to live there instead of moving to California. Ever since the day in 1859 when rumors of a great gold and silver strike in Washoe reached the California mining camps, there has been something legendary about Virginia City and the ore body beneath it. The legend was in the exaggerated accounts of the time in American and European papers; it gave humor and zest to *Roughing It*, and it colored the reminiscences of old-timers. It is canonized in the dozens of twentieth-century books and articles on the Comstock, biographies, popular histories, and fiction, which are likely upon occasion to distort perspective and fall into flamboyant interpretations of the " spirit of the times." C. B. Glasscock's *The Big Bonanza* is an example. Such a book is good reading, because it is a romance much more exciting and entertaining than mere objective history. This is true even of so well-documented a book as George Lyman's *Saga of the Comstock Lode*, the title of which indicates the quality of treatment given Virginia City in recent nonfiction.

Writers have combined the hero worship of the native-son school with the candid sensationalism of the early *American Mercury* school to give Virginia City an epic grandeur such as has for centuries glossed over the barbarities of the ancient Greeks and the medieval Normans. Dr. Effie Mack, in her scholarly and generally levelheaded *Nevada*, speaks of "the epic of Virginia City." She says, "To compose an *Iliad* of the pulsating life of Nevada's age of silver would require the master pen of a Homer." "Nevada's age of silver produced Titans." In the preface to *Ralston's Ring*, which is about the capitalists of the Comstock, Lyman asks:

What were they? Lilliputians or men of heroic mould?

To me they seemed made of the stuff which inspired the Norse sagas; of the fiber out of which the Lied of the Nibelungs was woven.

Theirs were the same problems: first the struggle with fire, water, earth, and air for bare existence. When those elements were subdued, the contest with men's greed, avarice, hatred, and duplicity. For what? For gold, plaudits, or supremacy, the goals of most human ambitions.

These enthusiastic quotations are from carefully written books. Elsewhere not only is the rhetoric more florid, but also the actual facts are inflated. Figures for population and the total production of the mines puff and swell as the years pass, and history is elaborated so that, for example, the Sutro Tunnel, which was a failure, is made "immediately and immensely profitable." Errors are merely good evidence of the legend that everything connected with the Comstock was great. Antiquarians can only footnote the myth.

Virginia City made Nevada famous yesterday. Transitory residents came, obtained their fortunes, and crossed on, eastward or westward. The city is the state's most important name, its greatest antiquity. Nowadays Reno and Las Vegas are the cities in the publicity, as again transients come, to stay awhile, before journeying on into the horizons. They are notorious today, but one can doubt that they influence history as Virginia City did or that eighty years from now they will be the thriving tradition that it is after eight decades. The story of Virginia City, queen city of the Comstock, is a chapter in the history of the American Dream.

Goldfield – The Twentieth-Century Boom

By the time important gold deposits were discovered in southern Nevada at the dawn of the twentieth century, the " Old West " had already been conquered by Pullman sleepers, Standard Oil cans, and electric-light sockets. Tonopah in 1900, Goldfield in 1902, Rhyolite in 1904, Rawhide in 1906, and a score of other camps started through the old life cycle of stampede, prosperity, and decline. Like the earlier Silver City and Gold Hill, they attracted colorful personalities, men loyal to their word of honor, and they presented oddities and contrasts in living that made them picturesque to Easterners and Californians. Their production of gold was astonishing, even fabulous. But their total character was something new under the Nevada sun.

In a desert setting, urban America had caught up with frontier America. The happy-go-lucky miner was gone, his place taken by the proletarian radical. From the start, the arrival of a capitalist aroused more gaiety among townsmen than the coming of the Fourth of July. The leaser (" lessee " was too fussy in a mining camp) and the operator eclipsed the prospector. The townsite promoter was more conspicuous than the earnest city builder. The press trained advertisement writers rather than literary journalists. As villain, the wildcatter replaced the gun fighter and the crooked mine superintendent. Personality was inefficiency and integrity a luxury.

Tonopah preceded Goldfield and survived it, but in the

years when Theodore Roosevelt and William Taft were presidents Goldfield was the capital of southern Nevada. It was the biggest boom town of expansive " New Nevada." Paralleling Virginia City, it was Nevada's second nine days' wonder. It gave wealth and prominence to its share of famous Americans. Its story is the story of Nevada mining in the first fifth of the century.

Except at its most luxurious, civilization in Goldfield was makeshift. In contrast to the towns of early northern Nevada, Goldfield was in waterless and treeless country, in a zone where even the sagebrush gave up trying to grow, in favor of the low shad scale and the giant yucca, which cast little more shade than a barb-wire fence. The first dwellings were camp tents, dugouts, adobes, and houses made of rocks, crate wood, or bottles stuck in mud. Ten thousand beer bottles would make a good two-room house. Kerosene cans were filled with stones and built up like bricks to make walls. They were cut open, flattened, and nailed shinglewise to make roofs for cloudbursts to rattle drops on. Hundreds of cheap duck tents were lined up like orderly mushrooms. Inside many the only furniture was bed springs that closed against the wall, a tiny stove, a trunk for a table, and a big box for a dresser. Some of the tents were boarded around and covered with tar paper, but during summer windstorms sand blew in and during midwinter blizzards fine snow filtered in. In these insecure cubicles miners' wives gave birth to babies, raised large families, and nursed them through epidemics.

The Rotunda Hotel was a large structure that looked like a circus tent. Since housing was at a premium, a privacy-loving married woman might have to share a bed with a nurse and a waitress. Men slept on billiard tables and in " the bull pen," a large tent full of cots. For a few weeks Miller's Annex was only partly completed because freight congestion was holding up lumber from California. Only the framework and roof were timbered. Heavy brown paper was tacked up for an outer wall and for bedroom partitions. Guests were glad to pay $4 for a paper-bound chamber that contained a bed, a cornhusk mattress, a washstand, a bar of soap, a hickory towel, and a kerosene lamp. Jokers tossed dogs and cats in through the walls. If a patron snored, a neighbor stuck his head through the wall to complain. People walked in and out without bothering to go to doorways. A drunk, full of liquor and tuneful song, was unable to sleep. He got up and blandly went the whole length of the hotel, bursting through every partition. When lumber and plaster finally arrived, the Annex looked like a bombarded fort.

Water was scarce for poor people. It was hauled in big tin tanks on wagons. A short hose was unhooked to fill pails at fifteen cents each. This meant that a thrifty miner's wife would bathe her whole family in the same tubful, then use it to mop, then to water a plant. One woman, who ran a boardinghouse, boiled the dishwater, skimmed it, strained it, and used it time and time again. Many a mucker or powder monkey cut a five-gallon can in half, poured a gallon in each half, stood with one foot in each section, and sponged himself with a towel.

In near-by Tonopah, a barber who charged fifty cents for use of his public shower used the same five gallons of water over and over again. A patron stood on a wooden grating that worked like the treadle of an old-fashioned sewing machine. He rocked back and forth under the shower water, pumping water from the sump barrel beneath to the perforated kerosene can above. The barber was able to hire out his five gallons as long as a week. When the perforations began to clot and plug up, he changed the water.

People hungered for something green. One wife had her husband spend a thousand dollars to bring in a load of green sod from Washoe Valley and make her a lawn. A sandstorm killed it. Another woman, who had grown up in the Rockies, went out of her way often to walk by the Palms Restaurant to see the dwarf Japanese pine trees in the window. An Italian was so desperate to see something green, it was said, that he set a post in the ground, cut leaves from tin cans, nailed them on, and painted the whole thing green.

There was no fire insurance in Goldfield because of the water shortage and the abundance of dry wooden shacks. When some tents and frame structures caught fire one day, men saved one building by smashing unopened beer bottles against the walls.

Fuel was scarce. Utah and Colorado coal cooked the meals and warmed the rooms, and when railroad strikes or freight congestion, or lack of locomotives because of line building in the Northwest, delayed the trains, the people stole coal from the smelters and timbers from the mines. They lifted the foundations of vacant tents and ripped from empty buildings the boards that would come off with the least noise. During the long winter of 1906, when snowdrifts lay unmelted for months, outlying buildings disappeared into miners' stoves, and shivering men bought seats around the hotel stoves. Families in tents huddled around their Perfection oil heaters, while the fumes of the kerosene stung their eyes and irritated their noses.

Later fine bungalow homes appeared on upper Sundog Avenue. They were made of pine, stone, and brick, with conventional red-and-green roofs and leaded windowpanes. The mine operators and merchants who lived there had all the luxuries of Los Angeles, including Japanese servants. Wives had the leisure to dress for dinner in beautiful gowns, give luncheons, teas, and whist parties, and attend musicales. Mrs. Charles Silvey Sprague organized Nevada's first chapter of the Daughters of the American Revolution. Mrs. Sprague was " a direct descendant " of both John Alden and Miles Standish.

Urban services, including ones unknown in the old days, moved in quickly, and modern, progressive social institutions were set up. In less than a year from its founding Goldfield had five hotels, five banks, a Turkish bath, a florist shop, local and long-distance telephones, two hospitals, a jail, laundries, bakeries, a post office that sold more stamps in one week than Sacramento did in two, and a soda fountain, all bright and shiny and attended by a sweet, homelike girl. Farewell to the days when men in Pioche and Carson City said, "Belly up to the bar!" There was a board of health and a street-cleaning committee. Several restaurants offered good food, but the Palms outclassed all others. In the balcony a piano and violin played selections from *La Bohème*. The menu announced trout and game in season, roast duck, quail on toast, broiled steak with mushrooms, and Roquefort cheese. The Hippodrome presented the road shows of the day, Nance O'Neil, Grace George, Weber and Fields, Kolb and Dill, Edna Goodrich, and the popular comedian, Nat C. Goodwin.

Goodwin was to play an important role in local mining history, as he had for thirty years in American theatrical history. This genial, witty New Englander had been a vaudeville artist at Tony Pastor's, then a star in comedies and farces, notably *A Gilded Fool*. He had played with headline actresses, toured Australia with Maxine Elliott and later married her and costarred in three great successes, *The Cowboy and the Lady*, Clyde Fitch's *Nathan Hale*, and H. V. Esmond's *When We Were Twenty-One*. Straining beyond his capabilities, he had played Shylock to Maxine's Portia, begun a decline, and lost his wife. Since Goodwin liked to drink, make love, and gamble — whether with cards or horses or mining stock — he found himself at home in the busy desert metropolis.

The crowds in the streets were evidence that the Spanish-American War had been fought. Khaki had entered American life. This drab, dust-colored fabric of canvas or drill was as hardy and cool and dirtproof in the Nevada desert as it was formerly in the Cuban campaigns, the Boer War, and the border skirmishes in the Punjab. Countless men wore it, giving a new, standardized look to the milling populace. One saw a man in a level-brimmed khaki hat, puttees, khaki trousers and shirt, sleeves rolled up above the elbows and collar flared open at the throat. Offhand one didn't know if he was a tenderfoot, miner, gambler, minister, mining engineer, surveyor, or crook. Sometimes one could size up a capitalist in a Panama and immaculate flannels, getting into a French automobile. And there was the coterie of old prospectors, informal and congenial, chewing over the past and declaring the new mines would never equal the Comstock, but none the less buoyant with hope of a big strike for themselves.

Chinese and Indians, who had contributed variety to the old camps, were negligible. The few Negroes were present only as porters. Preachers were disproportionately scarce, for a reason made clear by a Salvation Army adjutant: " In Gol'field, to safe souls is wery unbopular! " A few specimens of a new occupational type, automobile chauffeurs, waited for their employers to tell them to crank up.

Young men and old men were gathered from all the states and many countries. A great number were veterans of the gold rushes to the Yukon and the Rand, Australia and the Argentine. An equally large number were mineworkers fresh from labor strife in Idaho and Colorado. On the main streets were many virtuous middle-class girls, independent and unattached, who had come to town to work as stenographers for promoters and mining companies at the very good wage of $50 a week or to follow one other approved vocation: serving at lunch counters. The town matrons, respectable wives and mothers, showed the influence of Franz Lehar's popular operetta and of Maude Adams's current success in *Chanticler*. They wore Merry Widow hats, which were large, wide-brimmed sailors covered with flowers, and hung little red roosters on their hatpins or bosoms, or embroidered them in their ties.

The citizens of the camp were democrats free of artificial class distinction. Waiters gave a stranger tips on stock, and the cook leaned his elbows on the table and asked him if he thought the town of Kawich would make good. Jostling and conversing together were wildcat promoters, rich mine-owners, bankers and clerks, Eastern blue-bloods and Western red-bloods, ex-governors and ex-convicts. Nicknames were universal. Nat Goodwin said he wished to spend his last years on the desert. "Everybody here calls me Nat, and they all mean it. I'd rather be called Nat out here in Nevada than Sir Nathaniel on Piccadilly." An Eastern socialite spoke her mind just as divorcees do now in Reno:

I have just begun to enjoy the real freedom of living. I haven't got to call up Mrs. Grundy every time I turn around. . . . But the nicest thing of all is that my good friends here call me " Rose." If people in New York had addressed me so familiarly on such short acquaintance I would have fainted, but here it seems just the thing.

Or, as a druggist put in, " I don't care what Smith says of Jones; it's what Jones does to me that counts. We are all here to get rich, and your dollar is as good as mine."

The new Nevadans had energy and enthusiasm, the lively Bohemianism of mining camps the world over. " I like the West — I like this Nevada," testified Charles M. Schwab. " I like the men — their very bearing says ' do,' says ' inde-pendence,' says ' success.' "

Among the population were notable characters either at-tracted or produced by Goldfield and near-by Tonopah. "Fraction " Jack Stewart made neat little sums by locating fractions of ground that lay between already located claims. A company whose property he thus edged into would buy him out rather than drive two shafts, one on each side of him. He asked $30,000 for one small wedge. " I'll give you $1,000," said the mine operator. " All right," said Jack. " Let it never be said I let $29,000 stand in the way of a deal." Sam Dunham, founder of the Tonopah *Miner*, ex-sourdough and author of stirring verse, was still called " The Goldsmith of Nome." Wyatt Earp, hero of law and order in Dodge City and Tombstone, was a saloon proprietor in Tonopah. When highhanded peace officers belonging to a county political faction illegally threw Sam Dunham in jail for printing circulars against them, his friends went to see Earp. Earp declared he would open the jail and take Dunham out if the police did not. They did. E. A. (" Bob ") Montgomery was a Canadian who had farmed in Iowa before he took to prospecting. After several ups and downs and pork-and-bean grubstakes, he made millions when he found the Montgomery-Shoshone Mine in Rhyolite and sold out to the Charles Schwab interests. Having faith in the area, he poured part of his fortune into the promising ledge in Skidoo, built a hotel in Beatty. He drove about impressively in a new De Detriech automobile, worth $15,000 and capable of a mile a minute on stretches of good road. George Nixon, once a railroad agent in Wells, now a banker from Winnemucca, also a United States senator, was assembling a huge fortune. As senior partner to young George Wingfield he was getting control of banks and income properties and evolving the Goldfield Consolidated Mining Company. The millions he made along with Wingfield were to build the Majestic Theater in Reno and a home on California Avenue that was a show place patterned after the legation buildings in Washington — with a broad hall, spacious reception rooms, a state dining-room that had elaborate hand-carved walls and tile insets.

Wingfield was on his way to fame. Born in Arkansas, raised a cowpuncher in eastern Oregon, he had become a prospector and gambler. Once, when he lost everything in a Reno club,

George Nixon staked him, and his winning streak began in an all-night game in which he broke the bank. He went to Tonopah and went into partnership with a saloonowner. He opened a roulette table, played honestly, and saw to it there were plenty of cigars and drinks on the house. He fixed the limit of chances he would take. According to the law of averages, every play on the wheel brought him 5.26 per cent profits. He made $100,000 a year, and as he grew rich he formed the working partnership with Senator Nixon.

At twenty-seven years of age he was worth two million dollars and was important enough to be the object of conflicting interpretations. To persons on one side he was a cruel overlord, unconcerned with the sufferings of mineworkers and their families, careless of what happened to the money of the general public, and an adulterer with " the cold eyes and wooden face of a typical gambler." To the other side he was " a man of his word, generous to a fault, possessed of the mingled recklessness and honesty that mark a few of the best professional gamblers . . . the Jack Hamlin of a later day." In 1912, with commendable dignity, he refused an interim appointment as United States senator — Senator Nixon had died in office — because he did not want to be " just a white chip — a nobody — in Washington."

Walter Scott, alias Death Valley Scotty, was in and out of Goldfield. A combination of prospector and spendthrift, frontiersman and showman, he was a symbol of the era. By the fall of 1905 there was abundant local talk about him and he was attracting more national attention than any other mining man in southern Nevada and California. He was known for stunts, including the " Coyote Special " on the Santa Fe line. It had taken him from Los Angeles to Chicago in forty-four hours and fifty-four minutes. Before he was thirty years old this Kentucky horseman's son had punched cows on John Sparks's ranch in Elko County, ridden in Bill Cody's Wild West Show, and prospected in Death Valley.

He liked Goldfield as he did the other booming desert towns. In the words of a Goldfield paper, he was no fancy-dressing Diamond Joe or Coal-Oil Johnnie: he was a good fellow who was at home among common men with the bark on. He dressed in a blue flannel shirt, a red tie, khaki trousers stuffed into high boots, and a black hat. He drove into town, scattered money around, and sometimes played the high card. He had learned many lessons from the king of fake frontiersmen, the one and only Buffalo Bill.

From some of the things that have been said about me I would not blame people for thinking I am all kinds of a fool, but before they play that lead they had better skin their cards and look for something better. I reckon my critics never drank alkali water and lived on whang leather and Chukawalla lizards. If they had they might appreciate the taste of champagne and French cooking.

Did he have a mine? The question was as alive then as forty years later. The financial subsidy from Albert Johnson of the National Life Insurance Company in Chicago was not known then, and local prospectors and speculators tried to figure out the location of the mine:

It is certain that it is in either the Funeral Range on the east, or the Panamint Range on the west, which are boundaries of Death Valley. He has been known to cross the borax marsh in a westerly direction, and if so this would put him in the Panamint Range. If the mine is located in any one of the three canyons there, he would be well supplied with wood and water; if on the other hand he is located anywhere in the Funeral Range, unless it be close to some one of the very few springs that are known, he would need considerable assistance to keep himself supplied with water, or he would have but little time to dig out all the money he spends so freely.

Everyone had a " true story " of Scotty's mine. Scotty had a talc ledge on Furnace Creek twenty feet wide and running

$150 per ton. Somewhere near was a streak of rotten quartz so full of gold that a train of twelve burros carried ore with a net value of $175,000. Scotty's claims were guarded by men with Krag-Jörgensen rifles capable of throwing bullets several miles. Scotty had a fifteen-mile field glass to balk spies who tried to follow him. Six selected men dug his ore for him, and the foreman got a $500 bill whenever Scotty visited the camp. Scotty had a ledge with the rare nonmetallic element, tellurium, scattered through it in little kidneys. From a hole no larger than a flour barrel he took out $34,000 worth.

Many Goldfielders were ready to agree that

> Of Scotty's strikes, of Scotty's scads,
> Of Scotty's fakes, of Scotty's fads,
> Of Scotty's drinks, of Scotty's drunks,
> Of Scotty's thinks, of Scotty's thunks,
> Of Scotty's friends, of Scotty's folks,
> Of Scotty's jibs, of Scotty's jokes,
> Of Scotty tender, of Scotty tough,
> Mein Gott im Himmel! we've had enough.

Key Pittman, prominent lawyer, was a well-born Southerner who had joined the rush to the Klondike. But he chopped more wood than he dug gold and ended up fighting legal battles for abused democrats. He was counsel for Australians who attacked corrupt government in Dawson. He was the first prosecuting attorney in Nome during the lawless winter of '99. This was the time when the " Spoilers " of Rex Beach's novel were trying to usurp the rights of miners with placer-mining locations on the gold-filled sands of the beach. Pittman helped organize the " consent form " of government and stuck with the fight until the crooked judge favorable to the despoilers was removed, and the United States attorney, the court commissioner, and the court adviser were arrested. In Nevada he became an active silverite and went to the Senate in 1912, where he remained until he died in 1940, just after he had been elected for the sixth time. He fought for silver legislation, for Boulder Dam, and because of his unbroken service he gained seniority like any senator straight from the South and became chairman of the Foreign Relations Committee. He shocked the discreet English gentlemen of the Department of State by calling Hitler a coward and endorsing sanctions against Italy long before any other official said these things.

For nobodies and somebodies alike, Goldfield had saloons, long, narrow, and low roofed. It had the Glad Hand, the Three Wheels, the Grotto, many more, and the big four that occupied the corners at the intersection of Main and Crook streets: the Palace, Mohawk, Hermitage, and Northern. In these were sixty-foot bars with eight to twelve tenders, games that lasted twenty-four hours a day during good times, and a cashier's safe that was considered more trustworthy than the local bank vaults. Glasses clinked unceasingly over the bar. City men sipped cocktails and talked over the latest strike. Many a Goldfielder ate a Kentucky breakfast: a steak, a glass of whisky, and a setter dog (the dog ate the steak).

As ever, where mineral fever keeps a camp of fortune hunters at a high temperature, there was gambling. Conforming to type, gamblers were generous to charities and public causes. They had a quick wit and humor of the sort that keeps the world — and the wheel — turning, and they sized up men keenly and often gave them names to fit idiosyncrasies: Beefsteak Mike, Sheeny Jake, Dog-Faced Kid, Sure-Shot Dave. They participated in gambling for high stakes. One Easter Sunday a mining operator put $22,000 on the turn of a roulette wheel, and lost. One night a Tonopah man who had struck it rich three weeks before and sold his claim for $60,000 cash sat down at the little green table and played for two hours, losing his last $35,000. After his last $20 piece slid away from him across the table, he yawned, stretched, laughed sheepishly, and walked out under the star-swept sky. A young Swiss, who had inherited a nickel-plate plant in Norway, got off the stage during a stop, entered a club and joined a crap game with twenty-five cents. For sixteen straight hazards he lost, and each time he doubled the stakes, until he had lost $8,192. On the seventeenth hazard he presented a letter of credit from the Bank of England for £20,000, bet $16,384, and won. He played twenty or thirty minutes more and lost two or three thousand dollars. The stage was ready. He took his leave of the dealer, climbed in, and departed.

During the booming years of 1905–7 surreptitious crime included high-grading in the mines and fake assaying in the back streets. Goldfield winked at these, and there was one kind of out-in-the-open lawlessness that had a fair amount of social approval: lot jumping. The flimsy, portable houses facilitated fast work while a crowd gathered to watch. Anne Ellis, a miner's wife, saw a woman throw a tent foundation off a lot and at once drive on the lot a mule team pulling a tent on skids. She was prepared for quiet domestic life. Smoke was coming out of the stovepipe. Vigilantes had work to do. One night in Tonopah, for example, the circuit court held the townsite company's titles invalid. Two fellows armed with guns — allegedly backed by Tex Rickard — jumped a lot worth $13,000 and put up a cabin. Next day a committee of citizens rolled the cabin off the lot.

The "badman" was conspicuously missing. He was gone along with wild-hoorahing camp life and spontaneous Fourths of July like the one on Treasure Hill in the sixties. Normally, men no longer went armed. Cartridge belts and six-shooters were not standard costume. "The badman is an anachronism," said a local paper, "and 'shooting up the camp' is no longer tolerated as a humorous diversion of exuberant roysterers. . . . The good-natured jag is the rule and the fighting jag is unknown." The town was wide open and yet life and property were as safe as in an old American village. A citizens' committee and the determined discipline of the Miners' Union kept down disorder. Dude visitors looked in vain for men who looked evil and acted murderous; they found no corroboration for the stereotype in their minds. No howling dance halls and dives, no swaggering killers, no reeking lawlessness. At night the most conspicuous noises outside the window, instead of being drunken gunfire and the rumble of brutal profanity, were the rattle of roulette wheels, the voices of excited investors, the dull thump of distant dynamite, and the wind sweeping down from the volcanic wastelands above town.

There were fortunes to be picked up in Goldfield, but not by the mineworker except as he could steal high-grade ore. Goldfield was far from the placer mines of Tuscarora and the small claims of Unionville. The laboring miner was no audacious enterpriser. He was, at last, in his place. He was a proletarian — a chuck tender, drill sharpener, mucker, pumpman, cager hoistman. Unlike the Comstock miners of the sixties and seventies, he was class conscious when off duty. He was an Industrial Worker of the World and — as the next chapter will show — ready to take forcible steps to inherit the wealth of the land and help himself to the " pie in the sky."

The prospector, who was no mere working-class miner, often made neat little fortunes. He found a rich ledge and sold it to a millionaire operator, or he leased it to a capitalist for twenty-five per cent of the gross each month. Thus he avoided the tedious process of slowly building up his equipment as he dug more and more ore and shipped it to a custom smelter in Utah or California. The capitalist fully equipped the mine at once and hurried to extract all the ore he could before the lease expired. This system started in Tonopah in March, 1901. Three months after Jim Butler and his hard-up associates had made the first shipment from the Mizpah shaft, Henry C. Cutting of Reno approached Butler and asked for a lease. He said he would develop the mine and give Butler one-quarter of the gross output. With only a shallow hole in the ground, Butler had nothing to lose and a developed mine to gain. He accepted and gave Cutting a lease good until the end of the year. The idea spread, and by the middle of 1901 there were 112 leases in Tonopah, most of them on Butler's claims and granted by word of mouth. Twenty-five of these paid well. Five or six made their leasers rich. In the spring of 1907 leasers were doing most of the work in Goldfield. On just the Mohawk and Florence properties there were 250 leasers.

Leasing produced some of the miraculous new millionaires. A man with a little capital had a chance for staggering returns in a short time. "January" Jones went from poverty to wealth on the January claim. Zeb Kendall, ex-Kansas rancher, made enough to build Tonopah its Palace Hotel and establish the Zeb Kendall Brokerage Company. The Reilly lease produced over a million dollars in twelve weeks. The Lynches and Omearas leased Butler's Mizpah for thirty days and got out $640,000, with which they built a town on Silver Peak. The most famous was the Hayes and Monnette lease on the Mohawk Mine in Goldfield. The original leasers of the ground had lost over $100,000 in development. They had burrowed in three directions and found nothing. In 1906 along came G. H. Hayes, a mining engineer, and took a lease for the piece of ground, some 373 feet by 700. He persuaded M. J. Monnette, an operator from Cripple Creek, to take an interest. Their workers dug to the 80-foot level and drove a short drift that struck only low-grade ore. Their funds were exhausted. J. W. Smith, a Chicago cattleman, was in town to look after some mining interests. Accompanying him, curious to see the West, was another Chicagoan, Harry Benedict. Hayes showed them his claim and offered them an interest, but they refused. Next day, as they were on the train, heading for Illinois, they reconsidered, wired, and closed the deal with $5,000. Workmen ran the shaft down to 225 feet and drifted 100 feet, and found nothing. Back up at the 80-foot level they started a lateral, and in a few feet they drilled into a rich body of gray-black quartz containing streaks of gold from an eighth to a quarter of an inch wide. Bonanza! But only a starter, for they found other such ore bodies. Hayes and Monnette shipped to San Francisco one famous carload of picked ore that, minus moisture, weighed forty-seven and a half tons. After freight and smelter charges had been deducted, the check for the net proceeds was $574,958.39. Before the lease expired, the four partners made a million dollars apiece.

Extraordinary ore made such things possible. The average value of Tonopah ore was $40 per ton; of Cripple Creek, $30; Black Hills, $5; California, $5 to $20 per ton; but in Goldfield the ore averaged $100 to $500 per ton. Ore was not "shipping ore" unless it was worth $100 or more. One of the sights of Goldfield was piles of sacked ore awaiting transportation to the railroad. There were guards around some claims to keep passers-by from picking up rich surface rocks. Only — some ore bodies were shallow, some were hidden in the depths, some barely assayed. Mining was still pretty much the old game of guess and gamble, plunge and chance it. A poor man might be stunned with sudden riches. A rich man might be blighted by failure.

While Tonopah, first of the new boom towns, was developed largely by Nevada, Goldfield and its satellite towns were financed, built, and developed largely by outsiders from the East. Big money came in with a score of multimillionaires. A. D. Parker, vice-president of the Colorado and Southern Railroad, acted on advice of Thomas G. Lockhart, ex-Union Pacific brakeman and prospector whom he had grubstaked for years. He put money into the Tonopah Extension and into the Florence and Jumbo Extension in Goldfield. J. W. Woodside, C. R. Miller — later governor of Delaware, and John W. Brock, Philadelphia capitalists, all bought rich properties. William Andrews Clark, the Montana copper king who had bought himself a seat in the United States Senate, made heavy investments and built a profitable railroad to tap the new districts. Generally he worked through his brother, J. Ross Clark, who was a better mixer and rubbed elbows more winningly at the banquets given to honor the patron capitalists who were building up the desert boom towns. Others were Bernard Baruch, member of the New York Stock Exchange, and August Heinze, another of Butte's warring copper tycoons.

Most conspicuous of all was the youthful steel magnate, Charles Schwab. The presence of the wonder boy of United States Steel was an honor to Goldfield, Rhyolite, and Beatty. When Schwab and John Y. McKane visited Tonopah in a special train, all the whistles in town were tied down. It was McKane, an astute Scotchman from New Brunswick, who got Tom Lockhart to give Schwab an option on the controlling interest in the Tonopah Extension at fifteen cents a share. He himself owned properties in Bullfrog and Goldfield. Highly regarded, too, was another of Schwab's agents, Don B. Gillies, in charge of the Tonopah Extension. After time had passed and Schwab lost heavily on some investments, he made a public statement questioning the dependability of the Nevada bonanzas and suddenly became a turncoat renegade in the eyes of rabbit-bush boosters.

With big capital came influential and famous engineers to investigate and supervise, among them T. A. Rickard, future historian of American mining, and John Hays Hammond, confidant of international financiers and empire builders. Malcolm Macdonald, a native son of the Comstock, well known in the West as a consulting engineer, built the telegraph and telephone system in southern Nevada, developed the Montgomery-Shoshone Mine, and became president of the First National Bank of Goldfield.

Mines were capitalized on the " Colorado plan " of a million shares that had a face value of $1 but sold for a few cents.

At first the San Francisco Stock Exchange would not handle these issues. California was dreaming of the Comstock and refused to hear of good mines to the south. But when a new exchange formed in San Francisco to handle only Goldfield and Tonopah stocks, and when Eastern money, notably from Pittsburgh and Philadelphia, poured in to purchase them, the old Stock Exchange woke up, forgot the Gould & Curry and the Consolidated Virginia, and began to sell Mizpah, Mohawk, Florence, North Star. In 1905 Red Top stock sold for eighteen cents a share. A year later it was worth $2. Mohawk stock that sold for as low as ten cents was later worth as high as $20.50 in San Francisco and $21 in the East.

An observer of Goldfield mining noted that it was

tied down as tightly as Gulliver in Lilliput, a telegraphic ganglion in the world's banking and finance. Linked to civilization by Pullman cars, it is only next door, as it were, to Wall Street or the Bourse; differs from them hardly more than a manufactory from a salesroom.

But the anecdotes make clear that human values in Goldfield partly determined the course of local history. Among real mining men the word of honor of the open spaces held good, however exciting the crisis. A Philadelphia capitalist named Carstairs said to A. D. Myers, casually, on the street, " What'll you take for your 100,000 shares of Mohawk, cash? " " $400,-000," said Myers, one of the first prospectors in Goldfield. " All right — bring it to the bank Friday and get your money." On Friday Mohawk was worth six dollars a share, but Myers, although there was no written paper to hold him, went through with the deal. Charles Taylor gave George Wingfield and Senator Nixon a verbal option on the Red Top and Jumbo for $1,200,000. Before they took up the option the market value of the mines rose two millions, but Taylor did not welsh.

A Colorado man named L. L. Patrick held first option on the Combination Fraction. The initial payment of $5,000 was due and payable by 3:00 P.M. on a certain day. George Wingfield, Tasker Oddie, and Senator Nixon held second option and hoped against hope that Patrick would let his go, as the Combination lay between ground they were working to consolidate. Patrick was counting on money from partners in Chicago. He kept the wires busy while his partners dallied. Another person proposed to the Wingfield group that they cut the wires and get the option. They refused. The deadline drew near. The owners and the Nixon group were waiting, as Patrick sputtered and penciled more telegrams. An hour before 3:00 the wire came, saying that Chicago " has deposited five thousand dollars to the credit of L. L. Patrick to pay the first installment on the purchase of the Combination Mine."

Patrick went below the surface ore, which was worth only $28 per ton, and found bonanzas. In thirty days he took out enough ore to pay the $70,000 still due on the purchase, set aside $80,000 for development, and pay a first dividend. Later he sold to the Goldfield Consolidated for $5,000,000.

News stories, confidential reports, feature articles, rumors poured from Goldfield to the ends of the nation and stirred speculative fever in Bangor and Dubuque, St. Paul and Denver. The money of big men came pouring back, matched by the money of little men. From London to Shanghai the financial world talked of the Tonopah Extension, the Jim Butler, the Kendall, and the Mohawk. The San Francisco disaster in April, 1906, slowed things up for a while, and then as Californians found themselves flush with insurance payments they were hot to invest. The San Francisco Stock and Exchange Board opened in a temporary building and found itself facing a paper gold rush. Millions of shares passed through the hands of brokers. The floor was a turf of envelopes that had borne messages from clients. Brokers and clerks worked into the night to keep their accounts up, and finally the exchange had to adjourn for three days so that the brokers could straighten out the books.

Goldfield boomed more than ever. In 1902 there had been two men there. Now, in 1906, 30,000 men jammed the town and spilled over into the countryside. Prospectors, engineers, investors, and promoters stampeded from one spot to another throughout a whole vast desert area. Float rock and outcroppings that had lain for millenniums were looked at through magnifying glasses, ground up and panned, and melted white hot in crucibles. No longer were there secrets in the Anchorite Hills, the Toquima Range, the Silver Peak Range, the Skull Mountains. Men inspected every stream bed and canyon wall and alluvial wash. A hundred camps opened — Bullfrog, Bonnie Clare, Mazuma, Hornsilver, Manhattan, Transvall, Rosebud, Lida, Broken Hills, Goldyke. The founders did not incorporate cities, not even Tonopah. They incorporated companies and hastened to pillage nature and get on. Goldfield was their metropolis, a central dynamo of energy and inspiration.

" Goldfield is the greatest mining camp the world has ever known," cried a booster. " It produced more gold in the first year of its existence than was produced by any other camp in the same time. It will surpass the Comstock! " Nothing was wrong with Goldfield and everything was right. Oh, there was petty theft, lot jumping, bunco steering; labor leaders deported scabs; epidemic pneumonia was present, though not as in Tonopah during the winter of 1901 — but these things didn't matter. Better not publicize them and hurt the town.

For publicity, during the summer of 1906 Goldfield offered a purse of $30,000 and outbid competing towns for the forthcoming bout between Battling Nelson and Joe Gans for the lightweight championship of the world. Gans, a Baltimore Negro, nearly thirty years old, had won 145 ring battles and lost six. Nelson, born in Copenhagen, nearly twenty-four years old, had won forty-six and lost ten. The manager of the local committee was George Lewis Rickard. Before he set up his Northern saloon and gambling house in Goldfield he had been a cowpuncher, town marshal in Henrietta, Texas, a miner on the Yukon, a gambler in Circle City, Dawson, and Nome. Quiet, but popular and efficient, he set about to put Goldfield on the conversational map of America.

Financed by gamblers, mine operators, and promoters, Rickard's committee sent out 37,000 illustrated postcards and 30,000 circular letters. They assembled the $30,000 in gold, deposited it in the window of John S. Cook & Sons, bankers, and told the world to take a look. George Siler of Chicago was selected to referee. A big arena went up. The Tonopah and Goldfield Railroad rushed to lay sidetracks for three hundred Pullmans that would come in on the special trains from all parts of the country. Newspapermen and photographers rode in and diluted the throngs of mining men. The fighters themselves arrived and worked out, punched bags, and ran along the roads. The Biograph people and the Goldfield Athletic Club figured out the movie royalties. The usual prefight news jammed the outgoing wires. Gans had to get down to 131 pounds or at least 131½. . . . Nelson's manager, Billy Nolan, was unpopular because of his " take all that's loose methods." Locally, talk of the fight overshadowed discussion of the Mohawk Mine.

On Labor Day the great fight came off, in a town that had been blank desert three years before. In faraway Michigan and Alabama crowds gathered around newspaper offices to get the round-by-round bulletins. A total of 6,972 persons bought tickets worth $69,715, and shoved into the arena. At the ringside, before the battle began, Malcolm Macdonald of Tonopah gave each fighter a thousand shares of mining stock and said he would show his good faith by redeeming either man's stock for $1,500 after the fight. The fighters shook hands and the gong rang. Whatever happened, Nelson was to be paid $20,000 and Gans $10,000. The Dane and the American fought for forty-two rounds under the September sun. Nelson was strong, but rough. Many times Referee Siler had to caution him against butting with his head. Gans was clever and brainy. The crowd was on his side and thought him a gentleman. The fight ended when Nelson gave Gans a low, foul blow, in plain sight of everyone. No one murmured when Siler gave the victory to Gans.

The promoters netted $20,000. The stunt had worked. More than before, Goldfield was on the conscious mind of every American citizen over ten years of age. Fights continued on a minor scale. On the night of New Year's Day, 1907, for example, Bob Gans fought Kid Herman in a freezing cold wooden arena in Tonopah. The fingers of the telegraph operators at the ringside were blue with cold, and the seconds, instead of wiping off the fighters between rounds, wrapped them in heavy blankets. Power brought from the Sierras lit the 175,000 candlepower Cooper-Hewitt lamps that glared through the vapor coming from men's mouths. Gans won and slipped $12,000 into his pocket.

Goldfield told the world. James F. O'Brien, who had brought in a press by mule cart over ninety miles of desert and founded the *News,* used printer's ink judiciously to encourage investors and railroad builders. He was called " the man who made Goldfield." The masthead of the *News* announced: " All that's New and True of the Greatest Gold Camp Ever Known." In December, 1906, this proclamation, followed by the autograph signatures of a large number of representative men, appeared simultaneously in the newspapers of thirty American cities:

In the course of American progress it becomes necessary for a portion of our people to take upon themselves the burden of the development of its remote districts, and bring to our country the advantages of their hidden wealth.

We, the signers hereto, have undertaken this self-imposed task

TONOPAH IN 1903

PREPARING FOR A ROCK-DRILLING CONTEST,
GOLDFIELD (POSSIBLY LABOR DAY, 1906)

IN THE
RESIDENCE DISTRICT

*from a sketch by
Maynard Dixon in
SUNSET MAGAZINE,
February, 1906*

TYPES OF
PROMOTER IN
THE NEVADA
GOLD CAMPS

*from a sketch by
Maynard Dixon in
SUNSET MAGAZINE,
February, 1906*

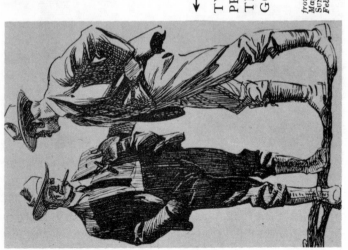

with every confidence that our effort will prove of great benefit to the whole people, and that the mining operations of Nevada will add greatly to our National wealth and bring great gains to those who shall lend financial aid.

Here, in the desert, we have builded cities in permanent form; here we have brought machinery, men and money, that we ourselves may be enriched and that we may secure for the uses of mankind the elemental treasure so bountifully bestowed by nature.

Goldfield, in the desert, is a city three years old, with a population of 15,000, with churches and schools; with four prosperous banks; with many paying mines and many more under development; with costly reduction works for the immediate treatment of ores; with a stock exchange where prices are fixed by men who have intimate knowledge of values; with its affairs in the hands of educated men and women.

Here is the greatest proven gold-mining district in the world, where operators and miners find prosperity and peace in an endeavor for common betterment.

Here we are located in the state of smallest population, with wealth sufficient for an entire nation. Here, we have sought the aid of the whole people, that benefits for the whole people might result. Here, have we prospered and given back to the development of Nevada the gains of our prosperity.

We began with prospectors and burros, and in a few years have builded cities, begun an unprecedented railroad construction, and are established on firm foundations for all time.

The possibilities of our Desert Country have not been unduly magnified, but are vaster than our utmost imaginings, and we point with pride to the appreciation which has marked our progress, growing daily in magnitude wheresoever our fame has spread.

We of Goldfield, who have sown our faith, have garnered golden harvest, in which we invite all people to participate.

In November Nixon and Wingfield had incorporated the Goldfield Consolidated, which united the Mohawk, January,

Laguna, Jumbo, Atlanta, Red Top, and others. The company was organized with five million shares, at a par value of ten dollars. Speculators were frantic to buy stock, Consolidated or any other. The Mohawk was producing $35 a minute, $2,000 an hour, $50,000 a day. In the last hundred days of 1906 it produced $5,000,000. High-grade stacked up higher and higher in gunny sacks, waiting to be hauled away. Brisk young brokers like Webb Parkinson traded energetically on the floor of the exchange and wrangled in verbal battles. Buying became so hectic that brokers sold stock from windows in the third story to men in the crowd below. Incoming and outgoing mail piled up in the post office, unsorted, and exhausted postal clerks went on strike. The postmaster had to pay for extra help out of his own pocket. The queues at the general delivery window were so long that men paid " loafers " five dollars to stand in line and get their mail.

In an atmosphere of cheery promotion and lush advertisement crooks and swindlers thrived. The villain at heart was a gentleman on the surface. He circulated in the Montezuma Club, the Palms, the Palace Bar. He called you by name and stood you for drinks, and you stood him. You respected him as one of the town's builders, a leading citizen. Too late you realized that he was a well-disguised jackal with sucker lists in his files (your name included) and indictments awaiting him in the East. He robbed thousands of people impersonally, politely, convincingly, selling them wildcat stock by mail.

Promoters with rascally motives flourished in Goldfield as never in old Virginia City, ingenious as its citizens were in fraud and chicanery. America was richer. Savings accounts were plump. Elaborate swindling techniques had been worked out by the camp followers of Wall Street. Post-office and telegraph services were quicker and the telephone had arrived. Suave crooks were so thick in Goldfield that they really needed badges for identification so that they wouldn't try to sell wildcat to each other.

At their least clever they salted mines by faking ore samples. A mining " expert " panned out a specimen for a victim. Under his finger nails was a mixture of clay and gold dust, which got into the water and produced real glittering gold at the bottom of the pan. Or he chewed away on a plug of tobacco loaded with gold dust and spit in authentic American fashion in the gravel he was about to pan. Tiny holes in shovel handles spilled out gold at the correct time to create high-grade and impress a sucker. If ore was to be assayed, a shotgun loaded with gold dust was fired into its surface, holes in dynamite were packed with gold dust before rock was blasted loose, high-grade was mortared to fine dust and sprayed on samples, or a solution of gold chloride was squirted with a syringe into specimen sacks, where it permeated the ore and gave a high assay.

More ingenious, they went into the neighborhood of mining excitements and took up hundreds of claims, thus breaking two conditions in the mining laws. They located claims before they had discovered " the vein or lode within the limits of the claim located," and they either did no work at all on the claim or else they chose a soft spot and ran an open cut without revealing " an exposed deposit of mineral in place." In this manner they got hold of claims that they could call annexes or extensions of real mines that were far away. They sold stock on their "mine," built up a price, and then sold their own stock and got out of the way. Some men located up to five hundred claims, tying up practically a whole district, and laid low. If a prospector made a strike, they claimed prior rights of location, contended in court, obtained injunctions, or started apex suits. That is, they alleged that a vein someone was mining came nearest to the surface on their claim and therefore, by American mineral law, was theirs.

If a mine actually was profitable, grafters made money on the equipment. They recommended machinery and mills more extensive than were needed and got rebates from the manufacturers. If the mine struck a bonanza and was worth owning, they mixed worthless rock with the high-grade, lowered the value of the output, beat down the price of stock, and bought it up.

Of the land pirates who sold scenery to trusting clients the headmaster was Jacob S. Herzig, alias George Graham Rice, who, like the rest, was a natural product of an era of speculation. A graduate of the streets of New York, this persistent scamp had stolen, gambled, forged, swindled, and tipped at race tracks since boyhood, when his first victim was his father. He spent time in the New York State Reform School and the State Prison before he went to Nevada. Once in Goldfield, he set up the L. M. Sullivan Trust Company. The titular head, known locally as "Shanghai Larry," was the former keeper of a sailors' boardinghouse in Seattle and recently the majordomo in the Palace Bar. No one knows why George Graham Rice chose Sullivan as his figurehead. Perhaps Shanghai furnished most of the $5,000 capital Rice needed to start with.

The L. M. Sullivan Trust Company acted as a brokerage house for the purchase of stocks on the current market, but such legitimate activity was incidental to its main functions. Rice bought several cheap mining groups, purchased advertising space all over the United States, and began to float properties. He started a news service about mining properties, especially about his own. Since he bought advertisements in Nevada and California papers, they printed his news. In order even better to dictate to the papers, he started the Goldfield and Tonopah Advertising Agency, which alone made him $125,000. Soon he had a huge business. Drafts, checks, and postal money orders, currency, and coin tumbled out of thousands of envelopes to pay for stocks at twenty-five and fifty cents a share. Rice did half a million dollars' worth of business a month. He employed scores of clerks, twenty-four stenographers, and a corps of copy writers. With the money entrusted to him as a broker he bought more claims and advertised them, and with the money that came in for stock in them he bought more claims. To raise the market value of these worthless stocks, he bought in and raised the price, and then dumped what he held on the sucker market. Thus, a potential millionaire, he lived a hand-to-mouth existence. His big promotions, all of them for the customary million dollars, dominated the Goldfield Mining Exchange.

Ever alert to publicity values, Rice got Governor John Sparks to become president of his mining enterprises, and he even persuaded the firm of E. A. Manice & Company, members of the New York Stock Exchange, to offer publicly stock for the Furnace Creek South Extension. His activity helped advertise all Nevada mines and encouraged the public to spend two hundred million dollars on stocks in 1905–6.

Dr. J. Grant Lyman, a former Saratoga tipster friend and an international swindler, came to Goldfield and — presumably on threat of exposing his criminal record — got Rice to promote the Bull Frog Rush Mining Company, which was a pure fraud. Eventual revelation of this combined with other things to end Rice's Goldfield career. He had taken in ten millions since coming to town, but as a broker and an aggressive crook who had to keep his swindles in motion he had to pay out huge sums each day. When bad weather held up the mails for three days, no sucker money came in, and drafts accumulated on the house for several hundred thousand dollars, the L. M. Sullivan Trust Company failed. It took with it the savings of thousands of small investors, hurt a score of Nevada brokers, and gave the state another black eye.

Rice's real name and his criminal past came out, and he left Goldfield with $500 and went to Reno. There he tried to start a Sullivan and Rice company, but being known for what he was he could not get started. Ever resourceful, however, he persuaded the former star of *A Gilded Fool* to let him create the Nat C. Goodwin Company. He borrowed a shoe-string starter, $10,000, and began to publish the *Nevada*

Mining News. With this he began to boom mines owned by the Nat C. Goodwin Company: the Bovard Consolidated, the Rawhide Coalition, the Rawhide Queen.

RAWHIDE was the climax in speculation, though not in production, of the Goldfield era. There was one good mine there, containing some bonanza ore that eventually produced a million or more. Around this ordinary good mine, vestiges of the " Old West " died while being used as stage props by slickers. Rawhide was just one of the many new camps being opened up all over the state, from Searchlight in the south to Seven Troughs in the north, but it is remembered more clearly than two-score more profitable camps, for five colorful Americans got into its brief history, George Graham Rice, Nat Goodwin, Riley Grannan, W. H. Knickerbocker, and Tex Rickard, and to top things off it received a visit from the notorious English novelist, Elinor Glyn.

Rawhide was discovered in 1907 and named after the rawhide mailbox of two near-by ranchers. With the usual precipitate rush made even speedier by Rice's promotions, five thousand persons stampeded in within a year. It was a miniature Goldfield but struck its inhabitants as promising to be second only to the Comstock. The Rawhide Coalition Company had high-grade in sacks piled up like cordwood. Some of the ore ran as high as $1,000 a ton. Stingaree Gulch was noisy with bawdy laughter and ragtime player pianos.

The Nat C. Goodwin Company promoted Rawhide stock at full steam, and with the *Nevada Mining News* to push it, sold abundantly. Effective publicity stories came out of the town. There was a boulder in the middle of the street that travelers turned to avoid. Finally it was blown to bits and found to be worth $300 per ton in gold. In March, 1908, the Rawhide Coalition Company put in a shot on one of its claims on Grutt Hill, about fifty yards from the main street. Mostly out of curiosity, the miners were investigating a knife-blade seam on a surface that miners working on the hill above had tramped over for many months. As the dynamite exploded it threw about fragments of a natural cache of high-grade. About $14,000 in gold ore blew over the hillside, and some of it was lost. One piece flew downhill and through the window of the Bank of Rawhide. The bank deducted the cost of the window and paid the company six dollars for the specimen.

Tex Rickard showed up after selling his share of the Northern. Before he left Goldfield he put up a sign in front of an outgrown church: " This Church Is Closed. God Has Gone to Rawhide." He drove from Goldfield to Rawhide by automobile in one day, a 150-mile feat worth exclamation in that age, and before going to bed he bought a lot worth $8,000. Ten days later his men completed building a new Northern, thirty feet by a hundred, and a dance was held. Three days after that the place opened with five barkeeps, two faro tables, two roulette wheels, and a half dozen other games. The presence of a man known everywhere since the Gans-Nelson fight was additional publicity for Rawhide.

Mrs. Glyn came during her visit to America in the spring of 1908. This unhappily married lady, eager for adventure, found Rawhide different from the European society she was used to. She knew the etiquette of social intercourse among people like Dr. Axel Munthe, the Duchess of Manchester, Cecil Rhodes, and Prince Hussein of Egypt. She was at home in the salons of English lords and American Vanderbilts. In Nevada she showed she could make herself at home in zinc-roofed shacks. She found a romantic world. Years later she recalled, " The men I met seemed to have stepped straight from *The Virginian*." There were some " 'dirty yellow dogs ' " but the mass of men were knights with courage, endurance, a rough sense of justice, and an abstract respect for honest womanhood. The miners treated her well. If they hadn't read *Three Weeks* they had heard of its essential theme, a married woman's right to love outside of marriage; and no miner within earshot of Stingaree Gulch could object to that.

One swain rode ninety miles across the desert to get some yellow daisies to put on the oilcloth cover at her banquet table. A "kind of bandit" called "Scottie," whose "lair" was Death Valley wrote her and asked her to visit there. He wanted her friends to escort her to a given spot. From there he would take her overnight to see the real West and then return her next day, " ' on the honor of a bandit.' " She wanted to accept this Robin Hood's tribute, but her friends said he was a desperate character and dissuaded her. Instead, the leaders in town planned carefully to give her the West she wanted to experience. Some shacks caught on fire, and she watched the fire brigade in action. When the sightseeing party had entered one of the largest saloons, masked bandits strode in and made all present put up their hands. They debated whether or not to take the handsome lady captive and hold her for ransom. They asked her what her name was. When she replied, "Elinor Glyn," they recoiled and told her to go free: she was too hot for them and would burn out of any place they put her. (Meanwhile down the street a real holdup took place in a saloon owned by one of the hoaxers, who lost a bankroll worth several thousands.)

In a formal ceremony the men of Rawhide gave Mrs. Glyn a gun as token of their esteem for her and *Three Weeks*. "We give you this here gun, Elinor Glyn, because we like your darned pluck. You ain't afraid, and we ain't neither." This Bret Harte touch thrilled her. And when Acting Governor D. S. Dickerson pinned a badge of deputy constable on her breast and told her she could arrest any boy in the state, and the crowd yelled and stamped, her emotions were exhausted. "Such chivalry . . . such innate aristocracy as in the mining camps of Nevada . . . a splendid community of *gentlemen*."

During the same spring, a minor event took place that produced the "literary classic" of the Goldfield days. Riley Grannan died and W. H. Knickerbocker preached a funeral oration over his coffin. A. Carlisle & Company, Reno printers, have made seven printings of a little seventeen-page booklet that contains the oration and a lengthy, flowery introduction, written, perhaps, by Sam Davis, Carson City newspaperman.

Grannan was a gambler and one of the most spectacular plungers the race tracks of America ever knew. As a youth he was a bellboy in a Louisville hotel. A rich sport backed him as a bettor at the tracks, and in his first year of betting he made $150,000. His rise to fame was rapid. He helped make the first form chart, with its useful data on the morning workouts of horses. As a result, he did not need to fix races.

As a bookmaker he stuck to the odds he had put on a horse, and unlike other bookies he did not shorten them and run to cover when the public snapped up his offering. He was well known from Saratoga Springs to old Santa Anita Park as "the Napoleon of the betting ring."

At forty-four years of age this huge and reckless bettor found himself broke at the Tanforan Track, south of San Francisco. The Rawhide boom was in the *Chronicle* and *Examiner*. He went to Reno and looked up Rice, who was an old Saratoga acquaintance. Rice staked him with $20,000, with which he started a gambling house in Rawhide. He caught pneumonia, struggled against it for nine days, and died on April 1 or 2, 1908. His last request was that he be buried in his home town, Paris, Kentucky, under his native bluegrass. His death was full-column news on the country's front pages.

Knickerbocker was another Southerner, born in Louisiana, who had preached in a Methodist church in New Orleans and then in one in Los Angeles. There his fervid eloquence won admiration, but his original interpretations of sacred matters did not. He was tried for heresy and acquitted, but resigned his pastorate and quit religion. He went to Tonopah, built the opera house, tried play production, and failed. He moved on to Goldfield, later to Seven Troughs, and made money in various ways, including Shakespearean readings. He turned up in Rawhide " to recoup his wasted fortunes " as a laborer cranking a windlass.

Ready to capitalize on Grannan's death as on Mrs. Glyn's visit, the Nat C. Goodwin Company put up $1,800 to give Grannan a funeral in Rawhide and ship his body to Paris for burial. Probably the company saw to it, too, that a California newspaper reporter took down in shorthand what Knickerbocker said, and that the whole occasion was put in pamphlet form. On April 3 the ex-preacher stood at the dead gambler's bier " in a tawdry theatre back of a bar-room . . . clad in the rough garb of a miner, facing the flotsam and jetsam of the west, and brought tears to the eyes of this hardened crowd of men and women with his somewhat embittered comments on life, pronounced over the cold clay of Riley Grannan."

The address was full of echoes from Shakespeare. Replete with sonorous phrases, assonant climaxes, and copious florescence, it was dynamic with the resounding triteness of nineteenth-century magniloquence. Formal, stagey, saturated with the melancholy of Hamlet, Prince of Denmark, it said little enough about Riley Grannan, whom Knickerbocker really didn't know, but did preach the inevitable fate long proclaimed by the classic tragedians.

When I see the ambitions of man defeated; when I see him struggling with mind and body in the only legitimate prayer he can make to accomplish some end; when I see his aim and purpose frustrated by a fortuitous combination of circumstances over which he has no control; when I see the outstretched hand, just about to grasp the flag of victory, take instead the emblem of defeat, I ask: What is life? Dreams, awakening and death; " a pendulum 'twixt a smile and a tear "; " a momentary halt within the waste and then the nothing we set out from "; " a walking shadow, a poor player that struts and frets his hour upon the stage and then is heard no more "; " a tale told by an idiot, full of sound and fury, signifying nothing "; a child-blown bubble that but reflects the light and shadow of its environment and is gone; a mockery, a sham, a lie, a fool's vision; its happiness but Dead Sea apples; its pain the crunching of a tyrant's heel. I feel as Omar did when he wrote:

> We are no other than a moving row
> Of magic Shadow-shapes that come and go
> Round with the Sun-illumined lantern held
> In midnight by the Master of the show.
> But helpless pieces of the game He plays
> Upon the checker-board of nights and days. . . .

Riley Grannan, Knickerbocker went on to say, accepted the circumstances surrounding him " as the mystic officials to whom the universe had delegated its whole office concerning him." He took both defeat and victory with composure. This made him a " dead game sport." He had reached the climax of human philosophy. Grannan wasted neither his life nor his money, for he constantly contributed to man's greatest task: scattering sunbeams in a world ever shadowed by gloomy clouds. Grannan was gone but not the need for his occupation. He was a public benefactor who smoothed the wrinkle from the brow of care, changed the moan into a song, wiped away the tear, and replaced it with the jewel of joy.

And now . . . I will say " Good-bye, old man." We will try to exemplify the spirit manifested in your life in bearing the grief at our parting. Words fail me here. Let these flowers, Riley, with their petaled lips and perfumed breath, speak in beauty and fragrance the sentiments that are too tender for words. Good-bye.

The time was about come to hold obsequies for Rawhide itself. Rice overreached himself again. Among other things, he boosted a worthless mine in near-by Broken Hills from nothing to $1.42½ per share. His tie-in with Goodwin was exposed. The Rawhide boom collapsed, aided by the failure of two banks and a real fire that burned down much of the town. Rice felt it wise to depart from Reno and Nevada. He went to New York and became B. H. Scheftels & Company, and behind the front of Scheftels he boomed the Jumbo Extension, the Emma Copper, the Ely Central (with a capitalization of $12,000,000), and other enterprises. He married a second wife without stopping to divorce the first, and in the course of some litigation he offered bribes to the jury. In 1910 he entered the Federal Penitentiary on Blackwells Island for using the mails to defraud. The next year he blandly made money on his imprisonment and his bad record by writing a magazine serial, "My Adventures with Your Money," which contained bragging about his exploits in Goldfield. He was out before the World War was over and playing his game again, in a suite with nine phones on two floors of a New York office building. Commission broker and dealer in securities, this master mind was promoting his own frauds in his *Industrial and Mining Age* and swindling purchasers of Liberty bonds. At least, Nevada was through with him.

The Rawhide fire burned down the New Northern, and Tex Rickard lost all he had made in Goldfield. He owned mining claims, however, and was soon making contacts in the New York of Delmonico's and the Waldorf, where he sold out to a syndicate and was a millionaire — until a crash took away his second Nevada fortune. Two years later he was back in Nevada, promoting the Jeffries fight in Reno with financial backing from Wingfield. The rest of his career was far from the Nevada which gave him his original fame. He went on to big-scale cattle ranching in Paraguay and the promotion of big-time prize fights: Willard *vs.* Moran in New York and Jack Dempsey's fights with Willard, Carpentier, Firpo, Sharkey, and Tunney. He built himself a

$100,000 Spanish hacienda at Miami Beach. A master ma‐
nipulator of publicity, a gambler who could lose all and win
again, withal a businessman, Tex Rickard was a representative
figure of an era in Nevada history.

The Goldfield Consolidated paid its first dividend in Oc‐
tober, 1907: ten cents a share. In 1909 it began making regu‐
lar quarterly payments of thirty cents a share or $1,066,000.
This was a prodigy in American mining history. Stratton's
great Independence at Cripple Creek had paid $1,789,000 in
dividends in one year, and Hearst's Homestake in the Black
Hills paid around $1,125,000, but this Goldfield property
was paying $4,500,000 a year! Underneath a surface area of
380 acres there were twenty miles of tunnels, all run within
a five-year period. Down in the Hampton stope in the Com‐
bination claim there was a ledge seventy feet wide, all pay
ore. Thirty feet of this averaged $200 per ton. One streak
was worth $500 to $1,110. It was telluride splotched with
free gold. It required no milling and was sent straight to the
smelters. Goldfield was world famous. Men thought it was a
metropolis with a great future. But in 1912 the production
of the mines began to fall away. By 1919 Goldfield was min‐
ing less than a million dollars a year. The Goldfield Consoli‐
dated paid a total of thirty million dollars to some six hundred
stockholders; and then it, too, like Riley Grannan, came to
the turning of good fortune, and with it died what was left
of Goldfield, "the greatest mining camp the world has ever
known."

Wobblies in Goldfield

The working class and the employing class have nothing in
common. There can be no peace so long as hunger and want are

found among millions of working people, and the few who make up the employing class have all the good things of life.

THE BEATTY *Bullfrog Miner* quoted this selection in 1905 from the preamble of the newly organized Industrial Workers of the World and editorialized that so far as Nevada went the declarations seemed too narrow. Nevada was a country where the poor men of today were the rich men of tomorrow. The history of Bob Montgomery and a thousand men who had grown wealthy in Nevada's mining camps during the past several years was sufficient refutation. " Here," concluded the *Bullfrog Miner*, " the worker of today becomes the employer of tomorrow, and such men do not all develop hoofs and horns."

The editor was too optimistic. There was spectacular trouble ahead in Goldfield. An event in the recent past had shown the melodramatic relations possible between miners and operators.

In 1900 Samuel W. Traylor became chief engineer of the Ely Copper Company. Once he had thoroughly investigated the property and the staff he returned to his offices in New York, where he was a consulting engineer. He was dissatisfied with the superintendent, Joseph Bray, who did not follow orders and spent from $20 to $25 a foot on crosscuts instead of $3 or $4, all that was really necessary; so he put in his brother John as general manager. John Traylor was an experienced miner, but Bray resented his presence there in a superior capacity.

He said John Traylor should get out of White Pine County and stay out. He had a bunch of tough men on his side, he was a member of the old Virginia City Miners' Union, and was going to organize an Ely union right away. Charles Moyer, head of the powerful Western Federation of Miners, came to Ely and the union was formally organized. A local bartender named Lloyd was made head. Traylor was or-

dered out of the county again. The union made no demands
for shorter hours or longer wages. Clearly it was a personal
matter with Bray, who was using the union as a tool.

Traylor stuck and trusted to his skill with the rifle and six-
shooter. He continued to live with his family in Ely and drive
back and forth the few miles to the mine. The route passed
through a narrow canyon where there was a squatters' settlement called Lane City. An imitation coffin appeared on
Traylor's doorstep at night. One morning he found his office
windows shattered. Strange breaks stopped the mill machinery, and once there was an inexplicable explosion.

One cold January day in 1903 seventy-five union men
gathered in Ely. At three in the morning a messenger woke
Traylor up and handed him a letter signed by the president
and secretary of the union: " You are to be out of White
Pine County in 12 hours." To this Traylor replied like a
true company man: " I won't be out of White Pine County
in twelve hours, or even twelve thousand hours, unless my
company orders me to leave."

Early in the morning, when it was ten degrees below zero,
Traylor bundled up and set out in a buckboard for the mine.
He took along an aide named James Gaskel. Gaskel was a
graduate of Brown University, where he had boxed and
played football. He was fearless, but knew nothing about
guns. At Lane City, below perpendicular walls, a group of
men and the secretary of the union rushed out and grabbed
the reins. Traylor pulled out his revolver and told the man
at the horse's head to let go. " If I am attacked, someone is
going to be killed. I may get it myself, but you can rest assured that some of you are going with me."

The leader ordered the gang away. " Let the bastard pass.
We'll get him later."

Traylor and Gaskel drove on to the office building at the
mill — a three-room shack containing an office, bedroom,
and engineering-room. Traylor called in the company's dep-

uty sheriff and phoned the county sheriff to tell him of the threatened lynching.

At seven o'clock three ore wagons filled with sixty or more irate miners, President Lloyd among them, drew up near the office. Lloyd appointed six burly miners to go to the office and get Traylor. They picked up a rope and approached. The company's deputy sheriff lost his nerve — or perhaps he was on the union's side and had to choose quickly — and ran from the building. Another young employee also ran away. This left only Traylor and Gaskel to face the gang.

Traylor let the men in and told them he was a friend of workingmen. There had never been trouble in mines he supervised in Arizona. But he would kill before he let himself be taken. The six men reported to Lloyd, who ordered the three wagonloads to rush the building.

The first miner in grabbed Traylor. Gaskel knocked him down. Traylor pulled his gun and shot the man dead. Another miner rushed in. Gaskel knocked him down and Traylor shot him through the heart. Another leader — Traylor shot him. A fourth unionist — shot in the shoulder, and later died. Two others were wounded. Traylor's spectacles were torn off on one side and hung swinging on the other ear and his eyes bulged out as he tried to see. The two defenders kicked the glass out of the window and slipped out. Traylor covered Lloyd and the rest while Gaskel hitched up the horses to the buckboard, and without hats or overcoats they whirled off toward Ely.

At a ford near Lane City they saw men in the road with rifles. They wheeled around and started up the other side of the canyon. Five miles up they came on two prospectors whom they got to go back and give misleading information. Then they made their return to Ely by a long detour around a mountain and got to Traylor's house about noon.

The sheriff escorted them from there to the jail by hiding them in the bottom of a prairie schooner and posting men on the rooftops to shoot at any insurrectionists. The frustrated miners (according to Samuel Traylor) prepared to fill beer kegs with dynamite, take them up the hill, and roll them down on the jail. A friendly rancher named McGill furnished fast horses and the sheriff and the two prisoners made a 140-mile flight in the zero weather, from Ely to Cherry Creek and from there to Wells on the Southern Pacific, whence they went to Salt Lake City to rest.

The community was on the mine operators' side, and a grand jury eventually exonerated Traylor for the shooting and sent two union leaders to prison.

This incident was a substantial sample of union terrorism for the newly prosperous Nevadans of 1905.

The Goldfield trouble in 1906–7 was caused by local and outside forces. The local cause was high-grading, which was being done on a scale unparalleled even in Cripple Creek, Colorado, and Kalgoorlie, West Australia. A majority of the men on the rich leases were guilty of it. Much of the ore was worth from $2 to $20 per pound. Men filled their pockets, dinner pails, or shirts. Or wore a harness just beneath their outside shirt, a sort of double shirt made in sections down which the ore could be dropped. A man could carry from forty to sixty pounds hidden away as he went off work, thus making an extra $20 to $50 a day. One mineworker made $100 a day for two weeks. The ore was a dark, porous formation with no gold in sight until it was roasted. In many a miner's shack or tent there were ore fragments roasting in the oven or on the back of the stove. Once they were hot, water was poured over them and the gold blistered out. Laborers earning wages of $4 or $5 a day put up $100 to $200 at the gambling tables.

An operator went into a leased mine one night and caught the seven miners and a watchman each wearing a canvas vest under his jumper. He took 210 pounds of ore from them, which assayed $1,100. The Mine Operators' Association claimed later that in the second half of 1906 at least a million dollars was high-graded from the Mohawk and that in the second half of 1907 not less than two thousand dollars a day from the Little Florence Lease.

Operators found it hard to get miners to work in low-grade mines and had to pay higher wages to get them. There was a long line of miners willing to pay to work at the rich leases. Sometimes the shift boss collected his percentage of the loot from the men working under him. The high-grade was sold in the forty to fifty fake assay offices in town. These fakers cheated the miners on ore values whenever they could before shipping the booty away by express.

The unions took no official stand on high-grading. They said it was a matter for the individual to settle for himself. But the practice gave the union both morale and a full treasury, and unofficially the leaders promoted it. A man who refused to high-grade was likely to lose his job on demand of the union; therefore, honest men stole to avoid being regarded with suspicion. A mine manager who was a member of the union made a miner unload high-grade at the point of a gun. He was summoned twice to the union hall, told he had no right to search a man, ordered to keep within the law, and threatened with violence and deportation from town.

Individual mineworkers argued that high-grading was not stealing. A worker had a right to help himself to the wealth of the world, which he was creating by his own labor. High-grade was part of a due wage. And there was plenty left for the owners: they did no work and got an even greater share, and, anyway, they had just stumbled on the mine.

Even some of the superintendents and owners argued this way. Saloonkeepers and gamblers were strongly for high-grading as good for business. The leasers were always eager to get out all they could before their deadline was up. They wanted no controversies that would close the mines or slow down the removal of ore, and they weren't concerned over the comparatively small amount the men could carry out. Not at a time when the Hayes-Monnette lease could produce four million dollars from the Mohawk in six months. Even if cases were taken to court, as a few were, either the justice of the peace or the jury would refuse to convict. There was sure danger of reprisals from union members. Besides, a new morality invades the courtroom in days of stockjobbing, frenzied finance, and get-rich-quick connivance.

The outside forces were huge movements in American labor which came to a jarring focus when high-grading was at its height. Involved were the American Federation of Labor, organized in New York in 1886, the Western Federation of Miners, organized in Butte in 1893, and the Industrial Workers of the World, organized in Chicago in 1905.

There were unions in Goldfield almost from the start. The Goldfield Miners' Union, No. 220 of the Western Federation of Miners, organized in 1904. Later in the year two other unions formed, a carpenters' local of the American Federation of Labor and a Federal Union. The latter was a local of Samuel Gompers's new organization intended to enroll all unskilled workers and frustrate any " one big union " some other organization might want to start. It collected small dues but gave its members no vote or voice in AFL government. In time, new craft unions were to be set up for its members to join. The newspapers excepted, Goldfield was friendly to the unions. Labor leaders belonged to the clubs and churches and fraternities and were elected to offices. In the camaraderie of the bars and restaurants and games, a laborer was as good as a millionaire. People still thought of the miner as " the honest miner " of Bill Stewart's repetitious but impassioned speeches before the Constitutional Convention. The mineworker was the foundation of Nevada's society.

There was no objection when the IWW was organized to include all wage earners, skilled and unskilled, and both the Goldfield Miners' Union and the Federal Union merged into it. As the *Bullfrog Miner* had said, many owners were recent laborers, and many laborers owned stock. When the telegraph boys struck, their dispute was settled peaceably, and Governor Sparks said the IWW was fair—nothing to be alarmed about.

But a new element kept coming in from Colorado, and the tenor of life changed. The militant strike of the Western Federation of Miners in Cripple Creek in 1903–4 was finally broken by the Citizens' Alliance, the State Militia, and the Cripple Creek District Mine Owners' Association. Strikebreakers were imported, and by means of a card system, the bull pen, and outright deportation, many union miners were forced to leave Colorado. As they departed, bitter with defeat, they saw more clearly than ever the application of the radical socialism preached by President Charles Moyer of the Federation and Secretary-Treasurer "Bill" Haywood, with their doctrines of the class struggle and the need for separate political action on the part of labor. These exiled veterans of the labor movement, joined by others from Idaho, were at first welcomed in Goldfield, where skilled workers were needed, but as they came to make up from a fifth to half of the local union membership they took things into their own hands.

They got even with scabs and antiunion men who came in from Cripple Creek and Telluride and the Coeur d'Alene camps. It was enough to say that someone was "a bad one." He was removed from Goldfield either by threats or by violence. From twenty-five to two hundred men were so deported. No one can say how many. Even a commission appointed by Theodore Roosevelt could not find out. But something went on and word got around. The local papers kept quiet because the union had warned them and also because as boosting organs they didn't want to print any news adverse to the reputation of the camp. So scabs got their warning, and if they were too slow in their reaction, "a trip

across the desert in a close fitting garb of tar and feathers "
speedily disposed of them.

The IWW members became increasingly highhanded and
dictatorial. In the spring of 1906 the owner of the Tonopah
Sun editorialized unfavorably on the local IWW and dis-
charged members on his staff. The IWW replied with a boycott on the paper. Therefore, the Goldfield union began a
sympathy boycott of the Goldfield *Sun*, owned by the same
man. Newsboys refused to deliver the paper. Stores and mines
that advertised in it were boycotted, and several mines closed
down. The printers' and the carpenters' unions, both AFL,
stuck by the paper, but the IWW placed a photographer in
front of the *Sun* office, snapped all persons who entered, and
then posted the photos with a notice that these persons were
unfair and should be run out of town. There were boycott
placards on the streets. Many business firms were threatened
with ruin and the whole town felt insecure. But many miners
opposed the boycott, and in midsummer, when the Western
Federation of Miners absorbed the mining department of the
IWW, conservative members thought they could hold in
tow the radicals in the ranks. The boycott ended when the
Sun was sold and became the *Daily Tribune*.

In December the Goldfield Miners' Union voted that no
less than $5 should be paid for any kind of mining labor.
This arbitrary act, tampering with the well-established $4
for an eight-hour day, was meant to take advantage of leasers
rushing to excavate before their contracts expired on the
thirty-first. The result was numerous strikes and lockouts.
The better-paid engineers and machinists lost money, as their
pay was higher than $5, but operators met the union demands
by lowering all wages to the straight $5. Conferences pro-
duced a compromise scheme. The union got the operators
to raise the lowest mineworkers' pay to $4.50, and to promise
political aid in two fights. One was against exorbitant railroad

rates, especially on coal. The other was against inflated food prices. Food costs were soaring. Merchants like Milton C. Ish could sell a wagonload of goods, even before it was carried into the store, to a line of customers on the sidewalk. Miners and operators agreed to make plans for a general store in which the workers would own at least half the capital stock. The union was unquestionably doing a good thing for the common man, for the whole community. There was moderation and good feeling on both sides.

Continuing on in 1907, Local 220 regulated the wages and hours of stenographers, nurses, household help, clerks, waiters, and barbers. An employer could demand only eight hours of work. He could not arbitrarily fire his help. He had to accept the closed shop. Workers paid regularly into a union insurance fund which guaranteed them a small income during sickness, strikes, or layoffs. The workers of the world were united! Organized labor was coming to the rescue of downtrodden humanity!

But the union went too far. Walking delegates went into mines and talked to workers on company time. Giving no reasons, union officers asked operators to fire certain miners. Gangs beat up scabs or members who opposed the business agents of the union and started them on the road to Tonopah. Antiunion people opened letters and found messages that were a skull and crossbones. Local 220 voted to call the blue label of the AFL " unfair " and only the red label of the IWW " fair." AFL carpenters who timbered in the mines got higher wages than IWW carpenters; therefore, they were blacklisted, intimidated, and slugged. Grocers and butchers were ordered not to sell to AFL mine carpenters. Being numerically the weaker, the AFL could only call names. The miners were radicals, agitators, I won't work's, trouble breeders, anarchists, and " hydrophobias."

A minority held control of the union. There were about three thousand members but meetings were called in a hall big enough for only three hundred. At evening meetings vote taking was delayed until after midnight, when miners who worked the next day had retired. A man not in sympathy with the leadership did not get recognition from the chair or was drowned out by jeers, hisses, and catcalls. The result was that the ordinary miner felt himself helpless and stayed away from meetings. With the chairman holding *Robert's Rules of Order* in one hand and a six-shooter in the other, all the average member could do was to vote a futile " No."

More and more the leaders preached the evils of wage slavery, the doctrines of the class struggle, the importance of class consciousness, the ultimate Marxist triumph of the laboring class over the capitalist class by revolution. " Go ahead and high-grade," they said. " Every time you can get your hands in a capitalist's pocket, do it. An agreement isn't binding. When you want a thing, take it. The capitalists are stealing ore, aren't they? The ore belongs to all of the people. Us workers have our rights, too. We do the hard, dirty work of digging the ore . . ." Snatch everything from the other side, urged the union speakers, regardless of " right " or " justice " — those bourgeois " alibis " for highhanded theft. Nevada was an isolated state of great wealth, a perfect setup for aggressive labor. The workers could get possession of all property. The red flag of anarchy, argued the leaders, symbolized more real justice than did the flag of the United States. It stood for universal brotherhood. In time of peace the workers must prepare for war.

At the time, Moyer, Haywood, and George A. Pettibone were on trial in Boise City, Idaho, for the assassination of ex-Governor Frank Steunenberg. The trial was sensational news the country over. Did the three leaders of the Western Federation of Miners plant the bomb that blew Steunenberg to pieces at his front gate because he had called out the militia to suppress the Coeur d'Alene strike? Young William Borah, prosecuting attorney, said " Yes." Older Clarence Darrow, second lawyer for the defense, said "No." On the walls of the Goldfield union meeting-room hung banners bearing mottoes in red letters: IF THEY MURDER MOYER, HAYWOOD, AND PETTIBONE, WE WILL GET A CAPITALIST FOR EVERY HAIR ON THEIR HEADS. IF THEY PACK A JURY TO CONVICT OUR BROTHERS, WE WILL PACK HELL WITH THEM.

Goldfield proletarians celebrated Bloody Sunday on January 20, 1907, to commemorate Red Sunday in St. Petersburg on January 22, two years before. On that day the czar's troops had fired on strikers and their families as they marched toward the Winter Palace to demonstrate, killing hundreds and wounding thousands. By order of the Goldfield union, all mines and leases closed, and all restaurants and saloons, during the two hours set aside for a parade and demonstration. Led by the newsboys, two thousand union members, all wearing tiny red flags, marched down Goldfield streets and then massed in front of the two-story frame shack that housed the union headquarters. Vincent St. John, a brainy radical, ordinarily quiet, leaned from the balcony, thrust his forefinger into the pale-blue sky, and gave them a militant speech. That evening there was another mass meeting. Resolutions denounced the Idaho trial, labeled the United States Supreme Court a tool of corporate greed and demanded that its members be elected by popular vote, and sent true revolutionary greetings to brothers of the working class of Russia, Poland, and Finland:

We have no enemy but the capitalist class!
Our flag is the banner that is dyed with the Martyr's blood of our class!
Down with capitalism!
Long live the international working-class republic!

St. John spoke again, elaborating with intensity on the Idaho trial: " If the working class stands by those three men, it will be one, too, three, and down and out forever with the capitalist class." He pointed to the banner lettered IF THEY PACK A JURY TO CONVICT OUR BROTHERS, WE WILL PACK HELL WITH THEM, and went on:

For my part, I mean every word that you can read on that red banner. But I care not whether they back out of their desperate and patent attempt to murder those men, or whether they turn them loose, or whether they kill them. If they convict Moyer, Haywood and Pettibone, the fall of the death trap will explode the percussion cap of the coming revolution in the country and fire the brains and hearts of every class-conscious worker to fierce revolt, and we will sweep the capitalist class out of the life of this nation, and then out of the whole world. If they turn white cheeks of fear at the rising storm, and let those three martyrs free, we will take them through the United States and with them at our head we will arouse the working class anyway.

Some time later a restaurant keeper named John Silva had a dispute with a waitress over a day's wages. Preston and Smith, the business agents of Local 220, declared the restaurant " unfair." A waiter and cook kept on working. A union crowd beat them up one night, took them several miles out of town, told them to keep on going, and fired a couple of shots for emphasis. Pickets marched in front of the restaurant, and when Silva came to the door to protest there was a bloody fracas. Silva was shot and killed, presumably by Preston, for he went into hiding.

Here at last was a flagrant union murder, and the community roused itself. Such things had happened at Cripple Creek before the mines were dynamited. The sequence might be repeated here. Goldfield citizens patrolled the streets, picketed miners' pickets, organized an extra fire department, and talked vaguely of lynching all the union leaders. Somebody shot at a banker. Persons unknown saturated several buildings with coal oil, but their preparations were discovered before they could strike the match. There was no proof that the union was involved, but rumors throve. The Esmeralda County coroner's jury held an inquest over the corpse of Silva, but did not name Preston. At the Montezuma Club businessmen and mine operators organized and agreed to employ no man who was a member of the IWW. They drew this up in a resolution and got over seven hundred signatures. Work in the mines practically stopped. AFL organizers got busy. They organized every craft in town except mining. They boycotted every firm hiring IWW labor. The IWW countered by boycotting every firm that employed anything but its own members. The sheriff and his deputies, with an eye to the total man power on each side of the controversy, ignored the Western Federation of Miners and its IWW members, and were therefore censured by the " capitalists " and praised by the "workers of the world." The town became an armed camp. Pockets sagged with six-shooters and automatics. Both sides purchased shotguns and rifles and imported supplies of arms and ammunition. The mine operators also brought in ex-convicts, thugs, and anti-union gunmen like " Diamondfield " Jack Davis, who toted a balanced pair of .45's, one hooked to the belt over each hip, and who, it was said, had been a terror to walking delegates in Montana, Colorado, Idaho, and Utah. When a nonunion miner escaped a mob of 150 by running into George Nixon's office, Davis and George Wingfield, with drawn guns, defied them to pursue him further.

Things stood deadlocked for two months. "Respectable people" did not leave their homes after nightfall. Guards patrolled business blocks. Men sent their wives and children from town. The tension held. The operators asked for peace and stability. They insisted that the Western Federation of Miners separate from the IWW and get rid of all members with un-American ideas. It was charged that the union was manipulating the stock market, that votes on vital issues were arranged in advance so that insiders could make astute purchases on the Goldfield Exchange and clean up small fortunes. It was said that the union leaders were co-operating with certain brokers to prolong the disorder. It was also rumored that the mines were not paying well, anyway, and the owners were so glad about the strike conditions that they were paying the labor leaders to string them out.

The union sustained its morale. When a man named Toplitz called street meetings of miners and referred to the patriotic shibboleths of the American capitalist class, there were cries of " God damn the Constitution! " " To hell with the flag! " The union said the operators were interfering with the rights of free American citizens to affiliate with whom they wished and were trying to kill the Federation of Miners.

But as time passed, miners who were husbands and fathers tired of tramping the streets looking for work. They got tired of keeping up their spirits by talking to each other, and they didn't like to have, one more evening, to face a wife at home in a tar-papered tent, boiling a soup bone she had borrowed from a neighbor. After losing forty-one days of pay, they voted to oust the IWW and reached an agreement with the operators. No strikes would be called with less than a two-thirds vote. All bans and boycotts were lifted, and guns were put away in closets and bureau drawers.

Peace settled on the town again. Hoistmen and timbermen went to work. Muckers shoveled away. Blacksmiths pounded. Black smoke poured from the stacks of the smelters. Diners in the Palms felt the dull shake of dynamite blasts far beneath their feet under the hill to the east. But the strike had cost the operators huge sums. Some were crippled, and much bitterness had been engendered. Many investors had lost faith in Nevada mines.

Preston and Smith were tried for the Silva murder, which by now was an isolated episode in the past. Silva had a gun, it seems, and maybe Preston, who did shoot him, shot in self-defense. At all events, Preston was convicted on his general reputation as a radical socialist and got twenty-five years for murder in the second degree. Smith got ten years for voluntary manslaughter.

Meanwhile, in November, 1906, the Goldfield Consolidated had been organized, and a new era in mining operations was under way. Leasing was to end in the middle of 1907, and steady, integrated mining was to begin. The miners' union would not find it easy to divide and rule one permanent, powerful company capitalized at $50,000,000. The company built change rooms. Miners coming off work had to undress on one side of a room, while a watchman and timekeeper looked on, put their work clothes in a locker, then walk the length of the room and around a partition to another locker on this side of the room, get their street clothes, and dress. The union called a walkout. It said that parading this way, naked, was degrading, intolerable, and un-American. It demanded and got two lockers adjoining for each miner. Beyond that, the union was blocked. It could not formally protest against the change rooms as a means of preventing high-grading. Although a few watchmen were corrupted, the income of most miners fell to their wages alone.

The end of the union's power was in sight. The Panic of 1907 came along. Banks closed. Mines reduced forces. Smelter prices went up. Cash left town. Unemployed miners sought work in Colorado and California. The operators could not meet the payroll in cash and paid the miners in drafts on San Francisco and Salt Lake City banks and later in company script with no stated deadline for redemption. Goldfield business accepted the script and it passed without discount, but a minority in the union claimed that the script was being discounted. They engineered a strike. The operators pointed out that the union had violated its agreement not to strike without a two-thirds vote, and closed the mines. Jack London came to Goldfield and made a speech. He said, "I am a socialist, but no anarchist." The union did not budge.

IN THE MOHAWK MINE, GOLDFIELD:
A LEDGE WITH $80,000 IN ORE IN SIGHT

STAGE FOR GOLDFIELD
IN A CANYON THROUGH LAVA

OLD MINE OFFICE,
VIRGINIA CITY

Farm Security Administration;
photo by Rothstein

At this point the Goldfield Consolidated played master politics. It got Governor Sparks to demand federal troops from President Roosevelt because there was danger of killing and dynamiting. The Nevada militia had never been reestablished after it went away to the Spanish-American War. No Esmeralda County authorities were consulted. It was an arrangement solely between the corporation and the governor. Roosevelt was reluctant. There was no evidence of actual insurrection. There were only future possibilities. But he was persuaded, and early in December three companies of the 22nd Infantry came to town. There was no disorder to quell, and the soldiers made no trouble for the striking miners. They shed some needed merriment by singing as they skated on the rink. "Come away with me, Lucile, in my merry Oldsmobile. . . ." They helped Goldfield when they spent money in the stores, saloons, and amusement places. They stole provisions from the quartermaster and sold them to hungry miners at cut rates.

Mine workers figured out that maybe the operators welcomed the script strike. Some thought they had promoted it. Either way, they had brought in the troops to break the union. With everything peaceful, Roosevelt felt he had been hoodwinked and sent his commission to study the whole history of unions in Goldfield. He proposed to withdraw the troops.

Wingfield, Nixon, Parker, and the other operators lined up the courts and the legislature and announced they would reopen the mines. The new wage, they announced, was $4, and no member of Local 220 would be hired. Not enough miners applied for work to man the mines. Governor Sparks called a special session of the legislature in Carson City, and it asked Roosevelt to keep the troops in Nevada. He gave a grudging yes on the conditions that the state would pass at once a state police bill and that the operators would abolish the card system of discriminating against former strikers. The legislature created the state police system, and toward spring the infantry departed.

Local 220 found itself facing a corporation that insisted on the open shop and had a state-paid, professional vigilante organization to help enforce it. The union struck, picketed, and intimidated, as of yore, but ineffectively. Courts gave sweeping injunctions against picketing and the use of threats. They even gave sanction to the card system. Index files stymied the followers of Moyer and Haywood. The employers cited their right to refuse to have business relations with any person or any labor organization.

Hell had not been packed full of capitalists. In Boise a jury had turned pale and acquitted the three martyrs, but public opinion was aroused against the general strike and labor violence. Mineworkers, consciously members of the working class, had gone too far. Victory went to the operators, who had been driven to class solidarity. The wobblies packed up and headed for new trouble in the Douglas fir forests of Washington and on the water fronts of southern California.

Dead Towns and Live Technology

NEVADA had hardly become a state when already it was strewn with dead towns where temporarily the course of empire had taken its way. Inevitably even the most flourishing mining camps reached their peak of production and began a decline. Cables and ore cars grew rusty. Sagebrush and shad scale crept over the dumps. The householder filled his traveling bags and his Saratoga trunk, pulled down the shades, and left behind him a furnished home. The merchant either gutted his store or cast an appraising eye on the shelves of goods and simply locked the door. The colored bottles in the drugstore window gleamed dimly through cobwebs. A big wooden boot dangled from a decaying awning to announce a shoemaker who no longer plied awl and hammer. The potted geranium in the restaurant window withered into a gaunt stalk, and the vase of wandering Jew dried into a curved yellow furl and blew down on the warping floor. Two-story business blocks stood useless in the bleaching sun.

A handful of people remained to work a low-grade mine or to wait, hopefully, for a revival. As they aged they became old-timers and joined the Society of Pacific Coast Pioneers, thus entering the peerage of "old boys" who had shared the adventures of pioneering. The badge and patent of the Society were as potent in Nevada as crosses, insignias, and garters were in European states. These pioneers remembered valuable unwritten history. They unconsciously built up myths. They had seen Mark Twain. They remembered things he once said. In Aurora they pointed out a half dozen cabins that had been the one he lived in when he was a dreaming hard-rock miner in the winter of 1861–2. They remembered Senator Nye; Lying Jim Townsend, a wandering compositor on the papers and a fabulous liar; John Mackay, ever generous to old friends and miners' widows. They had known Hank Monk when he drove for "Doc" Benton of Carson City. They remembered when . . .

Towns often died with dramatic speed between one census and another. Hamilton fell from 8,000 in 1869 to about 100 ten years later; Treasure City, from 6,000 to 50. In less than a decade Shermantown went from 7,000 to one family and Swansea from 3,000 to none. Belmont produced some $15,-000,000 worth of silver and lead between 1865 and 1885 and then collapsed. A smokestack stood on, 175 feet high, made of bricks hauled by ox teams the five hundred miles from Sacramento. Washoe City had 1,500 in the early sixties, when it was a complete community, with churches, schools, and sawmills. It was down to 70 by 1875. Thereafter it declined more slowly, until in 1919 there was one inhabitant, a saloonkeeper along the highway. The Nevada prohibition law of that year put him out of business. Reveille, in Nye County, was once a busy town of 400 persons. Its life ebbed when the price of lead fell after the Armistice, and its last citizen froze to death in his cabin during zero weather in 1923.

Eureka produced $50,000,000 in lead and silver between 1873 and 1896. At one time it was second only to the Comstock in production, but finally the mines struck more water than could profitably be pumped. The Richmond Refinery closed, leaving a dump of 700,000 tons of ore. The Eureka Consolidated closed, and most of the eight thousand inhabitants took the stage or the narrow-gauge railroad that connected with the Southern Pacific at Palisade. No longer were there five fire companies, two militias, a brass band, and a busy Opera House. Spent was the glory of the Eureka Hook and Ladder Company and the Knickerbocker Hose Company. Only the nine graveyards were as populous as ever, with simple pine slabs being added to mark the deaths of old men. A " wise guy " from Salt Lake City remarked that the town had enough graveyards to bury decently everything that ever died there, with the single exception of the town itself.

As economic and social life departed, buildings and improvements did likewise. Floods and cloudbursts gouged foundations, floated off outbuildings, and smashed in walls. Fires turned whole blocks into charcoal. With the coming of the automobile age, looters and wreckers rode in. They ripped up the board sidewalks and saloon floors and panned the dirt for lost coins and spilled gold dust. In Aurora this netted several hundred dollars. Under the floor of an assay office lay $2,500 waiting to be panned. The thick concrete that floored an old mill was worth $15 a ton because of the gold-bearing chemicals that had permeated it. Prowlers searched the walls and fireplaces of cabins, hoping to find a secret cache of money or metal. Legitimately or illegitimately there were valuable finds for souvenir hunters. The Henry Ford of Greenfield

Village sent an agent to collect old newspapers. He pulled some from cabin walls, where they had served as wallpaper. W. Parker Lyon, retired warehouse operator in Los Angeles, acquired hundreds of thousands of relics for his Pony Express Museum: gold-dust scales, Wells, Fargo ledgers, nickelodeons, joss-house ornaments, ladies' clothes, hand-drawn fire engines, barbers' chairs, and so on.

The boom towns of the new century relapsed even faster than the older ones. Hardly a brick marks the site of towns less than forty years old, Bullfrog and Bonnie Clare. The most enduring memorial in many a bonanza camp of the George Graham Rice period is a tin-can and bottle dump. Rhyolite, which was thriving in 1906, with two banks, a newspaper, a $50,000 school, and many stores and residences, is now a forlorn relic. The Overbury Block is the most conspicuous ruin, a three-story brick structure twelve windows wide across the front. Roofless, floorless, and mostly front and side walls, it barely suggests that once it housed six enterprises on the street level alone: a bank, a jewelry store, and four shops. The elaborate stucco station of the Las Vegas and Tonopah and Tidewater Railroad, after more than two decades of inactivity, is now a night club for Death Valley visitors who want to gamble in Nevada.

Goldfield, that marvel of the age, is a long way from being the town in which wobblies projected one of America's first general strikes. In 1923 a wind-blown fire burned out fifty-three blocks in the center of town. Nine years later two cloudbursts in close succession sent torrents down from the hills above town and washed out buildings. Some were saved by opening the front and rear doors so that the flood would wash straight through instead of piling up and boiling about. The Catholic church remains unfinished. Several churches are nailed shut. St. John's in the Wilderness has become a community church. Some years ago, the preacher, who served without pay, was also janitor of the Elks Club and the town's taxi driver. The X-shaped high school on Sun Dog Avenue is boarded up; so is the West Side school. The bulky red-brick grammar school with its high steps now houses all students in town. Scattered among vacated lots are rock foundations, shacks with walls missing, adobes with the plaster cement peeling off, and paintless frame houses weathered to a dark-brown stain. North of town, workers are tearing down the terraced mill of the Goldfield Consolidated. Soon all that will remain will be foundations and the huge fan of reddish-brown tailings on the flat below.

But Goldfield still exhibits the courthouse, built in 1907, and Firehouse No. 1, which has the WPA headquarters in the rear. Tex Rickard's home is kept groomed by the present owner. Its leaded, stained-glass window decorations and elaborate turrets that jut from the red roof are as startling now as they were thirty-five years ago, and their interest is undimmed when local mine leasers call their builder "Tex Richards." The four-story Goldfield Hotel remains to dominate the vista of chimney ruins and green-roofed bungalows. It is locked tight. After the war of 1914–18 a disciple of the wildcat age bought it of George Wingfield for a price between $20,000 and $30,000. He took pictures of it, of the mahogany lobby, the lambrequined lamp shades, the strongboxes behind the clerk's desk. He went east and mortgaged it, first for $100,000, and then for another $25,000. Then he stepped out and left this empty palace of a dying village in the hands of unhappy mortgagors. It passed through several hands and finally into those of a Californian who thought maybe the bipartisan boss of Nevada would be interested. He offered the hotel to George Wingfield, discounted to an attractive $70,000.

Tonopah, like Austin, has lived on in contracted form, a regional capital for prospectors, miners, and ranchers. Although it is the seat of huge Nye County, third largest county in America, it has never incorporated. Its five-story Mizpah Hotel is not conspicuous, because of the intact, active business

VIEW OF
PRESENT-DAY
TONOPAH

Frasher's Photos—Pomona, Calif

GOLD AND
SILVER ORE AS
IT COMES FROM
THE MILL

Farm Security Administration;
photo by Rothstein

Farm Security Administration; photo by Rothstein

ASSAYER PLACES CRUCIBLE CONTAINING
GOLD ORE IN FURNACE

district around it. Dugouts, shacks of flattened kerosene cans, unpainted frame bungalows and pillared mansions are there, as in 1906. Leasers are still working the Mizpah claim. The saloons and gambling houses and the red-light district have the flavor of old days. No fire or flood has destroyed ten thousand details, as in Goldfield, of the days when Key Pittman was a young man and Charles Schwab a hero from the East. Scattered cottonwoods and locusts have grown up to form green patches that complement the burnt-rock hills, and in summer the yards contain sunflowers, cosmos, and hollyhocks, and the screened porches are draped with rank, almost tropical banks of Virginia creeper. Tonopah survives, one of the most interesting towns in America.

A year or two ago a Nevada editor wrote, " The best investment the State of Nevada could make would be for the legislature to appropriate sufficient funds to plough under every ghost town in the state. Too much emphasis is being placed on failure and not enough on opportunity and success."

It is true that the weathered buildings in Rhyolite and Austin lack the dignity of relics in the Eastern states or in Europe, the ruins of churches and castles, the cabins in which great men were born, the halls in which the great men made speeches and wrote declarations. It is true, too, that the ruined hotels and banks and mills in the ghost towns served men only briefly, and not directly in the interests of culture and civilization. Certainly they are the epitaphs of a greedy race. Like the bones of cattle dead of thirst, they lie still and futile, symbols of waste and misspent life.

But one must remember what the editor has forgotten: that generations of men attempted to make a good life for themselves in a vast wilderness area. Men thought their cities would last forever. Their future was an Everlasting Yea. They tackled huge problems with energy that seemed boundless and a gusto that was unquenchable. In this sense the ghost town is a symbol of the faith that common men had in themselves and in their country. It is a tangible evidence of what Americans' hopes for happiness and security could lead them to do. Deserted prospectors' cabins, brush-mottled foundations, tumbled-in discovery shafts, and the red-brick hotels with the scars to show where the wooden balconies pulled off years ago — these linger from a virile past that built the base for the comfortable and prosperous present. The later generations of automobile tourists legitimately sentimentalize them. They are a genuine American antiquity as meaningful and significant as the trench mounds at Valley Forge and the white church at Lexington.

Gone are the days when the color of life was red. Nail by nail, brick by brick, the mining towns are crumbling, falling away, riding away in the auto trunks of souvenir collectors. But mining is still lively in Nevada. It is stronger economically and more useful socially than ever before. The hit-and-miss prospector still roams the wastelands, though he is no longer a representative figure, but the stampeder and mushroom camp and city builder has disappeared as a feature of Nevada life. The mining engineer, the industrial consultant, and the laborer remain. True, placer miners like those of early Gold Canyon and Bodie Wash and Osceola have their counterparts in the gullies of the Humboldt and Tuscarora ranges of present-day Nevada, but the simplicities of the gold pan and the rocker have always played a minor role in Nevada mining. Hard-rock mining with its shafts and tunnels has been the representative Nevada mining, and from the first months on the Comstock, when there were more gopher than Ophir holes, the key personnel in Nevada's industry have been mining engineers and metallurgists. They mastered the mining and reduction of native metals, the oxide ores, the refractory sulphides with their selenides, tellurides, arsenides, and antimonides. They worked out two early Western achievements:

the wet-silver mill, or Washoe process, and the dry-silver mill, or Reese River process. The final victory of survival belongs to them.

They have not captured the imagination of historians, novelists, or the general public. Men who examined ore specimens under microscopes, who traced geological formations, who made computations with scales and chemical mixtures, have remained as inconspicuous as the assayer himself. One ignorant Sandy Bowers, one lazy Jim Butler, one heat-crazed Jacob Breyfogle has taken his place in the epic of the West, and this is all right, for human interest must inevitably triumph when the story is told of the heroes of the frontier. But heroes are in the past now. Pedestrian and busy and important to present times is the engineer and metallurgist. Quiet, cold, efficient, college-trained, he is doing what he always did. Unglamourized, he is the subject only of brief mention in the technical journals or in the mining sections of Western papers. He continues the one enduring effort in the mining settlements: improvement in techniques for the profitable extraction of ore. Always in the background when mining was of public interest, now his interests are in the foreground, for the experts who follow mining.

For the technologist, the story of mining has always lain in fascinating (but not romantic) details. The physical mechanisms of the mine: shaft headframes, hoisting works, engines (steam, gasoline, electric), trams, pumps, lifts and cages and safety devices, shaft collars, timbering and cribbing, ventilation systems, drills. The plan of attack: tunnels, adits, levels, winzes, stopes, drifts, crosscuts. The lifeless but meaningful environment in the mine: the geological formations — strata, stringers, dikes, intrusions, veins, faults, shoots, displacements, seams, dips; and the rocks and minerals — trachyte, quartz propylite, basalt, scheelite, syenite, cinnabar, sulphurets of silver. The equipment and processes in the reduction works: roasting and blast furnaces, sintering machines, chlorination and cyanidation plants, stamp mills, ball mills, crushers, separators, settlers, amalgamation pans, amalgam safes, concentrators, agitators, Fagergen roughers, Kraut cleaners, Dorr classifiers, Moebius cells. The data on ore content, costs of supplies and equipment, water supply, shipping facilities, labor costs, demands in the industrial market, net returns per ton. These and other things are the " real inside story " of Nevada's search for nature's treasure. Its literature is not the dramatic and highly readable *Saga of the Comstock Lode* or *Gold in Them Hills*. It is *Cyanide Extraction of Gold and Silver Associated with Arsenic and Antimony in Ores* or *Geophysical Prospecting: Some Electrical Methods* or *Copper and Zinc in Cyanidation; Sulphide-Acid Precipitation*.

Everywhere, as Nevada's mineral production rises for the third time in history, old ores are getting new treatments and old districts are seeing new techniques. Boulder Dam power brings new activity to the lead and zinc mines of Pioche. The flotation process is working in the Aurora Consolidated and at a lead-zinc mine south of Ione. A cyanide mill twelve miles from Tonopah is at work on two million tons of silver-gold tailings that flowed down from early amalgam mills. Stimulated not only by new processes but also by the Depression and high silver prices under the New Deal, operators have reopened lead-silver mines in Eureka, the original Bullfrog Mine down south, the old Reliance Mine in Manhattan, the Hale & Norcross in Virginia City, and a hundred others.

Replacing the frontier miner with his pan, a huge dredger floats in a pond of muddy water below the old town of Manhattan and reaches down with clanking buckets to scoop up mud and gravel that contain gold particles. Soon a dredger will float on water diverted from Carson River and gnaw away at a third or more of the townsite of Dayton, biting out what remains of recently moved houses and uprooted fruit trees. Its buckets will reach down tens of feet below where the early Gold Canyon miners were able to dig; also they will recapture much of the treasure-filled tailings that ran off from Comstock mills above on the slopes of Mount Davidson. In the bottom of Bodie Wash, along which excited Aurorans followed Whiteman and his map of the Lost Cement Mine, a bulldozer, a power shovel, and a dragline are at work in rich placers, available only to workers of the contemporary machine age.

Tons of new equipment have been trucked into Virginia City, and the population has grown again. New shafts have been run, old workings re-explored, modern techniques experimented with. Virgin veins have been found. A cyanide process has proved cheaper than flotation. Ten or twelve mines are working the Comstock. Old names are preserved in one of the prosperously expanding companies, a merger of mergers: the Consolidated Chollar, Gould and Savage Mining Company. The most radical departure from traditional mining is the glory-hole method, which has made craters in Silver City, Gold Hill, and Virginia. The old square-set method was necessary because of crumbling rock; the lumber and labor required made it costly. The resulting rush for high-grade in the lower levels left much unmined rock near the top and also much metal-bearing waste in the square sets themselves. To recover this the Comstock Merger Mines Company, using a tunnel entrance, started in 1920 to slice out underground sections. At a cost of $3.13 per ton the company recovered ore worth $7.17, but milling costs took away profits, and the operation was discontinued. In 1933 W. J. Loring of Arizona, experienced in large-scale copper mining, looked over the Comstock, proposed a larger mill and the working of low-grade at the surface. In the following year his Arizona-Comstock Company brought in ten-ton trucks and gasoline-powered shovels on caterpillar treads. They took out seven cubic yards at a bite. Big-scale excavation dug a great terraced hole and recovered ore averaging $5.85 a ton, but did not find Woods's Store, that had fallen in long before with its burning stove and guardian dog. Mining costs were only $1.12 per ton, and milling, done half a mile downhill, was cheap. The Comstock paid good dividends again, and Loring's Cut became a big feature in the landscape.

But activity in Virginia City and Aurora is only a postscript to the old days. The representative new nucleus of mining activity in Nevada is the company town. Its origin is cautious and systematic. A mining magnate learns of a prospector's strike or of a small mine with rich prospects that is for sale. He takes an option. His expert geologists make a careful preliminary exploration. They estimate the size and richness of the ore body, all overhead costs, and outline necessary milling techniques. If they recommend favorably, the magnate takes up the option, and development proceeds. The town grows up. It is as orderly as the grounds of an automobile factory. About it there hangs no air of speculation or bumptious hope, no hint of a beggars' revel. The mine, the community, and the mill are a unit, blueprinted arbitrarily to fit the landscape and the mechanical requirements of the total plant.

A good example is Tungsten, which mines and mills sixty per cent of America's tungsten, required for electric-light filaments, X-ray targets, and certain hard-steel alloys. Tungsten is a standardized, stabilized town of 220 men laid out by the Massachusetts-Nevada Company in a low ravine that looks out across the Humboldt River Valley. The buildings have tar-paper sides, cleated with laths, and corrugated iron roofs, painted all over a dull-silver color. One low building houses the company offices, the store, and the post office. Across from it is the boardinghouse, which spreads out bounties of fresh food. Downhill are the garage, machine shops, a transformer, and the mills, one for working ore, one for reworking an accumulation of tailings. The final product is a yellow sand that trucks carry off in 400-pound steel drums. Above the store are a large rooming house and small shacks for miners and officials. There are a few Virginia creepers clutching at trellises near doorways, and a rosebush or two. Otherwise the only plants are low sagebrushes that look like short-clipped wool on the flanks of the ridges. There are no women. Wives and children, if any, live in shacks and auto trailers at Mill City, eight miles away. On a ridge above is a large green water tank, filled by lift pumps with water from the Humboldt Valley below. Up around a bend is the mine, supervised by one of Nevada's leading mining engineers, in which miners carefully separate barren country rock from scheelite — the tungsten ore — by flashing a fluorescent lamp. It makes the ore stand out in mottled, white patches.

In the company town, mining is no longer a romantic adventure or a titanic fight with resistant earth forces: it is a stable industry. Thanks to the extravagance and frauds of the past, mining failures loom large in the public mind, as failures in groceries or banking or merchandising do not. And thanks to the glamorous successes of the past, the Con Virginia and the Mohawk, the average small investor who does buy mining stock expects to get rich overnight and squawks loudly if returns are slow, even if steady. But the exhaustion of the big bonanzas, the slow evolution of corporation and stock-exchange laws, and the rise of efficient technology have taken mining away from wildcat speculators and from sleek promoters and given it to sober, trained investors. No industry is more in the hands of cautious engineers and astute businessmen. Someone once taunted Roswell Colcord, who had been an engineer in Nevada mines for a prolonged lifetime: "I don't see how you can call mining a legitimate occupation. When it's not gamble, it's fraud." Colcord replied in the same level tones he used when he was ninety-seven, "Legitimate? Why, it is as legitimate as raising wheat."

He might have added that it is safer than wheat raising. Figures for the comparative rate of return on capital invested in United States industry show mining far above other major investment fields: railroads, 3 per cent; insurance, 11 per cent;

national banking organization, 6 per cent; manufacturing, 14 per cent; mining, 182 per cent. Dun and Bradstreet have rated mining investments as being the best investments before the buying public, provided there is plenty of ore and it can be economically handled. A well-managed mine is as sure-fire as anything to invest in.

G. A. Joslin, formerly vice-president of the Mining Association of the Southwest, makes clear that a would-be investor must require careful investigation by engineers before he invests in a mining property. Good mines and prospects are not easy to find. Even if an investor pays an engineer a good fee only to get the report back that a prospect is worthless, he has lost nothing. The fee was a form of insurance against uninformed investment, in favor of a decision based on full technical information.

Of the development and equipment money spent on the advice of competent engineers but little has been lost and most of the money has yielded enormous returns. The development of mines and prospects when properly conducted is a legitimate business. The mortality is less than in an industrial business of comparable size, and the profits are larger.

Other defenders of mining point out that losses in mining are forty per cent less than in any one of the other four leading industries of the world: commerce, manufacturing, trading, and banking. And even agriculture, which is considered not only the base of civilization but also a steady occupation, is dependent on the weather, suffers violent cycles of prosperity, and is " much more speculative in most instances than a thoroughly prospected mining property, properly managed."

Not only is Nevada mining itself an industry. As a producer of strategic raw materials it is closely associated with a large number of manufacturing and technological processes. Nevada minerals have a heavy role to play in the war against the Axis. Manganese, mercury, tungsten, and even tin are being increasingly discovered by technically trained agents of corporations and of the United States Geological Survey. Many a prospector in the old days stumbled over ledges of unknown minerals that were neither gold nor silver and therefore of no interest to him, of no value, for that matter, until modern science created new and unprecedented demands. Nevada zinc goes into brass and is used in die casting and the galvanizing of iron and steel. Nevada lead covers cables, protects buildings with automatic sprinkler systems, solders electrical connections, and goes into linotype alloys. Its capacity for self-lubrication makes it an important component in bearings. Nevada copper helps carry the world's light, power, and communications, becomes refrigerator tubes and shell casings, and enters into the alloy called bronze. Silver itself is no longer a raw material solely for coins and tableware. It is a leading diversified metal. According to one authority, it surpasses even iron, aluminum, and copper. It surfaces automobile headlights, fills decayed teeth, and joins with lead in solder and cadmium in special bearings. It is a basic element in the films used by a million photographers and in the billion-dollar motion-picture industry. A new use is to line nonreturnable cans with a silver coat one-millionth of an inch thick on a base of copper-plate steel. Another is to serve as a germicide in municipal water supplies. Silver is a deadly killer of one-celled organisms. Under favorable conditions one silver molecule will destroy a living cell — as if a gnat were to kill a dinosaur.

Nonmetallic minerals are a growing division of the Nevada mining industry: alum; graphite, useful for paint pigment and foundry facings; gypsum, a principal product of Gerlach, used in plaster of Paris, fireproof building blocks, foundry cores, and land reclamation; fluor spar, used in steel smelting and in glazing pottery; marble, 99.5 per cent pure in a deposit near Nixon; marl, a natural powdered limestone, used to recondition soil in California; glass sand; dark-blue and green roofing slate; building stone; soda. There are several brucite mines. Brucite, a magnesium hydrate, is used to line open-hearth steel furnaces; piles of it lie drying in the sun along the railroad tracks at Luning. Limestone is abundant. Much of it goes from Sloan via the Union Pacific to sugar refineries in California, for it is the best sugar lime rock on the Pacific Coast. "It has a remarkably tough cryptocrystalline structure and retains its strength and coherence during and after cal-cining." The same deposit produces hundreds of thousands of tons each year of hydrated lime, burned lime, and dolo-mite, which is quarried to line steel plants. Diatomite, the silicon mass left behind by one-celled water plants that once lived in an inland lake, is common, and despite strong compe-tition from Lompoc, California, it is sometimes mined for use as insulation and silver polish. Borates are likewise common. For years borax was a major Nevada product along the marshes south of Walker Lake: Teels Marsh, Rhodes Marsh, Sand Springs Marsh, and especially Columbus Marsh. From 1874 to 1883 F. M. ("Borax") Smith made Nevada the leading producer of borax, until the discovery of colemanite in Death Valley shifted the leadership to California, where it has stayed.

Near Oreana, north of Lovelock, lies the only known de-posit of dumortierite which is of commercial extent and the required purity. This very rare mineral is an aluminum boro-silicate. It has high tensile strength. It has low heat-expanding and electricity-conducting properties. Even at white heat it is phenomenally resistant to expansion and electrical currents. It can endure a blasting heat and terrific physical stress and a violent range of temperature. It is the finest known material for spark plugs.

Bentonite, found in seven districts in Nevada, is a clay formed by the partial decomposition of glassy volcanic ash. It forms an emulsion in water and has a wide range of uses as a filler, plastic, and binder. It is put into paper, oilcloth, curtain cloth, linoleum, cordage, and rubber. It gives a better suspension to enamels in grinding frit for ground coats, adds strength to cement, and binds molding sands. It goes into soap, paste, glue, plaster, and pencil lead. It serves in the refining of fats and oils, the remanufacturing of old paper, the uniform dispersing of insecticides, animal dips, and plant sprays, the making of a stable suspension of particles in enamels and inks. An antiphlogistic in medical material, it is a constituent in salves and ointments that cure inflammation and in beauty clay. Its principal use is in the oil industry. It seals leaks in reservoirs and crevices in rock formations that allow drilling mud to flow out. Since it attracts water, it is used in clay filters to draw water from petroleum.

There is an important turquoise workings in the Austin area, which ships to Navajo artists in the Southwest and to jewelers in New York, Los Angeles, and Europe. In the Virgin Valley of semifrontier northeastern Nevada, between the desolate vistas of the Black Rock Desert and the huge antelope herds of the Mud Lake country, lies a bleak desert of eroded volcanic mud that contains a large deposit of big black opals. A black fire opal found there weighed seventeen troy ounces and is valued at a quarter of a million dollars.

Nothing of the magical, however, hangs over contemporary mining and milling. The uniform galvanized-iron buildings of the company town, the sturdy, plain food of the boarding-house, the banishment of wives and "bad" women to the nearest railroad or commercial town, the absence of flamboyant town life amid the mines, the efficient complication of the blueprinted plants, the totally workaday air — all these put mining on a matter-of-fact level where, engineers say, it should have been all the time. No rumors leak out — no tales of great strikes. No brokers rush to the telegraph office to buy a monopoly of the wires for a couple of hours. Visitors who come to the superintendent's office are not newspapermen ready for headlines or world travelers on the scent of excitement. They are geologists, professors from Columbia or Purdue. What news gets into the papers is of concern to financiers, mining operators, and unemployed laborers, but not to the general reader. It is abstract, written in a special, semi-technical jargon.

MINA (Nev.) Oct. 20 — Testing of ores from the Ashby and Garfield mines is proceeding at the Lucky Boy mill, operated by Champion City Mines, with treatment of a large tonnage from both properties projected if the milling process proves to be satisfactory.

The gold ore from the Ashby is said to be responding favorably to flotation, but the Garfield silver product is more oxidized and may require the use of cyanide. Shipments from both properties are being made to smelters.

Steady production of silver-lead-gold ore continues from the Lucky Boy mine, and development of ore is reported from several sections of the property. The mill has a daily capacity approximating 250 tons of ore but is now treating 175 tons.

For eighty years mining-town papers have been filled with similar news; so were the San Francisco, Sacramento, and Eastern papers. But with the grand and foolish days of mining speculation and public frenzy as dead as the towns of Treasure City and Rawhide, John Q. Public no longer reads such news.

V

WILD WEST IN NEON

Reno and Las Vegas as Villages and Outposts

THE TWO largest communities of Nevada are respectable, bumptious, and decadent. Each is a village, a frontier outpost, and a sophisticated cosmopolis. Each dominates an end of Nevada. They differ only in size and proportion. With its 23,000 inhabitants Reno is more the cosmopolis. Las Vegas, a quarter as large, is more the frontier town.

SEEN as villages, Reno and Las Vegas are the communities of homeowners with the "unsurpassed educational facilities" and "fine, strong church groups" that the booster literature truthfully refers to. Reno has fifteen churches, of which the Catholics, Baptists, and Methodists are prosperous. As you approach Reno from the south, sign after sign advertises "Harold's — World's Largest Roulette Wheel," but finally there comes a different sign: "The Churches of Reno Welcome You." In either town you may get gay on Saturday night and sing, "Hail, hail, the gang's all here! " at a cabaret, and next morning, just as likely, you raise your voice again, " All hail the pow'r of Jesus' name! "

The busy shopping districts are as self-consciously neon-lighted as any Billings or Oklahoma City, but the residential streets are modestly shaded, in Reno by elms and planes, in Las Vegas by poplars and cottonwoods. There are flower beds of asters, cosmos, petunias, snapdragons, zinnias, golden glow, and hollyhocks. There are lilac hedges. In summer the lawns are bright green and often they are shaded by old apple and pear trees. White picket fences enclose the less recent places. The houses, like those in any American small town, range from gewgawed Victorian Gothic through prairie-house types to the innovation from California: Monterey-Cape Cod. Kids play in yards and vacant lots and swim in the open-air plunges. There are Hoovervilles, but no slums. Crime is rare.

On the hill to the north the State University presides over the village of Reno. Despite the sagebrush and barren ridges in the distance, the immediate campus is kin to that of Middlebury College in Vermont or Grinnell in Iowa or of scores of other old-fashioned residential colleges. The quadrangle resembles that of the University of Virginia. The architecture is colonial, with tall white columns and red brick draped with ivy. The elms, box elders, and ashes, Manzanita Lake with its swans in summer and ice skating in winter, Gutzon Borglum's bronze of John Mackay the miner, the young men and women studying in the library and strolling along the sidewalks with books under their arms — these suggest a side of life in Reno that is in contrast to that represented by the postfrontier gambling of Center Street and the post-Hollywood novelty shops of Virginia Street. Until a decade ago a divorce suit brought by a faculty member was cause for scandal.

Townspeople are friendly in Reno and Las Vegas. Everybody talks to everybody else. Natives are as genial toward

bootblacks and bartenders as toward grocery clerks and milk-
men and popular preachers. Two drinkers at a bar brag about
their babies. On a cold day a taxi driver at the station says,
" Ride up in front. It's warmer here."

In Las Vegas, especially, a new resident isn't a stranger
long. Someone will clap him on the back. " You're a stranger
here, aren't you? Come on in and have a drink! " Anywhere
else such a greeter might be a " con man," but not in Vegas.
There he is just a citizen who has a town to share. "Everybody knows everybody else." He walks down Fremont
Street, nods to several dozen people, or exchanges joshing
remarks, or makes a serious inquiry or two. " How're ya? "
" Whatd'ou hear from Bill? " " Hear you smashed your garage door off th'other night! " This social compactness spreads
outward to much of Nevada. " Miles mean nothing here,"
testifies a radio dealer. " Reno's four hundred miles north.
You go back east and someone asks, ' Oh, you're from Nevada. Say, do you know Bob Jones in Reno? ' And the funny
thing is you do know him! "

Many divorcees sense this welcome. Those who weep from
homesickness on arrival gulp with sincere regret on leaving.
They can quickly establish acquaintanceships, if not romances, with natives, and they find opportunities for the sad
business of pouring out their life stories or the pleasant occupations of horseback rides, motor spins, and dinners out.

Inevitably there is gossip about private lives. Wholesome
village clans have much to say about the activities of fellow
residents. All are watched with the friendly sharpness that
Carol Kennicott came to appreciate in Sinclair Lewis's Gopher Prairie. So-and-so has left her husband again. So-and-so
won't be re-elected. So-and-so was with So-and-so at the
Meadows Saturday night. So-and-so was drunk on Virginia
Street in daylight yesterday. So-and-so said the other evening
that . . . And much more — the conversational traffic in private lives that is conspicuous in villages the world round.

Except for the university circle, culture is simple and un-original. Reno unquestionably has the advantage because of its size. Its Nevada Community Concert Association sponsors a season of well-known musical artists. A Little Theater presents dramatic productions. The crowded Washoe County Library displays a reasonable assortment of volumes, and there are women's clubs that print anthologies of Nevada poetasters. The Nevada Historical Society struggles along. An active Astronomical Society has explored the regions of Scorpio and Sagittarius through 5½- and 8-inch refractors and watched Venus and Mercury sink behind the Sierras. Down south, Las Vegas, which is a generation newer, has much less complicated culture. It has no urgent aspirations at all for culture but does label certain things as such. The movies are culture; so are the high-school plays and the church cantatas. One businessman says, "We have culture here. Rex Bell and Clara Bow have a ranch south of town, near Searchlight." Literature is available for five or ten cents a copy on the drugstore racks. A radio store carries a music side line of from ten to fifteen Decca swing records. No classical records are obtainable in any store in town. The county library is small and cramped. This in the state's second largest community! The fair explanation, however, is that Las Vegans who want cultural matters and luxuries, even some of the important necessities of life, buy them by mail or in Los Angeles.

Much of the social life is bound up in the rituals of fraternities, the Elks, Eagles, Masons, Knights of Columbus, the Eastern Star, the I.O.O.F. Standards of wit and humor are set in the Rotary, Lions, and Kiwanis clubs. Unofficially, an adolescent jest like this will make the rounds:

A fellow named Wood and a fellow named Stone
    were walking down the street.
Stone turned to Wood and Wood turned to Stone,
And they both turned to rubber when a girl walked by.

Or like this. A Nevadan will come up to a friend and say,

"You're a bum grocer!"
"Why am I?"
"Why, you don't know the difference between a blonde and a battleship."
"What is it?"
"I don't know either! Never been on a battleship."

Official humor is similar. A couple of Decembers ago the Las Vegas Lions gave Christmas presents to prominent members. The master of ceremonies, who is a man regarded by his fellows as quite a wit, gave a set of poker chips and a rack to a certain Protestant minister. He said he had heard the church services were rather sleepy, and here was a way to pep them up. He turned to a state legislator who had been trying to open up a new era for irrigation and settlement in the southern tip of Nevada. With Block 16 in mind, he said, "We hear you are trying to open up a new district," and handed the legislator a red light globe.

During the annual Helldorado in Las Vegas and the Fourth of July Rodeo in Reno, business and professional men wear beards and Western clothes. In Reno a kangaroo court roams the streets in an open truck. A dozen men are all judges, prosecutors, and executioners. They are disguised in seven-day beards, sombreros, and gorgeous red, yellow, and green silk shirts. They spot a friend on the sidewalk, some hapless optometrist or butane-gas distributor who is clean shaven and in ordinary business clothes. He is looking sheepish and pleasantly uncomfortable. "There's Rod McIntyre!" An eager vigilante, flushed red with the afflatus of village democracy, jumps down from the truck and slips a noose over Rod's ears. The judges call down from above. "Where's your whiskers?" "Where's your cow boots and ten-gallon lid?" "You're just begging for a necktie party, right in front of all these people!" "Get up here and explain yourself!" If a nonconformist is stripped of civilian clothes down to his civilian B.V.D.'s, the reason is he hasn't had enough pep and vim to be a vigilante himself!

Home folks use the telephone exchange frequently and copiously. They call up their friends whenever a question comes to mind or they have a bit of news to distribute. Suppose a man wants to talk to the house mover, gives what he thinks is the right number, and gets the confectioner instead. He chats on for a while, anyhow. Then he calls the operator and tells her laughingly about the mistake. If he likes her voice he asks her for a date. Finally he asks for the correct number and sees about getting his house moved.

Friends borrow cars and new skis and the owners don't mind. Eventually they'll borrow, in return, a shotgun or a riding horse. Everyone waves to acquaintances from his car. A Las Vegan in a convertible rides down Fremont Street and honks at fifty people in four blocks. Salesmen are folksy and genial rather than slick and hypocritical. They know their customers too well to want to cheat them. It is the California cities that are grabbing, grasping places. "Why, damn it all," a young assemblyman says, "L.A. was built to take your money away from you. Go down to their angel city with fifty bucks. They take it away from you. Go with forty. They take it away. Thirty. They reach out to snap it away. Take a dollar. They want it, too. Play safe, and go into town with just a dime or a nickel. They jump up and down and can hardly wait to sell you a two-cent value and clean you out!! "

Informality and congeniality, combined with frontier liberality, are symbolized by the free phones at the bars and lunch counters in Las Vegas. If one wants a taxi, or gets to quarreling with a fellow drinker about what the score was in the Rose Bowl last New Year's Day and wishes to call the sports editor of the *Review-Journal*, he just picks up the handy French phone.

Narrow-mindedness is always potential and sometimes ac-

tual. Professors at the university and instructors in the high
schools do not speak out freely on economic and political
subjects, as they could in a town fifty times larger than Reno.
Las Vegas saw mob action in 1940, a year in which hicks and
villagers the country over made illegal attacks on the Witnesses of Jehovah, in a wave of religious intolerance unparalleled since the Missourians warred on the early Mormons.
Three members of the sect, two men and a woman, were dis-
tributing tracts and playing their phonograph records of
Judge Rutherford's sermons. A crowd of "war veterans"
came on the trio in the car, pulled them out, grabbed their
bundles of tracts and several phonographs and burned these
on the street. They ordered the Witnesses to leave town and
threatened to use branding irons on them if they returned for
more proselyting. Police stood by and made no attempt to
interfere.

In contrast, naturally, kindness is just as potential, and no
doubt it is more often practiced. The people of Nevada's two
largest towns, like its other inhabitants, are notably liberal
minded and tolerant. One Reno man says of his town, "Here
are probably less hypocrisy and meddling and more freedom,
than anywhere in America."

Startlingly opposite to the Witnesses incident in Las Vegas
are the typical actions of the young, liberal District Attorney,
Wisconsin educated and a boyhood friend of the LaFollette
brothers. A Negro was arrested on the charge of a white
woman that he had tried to rape her in a back alley. The
Review-Journal rumbled that the D.A. better do something
about this quick, and ardent Caucasian democrats talked of
stringing up the outrageous Negro. Cool headed, the District
Attorney made a careful investigation. He found that the
woman was illegally approaching men on Fremont Street,
she had been a drunken hanger-on in a club the day of the hap-
pening, and she had pestered the Negro until he went off with
her. When they were together in the alley she saw a passer-by

and had a twinge of Nordic self-consciousness. "Rape! Rape!" she cried. The result was that the District Attorney released the Negro and had the court fine the woman five dollars for soliciting on the streets. Thereafter the D.A. referred to it as the case of the white girl who got fined for raping a Negro.

Provincial villagers under their surface sophistication, Renoites and Las Vegans dislike the spotlight when it points at unorthodoxies: gambling, vice, and divorce. Citizens are reticent about the "lurid" sources of local prosperity. The chambers of commerce are noncommittal. The mayors and police chiefs are evasive. Information and clues must be pried from one Nevadan or another. Some Nevadans are indifferent or disinterested, it is true. The moralists are covertly hopeless and tired of talking on these subjects or they have a rationalization which enables them to ignore the indirect source of their income, wholly or partly, and to dismiss the subject from their conversation. The Reno *Evening Gazette* expressed this same attitude at the time gambling was legalized in 1931.

The great part of Nevada's population is composed of men and women who never gamble and are not seeking divorce. Their attitude toward both these things is the normal attitude of most American communities. They are good citizens, uphold the laws, and raise their families to be honest, and upright in all things. . . . The real life of Nevada is not hectic, and this is something which the country ought to be made to understand.

The boosters, hopeful of attracting industries and millionaires, minimize the moral novelties. Publicity issued by the Reno Chamber of Commerce and the Nevada Department of Highways only hints at them and stresses, properly enough, things like housing and living standards, parks, educational facilities, and winter sports. One colored brochure, distributed by the Las Vegas Chamber of Commerce, does go further. Besides the usual praise for climate, churches, and accommodations, it contains puffs for the wide-open recreations of "this amazing playground" which is "still a frontier town" and for the advantages of Nevada's "'modern' divorce and marriage laws."

Small-town propriety has not been strong enough, however, to do anything about Reno's famous sign. Spanning the highway through town and clearly visible from all trains is a boldly lighted arch:

RENO

THE BIGGEST LITTLE CITY IN THE WORLD

In 1934, after hearing protests that the sign was distasteful and boastful, the City Council voted to change it to a mere modest RENO in four-foot green letters. But the change was unsatisfactory; the one-word sign seemed empty without its subtitle, and shortly afterward the immodest paradox was once again glaring out into the darkness. Six years later a new superneon arrangement increased its brightness fifteen times.

Certainly the towns have good orthodox matters to advertise. Each has an excellent dry climate, plenty of water, thriving commercial distribution, and normal public institutions, schools in particular. Each is in or near important cattle, farming, and mining country. Each lies close to scenic attractions. Las Vegas calls itself "Hub of the Scenic Southwest." Reno offers "100,000 Square Miles of Opportunity." Both hug transcontinental railroads and highways and thrive on tourists. After the Japanese raid on Pearl Harbor, the through railroads were prodigiously busy freighting war matériel to California; new army camps trained soldiers and fliers; local housing facilities were crammed tight. The towns hope to become bigger and wealthier and more powerful. What prosperous burgs ever thought otherwise?

"Slanderous" and "libelous" attacks, therefore, are grounds for limber activity by town builders angered by a

blotched reputation. Both towns have had run-ins with de-
tractors. Renoites have protested against numerous articles in
national magazines. Time and again they have had to say what
a local judge said in 1910: " This town is really as fine a town
as there is on earth. It ain't wicked. It only does things open
and aboveboard that San Francisco and New York do on the
Q.T. Why, even Reno's gambling is on the square! "

Recently Las Vegas has had two occasions to fight infamy.
In 1939 an Idaho legislator said publicly that Las Vegas was
the cesspool of the world. The Chamber of Commerce and
other civic groups invited him down at their expense. He
came, had a good, respectable time, and publicly changed his
mind. The following year *Look* published a photo-essay:
" Wild, Woolly and Wide-Open, That's Las Vegas, Nevada, where men are men and sin is a civic virtue." It was the
hodgepodge of fact and fantasy that Nevada subjects traditionally receive — melodramatic, sensational, distorted. According to *Look*, Las Vegas was " the most cockeyed and
self-consciously wicked place on earth . . . the American
Gomorrah." Its mayor conducted much of his official business in a bar. The Reverend C. S. Sloan of the Baptist Church
slept with his boots handy and responded to a marriage like
a fireman, and would perform his leisurely service, eight minutes long, " in almost any place — Pullman car, hotel lobby
or street corner — for $5." A picture showed him marrying
two eloping California youngsters outside the cab of a Union
Pacific locomotive. Mothers interrupted their shopping to
play slot machines in grocery stores. Block 16 (the segregated
prostitution section) was on " the official ' fun map.' " A
horse was a permissible means of entering a bar if you could
get him through the door — a hooliganism considered harmless by the Las Vegans. . . .

This five-page spread drew the wrath of many inhabitants
of the town. Letters besieged the Chamber of Commerce and
it campaigned against *Look* for a retraction or a future depic-

FREMONT STREET
LAS VEGAS

Union Pacific Railroad Photo

HIDDEN WELL RANCH NEAR LAS VEGAS

RIDING ON A TRUCKEE MEADOWS
DUDE RANCH, NEAR RENO

tion that would show the town as the residents saw it. Members of the Baptist Church, highly wroth, urged the Reverend Mr. Sloan to make the matter a personal one with the magazine. Sloan declared Las Vegas was not as wide open as indicated and was, instead, " a city of clean living and home loving people." President R. J. Kaltenborn of the Chamber declared his organization would attempt to compel the magazine to make some restitution for " the smirch on the good name of Las Vegas." He threatened suit. The Secretary wrote, " This office feels the part concerning sin being a civic virtue was a very unfair statement. We do have a beautiful little city and our schools and churches are as good or better than any in the Western country." Las Vegans did not get satisfaction from *Look,* but their protest may have benefited them. An article on Las Vegas commissioned by *Liberty* and entitled " Sin for Sale " did not appear in print.

THERE is a considerable amount of Western posing in Reno and Las Vegas. There are bellhops, orchestra players, lawyers, and merchants who confidently wear " Western " dude-ranch costume: cow boots, blue jeans, gay neckerchiefs, and Stetson hats. There is a good deal of talk in certain " higher " circles about horses and " cow ponies." The reason given for this Westernism is that it is what visitors want and it is good for business.

Reno's rodeo on the Fourth of July and Las Vegas's Helldorado in May call forth a rash of " atmosphere," including yoked oxen pulling covered wagons, old buggies, nineteenth-century frocks and bonnets, cutaway coats and top hats, and grizzled prospectors posed between belles. Many Western towns have such celebrations, and always after they close the antiques disappear. These old things do not really figure in the lives of the towns any more than the cow boots of the divorce lawyers serve any immediate practical purpose.

It is in other ways that Reno and Las Vegas retain real

Western flavor. On the streets are occasional old-timers, sombreroed cowboys, Mexicans, Piutes, ranchers. One can see a group of men bent over a specimen of rich ore brought in by an Indian or a hinterlander, wondering just where it came from and how much such ore is available. "Boy, if a fellow got hold of a claim of this stuff, he'd clean up plenty! "

Off just beyond the horizons of town wild and exciting events take place. A man and a domineering woman trespass on a miner's claim, intent on stealing a water tank. The two sides exchange shots and the miner falls dead. Or, mining partners dispute over their common holdings and one draws a six-shooter and slays the other. Or, in contrast, two men are digging at the bottom of an 85-foot shaft. They set eleven charges of dynamite and hurry up a ladder to a "station" 25 feet above. A charge goes off prematurely and blasts the lower man insensible with rock fragments. The upper miner quickly descends. The remaining caps may go off any second. He picks up his comrade, shoulders him, clambers to the station above, and slouches behind a muck pile. The ten caps go off harmlessly.

The towns contain numerous young men and women who are realizing the opportunity for old-fashioned careers that new-fashioned Nevada offers. Young men are rising in law, politics, medicine, and mining, young women in journalism, social work, social position. All a young person needs in Reno and Las Vegas is vitality and gumption and an absorbing interest in practical affairs. He must make his mark for himself. He can't get aid from his ancestors. Only a young person primarily interested in artistic or cultural work would find the towns too small and immature. There are unusual chances for female divorcees, of course, particularly if young and attractive. Female plaintiffs for divorce are sometimes looking around for No. 2, and young Nevadans are at hand, because of the disproportionately masculine population. One pretty, 30-year-old redhead who got divorced last year re-

ceived proposals from a linoleum manufacturer, an army offi-
cer, and a preacher, in less than a month, all of them contacts
made in Las Vegas.

The traditional "Western" word of honor holds. Many
a Renoite and Las Vegan has grubstaked a friend or acquaintance who wished to prospect for precious metals or the new
industrial materials like manganese and beryllium. He has
simply handed over $150 or more with the implicit under-
standing that he will own half of any mine found. The manager of such a nonfrontier enterprise as a chain retail store
testifies that the best credit customers in town, besides teachers and laboring men, are gamblers and prostitutes, who pay
debts promptly. Mormon farmers are slow paying but sure,
while products of advanced civilization, government and professional men, are the worst credit of all. Professional gamblers trust townsmen and lend to them on personal notes.
And vice versa. When the Las Vegas bank runs out of one-
dollar bills, because so many are taken out of circulation by
gambling, it sends a messenger to a leading gambler, gets
packs of bills in $100 lots, and uses them without a checkup
count.

The Nevada cities do not prohibit "indulgences" that belong in the Western towns of tradition. Law frees the individual instead of repressing him. The Puritan is out of power,
the democrat in power. It is assumed that men are fundamen-
tally good, that pleasure is justifiable, that necessity is no
crime.

Liquor is abundantly available, which is nothing novel in
America since 1934. There are about seventy-five bars in
Reno. During Prohibition, however, the two towns were
among the most wide-open places in the country. The reasons
were "protection," the isolation of Nevada from the main
federal enforcement headquarters, and local public opinion.
Bartenders served strangers after what Duncan Aikman
termed "probably the most casual . . . inspection yet to be

found in America." Evil results came, especially in Reno, where "Curley" Bill Graham and James McKay, gamblers and bootleggers, became benevolent despots.

There were some raids, inevitably. Belle Livingstone's Reno night club was visited by federal agents, who arrested three bartenders and seized liquor with fancy labels. After construction began on the dam in Black Canyon, Colonel George Seavers of San Francisco and several scores of prohibition agents raided speak-easies and roadhouses in Las Vegas and confiscated large quantities of booze. The Colonel said, "We're going to make this place safe for Hoover Dam workers."

The name callers got busy again. Dr. Clarence True Wilson, national director of the Methodist Board of Temperance, said Nevada was a combination of Sodom, Gomorrah, and perdition. Although the charge was too trite and stale to merit recognition, two Renoites replied. The Reverend Dr. Alfred J. Case replied, "This is just a forensic display of hot air." Mayor E. E. Roberts made a speech on Sunday night, March 29, 1931, in the First Methodist Church. The Mayor was in his eighth year of office. He was a former congressman and a leading divorce lawyer who claimed to have won more divorce cases than any other man alive. In his speech he made a proposal that got space in the nation's press. He said that the only way to drive bootleggers out of business was to "place a barrel of whisky on every corner and let every one help himself." The liquor would be made of good corn in a municipal still and be provided at public expense. A dipper would hang from the barrel. A sign would invite all to drink as much as they pleased but please not take any away. The scheme was no doubt meant to be fantastic but to get over a realistic principle, that drinking, like gambling, though socially bad, is "far more desirable when conducted in the open than under cover."

Most of America now applies this principle to liquor, but

only Nevada, best exemplified by Reno and Las Vegas, applies it also to gambling and prostitution, regulated by the most tolerant and sensible laws in the country. " We have six laws. Four are unconstitutional."

Men and women gamble in the " clubs " at any time of the night or day. In Las Vegas there are a dozen gambling houses, all busy, but especially the long-established Boulder Club and, across the street, Guy McAfee's newer Frontier Club. The clubs and slot-machine arcades are expanding. They gleam at night under fluorescent lighting tubes. In Reno there are about thirty-six clubs. Several of them, the Bank Club especially, are nearly always jammed with people. The least popular is the self-conscious Harold's Club, with women dealers and a hostess to explain the games. It advertises more than a hundred miles along the major highways but lacks authenticity because it is deliberately out to capture tourists. Nearly all the clubs are on the street level. From the sidewalks you looks through large uncovered windows to the brightly lighted interiors. The general atmosphere is that of any legitimate business patronized by the general public. The mood is that of an ultraserious carnival. There is none of the exclusive, aristocratic air of the Monte Carlo of tradition. The atmosphere is businesslike, lacking in style and glamour. It is " Western," lower middle class, proletarian even. The people are right off the streets and quite without pretension. As individuals wish, they are hatless, coatless, their shirts open at the throat. In summer there are many white pants and sport shirts. Old clothes and battered hats are common. The croupiers are genial fellows instead of the formal automatons of European casinos or Mexico's Agua Caliente of a few years back.

There are no steerers or criers. Visitors are never urged to play, and are at liberty to look on or linger. Women receive normal courtesies. No drinking is allowed except at the bar. The crowds are quieter than shoppers in a department store.

They are as quiet as church congregations. They are serious, concentrating. Only some stray extrovert pretends to be having a hilarious time.

Above the calls of the dealers and the undertones of the patrons rises the clangor of dozens of slot machines. They are mostly nickel ones, though there are some for dimes and quarters and four-bit pieces. Tourists play them. They furnish gay adventure for visiting schoolma'ams, maiden aunts, and gray-haired matrons. A few threadbare dopesters, secretive and wise, slouch near by. They watch the tourists waste their money, count their plays, and wait for the appropriate time to make a few plays for a jackpot.

There are circular crowds around the crap tables, where silver dollars are stacked up high. Nevada *is* a silver state. Dealers deftly rake in dice and coins with their dice canes. Assorted patrons play the big wheel of fortune, which gamblers despise, and roulette, which is a leading favorite with gamblers. It offers the player a fascinating variety of risks. A few card tables not in use are draped with green felt. Around the several in use sit experts, often roughly dressed, playing poker and faro. The latter is popular because of the equity it gives the players. Of all the games it gives the least percentage to the house, and dealers off duty prefer it even to roulette. The players intently clutch their cards and watch the plays by moving their eyes but not their heads. They speak seldom, in low voices, and smoke pipes or chew their quids in complete absorption in the game. The dealers smoke cigarettes carelessly and watch the circle of faces. In all these games the stakes are small. Plungers are rare. The clubs depend on the total bulk of ordinary plays as they come in half dollars, quarters, dimes, and nickels. Poker pots are rarely larger than ten dollars and in faro twenty-five dollars is a seldom-used limit. It is " small-time " gambling.

A casual watch at the tables sizes up the " characters " to be expected in an individualistic society: a stooped, sunken-cheeked old woman who smokes one fag after another as she plays faro; a Chinese tense over poker; a well-dressed, old-fashioned sport wearing a straw hat and playing self-confidently with angular gestures; a real cowboy — a contrast to the drugstore cowboys that drive the station wagons for the dude ranches — his face reddish, his eyelashes and brows bleached, who rolls in his seat as he flips his cards to the table top.

There are shills or dummy players in the room, playing with marked house money for a wage of three dollars a day, but a stranger cannot spot them. They keep the games going and thus indirectly entice patrons; they make the clubs seem busy and lively and interesting to tourists. On a winter day there may be more shills than genuine patrons. The clubs go in the red thousands of dollars in the winter to keep open and put up a good appearance.

Clusters of men and women watch the returns on horse races being held all over the country and place bets on races yet to be run. Seated at long counters the bourgeois tourists play keno. A house employee draws balls from a revolving wicket and calls off the numbers on them. The players place baby lima beans on numbers that correspond in columns printed on pieces of cardboard, hoping to line up beans all the way across the card and win the right to yell, "Keno!" The pay-off depends on the number of persons playing. A five-cent investment in chance may return $7.50 in less than ten minutes. It is more likely to return $0.00. Clubs that specialize in this game alone, like the Fortune Club in Reno, which calls it Bingo, advertise Big Feature Games at $25, $30, and $50, and free $50 and $100 drawings.

One hears tales of lucky breaks in the clubs. A bum borrowed a nickel and won the jackpot in a slot machine and then cleaned up a hundred dollars at poker. In Las Vegas, Producer Selznick stopped off for an hour's recreation after a long automobile trip, had a winning streak at roulette and took $3,000 in short order. A man signed a credit contract with the manager of a Sears, Roebuck retail store. He went down the street to a club and played the little cash he had. In an hour he was back in the manager's office. " Tear up that contract! I've got money! "

Presumably most of the gambling is honest. It is a legal, home-controlled business, steady and predictable, and it has a reputation to uphold. Fair dealing is an asset. Customers are plentiful and, if well treated, will continue to be. Dealers earn a good regular wage and can live well without cheating either their employers or the patrons. In Las Vegas, according to Max Miller, they earn seven dollars an eight-hour day. In Reno, they earn twelve dollars a day in winter and fifteen dollars in summer. State law prohibits bunco steering to any gambling game, " fixed " machines, sleight of hand, fraudulent dice or cards, and everything connected with lotteries: setting them up, selling tickets, aiding in their sale, or insuring them. Gambling by minors is illegal and the clubs, to assure themselves of continued good will from the public, have bouncers keep youths away. One would have a hard time proving any game crooked. Dice are guaranteed to be accurate down to 1/10,000 of an inch. The public is challenged on the wall of one Keno room: " $100 Reward for Anyone Who Can Prove These Balls Have Not Been Called Correctly. Equipment Open to Inspection at All Times."

In allowing open gambling Nevada is simply regulating what seems to be a desire for new experience and thrills ingrained in human beings. What in the original West was a moral anarchy is in the New West of Nevada a sociological pragmatism. When gambling was re-legalized, in 1931, Mayor Roberts said:

It's all nonsense trying to regulate people's morals by law. For eight years I've been trying to make Reno a place where everybody can do what they please, just so long they don't interfere with other people's rights. Now we can do lawfully what Nevada has always done under cover.

And Jim Tully, in town to cover the fight between Max Baer and Paulino Uzcudun, expressed his belief that Reno was "the last stronghold of personal liberty in America."

According to Anthony Turano, a Reno attorney, judges and college professors concurred with Roberts's opinion. Merchants were won over because of the good spending of the professional gamblers themselves and of the visitors brought in from other states. Regular gambling, it seems, does not excite people and hurt local trade as does a short horse-racing season. More important, Nevada towns were avoiding the evils common elsewhere in America, where gambling houses, lotteries, and numbers games thrive under cover and breed crooked police and corrupt city officials.

Nevada has not always been so wise. Its Puritans have had their try at suppressing "evil" and thus encouraging crookedness and antisocial activity. In 1909 reformers pushed through legislation that outlawed all gambling, beginning October 1, 1910. There had been gambling by license since 1879. The public revenue from licensing was lost, of course, and a sturdy chain of surreptitious joints began to build up that conducted every known skin game, including Chinese lotteries. Eventually there was "protection" and other corruption of political and social life. The swing back began in 1911, when an Act was passed, effective the first day of 1912. It retained much of the taboo. It prohibited gambling games with a single dealer — faro, monte, roulette, rouge et noir, rondo, tan, fantan, seven-and-a-half, twenty-one, hokey-pokey, craps, klondike; banking or percentage games played with cards, dice, or any device for money or any representative of money; any gambling game in which there was any percentage or reward to the keeper; slot machines, pools, and horse races. The law did allow certain gambling. It legalized poker, stud-horse poker, five hundred, solo, and whist when the deal alternated and no percentage was taken; social games played for drinks, cigars, and prizes under two dollars.

The legal fight was not over. In 1913 all gambling was outlawed again. In 1915 games were allowed where the deal alternated, and the sheriff was to collect license fees and pocket them. Unfortunately, as things worked out, the fees on licensed games were less than the bribes for unmolested illegal games. So matters stood on the surface, with undercover gambling an open secret, until 1931.

The evils of local corruption were one reason for the Act of 1931. The depression was another reason. A third was a resurgence of common sense, made easier by Nevada's spiritual nearness to the frontier. The bill passed the legislature on March 19 and was signed at once by Governor Fred Balzar, an old-style Nevadan. Gambling was legal immediately, and on the twentieth, even before the license forms had been printed, houses were thronged with players.

Speak-easy gaming places dropped the password ritual. Veteran roulette wheels and crap tables were moved into hastily rented ground-floor rooms. Before noon crowds were watching or playing, as poker chips clattered, slot machines click-clacked, and compressed-air drills beat a staccato on massive walls that were being torn down to enlarge quarters. Saturday night, the twenty-first, was a gala society night. Repressed Californians poured into Las Vegas and Reno and Cal-Neva resort, astraddle the state line on Lake Tahoe. In the swanky night clubs and hotels people appeared in fashionable formal dress to celebrate the occasion. In one Reno resort an entertainer imitated a movie première by announcing the guests as they arrived. Elsewhere a man gambled for more than thirty-three hours without once leaving his seat. He always had about $3,000 in front of him.

For a decade now Nevada counties and incorporated cities have issued licenses. Of the fees collected by counties a quar-

ter goes to the general state fund, three-quarters to the general
county fund. Fees from licenses issued by Reno, Las Vegas,
and other cities are split three ways: a quarter to the state, a
quarter to the county, and half to the town. Thus government gets its "take." In 1933 the revenue of the state was
around $69,000, that of Reno around $50,000. The fee is
$25 per table per month for certain card games, specifically
stud and draw poker, bridge, whist, solo and pangingue. Other
games are $30. The fee for slot machines is $10 per month.
There is no taxation or regulation for social games and vend-
ing machines. At a stroke the law removes graft, protects
juveniles from temptation, and provides public income and
regulated public recreation. There is a respectable role, then,
for Reno's two stores that specialize in gambling equipment
and her eight hundred slot machines — one to every four permanent inhabitants.

Prostitution must be recognized as a necessary part of Nevada's heritage, as from the first men have far outnumbered
women. Harsh critics condemn prostitution, but as long as it
is supporting the existing culture, the good that comes from
it must be seen, and the good that comes from having it out
in the open must have a fair hearing. If there are undesirable
aspects, then most of the criticism should be aimed at the society that needs prostitution so that it can have monogamists,
virgins, bachelors, and old maids.

In Nevada prostitution was legally segregated and supervised until January, 1942, when, at the request of army authorities, local officials closed down all houses. Designed to
protect soldiers and metalworkers until the Axis had been defeated, the ban was contrary to Nevada individualism and
common sense. County officers promised, however, to try to
change human nature and Nevada tradition for the sake of
nationalism and war. It remained to see whether more good
would result than harm. When Nevada "reformers" abolished prostitution in 1923, lumberjacks, miners, and ranch

hands encouraged hidden prostitution all over town. It was vice and truly vicious, as it is in most American cities. The system worked out in the consequent reaction made prostitution socially useful. Assuredly it did not corrupt the innocent. As Anthony Turano said, only the seeker and the moralist knew of its existence.

Prior to 1942 Nevada handled prostitution in a modified frontier fashion that cities like Los Angeles and Boston could well envy. When girls applied for a job they were fingerprinted. The prints were checked through the Federal Bureau of Identification for possible criminal record. The girls went through a regular medical inspection. They registered with the police as to where they roomed uptown when off work.

Since law forbade women to solicit on the streets, most of the time they were in one place under supervision; therefore Las Vegas and Reno, and other towns, were without delinquency problems, rapes, white-slave rings, and assorted morals offenses and perversions. Young people were protected by the police as well as by house cops. Townsmen said, with pride, that their wives and daughters could walk along residential streets at night without fear of attack. Preachers approved of the arrangement. They felt that the moral tone in town was good.

"Block 16" was a few blocks north of Fremont Street, Las Vegas. A stranger found it as easily as the near-by post office. There was a sequence of shacklike buildings, housing in turn Mexicans, Negroes, Japanese, and assorted whites in two-storied buildings. On warm days and nights the girls sat inside the open windows or on sidewalk chairs, or leaned in the doorways. The two-story buildings, with their downstairs bars, preserved the architecture and customs of the old mining towns, and, before them, of fancy houses along the lower Mississippi.

In Reno, the Riverside restricted district, a brothel on the European plan, was located with a little more difficulty, off

to the side on North Second Street. From the outside it looked
somewhat like the rear of a movie set, makeshift and unfinished. A few weak bare electric lights hung above an unpaved
parking lot in front. Inside, the "Stockade," or "Bull Pen,"
was a long, narrow, slightly bent lane between two low, con-
tinuous red-brick buildings. On each side there were about
forty "cribs," each with a door and window. A honky-tonk
bar blared faintly at the far end. The lane was a promenade
for male visitors. It was shaded by small trees. In the daytime
it looked tawdry. Illuminated at night by more bare electric
lights, strung on wires, it gave the purely visual effect of the
livestock pavilion at a country fair or of a debutante's garden
party with booths and concessions. At no time during the
night or day did it seem glamorous and enticingly sinful. It
was only banal.

Girls stood in their doorways or sat inside their windows
and leaned out through them on window sills. They wore
slacks, shorts, dresses, as they chose. To meandering males inside the stockade they called out the immemorial allures . . .
Hey, Slim, come here! I've got something I want to say to
you! . . . Come here, honey, I want to talk to you. . . .
Come on, dearie. . . . Their names were printed on a card
above their doorways: Lulu, Alice, Roberta, Edna . . . $2.
Inside was a room that resembled that of a schoolgirl. The
bed was made and covered with a spread. Pictures hung on the
walls — Woolworth lithographs, photos of movie stars, racy
calendars. The dresser bore the usual assortment of beauty
aids and a radio that broadcast popular music. The girls chat-
ted with one another from window to window, or knitted, or
read magazines, or sat and looked bored. A few held laughing
conversations with groups of males.

They were of all types, from girls that looked like your
cousin, through those that resembled the "fast" girls in high
school, to baggy older women who looked worn and hardened. One important characteristic distinguished them from

the scarlet women of the frontier. They did not look their profession. Since the jazz age gave cosmetology and "sex appeal" to all women, prostitutes have lost their monopoly on traditional means of allure. Rouge, lipstick, eyebrow pencil, mascara, slacks, shorts, form-fitting outfits, chorus-girl costumes — so universal are these in American life, including popular art and advertising, that only seeing a Nevada woman in a house of prostitution indicates her means of livelihood. When off duty around town these professional women dressed like ordinary working girls. Many of them wished to get married and settle down. Some married local men, raised families, and circulated in community life without meeting prejudice.

Technically they were in business for themselves. A girl paid two dollars a day to the owners of the stockade and pocketed all she made above that; Reno got only the taxes on the land and buildings. A man ambled to a doorway, the woman whispered something ecstatic in his ear, he nodded, they stepped inside, and the blinds came down. A few minutes later out he came and walked away. The blinds came up. "Come over here, darling . . ." And so on. Business it was, more aboveboard and honest than many a transaction in department stores. There were incomes for girls, profits for the syndicate which rented the space, fees for doctors, emotional release for migrant males, but no graft for the police.

Inside the entrance to the stockade sat a city policeman on regular duty in a windowed lookout. He preserved order, if necessary, checked on the medical records of the inmates, protected girls from sadistic drunkards, and enforced the rules scrawled on signs outside that cameras and curious ladies were forbidden.

There were other authorized places in Reno. The Cottage, for example, catered to a select clientele who liked shower baths, more privacy and less hurry, and would pay $3 and on up.

Today in Nevada, as on the old frontier, frank heterosexuality is all right. State law makes adultery neither an offense nor a felony. It is only grounds for divorce, rarely used. Extramarital sexual intercourse between adults is not advocated. Neither is it held against a person. Veterans of the Goldfield-Tonopah days well represent the attitude when they reminisce without ostentation or restraint. One sheepman, son of a Reno pioneer, who was in Tonopah in boom times, said recently:

Why, I went back there last year to a Fourth of July celebration. Was to be a big parade of old timers and old cars and wagons. Left rooming place to go downtown and watch. All the way kept meeting sporting women knew in nineteen o five, thereabouts. They come back to town to retire. Spent so much time talking with them about people used to know that never did see any of the God-damned parade!

Such a man feels that a prostitute has her place in life, but he shies at talk of homosexuality. For him, as for the Nevada statutes, it is the " crime against nature," something not in the Western, he-man tradition. A Hollywood " homo " or a New York Lesbian is an outrage against the way things should be. Such a man speaks scornfully of " parasite-like pimps," who are the only males meant by the Nevada statute that punished " habitual use of prostitution " — though, actually, none are ever prosecuted.

Prize fights in general are not an important element in the life of Nevada's two cities, but one particular fight is a page in the history of Reno. The battle of July 4, 1910, between Jim Jeffries and Jack Johnson was Reno's first and most successful advertising stunt. It helped give Reno and Nevada some of the notoriety that has lingered on through the decades. It would not have been fought if Reno had not been a Western city.

A postfrontier generation that was strong for Victorian respectability had clamped down on prize fights in nearly all of America, but Nevada, not yet through with cattle wars and gold rushes, sought profits and publicity and he-man entertainment by providing for glove contests. The law of January 29, 1897, was almost alone in the statutes of the states. Three big fights resulted, all made nationally prominent by the dynamic new journalism that William Randolph Hearst was giving Americans. The climactic fight was Reno's.

It was originally scheduled for San Francisco, but in middle June protests began to arrive in Sacramento in the office of Governor J. N. Gillett. The Governor wrote Attorney General Ulysses Webb that the fight must be stopped if it was a prize fight but could go on if it was only a sparring exhibition. Publicity for the fight increased and so did protests to the Governor. Public opinion was aroused. Metropolitan San Francisco wanted the fight. The rural hinterland of the state opposed it. San Francisco hotel men saw Gillett. The promoters, Tex Rickard and his partner, Gleason, called on Gillett, to no avail. They had already sold $130,000 in seats and run up expenses of $30,000 in advertising, and they had already started to build an arena. Blocked by political pressure, they looked about for another place to hold the fight. Salt Lake City was impossible: Utah laws forbade prize fighting. Oregon was out. Arizona was only a wilderness. Nevada towns saw their chance. Ely and Reno bid for the fight. Charley Stout, coproprietor of the Louvre, a Reno gambling house, offered a subsidy of $2,500 if the fighters' training camps were pitched in Reno ten days before the Fourth and said he was sure other gamblers would match his bid. Rickard kept the newspapers in suspense several days as to where the events would occur, and on June 20 announced Reno for sure.

Reno was front-page news for a fortnight and feature-story material in magazines for two months. There was a period of local prosperity, brief but vehement. Gambling boomed. Closed places opened. The limit went up. Saloons put in roulette wheels and other gaming machines. Fancy women gathered from all over the West, along with a small army of mendicants and petty crooks. Pullman cars were looted, hotel rooms robbed. It was almost a sign of disrespect if a pickpocket did not slip his hand into one's pocket. The hotels and rooming houses filled up so that by June 28 there was a serious housing shortage. The Golden Hotel placed three hundred cots for guests. Visitors kept pouring in. Special trains rolled in from San Francisco, Denver, Birmingham, New Orleans, St. Louis, and Chicago. Food became scarce. Visitors ate at a ragtime pace in crowded restaurants. One eating place with a seating capacity of 400 served 3,600 suppers. One café owner, it was said, had to stand guard over an exhausted cook to keep him from deserting, and at that the cook would prepare nothing but ham and eggs.

Special sports writers arrived to cover "the battle of the century." Jack London, Alfred Henry Lewis, Rex Beach, Battling Nelson, Rube Goldberg, Harry Carr, Georges Dupuy of France. London wrote of abysmal brutes in primitive orgies. He predicted that the fight would last no longer than thirty-five rounds. Western Union ran seventeen special wires into the pressrooms in Hotel Golden.

Ex-champions showed up: Tommy Burns, Corbett, Bob Fitzsimmons, the great Sullivan, Sam Langford, "the Boston Bone-crusher." Billy Delaney was there. It was he who had taken Jim Jeffries a raw boy and trained him to be a champion, but he and Jeffries had quarreled some years past and he was "in the Johnson corner." Foreign notables and rich patrons of sport came from Germany, Switzerland, Australia, England, and Spain.

Camp followers and assorted hangers-on and dopesters

were there in numbers, slouching about the training quarters, the bars, and street corners. On the surface they were, as usual, sardonic, sneering, incredulous, cold, and masked. Underneath they were really credulous, naïve, and childish. They believed everything, trusted in good luck, and sided sentimentally with the white contestant, Jeffries.

Meanwhile routine publicity flooded the sport pages and sometimes the front pages of America's newspapers. The veteran, James J. Jeffries, and the Negro challenger, Jack Johnson, were covered down to the last minutiae. The saline solutions used to toughen their faces, the fishing trips they took, their workouts, their remarks during interviews with crack reporters, revelations by their guards, their training-camp life — details of all these filled reams of copy. Americans read of the hexagonal arena speedily put up, with every seat good and a special section for women — a high balcony with a canvas top. For respectable females, who had first seen prize fights in motion-picture shorts, now showed a desire to see with their own eyes. Sensational! Equal rights were being pushed scandalously!

Betting on the fight became a leading occupation in Reno. Jeffries, called from retirement to defeat a black menace to white supremacy, was favored 10–6. Negroes felt a Johnson victory would gain them equal status. Southerners feared the dangerous exultation that would follow such a victory.

On the Fourth of July there were more than 12,000 visitors in a town of about 15,000 residents, and some 18,000 persons jammed into the arena. Women filled their balcony and scattered through the bleachers below. Their ostrich feathers got in the way. Their mere presence embarrassed fight fans who wanted to yell, " Kill the bastard! " The newspaper reporters did their best with the fight that followed, but it was a stupid fiasco. Jeffries, no longer a tough and resilient boilermaker, failed utterly to come back. He was slow, wooden, and over-cautious. He was a limp, tired, aged white man. Johnson, husky and young, even if "unscientific" in his technique, pushed Jeffries about and laced him. Johnson was a sportsman and a general in his strategy. He wore out Jeffries until his face was gory and his head bobbed and rolled on his great heaving shoulders. It was the butchery of an old bull. In the fifteenth round Johnson knocked Jeffries out. White men unduly exercised over the Negro question had to take their losses and swallow their pride. A wealthy lady cattle rancher was seated beside Bull Montana, the rough-and-tumble pugilist. She said, "Please show me the way out, mister, I'm crying so I can't see." "Madam," replied Bull, "you'll have to lead me out. I'm crying harder than you are."

The total receipts of the Reno fight were $277,775. The fighters received purses and bonuses of $121,000. Rickard and Gleason made profits of $120,000. This was big money, yet for Tex Rickard the future held a million-dollar gate.

Cosmopolitan Divorce Capitals

FORTY-ONE years ago, when Reno was a mere railroad town on the Southern Pacific Lines, William Ellis Corey sat in a box in a Pittsburgh theater and watched young Mabelle Gilman sing in the comic opera, *The Mocking Bird*. His blue eyes noted her slim waist, her dark hair, oval face, small mouth, and queenly grace. A few days later, at a fashionable swimming party, she watched him show off his athletic fitness and win a splashy race. Within the month he gave her a champagne party and took her on pleasure rides around Pittsburgh in a fancy big new car. Five years later Mabelle posed for a photographer in an ornate boudoir in Paris. The resulting picture showed her reclining on a sofa, and in the background, on an easel, stood an elaborately framed, life-sized likeness of William Corey.

These events, seemingly remote from Nevada, were preludes to a classic scandal that was to make Reno into the national symbol of divorce and one of the best-known small cities on the globe. Mabelle Gilman was just one of many singing actresses. She was a California girl who had attended Mills College, studied voice under a Madame Rosewald, tried out before Augustin Daly in San Francisco, and been signed at once for $50 a week. But Corey was one of the biggest names in the country. The popular magazines were full of his success story. He was a nine days' wonder right out of Horatio Alger. This native of Braddock, Pennsylvania, went to work at sixteen in the Edgar Thompson Steel Works and in a few years mastered steel-rail making. At twenty-one he was superintendent of the plate mills at Homestead. He was only one jump behind the other boy marvel, Charles M. Schwab. Armor plate was heavy and made boats clumsy. Corey developed a reforging process that increased resistance to gunfire and lessened weight, and every navy in the world put this armor on its warships. No one knew how to anneal armor plate accurately in the furnace. Together with R. A. Fessenden, Corey worked out a dependable process. Admired by Andrew Carnegie, he became president of the Carnegie Steel Company, the National Steel Company, the American Steel Hoop Company, and director on several Great Lakes railroads.

He exercised regularly. His carefully parted hair, his spectacles, the neat handle-bar mustache, the square shoulders and the firm stride as he walked through the steel mills all bore out his reputation for being methodical and painstaking. "The man with bulldog tenacity, who never gives up," he said, "is the one who succeeds." By the time Mabelle posed in Paris, Corey, not yet forty, was president of the United States Steel Corporation, the first billion-dollar corporation in history. He was a catch for any ingénue. Mabelle wrote her father the prophecy that someday she was going to marry a rich man.

However, Corey was married and had a grown son. Twenty years before, in his teens, he had married Laura Cook. They lived happily together and raised their son, Allan, until he was about ready for college. Then the papers began to pick up hints of the Gilman affair. Mrs. Corey heard rumors. Friends whispered things to her. The Paris picture was reproduced. Corey grew cold and distant. In May, 1905, when they were staying in New York, he told Laura that he was leaving her. He was no longer happy with her. He was sailing for Europe the next day. In a conference with Allan he said Mrs. Corey was a good woman but for reasons a boy could not understand he was leaving her. He went to Europe. Mrs. Corey, worried sick, lost forty pounds. She hoped for a reunion, but on his return he took separate apartments. His aged mother and his sister Addie pleaded with him. Carnegie took him aside and spoke to him. Tired and humiliated, Laura talked with her legal adviser and went to Reno " to rest."

The case was open now. Corey was quoted. He approved of the divorce, impossible in Pennsylvania or New York, possible in Nevada. He wanted custody of Allan. Friends said he and Miss Gilman intended to marry as soon as possible, and when she went abroad he paid her expenses.

In late July, 1906, Laura Corey sued for divorce on grounds of desertion, and asked for custody of the sixteen-year-old boy. Reporters crowded in to write up feature stories and make notes of everything said and done. Mrs. Corey wept. Addie, " sister by birth to William but sister by heart to Laura," spoke out in a dialogue quoted from Puget Sound to Tampa Bay:

Lawyer: Do you consider Mr. Corey a proper custodian for his son?

Addie: I do not.

Lawyer: Why?

Addie: For the reason that he is not a proper person for his son to associate with. He has no home, and his as-

sociates are not fit companions for a young man of
Allan's age. I do not think any New York man is
fit to have charge of a boy of his age.
Lawyer: Do you mean all New York men, Miss Corey?
Addie: I mean wealthy New York men.

Mrs. Corey's attorney, J. D. Redding, reviewed the story
of Corey's desertion and compared his farewell in the Lor-
raine on Fifth Avenue to Napoleon's in the Imperial Palace
when he entered Josephine's bedchamber and cried, " I am
going to leave you. The Pope of Rome shall divorce us.
Good-bye! "

On the first ballot the jury gave Mrs. Corey the divorce and
custody. There was plenty for the newsmongers to send out
under the Reno dateline: the embittered sister, the virtuous
wife, the manly son, the two-million-dollar settlement, the
sugar-daddy relationship with the actress. " Will he marry
Gilman? " asked the gossips. " Mabelle was a lively girl when
she was here," wrote a malicious San Franciscan, " and there
is no lack of material about her which would read well." Corey
celebrated the decree with a party at Delmonico's.

The public was overwhelmingly on Mrs. Corey's side.
Corey was the worst sort of immoral plutocrat. He was an
anarchist, undermining the Family, the basis of Church and
State, the foundation of Civilization. He was certainly as evil
as Napoleon the First. Said the weekly *Outlook*, " The wife
whom he wedded when he was without wealth and honor,
and the child she has given to him, he has deserted." And the
New York *Times*, even though Corey was president of the
company that made sixty-five per cent of all the steel in America, editorialized with vehemence:

He has treated . . . the most solemn obligations as " dicers'
oaths." If these things have nothing to do with him as a " business " man, what are the qualifications required in " business "
men? Can they be bankrupted in virtue, decency, self-respect;

can they repudiate their promises, fail in their trusts, desert their wives and offspring, and still be trusted and respected in business?

(But Corey was not exiled to a St. Helena, however much his critics wished to see such a thing happen. He gathered in more presidencies and directorships, waited nine months, and married Mabelle. A few years later the magazines featured pictures of them at their Château de Villeginis in the Valley of Chevreuse, and in New York City Mabelle Gilman Corey was a fashionable patron of the dramatic arts.)

This *cause célèbre* made Reno. William Corey was the villain. Laura was the heroine. Nevada divorce law was the fairy godmother. A " rest " in Reno had cured a wretched marriage for a noble woman. The world learned of Reno and easy divorce. Other Easterners went west. Reno was no longer just a wayside railroad town. It was a famous terminus. It was a focal point in American civilization.

And so it is now, thirty-five years later. Paralleling it on a smaller scale is Las Vegas, which was only a ranch when Laura Corey bought her ticket to Nevada. To these cities divorce clients and sportsmen come from afar. Autoists from all over America spend the night, breaking the long drive from Salt Lake to California. Their money and their willingness to let themselves go here, in cities where it seems to be the taboos that are illegal rather than the things tabooed, produce a peculiar combination of New York City and Hollywood. Any evening in the bars, clubs, and night spots one can find movie directors, state politicos, mining magnates, socialites from both coasts, nationally known businessmen, prominent sports and underworld characters, millionaires, artists, and foreign nobility. The average crowd is the mixture of big shots and small fry suggested in Edwin Corle's story of Las Vegas, " Apache Bar " in *Mojave*. A bartender or entertainer himself may be a fascinating unwritten biography or novel. One chef has been an Austrian labor leader, a spy during the World War, an author of fantastic fiction, and a friend of international socialists. He is a linguist, a mystic, a Rosicrucian, a student of Goethe and such books as the Comte de Saint-Germain's *Parallel English and French Text of the Most Holy Trinosophia*, and simultaneously a champion of the disinherited masses and of Adolf Hitler.

It is these non-Nevadans who help give the cosmopolitan, sophisticated, and somewhat cynical flavor to the cities. In particular they contribute to Reno a fame that makes it, though it is only a small town in size, one of the most famous cities in the world. Here are the latest in store fronts, drugstores, candy stores, coiffeurs, complexions, clothing ensembles, and female figures. This is the Reno that has improved on the night life of old times in Goldfield but has neglected the socially conscious labor solidarity that made it part of the history of the common man in America. This is the Reno that has been graced by the presence, from time to time, of people with big-time names: Vanderbilt, Morgan, Gould, du Pont, Colgate, Hoover (vacuum cleaners), Woodward (Jell-O); Eugene O'Neill, Sinclair Lewis, Robert Sherwood, James Swinnerton, the Fourth Earl Cowley, and Countess Kurt von Haugwitz-Reventlow.

For 18,000 inhabitants Reno had twenty-seven busy Western Union boys. It had railway passenger ticket sales and Pullman reservations equal in number to twice those of any American city twice its size, and a night life more animated than that in many communities ten times its size. Its service facilities are without parallel elsewhere. Ten years ago it had 127 lawyers. Now there are 180. There are seven or more corporation organizers. Cleaners and dyers, candy shops, florists, auto dealers, taxi companies are proportionately numerous. There are a dozen " dude ranches " and " riding academies " and as many night spots, including the Inferno, the Palace, the Ship and Bottle, the Riverside Hotel, and the place that ad-

RENO
AT NIGHT

WASHOE COUNTY
COURT HOUSE,
RENO

Nevada Photo Service—Reno

vertises on a road sign: "Reno's Famous Dog House — Divorcee's Haven." The special concentration of certain aspects of life in Reno is suggested by comparative data from the 1932 city directories for Reno (with about 18,000 residents) and Ogden, Utah (with about 40,000).

Ogden		Reno
72	apartment houses	69
12	clothiers, women's	13
16	beauty parlors	23
63	restaurants and lunchrooms	62
43	dentists	29
44	lawyers	127
45	doctors	43

Reno is the city where Catholic lawyers scramble to get divorce cases and the Y.M.C.A. is happy to fill its dormitory rooms by renting to divorce seekers. It is the home of high-comedy localisms that sound witty but often enough suggest heartbreak or cynical disillusionment: taking the cure (putting in the six weeks' residence), Alimony Park (the city plaza opposite the county courthouse), Bridge of Sighs (the Virginia Street bridge over the Truckee River), pouring a divorcee on the train (seeing her off after the decree), wash day (Monday, sometimes Tuesday, too, when default cases come up), the Separator (the courthouse), divorcee (meaning either man or woman, from arrival in Nevada until actually divorced), Divorcee Special (the noon train from the East), Dresden (a relatively sexless woman who lives to be looked at), six weeks'·sentence, the divorce business.

Reno is the victim of journalists and jokesmiths. "Renovate," says Walter Winchell, means to give unhappy marriage the quickest known treatment. *Life* and many myth peddlers tell of divorcees who kiss the courthouse pillars and throw their rings into the Truckee River. An *Esquire* cartoon shows a convertible coupé with the top down, a girl at the wheel, roaring along a desert road. A road sign reads, " Reno: 50 miles." Two wind-blown matrons sit in the rumble seat. One says to the other, "She's always going back to the scene of her divorce! " A drawing in *Pic* exhibits a sexy young woman, accompanied by a pudgy lawyer, as she leaves the Reno court-house after the granting of a decree. " Boy," she exclaims, tak-ing a deep breath that swells her breasts into her formfitting suit, " I feel like a new man! " This is the exciting burg of buried marriage but renascent romance that crops up in frou-frou fiction, in murder mysteries like Leslie Ford's *Reno Ren-dezvous* and romances like Elswyth Thane's *Remember To-day*, and in a " B " movie like *Reno*.

Las Vegas is similarly a permanent cosmopolis of tempo-rary habitations. It has its proportionate share of fashionable color and gaiety and prosperous activity, including a busy air-port. It supports a highly keyed up small-city social life. In an atmosphere of easy spending and one-dollar tips there is night life every evening, and, as the phrase goes, every Saturday night is a New Year's Eve. It was only a matter of time till Hollywood made *Las Vegas Nights*.

Obviously, divorce is the main key to the sophisticated side of the personalities of the cities. The divorce " trade " began unconsciously in Reno, but once it was recognized as a good thing economically it became a reason for legislative compe-tition between Nevada and other states.

In the early 1860's, when the population was in constant flux, stampeding from one mining camp to another, all over the West, Territorial Nevada sought to retain some people for the census and tax rolls by requiring only six months for citizenship. A divorce law was set up that was copied from the codes of several Western and Midwestern states. Approved on November 28, 1861, it was liberal in its provision, almost the same law as the one now in effect. By analogy with the citizenship law, it required only six months' residence. This same statute remained when Nevada became a state. For many years it was used only by Nevadans. During the great days of Virginia City, near-by Dayton, the seat of Lyon County, was known locally for the ease and eagerness with which it granted divorces. A visitor wrote that the mining inhabitants of this little wooden town with a red-brick courthouse were shocked at the person who was so stupid and blind as to cling to his first love, formed in the immaturity of youth, if he no longer cared.

Among the states of the Union, however, Nevada's divorce rate before 1900 was inconspicuous. Between 1867 and 1886 the state never divorced more than eighty-four couples in any one year, and the total for all the years was only 1,128. The United States Commissioner of Labor in a solemn study of marriage and divorce in the country did not raise a single eyebrow over Reno. "*Nevada*. The figures opposite this state have a very conservative character and in no way attract attention, the number each year being very small."

In the late nineteenth century, it was other states that had interstate notoriety. Maine, Rhode Island, and Connecticut ran small divorce mills for summer visitors; and Indiana attracted some people from over the state line — and also stimulated some diatribe writers in Ohio and elsewhere. In the 1890's South Dakota, with a six months' provision inherited from frontier days, was a national divorce center, and there was a colony of divorcees in Sioux Falls. South Dakota was the target then of adverse criticisms and court decisions, as in *Dunham* v. *Dunham* in the Illinois Supreme Court in 1896, which held a South Dakota decree void for a reason now familiar: the complainant was in residence merely for the purpose of securing a divorce and the defendant was not served with a process and therefore did not appear. Shortly after 1900 the state changed the requirement to twelve months.

In 1899 the Second Earl Russell came to Douglas County, on the shores of Lake Tahoe. With him was Mrs. Somerville (née Mollie Cooke). In due time they became Nevadans and got divorces in Genoa, the early Mormon settlement that was now a county seat. The Earl's grounds were desertion. Mrs. Somerville's were extreme cruelty. On April 15, 1900, the day after they got their decrees, they got married and started their return trip to England. The following year Russell was arraigned in the House of Lords on a charge of bigamy. Although an earl and a countess were involved, no great publicity came to Nevada.

But Nevada began to realize its possibilities in 1903, when California passed its law requiring a one-year wait after a divorce before a final decree and the right to remarry. " Once in a while California legislates for Nevada," said sagebrushers. A few people went to Reno to air their family troubles. After the Corey case burst upon the breakfast tables of America, rich and socially notable people started making the trek. Both shysters and reputable lawyers took notice. Reno did, too, for several hundred outside divorces a year left a million dollars or more each year and brought consistent prosperity to town.

By 1910 there were about three hundred divorcees a year. They definitely colored the life of Reno with their fashionable gowns and the gossip of New York, London, and Melbourne. Thomas's Restaurant near the Truckee River was nicknamed " Colony Café " and the " Delmonico's of Reno." Inside was the " Widows' Corner " where the prospective " grass widows " sat eating in huge stylish hats while tourists peeked at them, wondered at their daring, and laughed again at the cheap local aphorism, " United we stand. Divided we like it better."

The divorce business got ahead of professional legal ethics. Advertisements appeared in the Reno papers, " *Personal.* Absolute divorces, prompt attention, reliable experienced lawyer," with name and address. Solicitors worked the incoming trains. There were similar notices in Eastern papers. *Divorce Practice and Procedure under the Laws of the State of Nevada*, a pamphlet prepared by some enterprising Reno lawyers, was distributed through the East. It combined legal exposition and legalistic boosterism such as:

Here in Nevada the applicant, without deception or fraud, upon almost any charge from which lack of harmonious relations may be reasonably inferred, may apply to our courts and secure prompt results, by decree of absolute divorce, valid and binding in law.

A New York lawyer, eager to become an Eastern agent, placed this notice in theater programs:

> Divorce Laws of Nevada
> Have You Domestic Troubles?
> Are You Seeking DIVORCE?
> Do You Want Quick and
> Reliable Action?
> Send for My Booklet
> Contains Complete Information
> FREE
> Shortest Residence
> Address W. H. Schnitzer
> Counselor
> Correspondence Strictly
> Confidential

Reno's rise to notoriety was rapid. Local reform elements, clubwomen in particular, were stirred to take action. They forced the 1913 legislature to require a year's bona fide residence of either party. But local business slumped at once. Merchants, lawyers, tax collectors all felt a pinch. Hotel rooms remained vacant. Stores could not dispose of stocks of luxury goods. Churches lost in attendance and income. Discontent with the one-year law multiplied. Influential interests were stung too hard. In 1915 the zeal of the reformers recoiled upon them when a legislature that had been shown the light restored the six-month proviso. Seven years later this stand was reaffirmed by an initiative measure at the general election. Nevadans voted to require only six months. Reformers, conclusively deprived of their legislation, had to be content with rationalization.

In 1920 the Mary Pickford divorce "scandal," because of the prominence of Mary and her film-star husband, Owen Moore, refocused the spotlight on Nevada divorce. At that time Nevada law provided that a decree might be granted in the county where causes for the divorce action occurred, or in the county where the defendant resided, or in the county where the defendant should be found, or the county in which the plaintiff resided and the parties last cohabited, or in the county in which the plaintiff should have resided for six months. This meant, in one detail, that the residence requirement was waived if the defendant as well as the plaintiff could be found in one county.

On February 15, 1920, Mary Pickford took up residence at a ranch in Douglas County near the town of Minden, about fifty miles south of Reno. About three weeks later Owen Moore showed up in Douglas County with a party of photographers for the alleged purpose of taking mining pictures. He was served with a summons at Minden Inn, and in turn he appointed a lawyer to represent him in due form. The case was regularly tried in open court before Judge Frank P. Langan. The court satisfied itself of Mary's good faith: she had come to Nevada for her health, hoping to regain it in the Tahoe region. As for Moore's presence, which saved her many months of residence, she at first explained that he had come to Nevada to look for a coal mine, but at the suggestion of Judge Langan she changed this to a gold mine. She explained Moore had first gone to Virginia City, but failing to find proper accommodations there had come to Minden. The decree was granted.

There was a great outcry. Nevada was accused of winking at collusion (the manufacture of evidence), of openly flouting the law. Hostility was internal as well as external. The Nevada State Federation of Women's Clubs talked of getting the law modified again. The state's attorney general, Leonard Fowler, attempted to set aside the decree. He asked why Moore had not gone to Reno, where there were ample accommodations.

It is time for Nevada to show the nation that it does not countenance irregularity in court procedure, and that its morals are on as high a plane as those of any other State in this union. . . . The complaint will allege that the court had no jurisdiction because the plaintiff had no residence, and the defendant was brought into Nevada as a matter of collusion. Fraud has been committed and perjury has been committed. At this time, however, I am not prepared to say that any criminal action is to be brought against either Mrs. Owen Moore or against the defendant in the divorce action. This, in fact, is a matter for the district attorney of Douglas County to take care of.

The interest of the attorney-general's office lies chiefly in getting the decree set aside. The State is a third party to all civil actions, and, in this case, its dignity is at stake. . . .

But Fowler failed. There had been no collusion. Mary and Owen went their separate ways, happier by far because of what Douglas County had done for them. And the Federation of Women's Clubs failed to repeat what it had done in 1913. The initiative measure of 1922 was Reno's reply to the "reformers."

In fact, supporters of easy divorce were in the saddle, and with the reins in their hands they led "reform" their way. In 1927 the legislature in its last-minute haste before final adjournment passed a bill providing for an unprecedented three months' residence. By one vote the Senate had killed a bill to legalize gambling. It was considering an amendment to the divorce law that would add a new ground, two years of insanity in the spouse. According to the state constitution, the legislature should have adjourned at midnight, but after midnight on March 18 the Senate adopted the amendment. The Assembly would not concur. A conference committee was appointed but was unable to agree. A " free " conference committee was named. It agreed on the insanity clause, changed " six months " to " three months " in two places, and returned the amendment to the two houses, which passed the bill within ten minutes. This all happened well toward morning, and many legislators were sleepy. Some of them later expressed amazement when told what they had voted for. The " free " committee, of course, had not been authorized to make such a change, and even if so authorized, should have reported it unmistakably to the houses. Governor Balzar signed the bill before breakfast.

Defenders of the bill said that Nevada was forced into the law by competition from Mexico and France and cited a threatened three-month requirement in Wyoming. For either commercial or psychological reasons partisans of easy divorce argued much as did the Elko *Free Press*.

Divorce should be made as easy as marriage. When two people find they are not suited to each other, they should be given their freedom. The laws of our nation permit a man to marry in any State. The securing of their freedom should be equally simple.

How an imaginary State line can make a difference when a man is a citizen of the United States is impossible to understand. If Nevada can make men and women happier by a three-months' residence law, she should have it.

Some Americans benefited at once. Mrs. Sophia M. Ross, of Bayside, Long Island, and others who had already waited more than three months, applied for a court hearing, and received their decrees at once, in half the residence they had expected to put in. In the first forty-eight hours after the new law passed forty-eight divorce suits were brought.

Undeniably public opinion in Nevada was unprepared for this sudden amendment. There was widespread criticism of the haste in which this mercenary measure was passed. One paper accused the legislature of " parliamentary footpadism."

The Elko *Independent* said that a few foxy lawmakers had "hoodwinked the people of this State and sold their good name." Some Nevadans feared that the repute of their state would fall lower than ever. The Ely *Times* editorialized: "Nevada is already the most misunderstood Commonwealth in the Union, and the action of the legislature will further accentuate this unfortunate situation." Several papers warned that this "coup of the Reno business men who prey upon the nation's wedded failures" would fail of its intended effect. The Winnemucca *Humboldt Star* was of the opinion that lawyers would profit, "but apartment-house owners and merchants will lose unless the trade is doubled, and that possibility is doubtful." A judge said halving the time would kill the goose that laid the golden eggs. The Reno *Evening Gazette* warned that three-month residents would buy fewer motorcars and houses and would drop much less miscellaneous spending money along the way.

Citizens who were restless under George Wingfield, then in his heyday, whispered that he had connived to pass the law in order to fill his new Riverside Hotel with guests. It was pointed out that only a few hundred wealthy Americans went to Paris each year for divorce, attracted by the short, three months' residence and the secret hearing. And only two hundred or so Americans obtained Mexican divorces yearly, either after three days' residence or by mail. Also, few went to Cuba to exploit the one-day residence requirement. There was no dignity, Nevadans argued, in competing with such obvious rackets.

Suit was brought against the constitutionality of the Short-Term Divorce Act on the grounds that the legislature could not amend the initiative measure of 1922, but in August the Supreme Court upheld the constitutionality of the Act.

Because of the sly work of the "free" conference on March 18, the press of the nation had full opportunity once again to give Nevada traditional censorious treatment. Papers like the Providence *Journal* and the Philadelphia *Inquirer* and the Little Rock *Arkansas Gazette* spoke of dangers of last-minute legislation, sinister tricks, states that beg for unhappy marriages, and courts that turn the bench into a bargain counter. The Minneapolis *Tribune* remarked neatly:

This new law will be attractive to prospective or potential divorcees for two reasons: first, the length and cost of approach to a decree will be greatly reduced. Second: the pain of living in Nevada will be cut in two.

Thousands of Americans the country over, even in the South, discussed anew the old question: Should states' rights be abrogated in a matter where such shocking variations were possible, in favor of standardized federal legislation? Divorce had been a growing issue since the Civil War, as the rise of big industry and the growth of huge cities began noticeably to strain the restrictions of religion. Now divorce became an ever bigger issue as Nevada's action seemed to threaten the very fundaments of the American family.

Although Reno was thirty years entrenched in the American mind as a divorce capital, as firmly as Hollywood was as a movie capital, other states began to think competition was worth a try. As 1929 came in roaring and went out weeping and the Great Depression deepened, traditional attitudes toward divorce began to weaken. In 1930 Reno divorced 3,000 couples in return for an estimated $3,000,000. This was a tempting plum. When Idaho found her income from ore, cattle, and potatoes was slackening, she dropped the residence requirement to ninety days and hoped Boise would boom. When Arkansas had drought and a failure in the apple crop, her requirement fell to three months and Hot Springs got ready for prosperity. Florida threatened to pass a ninety-day law. Oklahoma and Arizona considered similar action to fight their depressions.

On May 1, 1931, the Nevada legislature lowered the requirement to six weeks and preserved the monopoly on short-term divorce. The initial result was a peak of 4,745 Reno divorces that year. Reno divorce had tripled in ten years; divorce in the United States had tripled in thirty years.

Other states liberalized and Reno felt the effects of competition. Washington, D.C., made divorce easier. Florida passed a ninety-day law, and the number of divorces, 4,842 in 1934, was over 6,000 in 1936. Georgia saw its big hotels in Thomasville, Sea Island, Savannah, and Augusta looming empty in the years of pinch, looked enviously at Florida's business and at the potential market in South Carolina — which allows no divorce — and lowered its residence requirement. In 1937 Idaho trimmed her ninety days to six weeks. New Mexico, Delaware, Hawaii, and the Virgin Islands talked of cutting down residence, and the Texas legislature considered an emergency bill to permit six weeks' divorce.

Some Nevada legislators proposed a thirty-day law, but they were talked out of it by conservative members of the bar who argued that the Nevada laws had been substantiated by Supreme Court decisions and were a sure service. Eastern lawyers would send clients to Nevada because they knew what to expect.

But Reno's volume of trade declined. In 1932, the year after the all-time record, Reno divorced 3,082 couples. In 1934 the figure was 2,854, and by 1940 the total was down around 2,000. Washoe County's golden age of divorce and publicity was waning. Its two famous judges passed out of service. Judge George Bartlett retired. Judge Thomas Moran died at seventy years of age. He had become a judge in 1911 and averaged 600 decisions a year until 1931, 1,500 a year until his death in 1938. In his lifetime he had granted 27,150 divorces.

The several thousand divorcees who each year spend several months in Reno and Las Vegas give permanence to the glitter and gaiety of the towns. These people need entertainment.

They want distraction. Their patronage supports gambling clubs, fancy bars, couturières, cuisines, high-priced gift shops, the growing facilities for winter sports, and those stylish perversions of the " Old West," dude ranches. They fill the roadhouses and resorts like Cal-Neva, which was once termed the nearest thing to an American Monte Carlo outside of Florida. Las Vegas has its Club 91, its El Rancho Vegas (a superswanky auto court), its Apache Hotel, and ranches near either the Colorado River or Mount Charleston. Reno has the State Line Country Club, the Tavern, the Cedars Club, and among others the Del Monte Guest Ranch and Farley's Dude Ranch. In 1925 Katharine Fullerton Gerould wrote, perhaps with truth, that pleasure in Reno was scarce, and unfashionable at that. " People with money and imagination go to Paris . . . for entertainment, distraction, civilization." But her strictures would not hold now, for either Reno or Las Vegas. Thanks to the steady growth and development of the state during the last twenty years, there is varied recreation, indoors and out, for every season of the year.

Princess Mdivanis and Cornelius Vanderbilt Juniors are not the only divorce clients in Washoe County, but it is the big names that make the bulletins of the press associations. Mrs. Orson Welles, Mrs. Jock Whitney, Esther du Pont Weir, the fifth Mrs. Tommy Manville, the Marquise de la Falaise de la Coudraye (Connie Bennett) are the news. They thrill local society matrons who associate with them at cocktail parties and lawn parties, where there is talk of wardrobes, polo, club life, and the private life of the society-page elite and movie-column galaxies. In this kind of high life Reno is far ahead of Las Vegas, though the latter has had its Baroness d'Oscarelli, Rhea Gable, and Mrs. Francis Lederer. One impressionable Reno lady told Duncan Aikman, " You know, the people who can sanely agree to disagree and to get their divorces a long way from home with a minimum of publicity are really the most civilized people we could hope to draw here." From these sterling-silver immigrants, well-to-do young Nevadans learn of spats and canes and riding to the hounds, and a few of them marry into the very best families in the country. Anthony Turano tells of a Reno working girl who married an English lord, a nurse who married an Eastern utility magnate, and an auto salesman who acquired a New York heiress.

Most of the divorcees, however, are unknown "names" with ordinary incomes, unhappy Does and Roes from Australia, Canada, New York, Pennsylvania, New Jersey, Massachusetts, California. There are waitresses, salesclerks, taxi drivers, butchers, preachers, teachers, dressmakers, hack writers, missionaries, garage mechanics. A few doctors, dentists, and lawyers come, and a few of them stay on as permanent residents. Many of the divorcees find it necessary to obtain temporary work so as to support themselves while they are acquiring residence. They work as waitresses, clerks, service-station operators, bookkeepers, or stenographers. Some men try prospecting in the desert. In Reno, a few take courses at the university.

Businessmen and lawyers try to provide entertainment that will be a healthy distraction for divorce clients and good advertisement for the "business." Clients have the opportunity to have a good time. They are offered private yacht trips on Lake Mead or Tahoe, moonlight horseback riding and midnight snacks, dining and dancing at roadhouses, swimming, hiking, cardplaying, skiing at Mount Charleston or Mount Rose, and, as their inclinations allow, gambling and drinking and temporary flirtations or love affairs.

In 1942 the total cost for a divorce, travel fares and living expenses included, was usually from $400 to $500. In practice, court fees were $31. The State Bar Association had set the lawyer's fee at $250, but in reality he charged what traffic would bear. In Las Vegas this was usually $100. In Reno it was $150. After 1946 legal fees went up, along with prices in general. Rich clients pay around $5,000. This is not a holdup fee like some charges reported elsewhere — $75,000 in Los Angeles, $100,000 in Detroit, $150,000 in New York.

Countess Kurt von Haugwitz-Reventlow, it is said, spent $50,000 in Reno. Estimates as to the state's income from divorce vary from one to three million dollars, the vast proportion of it being spent in Reno. Whatever it is, all the evidence indicates that Nevada owes considerable of its prosperity to its temporary residents. Permanent residents are loath to talk about this aspect of divorce, but from bellhops on up to bank presidents they are able to give accurate information offhand on fees, procedure, legal twists, and the Nevada philosophy of divorce.

The usual divorce comes after six weeks' actual residence with the intention of becoming a citizen of Nevada. If the defendant will not sign a power of attorney to a local attorney and a waiver of property rights before the six weeks are up, the plaintiff must wait thirty days more. If the spouse must be advertised for legally (in county papers), because no one knows where he is, the delay is 58–60 days beyond the six weeks. Most applicants do not need to wait beyond the minimum time, and their hearing in the judge's chambers takes five minutes or less. In one classic instance, Mayor Roberts appeared before Judge Moran as attorney in seven cases that were settled with decrees inside of thirty minutes' total time. In another, anecdote reports, he appeared in a successful suit a day for twenty-seven consecutive court days.

One can sit in the corridor outside the chambers on the second floor of the courthouse and see the attorneys and plaintiffs hobnob as they wait their turns. They don't have long to wait. Meanwhile they gossip, talk about parties, compose telegrams, or even pitch pennies at the brass " gaboon " on the tiled floor. Associated and United Press reporters angle for news stories. The divorcees wait nervously (as if legal obstructions might come up at the last minute) and rehearse their answers to the lawyers' questions. In Las Vegas the hearing is likely to be private in the judge's chambers. In Reno it is as likely to be held in the courtroom, where an alert bailiff sternly represses any whisperers or candid photographers in the audience.

Wherever conducted, the hearing is likely to be perfunctory. Often judge and attorneys speak so low that listeners hear only a few vowel sounds and s's. The attorney for the plaintiff asks questions that quickly establish his client's name, Nevada address, and the date residence was established. This last is so closely figured that the judge checks the total of days and weeks on a scratch pad. The client must show forty-two days of residence somewhere in Nevada. If he has been out of the state for three days, he must show a total of forty-five days, and so on. The client's witness, landlady or garageman or employer — who will probably get $10 for the service — testifies to his presence daily in Nevada for the six-week period. The client swears to the integrity of his intention to become a resident of the state. On rare occasions there is a slip here, as illustrated by a stock story.

Lawyer: Where do you live?
Client: New York City.
Lawyer: You mean you *did* live in New York City! You now live in Nevada.
Client: Oh, yes!

The client verbally recognizes the name of his mate and explains the need for an unconditional separation. Usually the mate has been cruel and has affected health by causing worry and nervous breakdown. The attorney asks convenient leading questions.

Attorney: Did not your wife repeatedly drink to excess and have affairs at home while you were at work, and did not your employer tell you about this?
Client: Yes.

Since Nevada courts award no alimony or child custody, if there are such matters to settle, the lawyers refer to an Exhibit A, perhaps an Exhibit B, too, and insert them in the court record. These are legal contracts that the lawyers have arranged. The judge mumbles his decree. Attorneys, client, and witness depart.

This routine, unorthodox to old-style Americans, has produced its batch of anecdotes about striking exceptions. After many a decree a divorcee goes downstairs and remarries at once or wires the former mate to go ahead with his marriage in some other state. Several local citizens have adjusted their patterns of life to the inherent possibilities of the county courthouse. One schoolma'am divorced the same lawyer three times, remarried him, and is now suing for separate maintenance. The proprietor of a confectionery, varying spouses, has married and divorced four times.

In some of the stories time and space and circumstance are compressed as in a stage farce — or a one-act tragedy. One woman remarried eleven minutes after she was divorced and was on an eastbound train in fifteen minutes. In immediate sequence the wife of an Eastern banker and a well-known author obtained Reno divorces. One waited for the other and they went at once to the county clerk's office for a license and then upstairs to be married by the judge who had given them their divorces. Two divorcees from the same city met and formed an acquaintance. Mrs. A. said, " I'm divorcing the meanest man on earth." Mrs. B. said, " I'm marrying the dearest man in existence." Mrs. A. mentioned her brutal husband's full name. " My God," exclaimed Mrs. B., " he's the man I'm going to marry! " The twice-married wife of a San Francisco psychiatrist divorced him in late December. Early in February a New York socialite divorced her husband. The next week the psychiatrist married her. She was his fifth.

Two women went to Reno together and got divorces. They returned home, where, by prearrangement, each married the other's former husband. A woman obtained a divorce, expecting to marry a popular tenor. As her suit was granted the tenor married a stage dancer, and the woman was left without the comfort of either her former husband or her intended replacement. A Philadelphia man sent another man's wife to Reno for a divorce, paying all her expenses. While there she met someone who was interesting and handsome and married him. One wife came to Las Vegas for a divorce, bringing her lover along for company. Six weeks later her husband, their daughter, and his wife-to-be arrived. All attended the divorce ceremony and later got in a car and drove off together. " You come in with the tied and you go out with the tied " — so goes a Reno jest.

A lawyer brought suit for a woman on the ground of infidelity. He assured the court solemnly that she wanted her freedom because her husband was an infidel. A six-foot-three Negro was in court before Judge Bartlett. The counsel asked the perfunctory question, " What did your wife do to you? " The man replied, " She done say she goin' to put poison in mah soup! She say, too, she goin' cut out mah gizzuhd while I'se asleep." " What was the effect of your wife's treatment upon your health? " asked Judge Bartlett, and the answer came, " Well, Judge, ah jes' nachelly lost mah appetite and I couldn't sleep."

" Lurid " newspaper anecdotes, taken at their surface value, have helped to fix several misconceptions about Nevada divorce that now lurk in the minds of many Americans. One is that most of the persons who go there to get a divorce already have another marriage lined up. The reverse is true. The very attorneys who tell the stories of immediate remarriage also estimate that fewer than one-fifth of their clients have another marriage in mind. The minority that do are likely to be persons long separated from their mates, finally determined on divorce only because another Right One has come along.

Another misconception is that divorce is always legally

easy. Actually, there are contested cases, heard behind closed doors. There are cases in which divorce pleas are refused. For example, pleas have been denied a husband who claimed his wife was extremely cruel when there was evidence that he, too, was guilty of extreme cruelty; a husband who claimed cruelty when he himself provoked the violence and misconduct complained of; a party that claimed desertion when there was evidence to satisfy the court that his invitation to his mate to return and live with him was not in good faith.

State law provides many grounds. They are:

impotency from marriage to present

unforgiven adultery since marriage

willful desertion of either party for one year

conviction of felony or infamous crime

habitual gross drunkenness contracted since marriage which incapacitates such party from contributing his share to the support of the family

neglect of husband for one year to provide the common necessities of life when such is not the result of unavoidable poverty

insanity for two years prior to the commencement of divorce action

extreme cruelty.

It is the last provision, the one most generally used, that is one of the striking details in Nevada divorce practice. In its day Nevada was practically the only American state allowing such a ground. In liberality it has been exceeded only by the " gross insult " allowed in Paris some years ago. Judges interpret " extreme cruelty " freely to mean cruelty to either party, physical or mental. Patriarchal Judge Bartlett was once quoted as saying:

Extreme cruelty is only statutory language. It does not necessarily mean cruelty in the accepted definition of the word, but may be reduced to the mildest kind of incompatibility. Under this provision two persons, who are no longer happy under marriage, can be freed from each other. That is as it should be.

This benevolent elasticity in the interpretation enables couples to find relief that many states' courts would never grant. An old man from Florida got a decree because his wife would not consent to bury him where he wanted. Swift Paine tells about Lady Heath, who divorced her husband, forty years her senior, because he humiliated her by declaring he would deny the paternity of any child born to them. The second Mrs. Jim Tully, who went to Las Vegas for succor, as had the first, said Mr. Tully had quarreled with her in the presence of guests, threatened her with bodily harm, and announced that if she didn't leave him he'd go to the South Seas. Converse M. Converse alleged that his wife drove a nail file into his ankle and several times angrily pulled out his hair by the roots.

Judge Bartlett in his *Men, Women, and Conflict* recalls, from the thousands of cases he has heard, husbands who dress well but refuse to bathe, who never pay bills, who are cranky about food, and who read at table, who refuse to kiss, refuse to speak for years on end, use profane language, or constantly bully their children. Some husbands force abortions on their wives.

There is sufficient evidence from judges and attorneys to correct a third misconception, that divorce clients are cheap, good-for-nothing people, determined to undermine the American home, that they are fair-weather marital partners, that they take divorce lightly. On the contrary, as Bartlett points out, for nine out of ten divorce is an escape from a cruel nightmare. It is the cumulative effect of years of ungovernable temper or ridicule, jealousy or nagging, that leads an individual to try to rescue some remaining happiness out of a ruined life.

Psychologically, divorce is a hard thing. On this point all observers agree. The " gay " divorcee is a myth. Many women are sent to Nevada against their wishes because their mate is dissatisfied and wants freedom. The majority of divorcees, clearly, are not on a lark. After years of thought, they are doing what they think is right. They are miserable to think that they have botched a part of their lives. They must find replies in their tortured minds to old notions of the eternal marriage. Their childhood teachings clash with their adult memories. They have the ordeal of revealing intimate details to their attorney. When he discusses the division of property and the disposal of children, they realize anew the rip they are making in their life's pattern. When their imaginations live through in advance the questions and testimonies of the trial chamber they feel sick and frightened. And after the divorce —What is ahead to look forward to? If they do silly or cynical things in Reno or Las Vegas, their motivation is a desire to forget the bewildering shift in their fortunes that brought them there. The seeming gaiety of life in the gambling clubs, the bars, and the dance halls only superficially covers a great deal of deep-felt sorrow and despair.

The evidence given in the hearings before humane judges rarely opens up the real issues between man and wife. " Extreme cruelty " covers a world of troubles; so does " desertion," which simply means that something was so unsatisfactory that one spouse packed up and ended the marriage himself, leaving it for the court to give legal sanction to what had already taken place. Another common ground, " neglect to provide," is likewise only secondary as a reason, and " infidelity " is a derivatory cause, not a primary one.

Granting that every case is different, the judges and lawyers and sociologists who have studied Nevada divorces (and divorces all over America, for that matter) find a few general causes repeated again and again. These include bossiness and overpossessiveness, constant complaining, and hasty marriage without sane discussion of such big issues as children and spending money. Too much " my " does damage a tardy " our " cannot repair. Money problems, in Bartlett's opinion, are a high-ranking cause. Let a couple live in a small, cramped apartment, he says, give them fewer physical possessions than their friends, and have the husband do a lot of growling about bills. In time, money will involve their relations with each other and with society. Affected will be their general health, sex life, recreations, conversations, and friendships. A gold-digging wife can wreck a marriage as fast as a penny-pinching husband, a prodigal husband as fast as a shrewish budget keeper.

Experts agree that, above all, marriage is destroyed by sexual incompatibility, which, in turn, is very likely to have a psychological origin in childhood complexes. Estimates in Las Vegas and Reno give it credit for as high as ninety per cent of all the divorces. Many times the clients themselves do not understand what is wrong and cannot explain it. A great many simply run on a sex rhythm that clashes with the other's. Sometimes a mate wants too much sex or too little, is too sensual or wants only outward affection. Because of this physical maladjustment and because nature's remedy — sex outside marriage — is in direct conflict with the standards of society, agonizing spiritual torture results. A man's reputation or career can be ruined by a selfish wife who demands every extravagance and gives nothing of herself in return. A woman finds her children small consolation, after her husband has taken the best of her youth and then run off with a young nurse.

The bench and the bar of Nevada have an articulate philosophical foundation for their statutes and practices. It was laid down during the late 1920's and early thirties, when Reno's fame was at its height. Above all, law must provide for human happiness. It must protect the individual against intolerable bondage. It must help men and women to avoid repressed, cramped, thwarted lives and instead lead expansive, vital ones in which emotional satisfactions are rich and enduring. The approach to marital disorder must not be narrowly ecclesiastical or legalistic; it must be humane, psychiatric.

As for the charge of church dignitaries that divorce is a social disease which should be wiped out, Nevada answers it by saying that divorce is a symptom and not a disease. And society cannot cure a disease by putting a taboo on the symptom. Divorce is the result of social and psychological problems. Wedlock is not meant to be a padlock. At the outset it is only a civil contract, as Martin Luther argued centuries ago. Not until the couple have established a stable spiritual harmony is their marriage a sacrament. They are the only agency that can make it holy. Civil marriage is only a social expedient devised to help society, and if it fails to make the individuals happy and to provide a good foundation for a home with children, then it should be dissolved quickly and quietly. This is only applying what our democratic heritage has stressed, that liberty and freedom are a good thing, and that each individual has a right to pursue happiness. The evils that pile up with some marriages are not the fruits of God's unfathomable will, not inevitable pain to be accepted with bent head. These marriages will dissolve themselves in one way or another. They cannot be saved by legislation, by stricter divorce laws, or longer residences, or the outlawing of Nevada decrees. If a marriage is congenial, a union that enhances the lives and personalities of the couple, if it provides a home for children that is happy and constructive, easy divorce laws cannot harm it. Compatible married love will weather storms; but for some unions divorce cannot be too easy.

Nevada assumes that mature individuals do not throw away happiness if they see it in sight. Hence the mere fact that a plaintiff comes to Las Vegas or Reno, or some other Nevada town, is evidence enough that the marriage is rootless. Or, as a lawyer puts it, the marriage is concluded *de facto* and the divorcee comes for *de jure* approval. To avoid unnecessary detail and scandal and embarrassment, therefore, uncontested pleas need state no bill of particulars, and, on request, judges must hear actions behind closed doors.

Men, Women, and Conflict, the one full-length exposition of Reno divorce, is kindly and knowing. It refers to Dean Inge, Margaret Sanger, H. G. Wells, Ernest Groves, Havelock Ellis, and Bertrand Russell and reflects their enlightened views.

In *Christianity and Divorce,* Frank H. Norcross makes a counterthrust at the prelates and ministers who have stormed at easy divorce as symbolized by Reno. Norcross, who is a Nevada lawyer now serving as United States district judge, meets Catholics and Episcopalians and other standpatters on their own ground, namely, Scriptural text and exegesis. His argument turns especially on certain fundamental statements by Moses, Christ, and Paul of Tarsus. Weakness number one in the churches' arguments against divine sanction for divorce is in the law of Moses found in Deuteronomy:

When a man hath taken a wife, and married her, and it come to pass that she find no favour in his eyes, because he hath found some uncleanness in her: then let him write her a bill of divorcement, and give it in her hand, and send her out of his house.

And when she is departed out of his house, she may go and be another man's wife.

Here is the redoubtable Moses allowing a ground for divorce: "uncleanness" in the King James Version, "erwath dabar" in the original text. This phrase is used many times in the Old Testament to mean nakedness, matter of nakedness, shameful exposure — in other words, incest or adultery. Furthermore, Mosaic law allowed divorce on other grounds. A man might appeal to the judge of the state, who spoke in the name of God. In Ezra, for example, the men of Judah and Benjamin, who have taken strange wives in marriage only to find they have increased the trespass of Israel against God, consume days in hearings of a mass divorce trial and, according to the law, put away all the foreign wives.

Judge Norcross gives detailed examination to the important statement attributed to Jesus, " What therefore God hath joined together, let not man put asunder," which, according to churchmen, is a clearly couched prohibition of divorce. This statement, says Norcross, must be taken with its whole context. In Christ's day the Pharisees dominated Palestine. Their usages were wrecking marriage and utterly degrading women. Under Rabbi Hillel, high priest and president of the Sanhedrin, they were interpreting Moses so as to allow divorce for every cause. This unrestricted freedom for men was bringing cruelty and grief to women. So whimsical were bills of divorcement that one of the disciples said to Jesus, " If the case of the man be so with his wife, it is not good to marry." When He said, " Let not man put asunder," he was being cross-examined by Pharisees who hated him for preaching kindness toward wives and all other underdogs and wanted to frame him. His answer was one of his clever verbal parries. Clever and also profoundly true, in the sense that a supremely noble marriage, based on mutual respect, love, helpfulness, forbearance, should not be tampered with. But nowhere, says Judge Norcross, does Jesus prohibit society to dissolve a union when it is intolerable to a mate. Here in essence, He agreed with the Pharisees that there were numerous possible grounds for divorce — but, the necessary judicial procedure should not be abused.

St. Paul gave permanent form to the misconstruction of what Jesus said, in statements such as " For the woman which hath an husband is bound by the law to her husband so long as he liveth . . . if while her husband liveth, she be married to another man, she shall be called an adulteress." About this statement, Norcross feels, there is no divine aura. It is just the prejudiced opinion of a man, a converted Pharisee, who still believed in the subordination of women.

So much for the case in reply to the theologians. Lawyers and judges in other states have repeatedly questioned the legality of Nevada divorces, and Nevadans have replied to them.

The legal attack on Nevada divorce has not been aimed at either the shortness of residence or the highly abstract charge of " extreme cruelty." Nor has the judicial proceeding *per se* been questioned, because the United States Constitution provides that " full faith and credit must be given in each State to the judicial proceedings of every other State." The one point of attack has been the legality of the residence itself.

Legal precedent built up in Reno has long since established that residence means permanency as well as continuity — actual abode of physical presence. A wife may acquire and maintain residence separate from her husband's. Partners to a marriage contract have the right to change their residence to get a divorce, provided the change is bona fide. It is not enough if the residence ends with the divorce. Yet generally it has terminated there at once — granted, even, that legal residence is often an intangibility hard to determine. The Nevada courts, like courts anywhere, can only inquire into the good faith of plaintiffs and accept oaths at their face value. The few rare accusations of perjury are leveled to help disbar some obstreperous attorney rather than to check what may be a rather general practice among clients. Right here, in the eyes of some influential Eastern states, is a weak link.

Eastern lawyers desirous of keeping divorce business at home cite to clients the classic case of *Andrews* v. *Andrews*. A Bostonian named Charles Andrews wanted a divorce. He went to South Dakota. Mrs. Andrews " signed " and was represented by an attorney. The divorce was granted. Andrews returned to Boston. In due time he remarried and had two children. When he died the first Mrs. Andrews reappeared and claimed to be his one and only widow and therefore heir to his estate. Her reason was that Mr. Andrews had never been a bona fide resident of South Dakota. He had not really established residence there: witness his return to Massachusetts for the rest of his life. The Supreme Court of Massachusetts upheld her; so did the United States Supreme Court.

The second wife was a bigamist and her children bastards and all three were paupers.

Another standard citation used to keep divorcees at home is the highly technical and legalistic *Haddock* v. *Haddock* case, in which the United States Supreme Court upheld the New York courts. The Haddocks married in New York and separated soon after. Fourteen years later Mr. Haddock got a divorce in Connecticut. Mrs. Haddock was notified by mail. Later he remarried. Eighteen years after the divorce, the first Mrs. Haddock sued for divorce and alimony, and won on the ground that she and her husband had residence in New York and therefore Connecticut could not legally hear her husband's suit.

Lister v. *Lister*, a similar case, involved Nevada. The New Jersey Court of Chancery found:

The Nevada divorce is absolutely void and is a perfectly plain case of gross fraud upon the laws of New Jersey, and also the laws of Nevada . . . a typical case of a fraudulent Nevada divorce . . . the defendant's pretended change of domicile was a fraud and a sham.

To give one more example, the recent Nancy Brill case in California turned on the same question. In 1934 Nancy Pierson Brooks married George Macy of the New York department-store family. The next year Mrs. Macy went to Reno and obtained an uncontested divorce, Macy being represented by counsel to make the decree legal. Still claiming Nevada as her legal residence, she went to southern California. In 1937 she eloped to Yuma, Arizona, with William H. Brill of Ventura, California. Shortly afterward he sought annulment in the Ventura court on the grounds that he was intoxicated at the time of the ceremony and that Mrs. Brill's Nevada divorce was invalid. The Yuma parson testified that Brill was sober, but the other charge won annulment. The California judge, taking the usual viewpoint, said that Mrs.

ANOTHER
GOLD STRIKE
IN THE WEST

Brown in the New York
HERALD TRIBUNE;
reproduced by permission

IN THE
WIDOW'S
CORNER

*Drawn by Dan Sayre Groesbeck
for HAMPTON'S MAGAZINE, 1910*

INTERCOLLEGIATE SKI CARNIVAL
AT GALENA CREEK

SKIING CROWD
ON SUN DECK AT MT. ROSE BOWL

Macy's Nevada residence was "purely simulated for the sole purpose of obtaining a divorce." Was Nancy Pierson Brooks now really Mrs. George Macy or Mrs. William Brill? She appealed the decision, seeking to set the annulment aside. Two years later, in 1940, the Third Appellate District Court of California decided that Nancy was still Nancy Macy and had never legally been Nancy Brill. She had never been a bona fide Nevadan and therefore she had to give up a husband she wanted and take back a husband she didn't want.

In practice, almost nowhere do judges question a Nevada decree where there is a cash settlement and a contract surrendering dower rights and rights to the other's estate. In most states they recognize a Nevada divorce if both parties have submitted to the jurisdiction of the court. And, of course, even in the states hostile to Nevada — Pennsylvania, New York, New Jersey, Massachusetts — a Nevada decree is as good as any, just so long as it is not contested, and few are.

Many Nevada lawyers claim that none of them are really contestable. Fowler V. Harper is on record as saying that the void divorce is a myth, a rationalistic casuistry. Nevada has jurisdiction over the subject of divorce within its boundaries, he explains, and over any person who brings a divorce action — if the other is notified — and is domiciled. Domiciled is enough, for the home or legal residence is indefinite in migratory divorce. A Nevada divorce has a legal effect, even if voided, he argues, for the couple are to all intents and purposes divorced. Whatever jurists may claim, laymen are not fooled. The law, Harper admonishes, had better catch up with practices. Collusive divorce is the rule, nowhere more so than in New York, where adulteries are often frame-ups. The practice of laymen and tribunals belies the theory of granting divorce on certain fixed grounds.

As for the desirability of federal control of divorce, most Nevadans and several sociologists are in agreement that modern life requires experiment and adjustment to changing con-

ditions and that forty-eight experimental laboratories in social legislation are needed. Home and family conditions vary
in a country as large as the United States, and if this geograph-
ical and ethnic diversity did not justify local control of divorce, the doctrine of home rule would.

WHILE the divorce business has continued to publicize Las
Vegas and Reno, a related legal service has developed to siz-
able proportions. This is quick marriage. As a county official
once grinned, " We knot 'em as well as untie 'em."

To expedite speedy matrimony the whole town tenders
information and free service. When a lovesick couple with a
California license plate on their car drive into a gasoline station, the attendant recognizes their errand at once. Along
with free air and road maps, he expects to donate aid in getting
married. He will volunteer information on where the county
clerk's office is, what the fee is, and where a preacher or justice of the peace is handy. If it is Sunday, noontime, or late
at night, he may make phone calls and make special arrangements. In the Washoe and Clark county courthouses special
signs make it easy to find the right room easily. If the clerks
are out to lunch they pin up notes telling where they may
be found. For, as a folder put out by the Las Vegas Chamber
of Commerce makes clear, " Marriage licenses are issued immediately upon application to the county clerk, 24 hours a
day, Sundays and holidays. No delay is required." This makes
elopement easy. Many a northern California couple has made
a fast trip to Reno, and the example of Hollywood celebrities
has given Las Vegas an increasing rush of ecstatic couples
from southern California. The county clerk displays on his
wall the applications of people like Francis Lederer, Jean
Parker, Carole Landis, Nelson Eddy, Max Rosenbloom, Har-
rison Hollway, Lola Lane, Helen Wills Moody, Ruth Etting,
Bela Lugosi, Artie Shaw, Richard Halliday, and Mary
Martin.

Restrictions and costs are reasonable. Boys under eighteen and girls under sixteen cannot be married, and parental consent is required for males from eighteen to twenty-one and females from sixteen to eighteen. A license costs two dollars. The fee for the ceremony is whatever the groom will pay, the general minimum being five dollars.

This whole setup appeals to many Californians because in their own state they must apply for a license and then allow three whole days to elapse before actually obtaining the license on the fifth day. Furthermore, they must take a physical examination to determine that they are free from venereal disease. This advanced legislation accomplishes its end. It prevents hasty, impetuous matrimony in California. It also deprives California of a considerable number of license fees and preachers' fees, and periodically a movement starts to repeal the law and keep the money in California. To date, however, the Nevada cities, and also Yuma, Arizona, have reaped a profitable harvest. So remunerative is the office of justice of the peace in Las Vegas that in the summer election of 1940 twelve men were competing for the office — the way men used to compete for the sheriff's job during Prohibition. In two years Justice of the Peace George E. Marshall had performed six thousand wedding ceremonies. His ritual took two minutes and six to eight seconds.

Marriages have long outnumbered divorces in Reno and Las Vegas. In Nevada during 1932, for example, there were 3,989 divorces (42 per 1,000 population) as compared with 7,088 marriages (76 per 1,000 population). At that, Nevada ranked lowest in the states for the ratio of marriage to divorce. In the same year there were 6.1 marriages in America to 1 divorce. Washington, D.C., had the highest ratio, 35.3 to 1; New York had 21.4 to 1; Nevada was lowest with 1.8 marriages to 1 divorce. No such national statistics are available for later years, but manifestly the ratio has been going up. In this same 1932 there were 4,453 marriages in Washoe County,

1,150 in Clark County. Two years later Washoe married 5,629 couples. In 1936 there were 7,602 weddings to 3,001 divorces. For some years Las Vegas continued to average 1,100–1,200 couples, but in 1939 there was a rise to 5,438, and in 1940 there was a tremendous increase. Reno's divorces in 1940 were down to about 2,000 but her marriages jumped to around 18,000.

Always the towns had experienced periodic booms in November and on January 1 and other special occasions, such as the passage of California laws, but in the summer of 1940 came military conscription. There was a stampede of young men seeking to avoid class Ia, those ready for immediate selective service. A rush for 1,254 licenses in June and 1,054 in July stimulated Las Vegas deputy clerks into unprecedented speed to service the queue waiting outside the office. By August the deputies in both Reno and Las Vegas were so efficient from meeting with rush patronage that they were able to issue a license in one minute and twelve seconds. In 1941 unsettled, warlike conditions continued to springboard marriage, and Utah took a turn at legislating for Nevada by passing a premarital medical examination law. Couples began to pour toward Las Vegas from over the eastern state line and burst upon the already excited county clerk. In the first six months of 1941 Washoe County granted 9,747 marriage licenses. Clark County was close behind, with 8,945. Over the three-day Fourth of July week end 588 couples crowded into Las Vegas, 640 into Reno. In the whole year of 1941 Nevada married just over 53,000 couples — a number of individuals equaling the total population of the state. On the estimate that each pair spent at least ten dollars, the state's wedding business grossed over half a million. Nevada marriage was in its Heroic Age.

Except for California's complaint against its own law that sends couples to Nevada to get married, there has been no out-of-state discussion, even by implication, of easy marriage in Reno and Las Vegas. The reason, no doubt, is that most states allow immediate marriage of adults and most Americans are predisposed favorably toward marriage (as not toward divorce). And elopement is romantically respectable. Even Catholics elope to Nevada and get a civil rite, just for the thrill and excitement, taking care later to have a priest repeat the performance, as a matter of routine orthodoxy.

Yet the contrast to the intermittent outcry against easy divorce is strange when one realizes that the case for six-week divorce is vastly better than the case for three-minute matrimony. Even granting that Nevada's fundamental reason for facilitating divorce is revenue, one can argue, as Judge Bartlett and other spokesmen do, that the law is humane, sociologically advanced, and profoundly moral in its spiritually regenerative effect on unhappy husbands and wives. But of all the knowledge that Nevada has of what wrecks marriages, none is applied, as it might be, to seeing that couples are properly launched at the start. There is nothing shocking in short-term divorce. There is something shocking in one-minute marriage licenses and two-minute wedding ceremonies, especially since a large proportion of Nevada divorces go to couples in only their second year of matrimony.

True to her old Western liberalism and her newer penchant for exploiting it, Nevada gives individuals full freedom, in as brief a ceremony as history has seen, but she might benefit individuals if she required prospective mates in the J.P.'s office downstairs to know what the divorcees upstairs in the district judge's chambers know too late — all the physiological and psychological information that constitutes scientific preparation for marriage. The same sociologists who advocate relatively facile divorce advocate relatively more difficult marriage. Nevadans of the bench and bar know a great deal that they are not putting to social use: how friends, time, interests, and money can wreck a marriage or hold it together; how mates should try to avoid discussion of things on which

they disagree; how each should be willing to make a 75 per
cent effort to make the marriage succeed and be happy to get
a 50 per cent return; how each should identify himself with
the other's problems and be tolerant of his weaknesses and respect his honesty of intention; how each partner should develop special interests that keep him busy; how loverlike
attentions, common sense, patience, a sense of humor, and
respect for individual differences can enrich a relationship.
Rita Halle investigated Reno for *Good Housekeeping* and
concluded that "marriage can profit from divorce."

But in Nevada it isn't benefiting. As long as the marriage
traffic keeps the silver dollars rolling in, Nevada will probably not act. Nonetheless, the time is ripe for some more
Western radical legislation.

The easy divorce and marriage that have come to play a
large part in the economic life of Las Vegas and Reno have
influenced the townspeople to view sex with a casual regard
different from the attitude of frontier days. In the era when
prostitution was the only extramarital life indulged in by the
average man, "respectable" women, young and old, were
thought of and spoken of with old-style chivalry. Marriage
was for family life and children. Courtship called for strict
continence, with sex a great privilege at the end of a patient
journey toward matrimony. But the Jazz Age and the Divorce Age have changed this in Nevada, as in America. Here
come people for a divorce who have perhaps for years hungered for companionship that their marriage hasn't given
them. Many isolated housewives confess that they have forgotten how to act in the company of males. Some of them
long for the stimulation of a fresh personality. What more
natural reaction than an experimental fling? What easier in
a community with a surplus of males, themselves lonely?
Here, with cultural entertainment meager, with the past to be
buried and forgotten, with six weeks to kill, and attentive

males to help kill it, easy-come and easy-go sex, quite apart from prostitution, is natural.

Tourists come through, including couples wanting a hotel room or auto-court cabin together. Whose business is it whether they are married or not? Couples come to get married — strangers — business. What does it matter whether they sleep together before or after the ceremony, or if they sleep together and call off the ceremony?

The result is an attitude among the floating population and a large proportion of the permanent population that is, even in modern-day America, conspicuously unconcerned about sex. The idea that sex is to be taken for granted characterizes certain classes and coteries in places like Palm Beach and New York and Hollywood, but here are small towns where the majority of the population is quite aware of sexual activity, even if they do not participate in it or publicly advertise its existence.

It seems to be assumed, whether true or not, that everyone is sleeping with everyone else. If a resident is visited by his good-looking sister, who lives in another state, and he takes her down the main street, or to a night spot, his friends smile when he introduces her as his sister. Barkeepers tell of candid suggestions made to them by divorcees. Virtuous divorcees tell of "shocking propositions" from local business and professional men, out under the desert moon, where their car could be easily recognized by passers-by.

Recently in Las Vegas a young "Mr. and Mrs." spent a night at an auto court that offered, in blue neon: "Marriages Completed in 30 Minutes with Minister or Judge. Wedding Chapel, Everything Arranged, including License. Open Day and Night." The next morning, ashamed to face their landlord, the couple drove down the street a block to get married at a similar place. The proprietor saw this and got mad. "The damn cheapskates. Why didn't they get married here?

They saw our sign. Damn *them!*" It didn't occur to him that the couple would be embarrassed.

To Nevadans sex is just one of the four basic wishes. Common-law wives get full legal protection, and the man who is just "living" with a woman is socially approved. The sentimentalism of a long, self-restrained courtship, the rites of the Victorian bridal suite, the romantic idealization of the physical union of two souls, are laughed at. Ironically, in view of their reputation in pioneer Utah, the Mormons are an exception, as they seem altogether sincere when they claim that the mate, the family, and friends are the three greatest values in life.

All this is part of the sophisticated side of Reno and Las Vegas. More evidence can be found in Max Miller's *Reno*. No outcry is needed. Nothing is going on that is not duplicated, however *sub rosa*, in other American cities. Probably, however, no other small cities are conspicuously this way. The New Morality, with its gambling, its contraceptives, its big-city leisure-class code, its flexible patterns for human relationships, and its casual view of sex and marriage, has reached a minor climax in the neon-lighted New West. It invites sociologists, not amateur and professional "reformers."

With their threefold personalities, Reno and Las Vegas bring to a dramatic focus certain American institutions and traits. Only a few blocks apart, sometimes across the street from each other, are village homes, modern public schools, sophisticated hotels, efficient chain stores, unmortgaged churches, gambling clubs, grassy parks, noisy bars, and courthouses that use assembly-line methods to assemble and disassemble marriages. Filling these buildings and the streets that join them are Americans who represent all the strata and crossstrata of the nation's life. From the country girl giggling and squeezing hands at the county clerk's office to the sleek hotel-lobby roué looking for a rich divorcee to exploit, from the florid cowboy with legs like parentheses to the Piute woman swathed in skirts and looking at a Love-Lure brassière in a shop window, from the hay harvester arriving in town for a big week end to the film star departing after a two-minute marriage — all America is here in animated mural.

FISHING, HUNTING, CAMPING, AND SKIING

Nevada contains a surprising number of good fishing waters. Among the best known and most dependable are the following.

Owyhee and Salmon rivers (near the Idaho line) — steelhead and Pacific Ocean salmon.

Bruneau River (west of Charleston) — trout.

Jarbridge River — trout.

Headwaters of the Humboldt River in the Independence and Ruby mountains (north and south of Elko) — trout. Especially notable in the Ruby Mountains is Lamoille Creek. Elko County claims to have 2,800 miles of fishable streams.

Creeks in the Egan, Shell Creek, and Snake ranges (north and south of Ely), for example, Lehman and Baker creeks near Lehman Caves National Monument — rainbow and Eastern brook trout.

Creeks tributary to Reese River in the Toiyabe Range (south of Austin), for example, Skull Creek — trout.

Creeks near National (north of Winnemucca), especially the south fork of Quinn River, Bilk Canyon, McDermitt Creek, and King's River — trout.

The Little Humboldt and Martin Creek (in Paradise Valley, north of Winnemucca) — trout.

The main Humboldt River channel — bass and catfish.

Pyramid Lake — cutthroat or black-spotted trout, which is a land-locked salmon. Black-spotted trout have been reported as large as sixty-five pounds, and never smaller than one and a half pounds. However, commercial consumption, dam building on the Truckee River, pollution from mills and cities, and spawn collection have started the species toward extinction. Francis H. Sumner of the United States Bureau of Fisheries, concluded recently, after close study, that " the Pyramid Lake cutthroat trout, as an economic entity and angling attraction, is doomed." In the past the trout has afforded sport to anglers such as " Pop " Warner, Herbert Hoover, Ray Lyman Wilbur, Zane Grey, Harlan Stone, and Clark Gable. Large fish are still caught, with spoons and lures. No bait fishing is done. Only a light casting rod is needed.

Truckee River — rainbow trout. Fly fishing.

Lake Tahoe — Mackinaw trout up to thirty pounds, silverside trout up to fifteen pounds, and large black-spotted or " Tahoe " trout. Fly angling is satisfactory only in the early spring season. Silversides take a wooden plug danced on the surface behind a speeding motorboat. The standard method is trolling with a metal, egg-shaped spoon of burnished copper or plated metal at the end of a twisted copper wire 75–200 feet long. The snell and hook is three feet from the spoon or directly attached. The bait is worms, minnows, grubs, or helgramites (larvae of caddis flies). As the season extends, a longer line is necessary. Either heat or a descending food supply takes the trout lower down.

Carson River — rainbow trout, silverside.

Lahontan Reservoir — trout, bass, catfish. The fishing is good only early in the year.

Stillwater Slough (northeast of Fallon) — catfish.

West Walker River, Desert Creek; East Walker River, Sweetwater Creek — rainbow and silverside trout. In lower Sweetwater Creek there are Eastern brook trout; the rainbows are higher.

Walker Lake — lake trout, perch, bass.

Topaz Lake — black-spotted trout, rainbow trout, Loch Leven trout from one and a half to ten pounds. The trout are caught with bait or lures, from boat or shore.

Creeks on the southeast slope of Boundary Peak (near the California line, west of Tonopah), such as Chiatovich Creek, Davis Creek, and Trail Canyon Creek — trout. These are approached from the Basalt-Fish Lake road.

Lake Mead — large-mouthed black bass from three to ten pounds, bluegill, crappie, trout, and catfish. The usual methods for the bass are offshore trolling or casting from the shore. Most fishermen find that sinking plugs in various colors with a line of 20–25 pounds' test are most satisfactory.

Colorado River below Boulder Dam — rainbow trout, bass, white salmon, catfish.

There are special regulations, agreed to by Nevada and Arizona, for Lake Mead and the Colorado River below the dam:

LIMITS

Bass   10 fish, but not over 15 pounds and one fish in one day or in possession. Not less than 10 inches long.

Trout   15 fish, but not over 10 pounds and one fish per day or in possession.

Catfish No limits in Lake Mead; 10 catfish, regardless of weight, in Colorado River.

Bluegill and crappie: 20 fish per day, but not over 20 pounds and one fish.

OPEN SEASON

Fishing allowed the year around.

LICENSES

Either Nevada or Arizona fishing licenses are good in all parts of the lake and river. A special nonresident visitor's permit, good for 15 days, is purchasable for $2. This is a double license, $1 for Arizona, $1 for Nevada; the visitor must purchase both.

For the remainder of Nevada, the state fishing regulations are as follows:

LIMITS

10 pounds or 25 fish, provided an angler may have 10 trout regardless of weight.

RESTRICTIONS

No fishing within 100 feet of any dam having a fish ladder, or within 500 feet of Quilici Dam near Dayton. Hours: 1 hour before sunrise to 2 hours after sunset. All fishing must be done with pole, hook, and line held in the hands.

LICENSES

Resident, $1.50; nonresident, $3; alien, $7.50. Required of all persons over 14 years of age. Issued free to residents over 60 years old. May be purchased from all county clerks and their agents, sporting goods stores, hardware stores, and so on.

In Nevada, counties still retain ultimate authority in setting the seasonal dates for fishing and hunting regulation, and the county commissioners can change the dates overnight; so local inquiry of the county clerk or the game warden is always advisable, or advance inquiry of the Nevada Fish and Game Commission, Box 678, Reno. These regulations are likely to be correct:

Churchill County: May 1 to October 1, including Lahontan Reservoir. No closed season on catfish.

Clark County: no closed season, the only fishing waters being Lake Mead and the Colorado River.

Douglas County: April 15 to October 1, including Lake Tahoe. Topaz Lake opens May 1. Closed Waters: West Walker River, canal outlet from Topaz Lake, Desert Creek, Edgewood Creek; also one mile above Douglas Milling & Power Dam on the East Carson River and below the dam to the county highway.

Elko County: May 5 to October 1, excepting Salmon River below Vinehard Dam and the Humboldt River, which remain open to November 15; all lakes open July 4 to October 1. Closed waters: Meadows of Lamoille Creek, and McDonald Creek from Sunflower Road Crossing to Bruneau River.

Esmeralda County: April 1 to October 1.

Eureka County: May 1 to October 1. Closed waters: Hunter Creek.

Humboldt County: May 1 to October 1, except Humboldt River, May 1 to October 31.

Lander County: April 1 to October 1.

Lincoln County: May 1 to October 1.

Lyon County: April 15 to October 1, except Lahontan Reservoir, May 1 to October 1. Closed waters: West Walker River and Desert Creek.

Mineral County: no closed season, including Walker Lake.

Nye County: April 1 to October 1.

Ormsby County: April 15 to September 15, including Lake Tahoe. Closed Waters: Ash Canyon and King's Canyon.

Pershing County: May 1 to October 1.

Storey County: April 15 to October 1. Closed waters: Truckee River.

Washoe County: April 15 to October 1, including Washoe Lake and Lake Tahoe. Pyramid Lake, March 1 to October 1. Closed waters: Truckee River from Asylum Bridge near Reno to Pyramid Lake.

White Pine County: May 12 to October 1. Closed waters: Cave Creek.

There are doves, rabbits, and quail in most Nevada valleys. Big-game animals are fairly numerous. There are 50,000 to 60,000 deer in Nevada, 11,000 antelopes (protected), 1,100 mountain sheep (protected), and 250 elk (protected). The principal hunting game are deer, sage hens, pheasants, and ducks. Among the best hunting areas are the following:

Ruby Mountains east of Jiggs (south of Elko) — deer, sage hens.

Off side roads between Wells and Elko and the Idaho line — deer, ducks, sage hens, grouse, Hungarian partridge.

Side roads east from U.S. 95 (from McDermitt to Winnemucca) — deer. National is a hunters' "headquarters."

Western Paradise Valley in the southern Santa Rosa Mountains — sage hen, grouse, deer. Martin Creek Campground is a convenient "headquarters."

Shell Creek Range, on side roads east from U.S. 50 (Wendover to Ely) — sage hen, grouse.

Pancake Range (south of Eureka), approached from Duckwater — deer.

Toiyabe Range (south of Austin) — deer, quail, grouse, sage hen. Good deer hunting was reported in 1941 on the Reese River Game Refuge and on Table Mountain near Kingston. In 1940 a forest ranger in the Toiyabe National Forest reported: "Probably the best hunting area is at the head of Reese River. Deer in this vicinity are too numerous and it is recommended that you hunt there for best results. Horses are necessary in bringing the deer out to the end of the nearest road. There are a few horses available in the Reese River District."

Pahranagat Lakes — ducks, geese, snipe.

Backwaters of Lahontan Reservoir — ducks and geese.

Stillwater Slough — ducks.

The agricultural valleys in the Reno-Fallon-Wellington area — chukor pheasants.

The Boundary Peak area between Montgomery Pass and Fish Lake, where automobiles can be driven up canyons such as Wyman, Queen, Trail, and Cottonwood — deer.

At present there is a closed season throughout the state on mountain quail, grouse, and all species of partridge. The state laws are as follows:

LIMITS

One buck with branched horns. One doe deer and one buck in Lander County's designated area; the same for a prescribed area in Nye County. Three pheasants. Ten valley quail, five cottontail rabbits, two mountain hares.

HOURS FOR SHOOTING

Sunrise to sunset.

LICENSE COSTS

Resident, $2.50. Nonresident, $10. Declarant alien, $10. Alien, $25. Deer Tag, $1. Doe Deer Tag, $2.50. Licenses must be obtained by all persons over 14 years of age, except resident citizens over 60, who may receive licenses free. Six months' residence in Nevada required before a residence license can be obtained.

The regulations for migratory game birds — shooting dates, hours, limits, guns, and duck stamp — are the standard ones worked out by the United States Fish and Wildlife Service, and can be obtained from the State Fish and Game Commission or the federal Fish and Wildlife Service, 271 Federal Building, Sacramento, California.

Since the Nevada county commissioners can make sudden changes in the dates for open seasons, local inquiry is a wise precaution. The following data, correct for 1941, are an approximate guide:

County	Deer	Pheasant	Valley Quail	Cottontail	Mountain Hare
Churchill	Oct. 5–Nov. 3	Oct. 12–13	Oct. 12–13	Closed	Closed
Clark	Oct. 19–Nov. 2	Closed	Oct. 12–26	Nov. 1–Dec. 31	Nov. 1–Dec. 31
Douglas	Oct. 5–Nov. 3	Oct. 12–13	Oct. 12–16	Nov. 1–Dec. 31	Closed
Elko	Oct. 5–Oct. 31	Closed	Closed	Nov. 1–Dec. 31	Nov. 1–Dec. 31
Esmeralda	Oct. 5–Nov. 3	Closed	Closed	Nov. 1–Dec. 31	Nov. 1–Dec. 31
Eureka	Oct. 5–Oct. 19	Closed	Closed	Nov. 1–Dec. 31	Nov. 1–Dec. 31
Humboldt	Oct. 5–Oct. 20	Closed	Oct. 12–26	Nov. 1–Dec. 31	Closed
Lander	Oct. 5–Nov. 3	Closed	Closed	Nov. 1–Dec. 31	Nov. 1–Dec. 31
Lincoln	Oct. 5–Nov. 2	Oct. 19	Oct. 12–19	Nov. 1–Dec. 31	Nov. 1–Dec. 31
Lyon	Closed	Oct. 12–17	Oct. 12–17	Closed	Closed
Mineral	Oct. 5–Nov. 3	Closed	Closed	Nov. 1–Dec. 31	Nov. 1–Dec. 31
Nye	Oct. 5–Nov. 3	Oct. 12–26	Oct. 12–26	Nov. 1–Dec. 31	Nov. 1–Dec. 31
Ormsby	Oct. 5–Nov. 3	Oct. 12–14	Oct. 12–19	Nov. 15–Nov. 30	Nov. 15–Nov. 30
Pershing	Oct. 5–Oct. 31	Oct. 12–14	Oct. 12–19	Nov. 1–Nov. 30	Nov. 1–Nov. 30
Storey	Oct. 5–Nov. 3	Oct. 12–14	Oct. 12–19	Nov. 15–Dec. 1	Nov. 15–Dec. 1
Washoe	Oct. 5–Nov. 3	Oct. 12–14	Oct. 12–19	Nov. 15–Dec. 1	Nov. 15–Dec. 1
White Pine	Oct. 5–Nov. 3	Closed	Closed	Nov. 15–Dec. 31	Closed

From one end of Nevada to the other, side roads lead off to campsites among juniper and pinyon pine, fir and pine, splashing streams, and high meadows. Sites for isolated, rugged camping are abundant. For an overnight dry camp along the transcontinental highways, there is always the sagebrush domain along the unfenced roadside. Developed campsites are limited in number but well equipped with tables, stoves, toilets, water, and recreational facilities, and are located in beautiful settings. A year or two ago, for some obscure reason, the public campground at Incline on Lake Tahoe, in Mono National Forest, was transferred to private hands, and so there is no free campground on the Nevada shores of Lake Tahoe. It is farther east that campers who want quiet and seclusion and hunters who want headquarters will find the offerings of the United States Forest Service, the National Park Service, and the Nevada State Park System.

Humboldt National Forest — north of Elko: campground on Jarbridge River; Gold Creek Public Campground on the road to Owyhee. South of Elko: Thomas Canyon Camp near Lamoille.

Toiyabe National Forest — north of Winnemucca: Martin Creek Camp at the north end of Paradise Valley. South of Austin: Big Creek Camp on the west side of the Toiyabe Range, Kingston Camp on the east side.

Nevada National Forest — a camp at Lehman Caves National Monument, southeast of Ely; a camp at Currant Creek, southwest of Ely on U.S. 6, the highway to Tonopah. In the Charleston Mountains just west of Las Vegas: Kyle Canyon Camp (complete with camp cupboards, and swings for children), Deer Creek Campground, and McWilliams Campground in Lee Canyon.

Mono National Forest — Galena Creek Camp on the magnificent Mt. Rose road between Reno and Lake Tahoe; Clear Creek Camp between Carson City and Glenbrook on Lake Tahoe.

Near Caliente — two state parks, Kershaw Canyon-Ryan Park, and Beaver Dam State Park, both amid beautiful scenery.

Boulder Dam National Recreational Area — improved camp-grounds near Overton and next to the water's edge on Hemenway Wash (at Boulder City), where campers may plug electrical apparatus into Boulder Dam power, paying in a slot machine.

Skiing is growing in popularity in Nevada and is encouraged by the State Highway Department, which keeps the necessary roads open in winter.

The Ely Ski Club has a warming hut, a variety of runs, and a power-driven ski lift costing $1 a day. They are located four miles south of Murray Summit on U.S. 6, southwest of Ely.

Twelve miles west of Carson City, at Spooner Summit, are a ski lift, a hut, practice slope, downhill runs, and a parking area for several hundred cars.

The Galena Creek course, eighteen miles south of Reno, is the best known in Nevada. It offers tobogganing, a racing course, a slalom course, marked cross-country trails, a ski jump permitting 165-foot leaps, a ski lift and rope tows that start at 7,600 feet and go up to 8,400 feet, a warming hut, and ample parking.

There is a new skiing development at Mt. Rose Bowl (formerly Grass Lake), near the crest of the Mt. Rose highway. In June, 1942, facilities included a new lodge and several good runs. Promised for winter were three or four rope tows and a constam T-bar lift.

In the Charleston Mountains, at Lee Canyon and Kyle Canyon, are sledding courses, jumping hills, and practice courses.

Nevada offers other important recreations: horseback riding at dude ranches, private flying at Reno and Las Vegas, and boating on Tahoe and Mead.

ACKNOWLEDGMENTS

For oral interviews or special information I am indebted to many persons and organizations, including the late ex-Governor, Roswell K. Colcord, Carson City; the late John A. Fulton, Mackay School of Mines, Reno; Professor J. A. Carpenter, Mackay School of Mines; the United States Department of Agriculture; the Nevada Agricultural Experiment Station; Mr. and Mrs. Ott Heizer, Lovelock; Mr. John T. Reid, Lovelock; Malcolm McEachin, Secretary of State, Carson City; Fred C. Greulich, Publicity Director, State Department of Highways, Carson City; D. G. La Rue, Superintendent of Banks, Carson City; Wayne McLeod, Surveyor General, Carson City; Roland Wiley, District Attorney of Clark County, Las Vegas; Clifford Jones, attorney, Las Vegas; Martin J. Scanlan, attorney and counselor at law, Reno; W. W. Hopper, President of the First National Bank of Nevada, Reno; Mr. Lester Nicholas, State Fish Hatchery, Verdi; Reno Chamber of Commerce; Washoe County Recorder, Reno; Las Vegas Chamber of Commerce; the County Clerks of Washoe and Clark counties; the State Bureau of Mines, Reno; Lois Johnson, Secretary of the Fish and Game Commission, Reno; the Forest Supervisors of Inyo, Mono, Nevada, Toiyabe, and Humboldt National Forests; the Regional Forester, Ogden, Utah; Edwin

Grabhorn, printer, San Francisco; Grant Smith, attorney and counselor at law, San Francisco; Mr. Felix Wahrhaftig, State Board of Equalization, Sacramento; Mr. Edward Wilde, Oleum, California; Dr. Lawrence Pence, Spokane, Washington; Mrs. J. B. Lillard, Sacramento, who ran through old newspaper files and collected much material pertaining to the Tahoe water controversy; Mrs. Leslie Curtis Kitselman, owner of Pyramid Lake Ranch; Sumner E. Perkins, mechanical engineer, Boulder City; Thomas C. Wilson, advertising agent, Reno.

I owe much to numerous libraries and their staffs, to Miss Caroline Wenzel and Mrs. Elsie Gibson of the California Room in the State Library, Sacramento; Miss Thea Thompson and her assistants in the university library, Reno; E. Chas. D. Marriage, State Librarian, and his assistants, Venie Robert and Laura Robins, Carson City; the Huntington Library, San Marino; the Public Library, Los Angeles; the college library, Los Angeles City College; the Bancroft Library, Berkeley; the Museum Library, Yosemite National Park.

My preparation of the manuscript has been materially encouraged and aided, at one stage or another, by Professor Kenneth Murdock, Harvard University; Professor Norman Foerster, Director of the School of Letters, University of Iowa; Professor Wilbur L. Schramm, University of Iowa; Mr. William A. Koshland, Alfred A. Knopf, Inc.; the late J. B. Lillard, Sacramento; Miss Faith Wiley, North Hollywood, California; Professor William C. Putnam, University of California at Los Angeles.

In my search for illustrations I have been helped by Professor R. P. Sharp, University of Illinois; Los Angeles Bureau of Water and Power; Las Vegas Chamber of Commerce; Transcontinental and Western Air Lines; Western Air Express; Frasher's, Pomona, California; Mabel Gillis, State Librarian, Sacramento; Boulder Dam Service Bureau; L. M. Engel, Nevada Photo Service; John Reid, mining engineer, Lovelock; two subdivisions of the United States Department of Agriculture: the Farm Security Administration and the Forest Service (offices in Washington, Ogden, and Ely); four subdivisions of the United States Department of the Interior: the Office of Indian Affairs, the Bureau of Reclamation, the Soil Conservation Service, and the Division of Information; Union Pacific Railroad; Title Insurance and Trust Company (Los Angeles); Reno Chamber of Commerce; California Historical Society.

For permission to reprint material still in copyright, acknowledgment is made to the following: The Arthur H. Clark Company for the selection from Jedediah Smith from Dale, *Ashley-Smith Explorations and Discovery of Central Route to the Pacific, 1822–1829;* Harper and Brothers for the selection from Mark Twain, *Mark Twain's Letters;* Houghton Mifflin Company for the selection from Franklin Buck's *A Yankee Trader in the Gold Rush;* Nevada State Historical Society, Inc., for the song, "Bound for the Land of Washoe"; G. P. Putnam's Sons for a selection from George Bartlett's *Men, Women, and Conflict;* Random House for the selection from Walter Van Tilburg Clark's *The Ox-Bow Incident;* Charles Scribner's Sons for the selection from the preface to George Lyman's *Ralston's Ring;* Yale University Press for the passage from William H. Brewer's *Up and Down California.*

For permission to use illustrative material, acknowledgment is made to the following: *Collier's* for the passage from *Rich Man's Refuge* by Frank J. Taylor; New York *Herald Tribune* for "Another Gold Strike in the West"; *Sunset Magazine* for drawings by Maynard Dixon. Other sources and courtesies are given in the credit lines accompanying pictures.

For pointing out minor errors in the first edition and making suggestions for changes or additions I am indebted to several correspondents, especially Professor Austin E. Hutcheson, Department of History and Political Science, University of Nevada.

Clues to much valuable but scattered newspaper material lay in the special index to California newspapers and periodicals in the California Room of the State Library in Sacramento. Invaluable for guidance and material were the *Nevada Historical Papers* (Carson City, 1913–26), *Highways and Parks* (Nevada Department of Highways, 1936–41), Dr. Effie Mack's *Nevada, a History of the State* (Glendale, California, 1936), Myron Angel's *History of Nevada* (Oakland, California, 1881), and the excellent production of the Nevada Writers' Project, *Nevada: a Guide to the Silver State* (Portland, Oregon, 1941). I have taken material from

hundreds of newspapers, magazines, and books, but aside from
those mentioned in the text or the copyright acknowledgments I
find space to mention only a handful that were especially en-
lightening:

ADAMS, ROMANZO: "Public Range Lands — a New Policy
Needed," *American Journal of Sociology*, 22: 324–351 (November, 1916).

BROWNE, J. ROSS: *Adventures in the Apache Country . . .
with Notes on the Silver Regions of Nevada*. New York, Harper,
1869.

——: *Crusoe's Island . . . with Sketches of Adventure in . . .
Washoe*. New York, Harper, 1864.

GOODMAN, JOSEPH: Series of recollections in San Francisco
Chronicle, 1891–92.

JAEGER, EDMUND: *The California Deserts: a Visitor's Hand-
book*. Stanford University Press, 1938.

SMITH, GRANT: "Highlights of Comstock History," *Pony Express Courier* (May, 1938).

STARKWEATHER, VIRGINIA: "Prospecting for Social Security,"
Survey Graphic, 75: 311 (October, 1939).

WHITE, LAURA A., *History of the Labor Struggles in Goldfield, Nevada*. M.A. Thesis, University of Nebraska, 1912.

In the library of the State University of Iowa, Iowa City, Iowa,
is a typescript containing the complete bibliography of my re-
searches into Nevada materials. It is my " Studies in Washoe Journalism and Humor " (1943).

INDEX

INDEX

[i]